the challenge of
RED CHINA

the challenge of
RED CHINA

GUNTHER STEIN

DA CAPO PRESS • NEW YORK • 1975

Library of Congress Cataloging in Publication Data

Stein, Guenther.
  The challenge of Red China.

  (China in the 20th century).
  Reprint of the ed. published by Whittlesey House,
New York.
  Includes index.
  1. Communism—China. 2. China—Politics and gov-
ernment—1937-1947. 3. China—Social conditions.
I. Title.
DS777.53.S65 1975   335.43'4'0951   74-34407
ISBN 0-306-70736-5

Published by Da Capo Press, Inc.
A Subsidiary of Plenum Publishing Corporation
227 West 17th Street, New York, N.Y. 10011

THE CHALLENGE OF RED CHINA

Author of

MADE IN JAPAN

FAR EAST IN FERMENT
(*Published in England*)

GUNTHER STEIN

the challenge of
RED CHINA

Whittlesey House
McGRAW-HILL BOOK COMPANY, INC.
New York   *London*

THE CHALLENGE OF RED CHINA

Copyright, 1945, *by* GUNTHER STEIN

First Printing

PUBLISHED BY WHITTLESEY HOUSE

A division of the McGraw-Hill Book Company, Inc.

Printed in the United States of America

ACKNOWLEDGMENT

The woodcuts in this book are by teachers and students of the Art College of Yenan University.

CONTENTS

Contents

Contents

Part Six: 3,000,000 FIGHTING ALLIES

Part Seven: WITNESSES OF THEIR WAR EFFORT

Part Eight: YENAN'S JAPANESE ALLIES

Part Nine: PERSPECTIVES OF A WORLD PROBLEM

Contents

Part Ten: ONE CHINA—OR TWO?

Chapter One

MOMENT OF DESTINY

THIS was the great moment the Chinese people had been suffering, fighting, and waiting for—year after bitter year. Japan collapsed and surrendered.

Enslaved China, so long under the Japanese heel, was free. And Free China, so long blockaded, was at last open to a new, peaceful world.

But that moment found the nation in greater danger and more deeply divided than ever—torn in two.

The drums of Japan's march of aggression ceased beating. But the angry rumble of China's internal conflict which had been ebbing and flowing as its steady accompaniment through fifteen years, did not die down. It rose. It threatened once again to swell into the frenzied fortissimo of open civil war.

Even before the Japanese laid down their arms, Chinese rushed to take them up to fight Chinese.

Would they still hesitate, desist? Would America and Russia unite in a decision to *make* them halt? Or would they fan the fire, unheedful of the consequences?

That fateful moment would decide the future of the hard-won peace of China—and of Asia and the world. . . .

The drama of disunity and confusion on China's political stage was floodlighted in a sudden, vivid flash—for all of us to see and, if possible, to comprehend its fateful meaning.

In the foreground—*Chungking.*

The drab wartime refuge of the internationally recognized National

Government of China, joyful at victory, was ready to return to provincial insignificance. Its leaders were packing up to move back to
Nanking, their former capital.

But that new air of brisk activity in military and government offices
meant more than breaking camp. Armies were reorganized and strengthened. The Kuomintang's political and administrative machinery was
tightened. It meant preparation for a new struggle. The watchword was
not Peace. It was Alert.

And—*Yenan.*

The lively little cave town in the barren hills of the Northwest, for
eight years the nerve center of "Red China" and headquarters of the
Communists' single-handed war against Japan, was equally ready to
become historical memory. For the Communist leaders, too, would
soon be on the move—away from the stranglehold of the Kuomintang's
armed blockade line along Yenan's little "Border Region"—to their
former war areas in the north where larger towns would fall to their
troops as the Japanese collapsed.

More than ever, the Communists were bracing themselves, planning,
organizing, strengthening their armed forces. Here, too, in spite of
elation at victory, the watchword was not Peace. It was Alert.

On the one side—*Chungking's China.*

To the 150,000,000 people in the villages and towns of the backward
interior which the Japanese never reached, victory meant little more
than an end to their fear of attack. It did not mean relief from conscription, crushing taxes, economic crisis, age-old feudal village tyranny
and bureaucratic rule on top. The people, stirring from political sleep,
were demanding democracy. Many would listen to the Communists
if they renounced their wartime pledge and began to agitate the masses
in the Kuomintang camp.

Chungking's China was expanding fast toward the coast and the
Lower Yangtsze as the Japanese Army surrendered to the advancing
Kuomintang troops. But those liberators would soon meet rivals, Communist-led armies with much political appeal to the masses, coming
from the enemy's deep rear.

On the other side—*Yenan's China.*

Behind the crumbling first-front lines of the Japanese, between their disappearing inner defense belts, the scattered Anti-Japanese War Bases of "Red China" assumed new significance. During eight years of bitter guerrilla warfare, they had risen like islands out of the sea of Japanese-occupied territories. Liberated by Communist-led troops closely co-operating with all strata of the population, they became regions of self-government under the Communist-initiated New Democracy.

The 95,000,000 people in those areas had derived social and economic progress from this new system and advocated it in neighboring regions. Many seemed ready to fight for it, if the Kuomintang tried to come back and to reestablish its regime in place of the popular New Democracy. . . .

At last, in the background—the *Vacuum* in China's political geography.

The country's most populous and developed areas in the north and center were left in a political void as Japanese authorities and puppet regimes broke down: long strips of strategic country along the coast, on both sides of railroads and motor highways, and key towns and large cities; all surrounded by the Communists' Anti-Japanese War Bases. The Communists would try to take control, bridging the gaps between the islands of their New Democracy, welding them into a whole; while the Kuomintang would try to forestall them. . . .

Scores of millions of people with divided loyalties and varying hopes and fears would be the breeding ground of intensified Kuomintang-Communist conflict: the masses, awakened to new political consciousness by years of alien suppression and apparently influenced by the ideas of the New Democracy which had grown up so close to them; the large forces of underground workers of the Communist and Kuomintang parties whose agitation was given free reign by the Japanese collapse; and many puppet collaborationists, anxious to save their skins by any switch that would help them.

Three large Chinese armies dominate that explosive scene:

Chungking's National Army, with some 2,000,000 conscripted troops,

3

well armed by the standards of Chinese conflict, had a good number of American-trained, American-equipped regular divisions and parachute battalions, a small air force and many American-trained pilots. And it was promised the aid of American air transport to help it in the race with the Communists for Japanese arms.*

Yenan's army had 900,000 hardened guerrilla soldiers, all volunteers from Liberated China; poorly equipped with arms they captured from the Japanese and their puppets during eight years of war, and with self-made land mines and hand-grenades; supported by 2,000,000 even worse armed but experienced militiamen; and effectively indoctrinated with the basic ideas of Yenan's New Democracy.

Wooed by both sides were the *"puppet" armies:* 800,000 men, trained and equipped by the Japanese, mainly for the fight against the Communists—but in their rank and file divided between pro-Communist and pro-Kuomintang loyalties.

And these are the two men of China's destiny, the only individuals looming large on the scene of potential conflict.

Chiang Kai-shek, the Kuomintang's party leader, and the President and Generalissimo of the National Government. A stern and rigid military figure in the immaculate uniform of a modern general; yet fundamentally a Confucianist soldier-statesman on the ancient patriarchal Chinese pattern. A lonely man who inspires respect rather than warmth. A leader who takes all responsibility upon himself, finds it difficult to delegate authority, and seems deeply sceptical of the political potentialities of the common people and of any political group other than his own.

It is his conviction that "China's destiny depends solely upon the Kuomintang," as he wrote in his book a few years ago. To him the Communists are bandits who must be made to submit to his authority.

Mao Tse-tung, chairman of the Communist Party of China, is Chiang Kai-shek's opposite in most respects. A broad, full-blooded peasant-intellectual in baggy pants and a soft cap, unconventional and easygoing.

* See *New York Herald Tribune,* August 8, 1945, "U. S. Will Help Chiang in Race for Foe's Arms—Accord Reached to Transport Troops to Meet Challenge of Chinese Red Leaders."

A radical popular leader of the present day, realistic and with a deep belief in the mission of his party and in the capacities of the common people.

He is willing to cooperate with the Kuomintang and all other political groups—on the basis of the principles of his New Democracy—in a coalition government. But he is ready to fight when he is attacked. . . .

The challenge of Red China must be judged on its own merits. There is no imaginable parallel in the present-day United States to the events that are taking place in China.

This argument, so often heard in Chungking, is baseless: The government in Washington would never tolerate an American Communist Party that had entrenched itself, say, in Wyoming, maintaining its own armies and government, issuing its own currency, and demanding from the President the formation of a coalition government of the Democratic and Communist parties as precondition for national reunification—and that the Kuomintang should therefore be given help to suppress the Chinese Communists.

Chiang Kai-shek, talking to Congressman Mike Mansfield, compared the dissident factions in China today with those in America at George Washington's time, thus admitting himself that China is still in the formative period of nationhood, as America was before the Declaration of Independence. But even this comparison needs qualification: China's revolution that is to lead her from semi-feudalism to modernism, is dragging on into its fourth decade, still undecided, still unwon. . . .

This moment of liberation from the foreign invader will push this long overdue revolution further: either peacefully, if the Kuomintang and Communist parties cooperate and if we try to help them unite; or once more with the violence of civil war.

Part One

A JOURNEY OF DISCOVERY

BULLET-LESS FIGHT WITH JAPANESE

Chapter Two

THE OTHER CHINA

PEARL HARBOR might never have happened if the two camps of China's National Revolution had not broken apart in the midst of success, after a short period of unity.

Nothing helped Japan more and did us greater harm in the Pacific than China's relapse into internal conflict in 1927.

Yet few people in the United States and Britain seem to realize what Chinese disunity has been costing us during all those years; how it came about that patriotic China today is split into two camps, with Chungking and Yenan as their centers; and why China has two armies, one Nationalist and one Communist, disunited in the face of the Japanese invader.

It was only recently that Washington and London seemed to become aware of the stake we have in Chinese unity: when American diplomacy, through General Joseph W. Stilwell, Allied Chief of Staff to Chiang Kai-shek, made a last-minute effort to reunite China for the final stage of the war against Japan and for a solid peace in Asia.

In 1924, when China's national revolutionary parties, the Kuomintang (Nationalists) and Kungchantang (Communists) came together in a firm alliance under Dr. Sun Yat-sen—to overthrow the war lords who terrorized and corrupted the country, and to liberate it from the imperialistic privileges which the foreign powers had arrogated to themselves—Washington and London regarded Chinese unity as a danger rather than a blessing; as a much greater danger, in fact, than the growing strength of Japan.

In 1926, when the united forces of the National Revolution began to sweep victoriously over Southern and Central China, the fear in Washington and London increased because of the inevitable revolutionary excesses which accompanied the long-delayed awakening of the Chinese masses to modern ideas of nationalism and internal reform.

And in 1927, when the movement reached the big commercial cities, Shanghai, Nanking, and Hankow, there was a sigh of relief at the *coup d'état* of General Chiang Kai-shek who "purged" the Communists and many progressive Kuomintang members from the camp of the National Revolution.

This *coup d'état* made the rightist wing of the Kuomintang, its newly created National Government at Nanking, and its purged Nationalist armies supreme in one part of the country. It caused the Communists—together with peasants' and workers' unions, with progressive Kuomintang elements and parts of the original nationalist fighting forces—to organize "Soviet" territories and Red armies in another.

It was apparently felt in Washington and London that the new Nanking government would be "amenable to reason." The new regime was much weaker than the united National Revolutionaries had been, and it was utterly dependent upon the financial support of conservative Chinese financiers and their foreign business associates in the international settlement and concession areas of the big cities. The leftist partisan movement, however, was not considered important. Cut off from Russian or any other support in the poor hill regions of Central China, it would soon peter out. . . .

There seemed to be no thought of the danger that Tokyo—more frightened than any other capital by the strength China had shown during those years of its short-lived unity—might utilize the new split for fresh aggression.

I first saw the Far East in 1932. The Japanese were completing their fightless conquest of Manchuria and their troops were in occupation of Shanghai's port areas outside the foreign-controlled parts of the city while China's Nationalist armies were fighting China's Communist armies.

I went to Manchuria. "Tell them in Nanking," some desperate patriots whispered to me, "that we can still resist Japan if they stop fighting the Communists."

I went to Tokyo. Only the split in China had made the conquest of
Manchuria possible, many Japanese told me frankly. For China would
have been expected to resist if her new unity had continued; and the
Japanese Army could not have afforded a fighting war. What it needed
was a bloodless conquest to raise its impaired prestige with the Throne
and Big Business, with the Bureaucracy and the people, by showing all
of them that heavy armament expenditure paid handsome dividends
and that a strong militaristic line of policy meant no risk of war. In this
way the Japanese militarists climbed back into political power after
more than a decade of eclipse, which was even more important to them
than the conquest of the Manchurian position itself.

General Koiso, then Japan's Vice-Minister of War and later one of
its wartime premiers, entertaining me at dinner, used Chinese disunity
as one of his arguments in defense of Japan's action.

We were kneeling in stockinged feet on the spotless straw mats of
Tokyo's fashionable Maple Club when he gave me his views on the
subject of China.

"A country where professed national revolutionaries fight each other
with hundreds of thousands of men," he said, "and where the government is using the plentiful foreign equipment of its army and air force
against its own people is not worthy of being a member of the League
of Nations. The fact that only a few solitary bandits fight the Imperial
Japanese Army in Manchuria shows better than all the investigations
you newspapermen and League delegates can make that Japan does not
act as an aggressor against another independent nation, but as a good
neighbor who does his sacred duty in establishing order for the thirty
million misruled and unhappy Chinese of Manchuria."

I went to Nanking. Prominent German Reichswehr generals in the
employ of Chiang Kai-shek were drawing up elaborate strategic plans
and drilling more and more troops. The most modern armaments and
large quantities of ammunition, airplanes, and pilots arrived from almost every country in the world. Merchants of death of all nationalities
did a thriving business. The Chinese troops I saw looked well drilled
and competent, their officers spick-and-span. Nanking gave the impres-

11

sion of a military camp and spent about one-half of its public revenue on the army.

All this was the National Government's effort against the Chinese Communists. The "Red Bandits" with their increasing areas and armies in Central China were Enemy Number One. Hundreds of thousands of National Government troops were fighting at the front. But it was not the front against Japan.

I went to Shanghai. Liberal Chinese told me in despair that their agitation for national unity and resistance against Japan was treated as a criminal offense by the Kuomintang government. Its secret police hunted down United Front enthusiasts and leftists, even in the foreign-settlement areas, torturing and killing many of their political prisoners.

Foreigners in Shanghai were divided in their opinions. Many sympathized with the authoritarian character of Nanking's internal policies and its attitude toward Tokyo. And of those who wanted to see China resist Japan few seemed to realize the close link between the Chinese Civil War and the prospects of world peace.

Some of the Old China Hands in the foreign business community were positively happy about the course of events. "You don't know the Chinese," one of them said to me when I told him of my reaction to what I had seen and heard on my journey. We were standing at the famous "longest bar in the world" in the old Shanghai Club, which was not the most appropriate place for the expression of the sentiments I had about the Chinese situation.

"You don't realize that it was high time for somebody to give all those Nationalists in China a good licking. No matter whether they are White or Red, they needed it. They were really getting uppish since 1924. Feeling their strength and getting nasty. Anti-imperialist, you know. Wanting to get things under their own control, like our International Settlement here in Shanghai, and to run their Customs and Salt Administrations, which we do much better. They were really getting strong before they split into two camps.

"Damn strong and cocky," he added with a sigh.

"But what about the Japanese?" I retorted. "Aren't they getting

12

even stronger and cockier, and much more dangerous than the Chinese?"

"Well, well—" He smiled superciliously. "Trying to frighten an Old Hand at the Far Eastern game with the Japanese bogey, eh? I tell you, those Japs will never be a match for us. Mind you, they're damn useful to business out here, as a matter of fact. And to peace, too, if you think of that.

"In what way? In several ways. They are buying a lot of stuff from us, those Japs, putting the Chinese in their place, checking the Russians. Pretty good job, I should think. And, you see, they don't touch us here in the International Settlement."

I did not go to Juiking. The Communist capital in Central China, like its "Soviet" areas with their ten million people, scattered over several provinces, was hermetically sealed off by the Kuomintang blockade. Nobody was able to go there. No objective information about the Communist areas was available. There was only Nanking's own version. The Red regimes were collapsing, government officials told me. The people in the Red areas hated and feared them for their cruelty. Their large but most primitively equipped bandit armies were wilting away under the powerful blows of wave after wave of modern Kuomintang troops. The Communists were virtually finished.

That was in 1932.

I had come under the spell of the Far East during those few months. I would have to return some day, I felt, going back to my new assignment in Moscow which the visit to China and Japan had interrupted almost at its start.

In Moscow I tried to learn more about the Chinese "Soviet" territories.

But Moscow seemed to have no direct contact with the Chinese Communists since Chiang Kai-shek broke with the Russian advisers of the National Revolutionary movement at the time of his *coup d'état* and sent them home most unceremoniously.

Stalin's policy of concentrating on "Socialism in one country" had evidently reduced the Kremlin's interest in China's internal affairs. The episode of close Russian cooperation with China's National Revolution seemed tainted with Trotskyism. The Communist International in which China had ranked next to Russia was in eclipse.

Anyhow, a regular Communist revolution on the purely agricultural basis on which the Chinese Reds had to work in their poor, isolated areas in the interior of Kiangsi province was not considered feasible in Moscow.

"How can you imagine Communism without a strong basis of heavy industries?" a prominent Bolshevik said when I asked about his views on the Chinese Soviet territories. "Lenin said that Soviet power plus electrification makes Socialism; and that is true, not only for us but for any country. Where industry is not developed in the economic structure of a country there can be no Communism and not even Socialism. A petty-bourgeois society of a progressive type is the best that can be expected of such a country if the suppressed classes succeed in getting into political control."

I returned to the Far East in 1934, not knowing that it would be for ten solid years.

At first I was assigned to Tokyo, but I followed Chinese developments and Japanese reactions to them with special interest and visited China once a year.

The fall of 1934 brought the "Soviet Republic" in Central China to an end.

Nanking's strategy, planned by Chiang Kai-shek's brilliant German generals, became increasingly successful. The Kuomintang forces built motor roads into the wilderness of the areas under the control of the Communists, put up blockhouses on every hill that was conquered, and attacked the Reds with vastly superior forces. The Communists, overestimating their strength, made the mistake of accepting the challenge to regular positional warfare. And the watertight blockade created a disastrous lack of salt and other essentials in the beleaguered areas. The Communists had to withdraw.

Over 100,000 Chinese Redarmists, party officials, and administrators evacuated all but a few hilly Soviet districts and started out on the famous "Long March" which was to take them over about 8,500 miles of almost roadless country during little more than a year.

The Nanking dispatches which were played up prominently in Tokyo newspapers described the "utter rout" in which National armies chased the "Red Bandits" from Central China through South and Southwest China, then over the high snow mountains and torrential rivers of the Tibetan grasslands, waylaying them on land wherever any troops could get at them in the wilderness and bombing them from the air. Nanking repeated month after month that the "final destruction of all Communist forces" had been achieved and that either Mao Tse-tung, the party leader, or Chu Teh, the Red Army commander, had "definitely been killed."

Eventually, at the end of 1935, Nanking reported that some "insignificant remnants of the Red Bandits," an exhausted rabble of starved and demoralized men and women, sick and in tatters, had reached the little Soviet Region which local Communist partisans had established some time earlier in the northwestern province of Shensi, around a little Kuomintang-held town called Yenan. . . .

Nanking continued its war against those remnants of the Red Army in the northwest. "Young Marshal" Chang Hsueh-liang, the ex-war lord of Manchuria, was ordered to annihilate them with his Manchurian army, which had to be kept busy because its soldiers and young officers were clamoring for action against Japan.

The Japanese militarists were anxious. "It is not true that the Reds were annihilated," the government spokesman in Tokyo said to me one day. "They are still quite strong. They have come close to North China where we have special interests. They have come on purpose. They are anti-Japanese and dangerous, especially with their agitation against harmony between Nanking and ourselves. And Nanking does not fight them properly any more. Anti-Japanism is increasing everywhere in China. Nanking must suppress both the Communists and anti-Japanism."

The Other China

Anti-Japanism grew indeed stronger over the entire country the deeper the Japanese penetrated from Manchuria into all spheres of the life of North China, using both military and political pressure to submit one part of the North after the other to their control.

Communist underground agitation contributed to its rise; but it was already a strong national movement. Chinese people of all classes and political creeds became more and more categorical in their demands on Nanking for the establishment of a genuine United Front embracing the Kuomintang, the Communists, and all liberal elements for national resistance against Japan.

The Manchurian troops which were supposed to fight the Communists became part of the movement. A fair number of them, soldiers and junior officers, had been captured by the Red Army or had gone over to it. After short political training courses, the Reds had sent them back to their regiments where they spread the idea of a United Front against the real enemy.

Fighting against the Communists slackened. Generalissimo Chiang Kai-shek went by plane to Sian, taking the Young Marshal severely to task for his failure to annihilate the Reds. Chang Hsueh-liang promised action. But his troops would not attack their compatriots any longer.

Once more, in December, 1936, the Generalissimo flew to Sian, threatening to relieve Chang Hsueh-liang of the command of his army. This time the Young Marshal sided openly with the demands of his men. He even confessed to having made contact with the Communists on the matter of a United Front against the national enemy.

The Generalissimo's reaction to this unsuspected confession made the Young Marshal lose his head. Chang Hsueh-liang and the equally anti-Japanese garrison commander of Sian, Yang Hu-cheng, took the Generalissimo prisoner. Part of the Sian troops were in a rebellious mood and wanted the Generalissimo put on trial. For some time his life seemed in danger.

The house in which he was detained became the meeting place of people who might well discuss the formation of a United Front: Chiang

16

Kai-shek, the exponent of the right wing of the Kuomintang which was in power; Dr. T. V. Soong, the most prominent liberal in the Kuomintang, who came from Nanking with his sister, Mme. Chiang Kai-shek, and her Australian adviser, W. H. Donald; General Chou En-lai, one of the Communist leaders whom his party had sent as its special representative, a former close collaborator of Chiang Kai-shek in the Whampoa Military Academy; and Young Marshal Chang Hsueh-liang whose Manchurian followers played an increasingly important role in the United Front movement.

What went on in the talks at that unusual meeting place is still a matter of controversy. But two facts are well established.

First, the Communists had no hand in the detention of the Generalissimo. When they learned of it over the radio, a special meeting of their Central Committee decided unanimously to send General Chou En-lai to Sian to intercede with the rash Young Marshal for the release of the Generalissimo in the interest of national unity against Japan.

Many Kuomintang officials I met later believe that the calm counsels of the Communist party and the diplomacy of their representative may actually have saved the life of the Generalissimo and that Chiang Kai-shek's friendly attitude toward General Chou En-lai during later periods of Kuomintang-Communist tension was due to a sense of personal obligation.*

Second, whether or not definite promises were exchanged, the talks in that peculiar setting at Sian had created an atmosphere favorable to a United Front when the Generalissimo was at last released on Christmas Eve, 1936, and returned to Nanking.

The Japanese were deeply shocked when they saw that the Sian Incident eventually led to the end of the Civil War and to a rapprochement between the various parties and groups in China. But I found them not without hope.

* W. H. Donald, in an interview with the Associated Press on February 25, 1945, confirmed that "Chou En-lai, Communist leader most prominently mentioned in current rapprochement attempts between the Communists and the Kuomintang, was actually the one man who enabled General Chiang Kai-shek to depart unharmed from the 1936 Sian kidnapping."

"A United Front between the Kuomintang and the Communists cannot last," a high-ranking Japanese told me one night at a dinner party in Tokyo. "Chiang Kai-shek is only marking time and trying to bluff us with a sham picture of internal reconciliation. He must realize that the Reds are a much greater danger to him if he cooperates with them once more than we shall ever be. You can be sure the Kuomintang and the Communists will never fight together. . . .

". . . Because they will always fight *together*. . . . Ha, ha . . ." he added, proud of his attempted pun.

The Japanese counted on the correctness of this opinion when they attacked China in July, 1937.

For two years or so there was the semblance of a United Front of all political groups of China in the war against Japan.

The Communists ceased all revolutionary activities and pledged themselves to fight the national enemy. The northwestern Soviet Region, renamed "Shensi-Kansu-Ningshia Border Region," became a local authority administered by the Communists for the National Government. The Red Army was submitted to the strategic command of the National Military Council in Nanking, which gave it the designation "Eighth Route Army" and confirmed the famous Red Army leader General Chu Teh as its commander. The Eighth Route Army was "permitted" to penetrate into the enemy's rear in North China after the withdrawal of the regular National Government armies and to organize there armed popular resistance against the Japanese.

Another unit under the leadership of the Communists and the strategic command of the National Government, the New Fourth Army, was officially established in Central China—from Red Army units that had stayed behind in thirteen small Soviet districts and had continued to resist the attacks of National forces since the main body of the Red Army went on the Long March.

But the terms of interparty cooperation were never worked out in detail. And the democratic reform of the National Government which was to lay a sound basis for complete national unification and for an intensified Chinese war effort did not materialize. The old Nanking

18

decree that pronounced the illegality of the Communist party, and in fact any party other than the Kuomintang, was never lifted.

I came to Chungking for the first time in the early summer of 1939 and found that the two parties were slowly drifting apart once more. General Chou En-lai, then the official Communist representative with the National Government, was no longer invited by the Ministry of Publicity to participate with Kuomintang spokesmen in the usual press conferences with foreign correspondents. Government officials told me privately that the Eighth Route and New Fourth Armies were not fighting the enemy. They hinted that sinister motives were behind the Communists' ever deeper penetration into the enemy's rear in North and Central China.

The Fifth Plenary Session of the Kuomintang passed a confidential resolution about "defensive measures" to be taken against "alien parties." Increasing pressure was being exerted on the few Communists in various parts of Free China outside the Border Region. Staff members of the representatives' offices of the Communist-controlled armies in several war zones under the control of Chungking were arrested. And the great Wang Ching-wei, second only to Chiang Kai-shek in the leadership of the Kuomintang and its government, had openly gone over to the Japanese.

In 1940, things were looking even worse. Armed clashes took place between National and Communist troops, some of them in sight of the Japanese. Each side blamed the other for having started them.

The Communists in Chungking said that General Hu Chung-nan, one of the Generalissimo's commanders in the Civil War, was surrounding the Border Region with large numbers of troops; that he was building up a strong blockade line around it; and that he had occupied about one quarter of the Border Region's territory which the National Government had recognized in 1937 as the special administrative and recruiting district of the Eighth Route Army.

News about the battle records of the Communist-led armies was suppressed by the Chungking censors. Since 1939 no foreign correspondent, diplomat, or military attaché had been allowed to visit Yenan, and the authorities in Chungking frowned on anyone's going occasionally to General Chou En-lai for information.

"We consider anybody who attends press conferences of the Communists an enemy of China," I was told by Dr. Hollington K. Tong, Vice-Minister of Publicity, after I had been to a tea at General Chou En-lai's office, together with a dozen other foreign correspondents and several American and British diplomats.

On January 17, 1941, it was officially announced in Chungking that fighting had broken out between Government troops and the Communist-controlled New Fourth Army on the south bank of the Yangtsze. The entire New Fourth Army, the statement said, had been disbanded. Its designation had been abolished. Its famous commander, General Yeh Ting, had been arrested.

We foreigners and most Chinese were dumfounded.

The Government explained further that the New Fourth Army had "acted in defiance of military orders to withdraw from the south bank to the north bank of the Yangtsze"; that it had "intended to stage a revolt" which was discovered in time; that not only the commander but also his entire staff had been taken prisoner; and that large numbers of New Fourth Army troops had been annihilated in the ensuing fight.

The Communists retorted: The New Fourth Army, in the interest of maintaining national unity, accepted Chungking's orders to withdraw its headquarters units from the south bank of the Yangtsze to the north bank, in spite of the fact that this would uproot its local guerrilla auxiliaries and endanger their families, since the Japanese would then be likely to occupy the evacuated areas.

The route prescribed by Chungking, the Communists stated, lay through especially strong Japanese positions along the broad river. It had proved impracticable for the withdrawal of the headquarters units of 10,000 men with their large percentage of noncombatants. After an unsuccessful attempt to evacuate over this route, a detour through territory held by Chungking troops had been proposed to their local com-

20

mander, who had approved it. But when the withdrawal began according to this arrangement, the New Fourth Army units were immediately encircled and heavily attacked by superior Kuomintang forces. The greater part of the 10,000 men and numerous women workers had been killed.

Was this to be the beginning of another internal conflict, at a time when the Japanese were slowing down in China and becoming increasingly aggressive against British and American interests?

The situation looked serious. All payments and supplies to the remainder of the New Fourth Army in Central China and the other Communist-led force, the Eighth Route Army in North China, were officially suspended by the Chungking government. A strict blockade was enforced on the Border Region. Once more, Communist-controlled China was cut off entirely from the rest of China, as in the days of the Civil War.

Shortly after the announcement of the New Fourth Army Incident, in Hong Kong, I received a copy of the December 27, 1940, issue of the Tokyo *Japan Advertiser*, an American-owned newspaper to which I subscribed. It contained the English translation of an editorial of the *Kokumin Shimbun*, written a week or so before the attack of Chinese Government troops on the New Fourth Army.

This is part of what the ultra-militarist Japanese newspaper wrote:

"Chungking is surely worried over the increasing influence of the Chinese Communists. Japan is in the same boat as far as this is concerned. . . .

"Reckless activities of the New Fourth Army . . . are becoming a menace to peace. . . .

"The Tientsin-Pukow Railway [Japanese occupied. G. S.] has been hard hit in its transportation. Activities of the Eighth Route Army are penetrating into North China and forming a cancer to the maintenance of peace. . . .

"The Chiang [Kai-shek] faction is now in a dilemma. . . .

"It is not altogether unimaginable that Japan, too, may be seriously

21

affected by the Communist influence if Chungking is not able to pacify the Communists."

Once more, in the midst of the Sino-Japanese War, Tokyo had demanded from the Chinese Government that it suppress the Communist armies. . . . Once more, the Kuomintang had taken action. . . .

It was not only the fresh rift between the two Chinas which worried Chinese liberals and foreign observers in Chungking: the war effort and the internal situation in the regions of the National Government were deteriorating badly.

The long duration of the Sino-Japanese War was certainly one of the main factors in the serious decline that became so evident in every field—military and political, financial and economic, administrative and psychological.

But it became increasingly clear that the perpetuation of the Kuomintang's rigid one-party rule and its lack of democratic contact with the people were at least equally to blame.

Chapter Three

STORMY PRESS CONFERENCES

OUR weekly press conferences in Chungking grew tense and heated as the Chinese crisis rose. They ceased to be mere routine conferences between foreign correspondents and officials and became dramatic side shows of current history. Some Chinese liberals wistfully called them "our only substitute for a parliament."

Every Wednesday afternoon the spacious auditorium of the Ministry of Publicity next to our Press Hostel was crowded to capacity. At a long, cloth-covered table and on rows of benches, almost a hundred people would be waiting for the Government spokesmen.

It was a strangely assorted crowd: a dozen or more foreign correspondents, some of the crusader type and others sharp, unemotional reporters; an ever-growing number of greatly interested observers from the embassies, American, British, Soviet, Dutch, and others; English-speaking correspondents of the official Chinese news agency and of some Chungking newspapers, with a sprinkling of liberals among them; a large group of recorders, censors, and stern-faced, silent observers from various Chinese Government organizations; and some thirty Chinese boy and girl students of the American-staffed School of Journalism of the Ministry of Publicity, attentively watching the strange phenomenon of open political discussion.

The three Government spokesmen would take their seats at the head of the table, Publicity Minister Liang Han-tsao presiding. The agile little man, glib and all too anxious not to offend the powerful forces of reaction in the Kuomintang, was inclined to conduct the conferences as Sunday-school classes on the superiority of Oriental over Western conceptions of society and democracy. He resented any questions we asked on concrete problems and sidetracked them to the best of his limited ability. Dr. K. C. Wu, the urbane and somewhat supercilious Vice-Minister of Foreign Affairs, kept himself in the background unless he felt he had to help the Minister with a sharp outburst against our stubborn questions. Dr. P. H. Chang, the able and friendly secretary to the Cabinet, tried to inform us as best he could but was, like the others, not often free to talk frankly.

The United States Navy was drawing closer to the China coast and China would soon be needed as the main Allied land base against Japan.

Many American and British lives would depend upon China's readiness to achieve reform and national unity for her fullest possible cooperation in the final war effort.

Yet things in China were going from bad to worse. The lack of democracy and free speech in Kuomintang China paralyzed the people's spirit and the war effort in general. The economic and financial crisis rose and nothing effective was being done to combat it. The grossly inequitable distribution of war burdens among various strata of society led to increasing popular dissatisfaction. The pathetic undernourishment of the Kuomintang soldiers and the delay of urgently needed army reforms weakened China's military power more and more.

The movement for democratic reform among Free China's liberal intelligentsia and even inside the Kuomintang party and government was suppressed instead of being made useful. And the dangerous rift between the Kuomintang and Communist parties, which had so much to do with the general crisis, grew deeper and apparently threatened once more to lead to civil war.

Those were the problems around which our hot discussions at the press conferences turned. We wanted concrete information on the measures that were supposedly taken to solve them. And we wanted the right to report according to our own observations. For our messages were heavily censored or completely suppressed by the Government. One aspect of the crisis after another became taboo to us as to the Chinese press. Our urgent requests for relaxation of censorship were ignored—like those of the Chungking newspapers.

The Kuomintang-Communist issue seemed of special importance to us. It was the only one we were not able to judge for ourselves. We knew one-half of patriotic China, the "Free China" of the Kuomintang government in Chungking; but not the "Liberated China" of the Communists in Yenan which Chungking kept hidden behind a tight wall of blockade.

All we heard in Chungking about those forbidden areas and the Kuomintang-Communist conflict in general were incomplete and highly controversial statements by the two parties. The Communists claimed they could help the Allies to a large extent and that their anti-Japanese fighting strength was continuously growing in a bitter and successful struggle with the enemy. But the Kuomintang government in Chungking insisted that the Communists had ceased fighting the Japanese in 1937 and had expanded their armies and territories for the purpose of overthrowing the government of the Kuomintang. The Communists suppressed and terrorized the people. They planted huge quantities of opium for sale in Kuomintang areas. They took orders from Moscow and had secret dealings with the Japanese. They were disobedient, undermined national unity, and sabotaged the war effort. They had to be treated as bandits and traitors until their armies and governments submitted unconditionally to Chungking.

The Communists invited anybody, correspondents, Allied diplomats, and military observers, to come to Yenan and find out for themselves. But the Kuomintang government allowed nobody to go. The conflict between the two parties, we were told at the press conferences, was a Chinese family affair and of no concern to foreigners. The Communists were disobedient. No question of national unity was involved.

Our increasing grievances against the censorship and the manner in which the press conferences were conducted contributed much to the crescendo of journalistic fervor which rose from one Wednesday afternoon to another. It led to a climax through the suppression by the censors of a collective interview we had with the Communist representative in Chungking.

Another armed Kuomintang expedition against the Communists was rumored. To hear about the Communist attitude, we went to see old Tung Pi-wu, who had been a veteran of the early Kuomintang and a close collaborator with its founder, Sun Yat-sen.

"The Communist party of China has no fundamental quarrel with the Kuomintang," Tung Pi-wu said, "for we subscribe equally to the basic ideals of Dr. Sun Yat-sen's Three Principles of the People which charge all political parties in China with the promotion of the country's national independence, the realization of constitutional democratic government, and with sincere efforts for a profound improvement of the people's livelihood. Nothing the Communists have done since the war broke out in 1937 has infringed on these principles, as you could see for yourselves if you went to investigate on the spot."

Tung Pi-wu expressed the hope that for the sake of victory and national unity all problems between the Kuomintang and Communist parties would be solved peacefully, and he added that Yenan was sending another special delegate to Chungking to negotiate a fresh understanding.

All our messages about this interview were withheld by the censor. Our editors wanted information about the growing party strife which caused unusual concern in Washington and London. Yet our protests at the press conference were without results.

We decided on action. One afternoon in February, 1944, six of us sat together in the Press Hostel in the room of Brooks Atkinson of *The New York Times* and drafted a collective letter to Generalissimo Chiang Kai-shek requesting him to let us go to Yenan. Every correspondent in the Press Hostel signed and Atkinson, as president of the Foreign Correspondents' Club, was to hand the letter to the Minister of Publicity after the next press conference.

The meeting was typical. These were some of the questions and answers exchanged between us and the spokesmen:

QUESTION: The official Chinese news agency *Central News* reports every day in detail about the "great and bitter cleavage" between the

Democratic and Republican parties in the United States. May we be allowed to report similar things about the two political parties in China?

ANSWER: If your government asks us not to let our correspondents in the United States talk about these matters, we shall certainly stop them.

QUESTION: Is it true that recent pamphlets which were allowed by the censorship to circulate in Chungking have again called the Chinese Communist leaders "bandits, war lords, traitors, and disillusioned ambitionists"?

ANSWER: This was not for publication abroad but to show that the Chinese Government was being misunderstood.

QUESTION: We are told officially that the Communist troops are not fighting the enemy. But the Japanese continue reporting battles with them, even with the New Fourth Army which was supposed to have been disbanded by the Chinese Government three years ago.

ANSWER: If you want to believe the Japanese, go ahead.

After some futile discussion about the suppressed messages, Brooks Atkinson presented our letter for delivery to the Generalissimo.

The following Wednesday the Minister of Publicity opened the conference with a lengthy speech in his usual Sunday-school manner.

"It is not in my power to release your cables about your interview with the Communist representative. You must take note of the fact that on certain issues there is a difference between European and Oriental conceptions. . . . As you all know, the Chinese political system is built upon principles of family relations. The family system developed into the state system. Our relations with the Communists must be regarded as a family affair. . . . The elders will not try to publicize disputes in the family when some juniors are recalcitrant."

That sounded both familiar and ominous. But then the little minister raised himself and continued with solemn emphasis.

27

"After long consideration we have arrived at the conclusion that the time has come for some facts to be made known to friends abroad. We know that our foreign friends are interested in getting at the real situation, because it concerns them as well as us.

"The Generalissimo has therefore instructed me to convey to you the following message: 'It has also been my idea to invite the foreign press to visit Yenan. . . . The Government will send you formal invitations when the time comes for this plan to be carried out.'

"The Generalissimo's only conditions are that you also visit non-Communist areas in the Northwest and that you stay for at least three months in Communist-controlled territory."

Had we won at last? I looked at the beaming face of one of my colleagues who seemed to think of a nice "lead" to be used from Yenan, something like, "The first white man to set foot on the red soil of the Communist capital. . . ."

We never knew during the next three months whether we could really go to Yenan. Heavy odds were laid against our success at parties in Chungking's diplomatic salons where our crusading at the press conferences had long been a favorite topic of conversation. And the Chinese liberals were doubtful, too.

Almost every week we heard of rumors that the journey was to be called off. Powerful people behind the scenes, especially at anti-Communist Kuomintang headquarters in Sian, we heard, were by no means pleased with the prospect of our investigations in the other half of China and tried to have Chiang Kai-shek's promise canceled.

But the Generalissimo kept his word. We left Chungking on May 17, 1944, envied by diplomats and military attachés and by many liberal Chinese who would have liked to go with us. Only six of the foreign correspondents who had applied for the journey were able to take a trip that would last over three months.

We traveled in the safe company of eight picked representatives of Chungking newspapers and four government officials, wearing badges, "Chinese and Foreign Correspondents' Party to the Northwest."

28

During our short flight to Paochi, the only civilian airfield near the Communist-controlled Border Region, I had a busy time sorting out my "terms of reference."

I had with me long lists of accusations against the Communists given me by high-ranking Kuomintang officials in last-minute off-the-record interviews and specially written memoranda. I had even longer lists of detailed questions to which Chinese and foreign friends in Chungking wanted replies. And the censorship rules for our reports from Yenan had arrived at the very moment of our departure in a letter from Minister Liang, which said: "Anything hindering the consolidation of Chinese unity or a settlement of Kuomintang-Communist difficulties by political means will be deleted. On controversial points the Government should be given an opportunity to rebut."

In Paochi three important return passengers were waiting for the special plane on which we arrived: Lin Pai-chu, a white-haired Communist leader in a thick, homemade woolen tunic and proletarian cap, the chairman of the Border Region government who, like his old comrade Tung Pi-wu, had once been a prominent Kuomintang member in the days of Sun Yat-sen; Dr. Wang Shih-chieh, a high Kuomintang official in correct diplomatic attire, reminiscent of his recent "good-will mission" to Britain; and a general of the National Military Council in Chungking. The three men had started negotiations in Sian a few weeks earlier and were now on their way to Chungking for more detailed talks about a Kuomintang-Communist rapprochement.

They stood stiffly and somewhat forlorn at the edge of the airfield, behind a cloth-covered table which looked out of place on the green ground alive with spring flowers. Old Mr. Lin Pai-chu, the Communist, was apparently glad to see us, and I felt he would have liked to talk. But the general looked gloomy and forbidding. And Dr. Wang, in spite of our old acquaintance, was as uncommunicative as he was stern.

The question of how negotiations were going died on my lips. A swarm of local officials around the three silent men were evidently perturbed at our intrusion and we were whisked away to the train for Sian.

Chapter Four

A POLITICAL CRIME MYSTERY

ARE you a political detective?" one of our local guides in Sian asked me when they took us on a thoroughly conducted tour through the "Labor Training Camp for Ex-Communists." My interest in facts seemed to annoy him.

Sian, that grim bastion of anti-Communism and anti-Liberalism at the gateway to Yenan, is not used to independent newspapermen and has a deep suspicion of foreigners of almost any kind—as the resident missionaries are made to feel every day of their strictly supervised lives in hospitals, schools, churches, and foreign relief organizations.

I could not make up my mind, either in Sian or during the following two weeks of our journey through parts of the Kuomintang's blockade belt around the Communist-controlled Border Region, whether I felt more like a political detective or like a suspect of political crime. But all the time it was as though I were moving through the pages of a somewhat confusing mystery thriller of a new political variety.

The reception we had in Sian and the rest of General Hu Chung-nan's domain was somewhat like that of royalty from potentially hostile nations. Elaborate official welcomes were held for us wherever we went, with bands, parades, and well-staged popular demonstrations. Endless numbers of empty, solemn speeches were addressed to us. We were given lavish banquets twice a day, special theatrical performances, and comfortable trips to local sights.

Sian, like every town we passed, was on its toes. The streets had been especially cleaned, beggars and stray dogs turned out, and many Allied flags and welcoming banners decorated our path.

It was most difficult to find time to do our work. We were kept busy

30

with entertainment and constantly surrounded with an embarrassing solicitude for our comfort and pleasure and with a poorly veiled suspicious watchfulness. Each of us, as a rule, had one or two or three hosts with him. The Sian authorities had mobilized a large number of special rickshaw men who tried to force free rides on us and followed us anyway whenever we succeeded in sneaking out of the Guest House alone.

Foreign missionaries on whom we called were thoroughly questioned by plain-clothes men immediately after our visits and begged us not to make things more difficult for them by quoting them personally on what they told us about the Kuomintang and the Communists. And certain Chinese in Sian had been given orders not to leave their houses during our visit.

Wherever we went, our final destination was politely ignored in the public speeches given to us. The names "Yenan" and "Communist" were never mentioned and the common people in the smaller places had been given to understand that their particular area was the goal of our journey.

All our hosts appeared at first reluctant to talk even privately about their Red neighbors. But it did not need much provocation as a rule for a veritable hailstorm of accusations to be let loose against them. They usually warned us that our journey to Yenan would not enable us to find out the truth we sought since the Communists had cleverly extinguished all evidence of their crimes in careful preparation for our visit. "You may even get a favorable impression of the Communists," one of our hosts told me, "but it would be an utterly wrong impression."

"Is there a blockade against the Communist-controlled areas?" we asked in Sian at a formal meeting with the provincial governor and the highest ranking local officers in which our free habits of questioning caused considerable raising of eyebrows and disapproval on the part of some of our Kuomintang colleagues and government guides.

"To avoid trouble, we drew a line around the Border Region and built a ditch along it and little houses for a few dozen soldiers each; it is only a protective line," the Governor said.

31

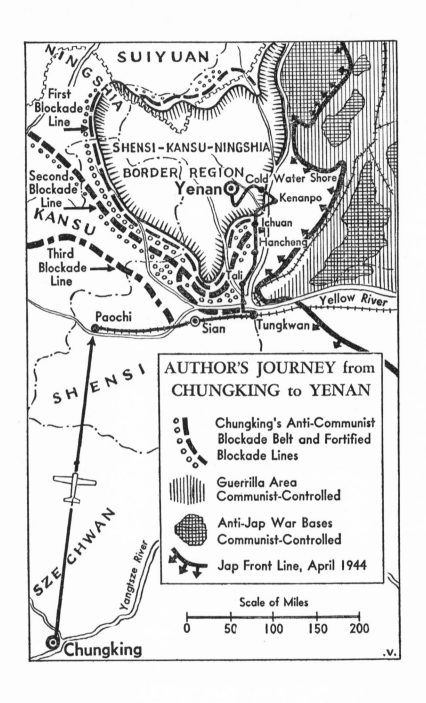

NINGSHIA

SUIYUAN

First Blockade Line

SHENSI – KANSU – NINGSHIA

BORDER REGION

Yenan

Cold Water Shore

Kenanpo

Second Blockade Line

KANSU

Ichuan

Hancheng

Third Blockade Line

Tali

Yellow River

Paochi

Sian

Tungkwan

SHENSI

AUTHOR'S JOURNEY from CHUNGKING to YENAN

Chungking's Anti-Communist Blockade Belt and Fortified Blockade Lines

Guerrilla Area Communist-Controlled

Anti-Jap War Bases Communist-Controlled

Jap Front Line, April 1944

SZECHWAN

Yangtsze River

Scale of Miles

0   50   100   150   200

Chungking

.v.

We said we had recently been told in Chungking that there was definitely no blockade at all.

"Blockade is a term used by the Communists," replied Major General Lo Tse-kai, Vice-Chief of Staff of General Hu Chung-nan, the Strong Man of Sian, who was absent. "Call the belt a protective area. That's what it is. It was established because the Communists failed to obey military orders. Wherever there are Red troops with organizations, doctrines, and propaganda methods entirely different from ours, there is danger that the whole area may be sovietized. Moreover, the Red troops have the slogan 'No hard fighting; retreat when the enemy comes,' so that we have to keep in mind the possibility of the Japanese marching through Yenan to Sian. The Communists would not be likely to offer resistance. Therefore, the protective belt is actually more against the Japanese than against anybody else."

"What are the main points of difference between the Government and the Communists?" we asked.

The head of the provincial Kuomintang, an important man in the national party hierarchy, took his turn. "The Communist party is an international organization, while the Kuomintang is a national party advocating democracy. The Communist platform is class struggle, while we believe in class harmony. The Government is doing everything to achieve national unification and a thorough enforcement of orders essential for progress and for the war, while the Communists consider all this detrimental to the development of their influence. To the Communists, national unification is a mere pretext for achieving their own ends."

"Are you optimistic about a solution of the Communist problem after the recent preliminary negotiations here in Sian which are being resumed in Chungking today in a more formal manner?"

"As Governor of Shensi province of which Yenan is a part, I hope of course that a solution may soon be found; for only then can opium suppression and conscription to the army be carried out in the Communist-held territories."

"Are the Communists really growing opium?"

"I just wanted to talk about that. It is a ticklish subject, one of those family scandals one does not like to discuss. A long list of districts where opium is grown in the Border Region will be given to you. But the Communists have removed all evidence. You will be unable to locate any poppies or any place where opium stocks are hidden. The Communists have even taken down defensive structures along the Border Region and changed slogans of hostility toward the Government on walls and houses into slogars of cooperation and national unity."

I said I would like to know about the twenty-four cultural leaders with Kuomintang affiliations whose death at the hands of the Communists was reported last March in advertisements in the leading Chungking and Sian newspapers in connection with an official memorial service held in Sian.

"You will get the names. The memorial service was held here," the Governor replied. "Not entirely under party and government auspices but primarily by the bereaved families and friends. It is true that the Communists killed them and that they arrest anybody who is discovered as a Kuomintang member and even put such people to death."

One of our official guides from Chungking spoke up: "I hope you won't publish all these things right now so as not to endanger a political solution with the Communists. And please don't regard this as political propaganda of the local authorities here. The whole problem is internal and has not been propagandized in the past. We still want to adhere to this policy."

The conference ended somewhat unpleasantly with the discussion of the case of a Free Frenchman and a Swede who had escaped from Japanese-occupied Peiping through the Communist areas to go to Chungking and had been detained in Sian for the last nine months, without trial, for alleged espionage.

We took up the matter because diplomats and other foreigners in Chungking were concerned about it, especially since there had been a previous case of three completely innocent people, two Frenchmen and a Dutchman, who came the same way and had to spend a few bad weeks in Sian, apparently on account of the favorable impression they gave about the Communist areas. They were at last released—the elderly Dutchman with a broken collarbone.

But it was probably not our business to probe into such delicate matters and we respected our host's "sincere hope to refrain from further discussion."

On another occasion Major General Lo Tse-kai completely discounted the military importance of any possible understanding that might be reached between the Government and the Communists. Irritated by our continued questions on the Communist problem, he said, "We never had too much military strength in this protective belt against the Communists. And as for them, you cannot expect the Communists to fight the Japanese anyway. The most important result of a so-called agreement with the Communists would be that they might in such a case refrain from future attacks on our own troops at times when the Japanese launch offensives against us."

"What makes you expect that the Communists would not fight the Japanese even in case of a fresh Kuomintang-Communist agreement? Was it not generally recognized that they fought very well indeed, at least after the first agreement on national unity during the early stages of the war against Japan?"

"Even in the 1937 campaign they did not do much. And during the last six years the Communists did no fighting."

"Do you really mean this?"

"I say they did *no* fighting," he replied sharply, his face reddening.

"Why, then, do the Japs so often mention offensive and defensive operations against the Communists in their war communiqués?"

"Whatever units the Japanese claim to mop up or engage behind their lines are Government armies, not Communist troops."

"But Japanese war communiqués always differentiate clearly between Government and Communist forces."

"If you believe in Japanese propaganda, what use is it for America to fight in this war?" He was very excited. "This concerns international affairs," he concluded, "and I refuse any further discussion of the subject."

"May we assume that you are speaking for your chief, General Hu Chung-nan?"

"Yes, of course. What I have said is entirely based on reports turned in at headquarters."

Our first actual witnesses against the Communists were the inmates of Sian's famous Labor Training Camp.

Our official program said: "The Camp was established by the National Military Council in 1939 to give short-term training courses to certain homeless youths who fled to Sian from the Communist areas. Through labor service they are taught some productive technique or trade so that they may participate in the nation's wartime work."

The camp is a very big, walled place with nicely ploughed fields and parade grounds, dormitory and classroom barracks, Spartan and of a breath-taking cleanliness. Every square inch seemed swept and smoothed. Some of us instinctively put our cigarette butts into our pockets during the tour of the grounds. An atmosphere of rigid discipline and sternness reigned everywhere. I had never experienced anything like it in China.

We saw hundreds and hundreds of hard, impenetrable faces of men between twenty and thirty-five in gloomy classrooms and spoke to some on a joyless playground. One of those men trembled so pitifully and got so hopelessly confused when I asked him about his political past that I did not have the heart to go on.

We looked into an empty girls' day room where an exhibition of knitted things was prepared for us. On the walls was a strange combination of amateurish portrait sketches: Mme. Chiang Kai-shek; her radically democratic sister, Mme. Sun Yat-sen, who courageously upholds the true meaning of her late husband's political teachings and her opposition to the present course of the Kuomintang; Mme. Curie of radium fame; and Mme. Kollontai, Soviet Russia's ambassadress to Stockholm.

Somewhere, there was a "wall newspaper" in English, *The Bonfire*, Vol. 2, No. 5. But we met nobody in the camp who understood English. One of its items was an article, "Message from a Martyr," dealing sympathetically with Pastor Martin Niemoeller, one of the most famous prisoners of Hitler's concentration camps. Another article opened: "With great rapture we students of the Northwest Youth Labor Camp welcome the arrival of the American-British Journalistic Mission."

In the auditorium, decorated with Allied flags, banners of welcome in English, and large pictures of Chiang Kai-shek, Roosevelt, Churchill, and Stalin, a horseshoe table was covered with tea, cakes, candy, cigarettes, and flowers. On the inside of the table several dozen men and some girls were standing stiffly at attention when we came in, sitting down just as stiffly when we, with a large number of guides and camp officials, took our places opposite them.

I filled page after page of my notebook with their stories. In the people who told them there was something that puzzled me for weeks: they were so tense and grimly self-condemnatory, so sad and yet so anxious to praise the camp which could not possibly be a tolerable place for any unbroken human being. They looked well enough physically, many of them were obviously intelligent, and a few seemed to have the characteristics of strong personalities. But they impressed us like marionettes, and some of the stereotyped life stories and accusations against the Communists I heard sounded memorized rather than experienced.

Why had they first joined the Communists? I asked one after the other. These were some typical replies:

"When the Japs came to my home I heard our people praise the Red Army and made my way there to join it. . . . I went there to help my country, although I was not a Communist at first. . . . The Communists in our university advocated liberty and equality and I believed them. . . . I first joined a guerrilla group at my native place and we all went over to the Communists to fight together with them. . . ."

And why had they left?

"I wanted freedom there, but since I did not care to join the party I felt the loss of freedom in Yenan was not worth while, and now I have been here in the camp for two years and feel free. . . . I studied medicine in Yenan but did not find a 'way' there, as the old Chinese saying goes. Things were not what I had thought. Their chief aim was

37

to gain strength but not to fight, and they planted opium. I heard that this labor camp was very good and came here voluntarily, a year ago, to fight for my country. No, I did not try to join the army; I had gone too far wrong and felt I was too much in need of thorough ideological training. Yes, here I have found my 'way.' . . . I had thought they were fighting the enemy. Discipline was bad in their army. They planted opium. I came voluntarily to this camp because I wanted to be trained. No, if I had the choice between leaving here tomorrow and staying another year I would certainly stay on. . . . I was a staff officer under the famous general, Ho Lung. I liked him very much personally but disagreed with him and left because I was forced to fight Government troops."

Who were all those people? Why did those strong young men not join the army, having forsaken their Communist sympathies but being as patriotic as ever? What gave their faces that strange, frightened expression which I had never before seen in easygoing China? Were they some of the thousands of progressive students and intellectuals from all over Kuomintang China who were caught in Sian on their way to Yenan year after year or arrested in their homes and colleges for "dangerous thought"? Months later I was to hear the inside story of this mysterious camp.

Other witnesses against the Communists came to see us at our Guest House, with special guides who always knew the replies to our questions better than the witnesses themselves. They spoke indifferently and in vague terms of Red suppression of the peasantry, of Communist Army units running away from the Japanese, of their attacks on Government troops, of wholesale Red murder and robbery. All of them failed when it came to actual concrete details, and some looked frightened rather than anxious to talk to us. The faces of their guides might have frightened anybody.

I was getting a bit homesick for Chungking. Its stuffy atmosphere seemed almost free and easy to me by comparison with that of Sian.

Chapter Five

THE STRONG MAN AND HIS REALM

LIEUTENANT GENÈRAL HU CHUNG-NAN is the Strong Man of Sian. His name is hated by the majority of patriots all over China as a symbol of authoritarian anti-Liberalism and militant anti-Communism.

His well-equipped armies of four or five hundred thousand men, among the best in China, have for years been surrounding the small Communist-controlled Border Region—while the lack of good troops at the war fronts permitted the Japanese to penetrate farther and farther into the country.

On the off-chance of meeting him in person we made the short trip to Tungkwan at the edge of his vast domain. Tungkwan, an ancient fortress in the Yellow River bend, was destroyed by enemy artillery five years ago. Since then the small Japanese positions on the other bank have been practically inactive. This is where Wendell Willkie and other traveling dignitaries used to be shown the "front" in recent years.

The front atmosphere of Tungkwan was as peaceful and unreal as I had found it on a previous visit with the British Parliamentary Mission to China, a year and a half before. Not the slightest change was visible. The Generalissimo's trim and modest son, Captain Chiang Wei-kuo, was still in command of a crack company of Hu Chung-nan's soldiers.

He showed the guests through the same spick-and-span underground trenches and machine-gun nests, making us peer through binoculars at one or two Japanese soldiers supposed to be on the same hill feature across the river. In the same old ruins of the town with its tidily piled-up rubble there were again many Allied flags and banners of welcome. The slogans on the walls in large English letters announced (it was in

May, 1944), "The whole Axis crumbles," "Rioting in Tokyo," and similar hopeful anticipations.

Again there was neither gun nor rifle shot. We sat just as peacefully as last time in the same old rickety building of the "Social Club" with its funny little bar, maps, and pictures . . . a single mile from big Japanese guns.

It was like seeing an old movie again.

A hushed silence fell on the room: The General was coming. . . .

Hu Chung-nan strode in, surrounded by a swarm of aide-de-camps. Introduction, shaking of hands, polite phrases.

I watched him intently for about half an hour. Was this the famous Strong Man the Generalissimo was supposed to be grooming as his possible successor? The man whose awe-inspiring name is whispered like that of only one other person, the grim chief of Kuomintang China's Secret Police, Tai Li?

Hu Chung-nan is a small man in his early forties. A bit fat, with flaccid, feminine, late-Roman features. Long artist's hair showed beneath his military cap. A shrewd and almost shy smile accompanied the soft, actorlike gestures of his fleshy hands and the strangely restless, birdlike movements of his head.

"The first duty of a military man is to fight the enemy," he said at the beginning of a short welcoming speech. With these words he parried the questions in our minds about his blockade against the Communists and the occasional fights along the Border Region. And when we finally asked them, he said politely, "With a big campaign on in the neighboring province of Honan and being very busy, I want to refrain from any political comment."

He seemed extremely worried. Next door, in Honan, a very large and reputedly very good Chinese army under another well-known Strong Man somewhat of Hu Chung-nan's type was quickly crumbling before an enemy offensive. The large province was being lost almost without a fight, and General Hu Chung-nan had arrived with a few divisions in a late and vain attempt to help his neighbor.

Would the Japanese push on to Sian, into Hu Chung-nan's important domain? Was that the final aim of their Honan offensive? Had their desire to gain control over the Honan stretch of the Peiping-Hankow railroad, and thus to complete their trunk line between North and Central China, been no more than a secondary objective?

Past experience seemed to indicate that the Japanese were satisfied to leave General Hu Chung-nan undisturbed. They could have attacked and beaten him long ago. There were only one hundred miles of easy ground between the Japanese positions opposite Tungkwan and the large open city of Sian. And foreign observers felt that Hu Chung-nan's troops might have been too thoroughly indoctrinated against their domestic enemy to do their best in a fight against the Japanese.

It had been a postulate of political strategy with Tokyo, so far, to keep the Sian zone of Kuomintang-Communist conflict undisturbed; for if the two Chinese camps were separated territorially they might at last compose their quarrels and draw together politically. That would open the way to a thorough change of the political character of Hu Chung-nan's troops and to their activization against Japan. And, far beyond that effect, it would greatly strengthen the Chinese war effort all over the country. Japan would not take such a risk unless she had to. . . .

But a new factor had come into the picture—the Chungking negotiations between the Kuomintang and the Communists with America's wish for Chinese unity as their background. Would that new factor be sufficient provocation to the Japanese to attack Hu Chung-nan?

In their broadcasts the Japanese threatened openly that they would have to launch a large-scale offensive against Sian and Northwest China in general if those negotiations led to an agreement between the two Chinese camps. And certain Chinese officials in Chungking and Sian were echoing those Tokyo broadcasts in confidential talks with foreigners: "This is not the time to come to an understanding with the Communists. It would make the Japanese jump at our necks."

Clearly, General Hu Chung-nan had reason to worry. And our appearance at this critical time, with the Generalissimo's permission to go to blockaded Yenan, must have been most unpleasant to him, for he had strongly advised against our journey and apparently been responsible for its delay.

We traveled north along the Yellow River through a strip of hilly country that is both defense line against the Japanese on the other bank and blockade wall against the near-by Communists.

The population seemed somewhat more thoroughly mobilized than in any other front or rear zones I had seen in China. But it was evidently a disciplinarian and not a popular mobilization—a mobilization based on suspicion rather than trust of the people, on rigid control from above rather than on any attempt to enlist the voluntary cooperation of the people. The ordinary men and women and youths I saw there impressed me as even more apathetic than elsewhere in China, as though they were bewildered by their contradictory double task of facing an external enemy and an internal foe.

The local officials were mostly picked Kuomintang men from other provinces who had gone through special training in Chungking and Sian. They seemed outwardly more modern and in some ways somewhat more active and efficient than local officials in other parts of China. Yet, facing two ways with much fuller consciousness than the ordinary people, they gave the impression of politically split personalities. I often felt tempted to ask those officials whom they meant when they talked about the enemy—the Japanese or the Communist "bandits."

The way they discussed the problems of popular mobilization, of developing the economy of a backward area, and of educating the masses was evidently that of stern, authoritarian taskmasters who were ignorant or contemptuous of the intelligence and potential initiative of the common people. Their policies seemed to me typified by a little scene we witnessed in a stuffy primary school in one of the towns that gave us a showy, royal welcome for which all the population had been mobilized. Children in uniforms were sitting stock stiff with their hands firmly folded behind their backs, shouting in unison: "Is it good to breathe fresh air?" And then: "Hao" (it is good).

At Tali, a trim little town, our host was the active and reputedly conscientious Prefect Chiang Chien-jen, a remote cousin of Generalissimo Chiang Kai-shek. Part of his special area had once belonged to the original Communist-controlled Border Region and he confessed with some hesitancy that the Communists had been driven out of it after the war with Japan had begun, which means after the Kuomintang-Communist agreement of 1937 on the limits of the Border Region.

"The defense of the river against the Japanese made it necessary," he said. "But we drove the Communists out mainly by the force of the people's organizations. It was rather easy to drive them out. They did not fight."

A large number of blockhouses manned by numerous members of the "People's Militia" was a special feature of this area. We inquired about the organization of the militia, and that brought about one of those minor press-conference crises we experienced at almost every place.

"Their task is to preserve peace and order. They must provide their own uniforms; they mostly bring their own rifles and normally get neither food nor pay when they are mobilized and away from home. If they are too poor to maintain themselves, other people help them. Their main function is to guard against bandits."

That struck a familiar note with those of us who knew about the old Chinese institution of people's guards by which rich landlords strengthen their economic and political power, resisting bandits at one time and fighting or threatening enemies, competitors, or tax collectors at another.

"Are they still equipped and maintained by local landlords?" we asked.

There was a moment of consultation and one of the officials replied hotly, "As this area is organized mainly against the enemy, I hope you will ask other questions than whether the landlords have an influence over the militia."

The least scholarly and benevolent type of old landlord gentry seemed even more evident in the administration of those "model districts" than elsewhere in China, and they looked at least as prosperous and arrogant as I had often seen them in other parts, against the background of an especially poor and depressed peasantry. Even some of our Kuomintang colleagues were embarrassed by those men, especially when they were introduced to us as "the people's representatives."

An incident with one of them, although small in itself, seemed so characteristic of the atmosphere in the blockade belt that most of us referred to it in the travelogue messages we sent to our papers. At the usual elaborate banquet in a little town I had been sitting next to a big, elderly man in a heavy silk jacket, the Agricultural Commissioner and "head of the Peasants' Union," whose personality reminded me of several speeches of Generalissimo Chiang Kai-shek against selfish and corrupt rural gentry.

Next morning, while we and our hosts were walking paradelike through the streets of the little town which were lined with row after row of well-regimented people, he told us that he owned much land but that he worked himself in his fields and was "practically a farmer." To demonstrate how he wielded the hoe on the fields, he swung his walking stick with his pale, flabby hands, when two little children ran in our way to have a better look at us. The landlord's "hoe" suddenly turned back into a stick and hit one of the kids. The modern-trained, intelligent magistrate noticed our instinctive reaction to this significant little incident and was greatly embarrassed.

A few of us then asked the head of the Peasants' Union, who seemed to be a man of special importance, whether we might walk alone through the town for a little while to talk to some of the people. He seemed somewhat shocked but gave instructions to a swarm of equally surprised officials to leave us alone, and we went off unguided.

We visited a little grain shop and talked to the owner, a shy and friendly man. He had just begun to discuss his business problems, telling us that prices on the whole were now about four hundred times as high as they had been before the war and that things were becoming more difficult, when a bespectacled young man in the uniform of an official slipped in silently without as much as a nod, sat down in the back of the dark shop, and ardently took notes of what was said.

44

The excessive politeness of our hosts was no deterrent to the clumsiness with which they made us feel their suspicion.

In a little town one of us asked for the address of the only foreigner, a Norwegian lady missionary of whom we had heard. She was an old and apparently useful resident of the town, but there had been no room for her at the big banquet we were given the night before. A local official, before giving the address, asked bluntly, "What are you going to ask the missionary lady?"

At another place the shopkeepers had evidently been prepared for our visit, since it must have been noticed that we took an interest in the price situation. When we wanted to buy a few things they quoted prices which made us gasp, prices in cents while we were used to prices in tens of dollars. And we were assured that consumers' goods were really very cheap in the town. I was offered matches at twenty cents instead of the usual three or four dollars per box. And Dr. P. C. Hsieh, our number one guide from Chungking, was given a tube of Shanghai-made tooth paste for forty cents, although he protested with considerable embarrassment that the normal price was around one hundred dollars.

Witnesses against the Communists were produced almost everywhere. In the little town of Hancheng two farmers were to tell us about the atrocities of the Reds who had been in their villages for a few days during the time of the Civil War.

"It was in September, 1935," one of them said. "The Reds stayed in our village one night, drove away cattle, looted a house, and shot my father, who was the village chief. No, I did not see how it happened. I had escaped. But I saw my father's body later."

"How did you know the culprits were Communists and not ordinary bandits which, we heard, were so numerous here in 1935?"

"They wrote texts on the walls, saying they were Communists."

"Why do you think they invaded your region?"

"They were sabotaging our patriotic war of resistance."

"But the war of resistance started only in 1937, almost two years later."

There was silence, and the official interpreter who had thought-lessly translated what he was told, tried to explain: "The man made a mistake. He came here a long way on his own initiative. He was very eager to tell you about his experiences. It is true, the Reds have not been here since the war began."

The other man told us that the Communists had burned the coffin with the corpse of his uncle that was being kept in the house for an auspicious funeral date.

"Why did they do that?"

"Because they thought my uncle's family was the richest in the village. They also killed a man in the neighborhood who they thought was the village head, and they burned houses."

"What did you see yourself?"

"Nothing. I had escaped. When I returned I found my uncle's house burned. No, I did not see the man they had killed or any other corpses."

In Ichuan, the last outpost against the Border Region, where popular enthusiasm was so well organized that hundreds of shopkeepers and other townsfolk literally leaped when we arrived, while cheer-leaders made them shout welcoming slogans at us, we saw a "Relief Camp for Refugees from the Communist Areas." There were some twenty ragged men in a little building, deserters from the Eighth Route Army.

The first man I talked to was an amusing type of genuine vagabond. He was frank and humorous in his confession to an equally profound dislike of hard work and of the dangers of war and stated laughingly that he had on a former occasion deserted from the Government Army. Then, he said, he was "taken" by the Communists at a peasants' meeting and enrolled in the Eighth Route Army.

"I don't know how long I have been here. I ran away from the Border Region some time ago because they worked me so hard. I had to plough two *mow* of land in the time I needed to do one. Therefore I ran away and came here."

"Did the Communists punish you when you worked too little?"

46

"No, they did not punish me." And he added, really serious for the first time, and most indignant, "They *criticized* me."

Another soldier had been partly paralyzed from childhood. His neck was stiff and his left arm dangled weakly from a low shoulder. He had been conscripted into the Eighth Route Army, he said, and ran away because they planted opium. "Every company has to grow forty *mow* (about thirteen acres) of opium poppies."

Still another, a strong, normal fellow, said he had voluntarily joined the Eighth Route Army when the enemy occupied his village in North China and fought the Japanese with his unit until 1942, giving details of several engagements. They had then been sent back to the Border Region for land reclamation work.

"After one month I disliked having to reclaim land instead of fighting," he said. After some rumination he obliged the camp officials with an afterthought: "They also planted opium. I ran away."

Poor chaps, they were to be sent once more for land reclamation: to the bleak, blockhouse-dotted Yellow Dragon Mountains which we had just passed. A few years of work in a labor company was the means of reforming all those deserters from the Communist side, the camp commander told me.

The chief of the local Anti-Smuggling Service joined our group and whispered to some of the deserters for a while. Suddenly, one spoke up on his own initiative.

"The Native Products' Company, a government enterprise of the Communists in Yenan, handles all the opium business. But the company does not exist now. It has been closed down for a while because you foreign correspondents are coming on a visit."

"Did you hear that yourself in the Border Region?"

"No, I heard it from a man who arrived here yesterday."

We asked to see that man and he came after the other had talked to him in a corner. Yes, the company had been suppressed, he said, for the time being. No, he did not know why, he had never heard of foreign correspondents' coming to the Border Region.

Still another deserter volunteered, "Everywhere off the main roads

47

in the Communist areas opium is planted in great quantities. For the Reds need national currency from the smuggling trade since the Government stopped all payments to their armies. Each company or brigade of the Eighth Route Army has a special economic officer whose main task is to see that enough opium is grown. But those economic officers have been taken away now because of your visit."

"What were you taught about Communism?" I asked the group.

"Only to oppose the Kuomintang. No, we don't know what other aims they have. We were taught only to fight the Kuomintang.

"No, nothing at all about fighting the Japanese," they added in a chorus.

The Anti-Smuggling chief gave me three badges of deserters from the Eighth Route Army and a little scrap of paper supposed to be a certificate for the export of 5.4 ounces of opium from the Border Region.

These were my last impressions of the Sian-controlled protective belt against the Communists.

In a popular library the picture of Generalissimo Chiang Kai-shek still hung side by side with those of Chamberlain, Daladier, Mussolini, Hitler, and Goering, as in the old days of Munich. At a lonely street corner was a large English-written wall newspaper which sternly reminded the Allies that they would neglect their obligations under the Four Power Pact if they "failed any longer to treat Japan as their Enemy Number One."

By way of contrast, I found among the local Kuomintang officials in that little outpost Ichuan an especially vitriolic hatred of the Chinese Communists which seemed to dominate their thinking completely and to leave little room for strong feelings against the Japanese.

"How can you ask whether the Communists are in any way Chinese patriots?" one of them snubbed me. I had asked him whether patriotism might not be a common basis for an eventual understanding between the two political parties.

But when we asked one young official what the ordinary people in this area thought of their neighbors, he told two of us privately, "Many think that the Communists are just Chinese people like ourselves. And I agree with that opinion, although some here have quite different ideas about Communists."

Somewhere on our way, out of earshot of the officials, we had got a similar reply from a little shopkeeper.

Chapter Six

"OUR OWN GOVERNMENT IS TO BLAME"

THE official program for our gradual approach to the Communist-controlled Border Region included a detour to the headquarters of Marshal Yen Hsi-shan, the last of the semi-autonomous war lords of China.

None of us knew what to expect from that visit. Even to high government officials in Chungking the Old Marshal had seemed little more than an historical memory. He was the man who at the time of the Revolution of 1911 rose from an innkeeper's water carrier to "model governor" of Shansi province. With his strong provincial armies he fought Chiang Kai-shek in the early nineteen thirties and almost emerged as China's leader instead of Chiang. During the war he lost most of his province to the Japanese but was supposed to have been on fairly good terms with them for some time.

Was he still alive? some people in Chungking had wondered. He must be. His name continued to rank high on the list of dignitaries of the Kuomintang. It was still among those adorning Chungking's dormant Council of State. And it figured among the country's highest military leaders; for Marshal Yen is Commander in Chief of the Second War Zone that comprises so much of the Communist-controlled areas. Nobody seemed to know how much of his old province of Shansi was still in his power, what his rule was like, or where Kenanpo, his headquarters, was situated.

Courtesy had apparently demanded that we call on the old gentleman before visiting the Communist-led armies, nominally under his command.

We crossed into Shansi province on a narrow suspension bridge over the Yellow River, scaled steep hills on our mules, and reached

Kenanpo—a strange, well laid-out settlement of two thousand caves cut into the soft loess earth of a steep hilltop, overlooking a grandiose scene of desolate mountains high above the river.

The marshal is a shrewd-looking, mild-mannered man of sixty-three who seems older than his years and as unwarlike as any Chinese I ever saw. He began at once to tell us about the paternalistic social theories he applies to his feudal fief of one million people; and so did the military officers, government functionaries, and intellectual advisers of his official family who treat him with the deferential obedience due an old-fashioned, benevolent Chinese father.

Yen's writings on social reform are a strange blend of "improved" Confucianism, Socialism, and Sun Yat-senism. They aim at "abolishing the proletariat in China" and, meanwhile, at protecting his own peasant retainers against the ideological influence of the Communists across the border. The "almost complete" set of Marshal Yen's works each of us got as a present must add up to some three million words. It is the gospel everybody in Kenanpo is supposed to follow.

One of the first things we were told was, "The Kuomintang has no real authority here; the party and its Youth Corps exist only nominally; they are free to establish themselves anywhere in our areas but are given to understand that it is better for them not to do so."

There were no Kuomintang party flags anywhere, none of the usual pictures of Chiang Kai-shek and Sun Yat-sen; and none of the official Kuomintang rites were observed at the public meetings we attended. Old Yen's own picture in marshal's uniform dominated the scene.

Yen Hsi-shan has his own currency, discreetly called "cooperative certificates." He raises heavy taxes according to his own ideas. The *gendarmerie* in his area is entirely his own, like his troops. His military and civilian officers are not appointed by Chungking but exclusively by himself.

The landlords under his rule had to reduce their rents from the former 50 or 60 per cent of the tenants' crops to a mere 5 per cent and were thus forced to work or leave. Yen's own taxes took the place of the rents, and he seems to be the only landlord now in the poor valleys around Kenanpo.

The merchants had to surrender to Yen's monopoly administration all "domestic" trade and all their "outside" commerce with the Japanese, Kuomintang, and Communist regions. They, too, were thus forced to go to work or leave and the marshal became the only merchant in his area. He prides himself on being more "thorough" in his social reforms than his Communist neighbors. He prohibits the smoking of cigarettes and prescribes suicide for officials who fail in their duties.

Marshal Yen does not like the Communists. Early in the war against Japan he sensed the upsurge of popular enthusiasm for a really progressive nationalism. He collected United Front elements from various radically democratic groups, encouraged their hopes for a political new deal in his "model province," and organized them into a high-spirited New Army, by the side of his old provincial army of mercenaries and conscripts.

But the New Army took his vague progressive ideas too literally, objected to his feudalistic paternalism and his lax methods of fighting the Japanese, revolted, and finally went over to the Communists after bitter fighting with his old-style troops. The New Army still exists and, as I found out later, seems to have built up a distinguished record of successes against the Japanese, in close alliance with the Communist Eighth Route Army.

We asked whether there had been any incidents between Marshal Yen's troops and the Communists recently.

"In the past three or four months there were eighty-six conflicts," he said. "We had seven hundred casualties and one regimental commander was killed. Recently, for example, there was a fight at the Feng River. We were ordered by Chungking to send some troops through an area held by the Communists in order to assist the Government armies in their defensive against the Japanese in Honan. The Communists stopped us, and that was how the conflict arose."

But one of Yen's aides, a liberal English-speaking professor at his university near Kenanpo, had previously given a few of us an entirely different version of this conflict. "We needed more food supplies," he said, "and therefore took a number of villages in the relatively fertile region of the Feng River; some from the Japanese and some from the Reds. The Japanese did not resist, but the Reds fought back when we came in, and we lost almost a whole regiment. However, where we let the Communists stay in their positions in Shansi province, relations between us and them are quite good now."

I asked Marshal Yen in a private interview what he thought of the Communists, of their practices and their conflict with the Kuomintang.

"The administration in the Communist-controlled areas is rather good," he replied. "The chief weakness and mistake of the Communists is that they think only of their party and not of the people. They train the people with the objective of dying for the party but not with the aim of improving their own livelihood. Superficially, the attitude of the common people in the Communist-controlled regions toward the administration is good. But if one talks to them privately, the people will weep about conditions."

He thought for a little while and drew his chair a bit nearer mine, as though he wanted to take me into his confidence. "If you are going to judge the Communists from the point of view of whether they are improving themselves, you foreigners must come to the conclusion that they are good because they *are* progressive.

"However, the more progressive the Communists are, the more the Kuomintang is afraid of them. The Kuomintang must reform itself. The Communists, on the other hand, should abandon their attempts at overthrowing the Kuomintang by force and should concentrate on the improvement of the livelihood of the people in their areas.

"As friends of China and as our allies who are worrying about the Kuomintang-Communist conflict, you should urge the Government in Chungking to improve and the Communist party in Yenan to abandon its expansionist policies."

"Have the Communists been expanding into Kuomintang regions recently?" I asked.

"It is true that they have slowed down in their expansion. And the demand of Chungking that the Communists should withdraw from their present Border Region in North Shensi is unreasonable. But no-

53

body is sure that the Communists have definitely abandoned their policy of force for the future.

"Look at me," he said. "Why does the Government allow me to do what I am doing? Why does it let me and some other provincial leaders in China have a certain amount of force and power of our own? Why are none of the officers under me and none of my civilian officials sent by the Government in Chungking? Why can I collect my own taxes?

"And why, in spite of that, do I get from Chungking regular monthly cash payments for the wages of my troops, special payment for their uniforms, and a large quantity of food as well as bullets— all of which the Communists don't get?

"Why all this? Simply because the Government knows that I do not want to overthrow it by force although I am also critical of the Government and frequently send my criticisms to Chungking. This shows the Government that I want to help it improve but that I don't want to overthrow it."

He spoke about the great strength of the Communists and I asked him to what he ascribed it.

"The reason why the Communists today have such powerful forces is that so many people are following them. And the reason why so many people are following them is that our administration, the administration of the National Government, is bad."

Then, with more emphasis than he had used before, "We have to blame ourselves for the present situation with regard to the Communists. Only by improving our government all over China can we prevent the ordinary people from following the Communists any further."

I asked whether he thought that Chungking was reliably informed about the Border Region and the Communist-held areas in the enemy's rear.

"No. The authorities in Chungking cannot get reliable information about the Border Region, because their investigators are men who pick up only the bad points. The reason for this is the hostile mentality of those investigators."

54

"Our Own Government Is to Blame"

At last the time had come for us to see for ourselves what was going on in the Yenan regions.

After several days at Kenanpo, crowded with talks and the usual receptions, banquets, mass meetings, speeches, and theatricals, the kind Old Marshal and his retainers saw us off one early morning on our ten-hour ride north along the Yellow River.

We went over a practically unused route on which we had decided only a few days before, instead of taking the main road to Yenan via Ichuan according to the official itinerary.

It seemed more tempting to approach the mysterious land of the Communists through a back door.

"We will find them just as Chinese on the other side," one of my colleagues said on the ride when we were wondering what to expect. "Things may be better in some respects and there will be other labels. But Chinese are Chinese. You will see, fundamentally the difference won't be great. . . ."

Part Two

THE DOOR TO YENAN OPENS

EIGHTH ROUTE ARMY SOLDIERS IN PRODUCTION WORK

Chapter Seven

CROSSING THE LINE

I CROSSED many frontiers in my twenty years as a foreign correspondent, but none ever seemed to me so forbidding as the lifeless, closely blockaded border between the two halves of China. We stopped in a wild gorge of the Yellow River where a group of Marshal Yen's military and civilian officers had assembled to bid us farewell.

On the steep, bare mountains on either side were grim-looking blockhouses, trenches, and a few sentries. No human habitation was visible at. this river crossing which had seen much trade in peaceful times.

The day before, a soldier with a white flag of truce had announced our coming to the Communists who expected us from the other direction, and a heavy barge was brought down the river for the rare occasion of contact between the two sides.

The sixteen boatmen had a hard task rowing us across the rapid torrent. They pulled with all their might in a fast, beautiful rhythm, chanting an ancient river song that sounded like the prayer of primitive men to the wild elements.

On the other bank four solitary figures moved slowly along the foreshore to meet us. Shy, friendly smiles, awkward handshakes, and an almost embarrassing minimum of simple words of greeting were our welcome on Communist territory. There was none of the usual scraping and bowing, no exchange of name cards and of solemnly mumbled phrases of courtesy.

We had become used to large reception committees, bands, parades, and rows of cheering crowds at every place we passed, so that we were both perplexed and relieved at the contrast.

Crossing the Line

"The name of this place is Cold Water Shore," one of the Kuomintang men in our party remarked with an ironical smile.

We climbed up the steep bluff in silence, following the four quiet, blue-uniformed comrades to a prehistoric-looking little village.

A few groups of caves with walled-in farmyards and mud-built stables in front of them; a dilapidated shrine that seemed to serve as a speaker's platform for village assemblies; some children playing on the steps of a little temple; and an Eighth Route Army soldier patrolling the top of a ridge, high above the village: this was the place where we settled down for our first night in Communist China.

Some peasants had cleared for us their brick-built family beds, each big enough for four or five people and taking up most of a cave. Tidily piled up along the walls were their tools and household utensils, bundles of dried vegetables, and jars of preserved food. The pleasant, earthy smell of herbs in our cave at Cold Water Shore will always be associated in my mind with that first night in the Border Region.

We stretched out comfortably on the clean straw mats that had been spread out for us in the little farmyards in front of the caves. Washbasins with steaming noodles, vegetables, and scrambled eggs were brought for our evening meal, without apologies. It tasted delicious after two weeks of banqueting on rich Chinese food.

Peasant women quietly continued spinning, cooking, and nursing babies in the yard and took little notice of us. Men came home from the fields, gave a friendly nod, put their tools in a corner (the tools seemed unusually new and of a modernized shape), and looked after their cattle. Life went on as usual. Nobody made a fuss about us.

Next morning soldiers arrived with horses and mules for our five days' ride to Yenan—weather-beaten, well-nourished men in hemp sandals and baggy blue cotton uniforms with the red collar tabs of the regular Chinese infantry.

The red star on the caps of the Communist troops was replaced by the white star of China's national flag when the United Front against Japan was formed in 1937. But those red collar tabs—somewhat larger than the regulation size in the Kuomintang Army and shining redder because they are worn without the usual insignia of rank—seemed to have special significance, like the bits of bright red cloth that showed through the cartridge belts of some of the soldiers, as though they indicated the special character of the Communist troops and their connection with the past.

One of the soldiers was Wang Chen, a pale, wiry, proletarian-looking man in his middle thirties, with protruding teeth, intelligent eyes, a ready laugh, and a big, warm handshake.

He welcomed us with simple friendliness, standing at attention, his hand at his cap, "in the name of Comrade Chu Teh, my commander in chief." He assigned to me a big horse captured from the Japanese.

The soldiers, who showed us the way over narrow paths up and down steep hills and through canyonlike valleys, carried Japanese rifles or Mausers and some of them had the long Samurai swords of Japanese officers slung over their shoulders like guns. They were lively and cheerful and often broke out into melodious guerrilla songs.

The land was poor and in many places semibarren, dry, yellow, and treeless. "The whole Border Region is like this," Wang Chen said. "This poverty of the soil and the resulting backwardness of the people are the main problems of our rear base. But we are tackling them like every other problem."

There was definite evidence of progress in comparison with what we had seen on similar land in the adjoining Kuomintang areas. A part of the semibarren hills much greater than on the other side was green with young wheat and millet. The reclamation of virginal or long-abandoned land had been going on here for five or six years.

Frequently we passed large groups of peasants ploughing and hoeing on gradients so steep that they could not use their oxen and horses. "Those groups are 'Labor Exchange Brigades,' one of the many forms of voluntary cooperation we encourage," Wang Chen explained. "They have made a great deal of difference to the livelihood of the people. For twelve people working together can do at least the same amount as sixteen working individually. Most families have much more land now than they used to have, and bigger crops. We had good weather for a number of years, which made land reclamation very

61

profitable. Most of the peasants here are still somewhat superstitious and they say, 'There has been plenty of rain since Mao Tse-tung came.' "

The farmers looked better fed and better clad than those I had seen in other parts of China. They seemed to have more livestock. Cotton growing had been introduced for the first time, and spinning and weaving revived. Schools seemed more numerous and there was in general more activity in these still poor-looking little cave villages than in those we had passed on the other side.

The village magistrates we met gave the impression of a new type of keen, practical people of the poor peasant type. Most of them were Communists, local men who had carried out a vigorous agrarian revolution years before the Red Army arrived from its Long March, at the time when the present Border Region was still a "Soviet District." But we were told that elections to the People's Political Councils, which Yenan introduced everywhere, were free and democratic and that Communist party members were never allowed to take up more than one-third of the seats. If more were elected, they had to give up their seats to nonparty candidates who had the next highest number of votes.

Of the men who sat on the councils with Communists many were said to have been former members of the Kuomintang. And we were told that a good part of the new "activists" instrumental in mobilizing the people for an intensive production drive, for education, mutual help, a greater interest in self-government, and all the other policies of Yenan's "New Democracy" were not Communists themselves.

It was all too new, and impressions were too incomplete to judge the truth of all the claims to progress that I heard. It seemed somewhat too good to believe. But the atmosphere in those little cave villages on the way did seem different from that on the other side: more lively and without any visible signs of regimentation.

The personality of Wang Chen interested me more than anything else during those refreshing days on horseback. There was something unusually impressive about this plain, unhandsome, modest soldier who was said to be a brigadier general and garrison commander of one quarter of the Border Region, including Yenan itself. He spoke with equal enthusiasm about his many battles with the Japanese and the economic and cultural progress of the peasants in his area.

It took me months of later acquaintance to realize fully how much he personifies Chinese Communism in its past and present phases and what a typical part he has been playing as one of many ordinary fighters. For Wang Chen, in spite of his sterling qualities, seems no exceptional man.

One afternoon I succeeded in getting his life story from him, although he did not want to talk about himself. He told it simply and without hatred for his former class enemies.

As a boy he had suffered grinding poverty and feudal suppression in his little village in Hunan, in Central China. His thirst for liberty and knowledge and his hot, rebellious temper had made him run away to the big city where he kept body and soul together as a water coolie and then as a vegetable peddler, until he found a comparatively well-paid job on the Canton-Hankow Railway. Night-school studies and trade-union work increased his awareness of the social injustice that kept the Chinese peasantry in backwardness and fired his hatred of imperialistic Japan. He joined the Communist Youth and then the Kuomintang when the two parties began to cooperate in the National Revolution. During Chiang Kai-shek's *coup d'état* of 1927 the Kuomintang purged him from its ranks. He was among the railroad workers' guards who opposed force with force, was wounded, and had to flee for his life from one underground hideout to another.

Wang Chen's military life started in 1929, when he did as so many peasant rebels had done before him through the ages of Chinese history: he went into the hills of his native province and organized peasants into a small band of partisans. The first Red division developed out of the merger of many such bands and he joined up as a sergeant. He was wounded four times during the stormy years when the new Chinese Soviet Republic opposed strong Kuomintang armies; and two more times on the Long March on which the Sixth Red Army which he helped to lead as a political commissar lost nine thousand out of its twelve thousand men.

The Long March of 8,500 miles, with its ceaseless fighting during twelve grim months of almost incredible hardships, was Wang Chen's staff college and he knew then that he was preparing himself for the eventual fight against Japan. "To resist the national enemy had been our real aim ever since 1931," he said, "although our struggle for survival was still with the forces of the Kuomintang which fought us instead of Japan.

"But for me the Civil War ended already in 1935. That year, when I arrived here in the Border Region with my exhausted troops, Comrade Mao Tse-tung had started the United Front movement. As a result of it, he gave orders to launch no more counteroffensives against the Kuomintang armies even though they continued attacking us from Sian. I was to train the brigade of which I was then Vice-Commander for the war against Japan, and to educate it politically to United Front cooperation with the Kuomintang. We were ready when the war with Japan broke out. There was real cooperation with the Kuomintang for some time. We covered the southward retreat of the regular Kuomintang troops from the north and then advanced north ourselves behind the enemy lines. I gave up many of my steeled veterans of the Long March as cadres for the fresh units that were formed there by peasant and worker volunteers in the Japanese rear. But my brigade also grew. We were in many battles against the Japanese in North China. Until," he sighed, "we were called back here. . . ."

Why was Wang Chen's crack brigade in the Border Region today instead of continuing its fight against the Japanese at the front?

First of all, it was necessary to guard Yenan against the Japanese who hold strong positions on the opposite bank of the Yellow River, a little farther north than where we had crossed it. They tried at frequent intervals to force the river and march on Yenan, a city they seem to hate more than Chungking. Moreover, as long as relations between Chungking and Yenan are not so good as they were for a short while at the beginning of the war, the Communists feel they cannot count on assistance from General Hu Chung-nan's troops around their Border Region in case of a large Japanese offensive.

"Hu Chung-nan helping us? Never!" Wang Chen said.

Their second task is to guard the Border Region against those same Kuomintang armies of Hu Chung-nan in the blockade belt which are supposed to be ten times as numerous as the forty or fifty thousand men the Communists are now keeping in garrison.

"And our third task," he said with emphasis, "is to hold an elite force in readiness for the Allied counteroffensive against Japan."

I came to know Wang Chen well enough later to believe him when he expressed a longing for that day and when he talked with warm understanding of the impatience of his men for the fighting front.

Chapter Eight

SOLDIERS WHO FEED THEMSELVES

WANG CHEN and his brigade of ten thousand men were given yet another duty when they came back from the front. They won a new kind of victory of which they have reason to be proud. They carried out the order "Feed and support yourselves; lighten the burden of the people; lead the way in a great production drive."

Wang Chen seemed full of enthusiasm and activity when we came to the scene of his brigade's battle for production, the area of Nanniwan. The old revolutionary and soldier showed an entirely new side, as did so many military commanders later in Yenan: he appeared to be the born leader of a great production enterprise, a pioneer farmer and educator.

What I saw in Nanniwan put life and truth into every word of his absorbing story.

"You have seen how poor this Border Region is," he said. "You have seen the blockade belt that surrounds us and you know that the Government in Chungking gives us neither pay nor food. You realize that we are facing the Japanese across the Yellow River. You will understand the choice that stood before us when we were recalled from the front. It was between two things—either to live in semistarvation and thus weaken ourselves and the war effort, while at the same time having to burden the people with demands for our minimum needs; or to do what no army has done before as far as I know: to work for our own subsistence while training and standing ready to fight at a moment's notice.

"I put this alternative frankly before my troops at the time. There were many different opinions. Their minds were bent on fighting the

Japanese. A good part of them did not like the idea of reclaiming land and doing peasants' work while the war was still on. We had many discussions. But at last we were united in the decision that Comrade Mao Tse-tung's order was correct under the existing conditions. Only a few may still fail to understand fully why we have to be in Nanniwan a while longer and do farm work in the hills instead of returning to the front."

I thought of the deserters from the Eighth Route Army on the other side and, watching his reaction, handed Wang Chen the identification badges of three deserters which I had been given in Ichuan by the chief of the Anti-smuggling organization.

"Yes, those were my men," Wang Chen said without hesitation when he saw the names on the badges. "Maybe they were some of those who did not understand or maybe our work was too hard for them. I don't really mind their running away. It makes no difference on which side they stand against the Japanese, whether on ours or on that of the Kuomintang—if only they are made active in the war effort."

And he continued his story.

"About a hundred years ago a great uprising of local Moslems against the suppression of Peking led to the depopulation of this large area of Nanniwan. All the land on the hills and most of the fields in the valleys went to waste. When I led my troops here to start our first army-production project four years ago, there were no caves or houses for us to live in, there was no food to buy, there were no tools, and no farmers whom we could ask to work for us.

"The Border Region as a whole was so poor at that time that we could not bring enough food and scarcely any implements. We received little money from the government in Yenan. Right from the beginning we had to provide for ourselves almost everything we needed. We cut down wood for primitive shelters and dug a few caves. We reclaimed a bit of land each to get some vegetables. We didn't have enough to eat in the meantime.

"To have something to exchange for the goods we needed most urgently we cut hard pines, which the people in the adjoining areas like

67

for coffins, and sold them to the villagers. The magistrates in the areas through which you rode helped us borrow some old tools from the peasants who were ready to assist us as much as they could.

"Our tool problem was solved at last when one of my soldiers, young Company Commander Liu, discovered a big, old iron bell on the top of a hill in a long-abandoned temple. It was too heavy to bring down and I don't know how it ever got up there. Liu dug a big hole underneath and smelted it on the spot, and we found some blacksmiths who were willing to teach our men how to make tools from the two thousand pounds of iron we got from the bell and from scrap we collected in the distant villages."

The temple bell of Company Commander Liu and how it helped to reclaim thousands and thousands of acres of land has since become the subject of one of the most successful stage plays and folk-dance dramas all over the Communist-controlled regions. We saw it acted with spirit and talent a few weeks later in Yenan.

"We produce more tools now than we need and sell them cheaply to the farmers. But first of all we replaced every implement we borrowed with a new one. Yes, those nice strong hoes you saw at your first resting place at Cold Water Shore came from our army blacksmiths.

"There were many more difficulties to overcome. One of them was that I knew too little of production myself. But we solved this, like all our problems, in a democratic way. I asked each and every one in my brigade to offer me their knowledge and experience, to criticize the plans I made for them, and to suggest changes. We discussed everything together, just as we did all the work together. For there is only one distinction of rank in the Eighth Route Army, in war as in work: our cadres, as we call the officers, have to work harder and better than any other comrades, no matter what the job may be."

Today, over 35,000 acres of former wasteland are under cultivation in Nanniwan. This year's harvest will yield on an average somewhat more than 1.1 tons of millet, rice, wheat, corn, vegetables, cotton, hemp, and tobacco to every one of the ten thousand officers and men on this vast "revolutionary property," as they call it proudly.

Each ten men have raised one cow, ten sheep or goats, and five pigs, and each company owns at least one hundred chickens and many ducks and rabbits.

Wang Chen's brigade does not spend a cent of the taxpayers' money any more. On the contrary, it helps the people in many ways.

The soldiers of his brigade and of the other units of the Eighth Route Army that have followed its example, in the Border Region as well as in some parts of the Anti-Japanese War Bases in the enemy's rear, now seem to be the best fed in the whole of China. Owing to the great improvement in nutrition, sickness and death rates are said to have gone down greatly in spite of the pathetic lack of medical supplies.

The people have greater respect than ever for this army which supports itself to such a large extent. "Instead of demanding aid or taking things away from poor peasants," many farmers told me later, "these new soldiers help the peasants."

This is part of Wang Chen's order to his brigade, dated February 5, 1944:

"I. In execution of the policy of Chairman Mao Tse-tung, our food production last year twice exceeded the quota assigned us by Division Commander Ho Lung. Our production quota this year is twice as large as our actual production was last year. But we must exceed it by at least one-third and produce a total equivalent to 13,000 tons of millet.

"II. The period from March 10 to the end of October is to be devoted to agricultural production. But due to rain and the intervals between ploughing, hoeing, and harvesting, there will be about fifty days during that period which are to be given to recreation, military training, and anti-Japanese political education.

"III. With the exception of those engaged in medical, industrial, and transportation work, all members of the brigade, both cadres (officers) and rank and file, must on an average cultivate five acres of land.

"IV. In order to carry out the duties of developing production, guaranteeing supplies for the army and the government, of taking into account both public and private interests, and of building up revolutionary property, so as to persist in unity with the people in armed resistance against Japan and in the protection of the Border Region, the following distribution of each member's production, estimated at an average of 2,440 pounds per head, is to be carried out: 30 per cent for the self-supply of food to this brigade; 4 per cent for its self-supply of clothing; 33 per cent for the food-reserve fund of the army; 33 per cent as each member's private income which, on the basis of prevailing food prices, can be drawn in cash and either invested in cooperatives against interest, remitted home, or used for personal needs.

"V. Since the production movement is a sacred task in the revolutionary cause, cadres and men and political workers in every unit must thoroughly carry out their mission in close solidarity and with mutual encouragement and help. . . ."

(Signed) WANG CHEN
Brigade Commander and Political Commissar

The crops looked excellent in Nanniwan and may have turned out larger than these estimates. But even if they were only normal, Wang Chen's brigade, in 1944, will not only have fed itself plentifully and put in one year's reserve ("for the counteroffensive," he said enthusiastically when I asked about its use), but it will also have provided an equal amount for the market from the one-third of the crop out of which the soldiers get their private cash income.

"Our production will continue to grow and we shall reclaim more land every year," Wang Chen said. "After the war Nanniwan will easily support 200,000 people—wounded soldiers and refugees from famine districts in Kuomintang regions like Honan. Many starving people from Honan are already smuggling themselves through the blockade lines into the Border Region because they know that we will help them to settle down." (I was to see a good number of them later.)

Those days in Nanniwan were one of the most encouraging experiences I ever had in the Far East.

We saw rows of white-clad men in their undershirts and pants reclaiming marshes and dry hill land or working in well-cultivated fields.

70

"This is the company, or battalion, or regimental commander," Wang Chen would say, picking out one of the hard-working men and demonstrating proudly his labor-hardened, calloused hands. Or, "This one joined the Red Army when he was twelve, on the Long March; he is a company commander now and one of my best men before the enemy as well as in agricultural work."

We saw tidy dormitory caves and dining rooms and social clubs, a hospital and a sanitarium, all built by the men themselves. We saw workshops in which disabled soldiers and soldiers' wives spun and wove and sewed all the uniforms for the brigade; blacksmiths' and printing shops; and small plants manufacturing paper, soap, and alcohol.

We met some of Wang Chen's popularly elected "Labor Heroes." One was a Japanese war prisoner in Eighth Route Army uniform who helped the Nanniwan project with a new type of pump he devised, with a modern beehive he designed, and with many odd jobs. He seemed just one of the Eighth Routers, happy and natural in an entirely un-Japanese way and violently opposed to Japanese militarism.

We saw the officers and soldiers beam when Wang Chen came into sight. That and nothing else, as a rule, was their salute to their brigadier general of whom Division Commander Ho Lung told me later that he had to bawl him out sometimes for being too rough and strict with his men. Wang Chen himself had confessed to that fault and told me he was trying to improve himself. But it was evident that the men were very fond of him.

Wang Chen's hands were just as calloused from labor as those of his troops. An American doctor at the International Peace Hospital in Yenan told me afterwards that he had to put the brigadier general's big toe in a plaster cast recently because he dropped a heavy bag of coal on it while helping his soldiers with their work, as every officer does.

But the men of Nanniwan are still primarily soldiers, and probably among the best anywhere in China.

Wang Chen was greatly surprised when I asked him whether the fighting qualities of his men had deteriorated in the course of their production work.

"They are better than ever," he said. "First of all, they are much healthier and stronger. They never had such good food in their lives, nor so much physical exercise. Secondly, they have a full five months of military training in winter—hard, realistic training and nothing else; and one full month of military training in summer during the dull agricultural season. Even during the months of work in the fields there is not a day when they don't practice hand-grenade throwing, bayonet tactics, and all sorts of other techniques in their rest periods. You have seen them take their rifles with them to the fields. They are always ready for action."

We visited one company after another in their tidy cave headquarters. The arms were kept splendidly. For two days I myself counted how much of their equipment was Japanese and wrote down the markings in detail. It was obviously true that more than one-third of their rifles, two-thirds of their machine guns, and most of their artillery had been taken from the enemy.

"All this was captured by my brigade," Wang Chen said.

Every one of those mountain guns had its own fascinating story. A good many we heard from men who participated in their capture, and there was always mention by name of the soldiers who had given their lives in those fights with the Japanese. The memory of the dead seemed alive everywhere. The brigade had very large casualties in more than three years' battles.

These troops are now specialists in Japanese arms. They have learned their use thoroughly. Japanese war prisoners whom they helped to unlearn their Fascist ideology and who joined them as fighters against the militarists in Tokyo, assisted them much in this kind of training and also taught them the tactics of the Imperial Japanese Army. During the final counteroffensive they hope to take large quantities of arms from the Japanese and to turn them against the enemy the moment they capture them.

"The brigade specializes in night operations, at which our men everywhere are very good," Wang Chen said. "We continue giving them the hardest training in all the most difficult physical tasks and they make steady progress."

72

He read from his notebook some of the brigade's present performance records. In rifle shooting the cadres and men, including doctors and nurses, cooks and transport workers, average 95 per cent hits on a target 1 yard in diameter at a distance of 110 yards. Their average at well-aimed hand-grenade throwing during rapid advance, in fully equipped state, is 43 yards. A bayonet charge over a distance of 165 yards, with five handicaps and seven targets and the throwing of three hand grenades, takes 96 per cent of the men only one minute or less.

At our request a few platoons were sent at a moment's notice into a sham skirmish. It was an impressive performance of strength, speed, and skill.

Wang Chen is also an enthusiastic teacher of nonmilitary matters and very keen about the cultural progress of his men. Like all Eighth Route Army cadres, he is an all-round leader.

Nanniwan was just as much a busy school as a huge productive enterprise and a model military training ground.

"We have turned the monotonous existence of the Chinese soldier into a full and rich life, and we continue improving our cultural and political standards in the brigade. Our degree of literacy has become quite high. Only 20 per cent of all men read and write fewer than five hundred Chinese characters. Forty per cent know between five hundred and one thousand. And the others know more than one thousand and are fully literate in spite of all the difficulties of the Chinese script. One-third of all the time we give to education is devoted to cultural matters."

Great stress is laid on the democratic system of free and frank discussion. In a number of talks with plain soldiers I noticed that even those who still read comparatively little have a standard of general knowledge and a vocabulary far above those of the common people, which seemed due to their frequent discussion meetings.

"Last summer, when Comrade Mao Tse-tung asked me to intensify the political and cultural education in my brigade, I told him that I was still only semiliterate myself," Wang Chen said. "But Comrade Mao insisted that I do it and learn in the process. I had long discussions

73

with intellectuals in Yenan, told them about my investigation of our cultural shortcomings, and worked out together with them a concrete educational program. The party then enlisted well-known writers to come to Nanniwan on prolonged visits and help us, which they did."

I asked about the contents of the political education given to the brigade.

"It has the two objectives of inculcating hatred against Japanese militarism and raising national self-confidence. We have outgrown the old methods of an abstract revolutionary education. In all we teach we start with simple, concrete examples of what crimes the soldiers themselves know the Japanese have committed in Chinese villages or with examples of the practical, democratic cooperation between our brigade in Nanniwan and the people in the surrounding areas.

"From such examples within the experience and understanding of our men we deduce the political principles that guide our army, our administration, and the Communist party in their policies of war against Japanese militarism and in the practice of our New Democracy.

"The expression of everybody's views plays a large role in this education. And it has to be really free, in order to be useful. We blame ourselves, and not our men, for wrong opinions they may hold. We try to convince them, not by order, but by discussion."

Chapter Nine

NOTES OF DISCORD

SOME of the accusations against the Communists I had heard on the other side began to fade into comparative insignificance before the reality of Nanniwan. All of us felt that way.

Yet I kept them in mind all the time.

The opium question ranked first, because it loomed so large in Chungking's case against Yenan.

We arrived in the Border Region from a direction in which the Communists had not expected us to come and thus passed through those "remote and almost inaccessible territories" where, according to the Governor of Shensi in Sian, large quantities of opium were produced by the Communists.

All of us watched out for poppies every day and every hour. Wang Chen repeatedly suggested to our Kuomintang colleagues and ourselves that we go off on our own anywhere, for any number of days, to look for poppies. Nobody accepted his offer. We had covered sufficient territory, anyway, and the hilly country over which we came gave us wide vistas.

Our whole group always stayed together and none of us saw a single poppy. But several weeks later, when our Chinese colleagues and three of our National Government guides had returned home, the Kuomintang-subsidized *Meng Li News Agency* in Chungking carried the following dispatch from Sian:

"The Press Party of Chinese and Foreign Correspondents visiting the Northwest, on their way from Shansi province to Yenan, changed their route at a moment's notice and instead of taking the Yenan highway via Ichuan, as was decided for them by the Yenan authorities, crossed the Yellow River in West Shansi and passed through the most secluded and lonely villages before they got on the main road to Yenan.

"Over all the area through which they traveled, poppies grew so luxuriantly that they formed a spectacle.

"A certain correspondent recently wrote from Yenan to the' Shensi Branch Headquarters of the San Min Chu I (Kuomintang) Youth Corps and in his letter he described in detail what he had seen and heard. Together with the letter he sent a poem which reads as follows:

'Everywhere grows a wonderful flower of which I do not
    know the name;
I got off my saddle and respectfully asked the Elders;
They shook their heads, waved their hands, and kept silent.' "

Was this the kind of information on which Chungking's accusations against the Communists were based, the type of intelligence that was given to the Generalissimo?

I also watched out for those anti-Government slogans the Communists were alleged to have changed for our benefit into slogans of co-operation with the Government. In a little town where we passed the night one of our Kuomintang guides told me privately that he and several others had found slogans on house walls which read, "Reactionaries who dare to fight the Border Region must be driven back," "The Kuomintang is detrimental to the people," and another which was partly defaced, "Down with the Kuomintang."

A little while later we had a press conference with the local magistrate in the presence of Wang Chen. There was also a young Communist party official from Yenan, Chen Chia-kang, whom I knew during his years in the Communist Representative's office in Chungking.

Without mentioning how I had come to know about them, I asked the magistrate bluntly when those slogans had been put up. He said he was not aware of any such writings, but if they really existed, the third one would probably date back to the Civil War and the others might have remained from the summer of 1943, when the whole Border

Region was alarmed at the prospect of an imminent attack by Government troops. He would investigate and reprimand anybody he found responsible for counteracting the policy of the authorities in Yenan whose aim it was, in the interest of national unity, to achieve cooperation with the Kuomintang and to avoid all provocation.

Chen Chia-kang, normally gentle and mild, rose to the occasion with an almost passionate speech. "In the period of the struggle with the Kuomintang," he said, "such slogans were widely used as a matter of policy, but that policy has been abandoned since the United Front was created against Japan, and it is not the aim of Yenan any more to defeat the Kuomintang. We realize fully," he exclaimed, addressing himself to his compatriots, "that the slogan 'down with the Kuomintang' would be just as harmful to our country as your slogan 'down with the Communist party' "—which, as we all knew, is still used in wide parts of Kuomintang-controlled Northwest China.

I suggested having a look for ourselves. We took lanterns and all of us went searching through the sleepy main street of the little town.

At last we found over a shop two little slips of red paper such as Chinese people paste on their doors or walls, sometimes with classical quotations and sometimes with private expressions of opinion. The third slip of red paper had been completely scratched off and bits of it were still lying on the ground. Evidently all the papers were old and faded and had been inconspicuous among newer and much larger slogans of a positive and practical nature, connected with the Border Region's propaganda drives for increased production, education, and intensification of the popular war effort against Japan.

We resumed our conference by candlelight in the courtyard of the magistracy, in an atmosphere of considerable tension.

Wang Chen spoke, at first calmly and then with vehemence. "It is fortunate and important for the Chinese Republic that you correspondents have come here and that at the same time Comrade Lin Pai-chu went to Chungking for negotiations between the two parties. I want to assure you again that you have the right to investigate freely every phase of our work here, and you are most welcome to do so. But to drag out old Civil War slogans is harmful. I do not hesitate to criticize anybody who in front of foreign friends tries to sow discord, and I say frankly that such activities are the work of spies rather than of newspapermen.

"All over the world the Fascist forces are weakening and the forces of democracy are gaining strength. This is very fortunate for China. But it is regrettable that some people in our midst are still sowing dissension. As garrison commander of this area, I feel responsible for the fact that such old writings have been kept on houses in this town, and I shall investigate the matter. But I want to tell you that such slogans have only one significance now, a great significance, and that is that they tell something about the history of the relations between our two parties."

Wang Chen's sincerity made an impression on everybody although his Hunanese hot temper and his oft-expressed wish for national unity had for once got the better of his usual reticence on the delicate matter of Kuomintang-Communist relations.

From the first day we had watched the relationship between the Kuomintang men in our party and the Communists, anxious to see them develop in a friendly way. Our leisurely horseback rides across pleasant hill country, the improvised wayside meals in the day and the long evenings with plenty of good, plain food and local-made liquor at quaint resting places seemed to offer singular opportunities for personal contacts. They might help a little toward an understanding between Chungking and Yenan, for which all of us hoped. . . .

The head of our party, suave Dr. P. C. Hsieh, with whom we had had no difficulties so far, belonged to the group of Dr. Sun Fo, the leader of the progressive wing of the Kuomintang, and called himself an open-minded liberal. And Wang Chen was certainly a sincere patriot and a likable man. They should have been able to get on well with one another. . . .

I was always glad when I saw them together, absorbed in conversation or exchanging friendly remarks at meals over their cups which both of them liked. Yet I sensed some tension between them and between their two groups almost from the beginning.

78

Now that Wang Chen had made that sharp speech, I wondered whether something might not have happened before of which we did not know; whether there was not more behind his excitement than the three slips of red paper.

There was more behind it.

The next day, when Wang Chen, Chen Chia-kang, and I were resting on a hilltop after a strenuous ride, Wang told me what had been on his mind for some time and had contributed to arousing his temper the night before.

"When I first spoke at some length with the Chungking government officials who are the leaders of your party, they irritated me deeply by saying, 'Those foreigners are of no account,' and, 'It is for us to lead the group of newspapermen; they have no individual right of going about as they please; they must obey discipline and all arrangements for them must be through us.'

"The second day I visited the two officials in their room. They tried to give me a lesson, saying, 'You are too warm-hearted to the foreigners, as though you thought they might be useful to the Communist party.' And then they gave me accounts of all of you. This is what they said, and it was mainly the responsible leader, Dr. P. C. Hsieh, who spoke.

" 'Among the foreigners there are an American priest, another American who works for the Kuomintang Publicity Board, a Russian *Tass* correspondent—and the other three are just Jews. Without morals, without knowledge, and without culture. No use whatsoever. As you know, Jews are like that. They are only newspapermen, trying to make a living, working to get dollars and pounds. Even among each other they compete fiercely because news can be sold.'

"I was boiling with anger," Wang Chen said, "although I restrained myself. I told them I am a son of China, a Communist soldier who fights against Japan and against international Fascism of any kind, and that I don't like it at all to hear anybody propagating Fascist ideology.

" 'You have spoken like Tojo and Hitler,' I told the Kuomintang men, 'and what you have said is an insult to me and to the foreign

79

friends of our country.' They both stood up and said in unison, 'Please don't misunderstand us. China's problems are internal problems, a family affair which we should discuss among ourselves but not with foreigners.' I walked out angrily without another word.

"I brought the matter up several times in front of all the Kuomintang correspondents, some of whom seemed shocked. I wanted to nail down the two men to their statements, and they never denied a word."

The night before we left Wang Chen's Nanniwan headquarters on the last short stage of our journey to Yenan, some of his soldiers and their wives gave us a beautiful folk-dance performance in front of the local headquarters under a moonlit sky, with a large gathering of troops around us.

Wang Chen was called to the telephone. And when he came back he jumped on a table and shouted, in a voice vibrating with emotion, "Friends, the second front has been opened! Europe has been invaded! American and British troops have landed in France!"

And then, still louder and shaking his fist, he roared to the resounding threefold echo of his men:

"Down with Fascism; long live Democracy!"

Chapter Ten

THIS IS YENAN

YENAN looked rural, peaceful, and innocent; like the primitive campus of a medieval institution of learning rather than the headquarters of the military and political forces of Chinese Communism.

The sun played a serene allegro of rustic harmony on a semibarren yet peculiarly attractive scene.

A thousand-year-old pagoda was shining tall and yellow on a hillock over the junction of three narrow valleys, treeless and strangely void, with a mere sprinkling of low houses. Near by, an ancient city wall, hiding the empty site of old Yenan; its mud-and-brick houses pulverized by Japanese bombers, with only a few half-ruined stone gates standing by the road; much of its rubble washed back into the soil by heavy autumn rains and turned into fertile patches green with flax.

Tall ranges of boldly shaped hills glistened in the rich yellow of their dunelike loess soil and the fresh green of slanting wheat and millet fields.

In contrast to all the light and color, innumerable little cave entrances gaped black out of the hillsides—rude gashes of prehistoric-looking dwelling caves, above them thin columns of kitchen smoke rising through invisible chimneys out of fields which are their rooftops —and long, regular rows of arch-shaped openings into the modern cave structures of government institutions, schools, and hospitals—cut tier upon tier into glittering façades of pared and smoothed yellow hill surface, like big buildings half-buried in landslides.

Sheep and goats, cattle and horses grazed in the valleys and on the hillsides. Peasants in wide-brimmed straw hats worked in well-kept fields. Blue- and white-clad people crouched on stones in the shallow

81

rivers, washing clothes, babies, or themselves. Little caravans of donkeys, mules, and horses with heavy bags and bundles, their bells tinkling and their traditional red tassels swaying, moved slowly over the dusty mud road, past unhurried officials, students, and soldiers in faded blue cotton uniforms. Blacksmiths in open shacks forged tools for farmers. Workers made bricks by the roadside. Tradesmen were busy in little stalls and shops. Children played in a big schoolyard.

We stopped at the Government Guest House, a pleasant garden compound of caves and little brick houses. A few people received us in a friendly, natural manner.

Each of us got a simple little room, brick-floored, with paper windows, a makeshift bed of boards, a big new desk, and some flowers, and we were left alone to settle down and rest after a long journey.

The Communists did not seem so keen or so good on propaganda as I had thought. Very little happened the first few days. They seemed glad that we had come and were willing to help us in our work. But they did not go out of their way to impress us and showed a calm reserve. Their attitude seemed to be, Use your own eyes to find out about us.

They were evidently suspicious of our Kuomintang guides. Dr. Hsieh's anti-Semitism and anti-foreignism, which they called Fascism, seemed to have made a strong impression on them. Some of the Kuomintang members of our party looked uncomfortable. At the beginning, the atmosphere between the two Chinese groups was somewhat tense in spite of outward mutual amity. It was reminiscent of the pet phrase of the Minister of Publicity in Chungking about the Kuomintang-Communist conflict being a "family affair."

One of the elements in the atmosphere of Kuomintang-Communist tension in our Guest House was an actual family affair. It concerned one of our guides from Chungking whose brothers, like many upper-middle-class families in China, are split between followers of the Kuomintang and Communist parties. Our guide and two of his five brothers belong to the Kuomintang and work for it in Chungking, while the others are Communists living in Yenan. The three Communists, apparently, did not care to see their right-wing Kuomintang brother and were rather formal when they visited him at last; and this gave rise to some agitated speculation in our Kuomintang group about alleged Communist party pressure on the unfortunate heretics.

We kept in the background for a while, spending much of our first days with two foreigners we found in Yenan. Michael Lindsay, an English economist who escaped from the Japanese in Peking the day of Pearl Harbor, has been helping the Eighth Route Army with technical radio work ever since. And an American doctor who calls himself by the Chinese name Ma Hai-teh has been working for six years at one of the local hospitals. Both said they were not Communists but gave very favorable opinions about the Border Region and the Communist-controlled Anti-Japanese War Bases.

My days and a good part of the nights were soon crowded with work. I worked harder than I had ever done in my journalistic life.

I had to clear up many doubts and get at the truth behind all my strong and surprising impressions of a life that seemed entirely new to Asia. For hours and hours I interviewed individually Communist and non-Communist leaders and responsible officials, without much regard for their time, I am afraid. In fact, I cross-examined them, going unceremoniously into details of their political life stories and asking disagreeable questions based on Kuomintang accusations of the "bandit" variety. I had never met anybody in the Orient who would allow himself to be interviewed in such a manner. But the people in Yenan did not seem to mind.

I visited government offices, army organizations, factories, model farms, colleges, schools, hospitals, the court, and the jail and dropped in on meetings of self-government bodies. I talked to many plain people, especially non-Communists. And I kept on thinking up new lines of critical approach, probing into details of various aspects of Yenan's political system and practice, on the basis of my experiences in other parts of China and what knowledge I had of Russian Communism.

I was completely free in my investigations, able to go wherever I wanted and to see anybody I desired to talk with. No questions were barred and no replies refused.

The political scene of Yenan reflects the calm and simplicity of its rustic setting, just as its political life goes on at a retarded but steady village tempo.

In the foreground is the headquarters of the Communist party, The Yang Family's Hill, as everybody calls it by the ancient name of its site.

It is a rabbit warren of neat, whitewashed offices and dwelling caves, connected by steep paths and steps through terraced vegetable plots; with a small secretariat building of modern architecture from which the Central Committee directs the work of a million party members; and with a big stone-built auditorium, where Roosevelt, Churchill, and Chiang Kai-shek share the walls with Marx, Engels, Lenin, and Stalin. (The pictures of the non-Communist Big Three all looked a bit faded, like the others, and apparently were not just put up for us.)

Party headquarters is a calm but busy place where the teamwork and the private lives of hundreds of responsible party functionaries seem to merge in a peculiar pioneer atmosphere of unsophisticated, self-assured enthusiasm.

The fifty-year-old man in a baggy tunic, tall, massive, good-natured, and somewhat awkward in his speech and movements, with whom the people in headquarters seem to be on warm and affectionate terms, is Mao Tse-tung, chairman of the party and the outstanding personality in Communist China.

Mao Tse-tung still looks and acts like the peasant he was and the schoolteacher he became—easygoing and simple, thoughtful and precise. His unusually powerful forehead, his penetrating eyes with their air of deep concentration, and the calm and clarity of mind which his mellow personality seems to express mark him as a mature statesman of ability and a popular leader. He is poles apart from the stern, rigid, and care-burdened military figure of Generalissimo Chiang Kai-shek in Chungking.

A short distance up the valley is Army Headquarters. Everybody refers to it as The Wang Family's Plain, the ancestral name of another old landlord's estate near the Yen River where blue-uniformed sentries guard a low brick gate in front of a large compound similar to that of party headquarters.

It is the nerve center of the Communist fighting forces. In caves with incredibly primitive radio equipment, daily operational reports are received from the far-flung Communist war fronts in the enemy's rear in North and Central China.

The maps of the simple war room in a little mud building give a picture of one of the most complex constellations in military history. They show the scattered areas of thirteen large and many more small Anti-Japanese War Bases which the Communists have liberated from the enemy—areas supposed to have a total population of 80,000,000 to 90,000,000 and more than 2,000,000 militiamen. They specify the latest dispositions of the large, mobile regular forces of the Communists, alleged to be about half a million strong.

They give in detail the array of several hundred thousand Japanese troops and their innumerable Chinese puppet soldiers, showing how the enemy is hemmed in by the Communist positions—in thin strips of territory along railroads and motor roads and in narrow circles around the big towns and cities.

The hundreds of staff officers who live and work in the caves at headquarters were very busy. For field commanders were arriving all the time from the various parts of the front, having traveled for months on foot and horseback and crossed dozens of heavily fortified enemy lines through breaches made by Communist troops. It seemed that plans were being laid during the summer for Communist operations in connection with the Allies' final counteroffensive against Japan.

General Chu Teh is the Commander in Chief. He is broad, heavy, and remarkably strong at fifty-eight; a man of few words whose clever, deeply lined peasant face is known and beloved by the troops and people for its irresistibly warm and cheerful smile which puts everybody at ease; a forceful revolutionary warrior turned strategist and popular leader.

"He appears clever and honest," one of our Kuomintang colleagues remarked to me, evidently surprised at his own impression.

A third center of power seems to be budding in the self-government institutions of the New Democracy which have been created by the Communists.

In the middle of the town in a walled-in compound with gardens and vegetable fields• stands a big barnlike assembly hall marked People's Political Council. It is next to the solid stone bungalows of the government of the Border Region. Here legislation is passed and administration carried on by men and women who are said to be freely elected by the entire population and to represent all its classes.

Strangely enough, there seems to be only one restriction on the people who elect the councilors, and on the councilors themselves who then elect their standing committee and the heads of the Border Region government: as we had already heard on the journey, Communist party members must not occupy more than one-third of the available seats! Two-thirds of all the members of the People's Political Council and its standing committee and of all the responsible officials in the government must be non-Communists.

Stranger still, Communists in all those elected bodies and everywhere else have strict orders from party headquarters to facilitate the work of their nonparty colleagues in every possible manner and to further the development of the New Democracy in which its Communist initiators seem to have restricted themselves to a one-third minority.

The picturesque background of Yenan's political scene is in the big popular meetings, theatrical shows, and folk dances which are alive with a rustic communal spirit.

Inconspicuous men in the badgeless blue cotton uniforms of common soldiers, chatting with people they do not seem to know, were introduced to us as famous military commanders.

Others, dressed in the same crumpled cotton pants and tunics as the crowds of clerks, students, and simple labor heroes with whom they

86

joked or carried on serious conversations, turned out to be outstanding party functionaries, high government officials, or eminent professors.

Famous women revolutionaries and novelists, educators, or actresses were part of gay groups of peasant women and factory girls, secretaries, students, and schoolteachers in the same simple garb—cotton trousers and tunics, shirts or blouses of blue, gray, khaki, black, or white, all with those strangely beloved soldiers' caps which seem to have become part of the men and women of all ages in this mysterious New Democracy.

When I walked through the empty-looking valleys of Yenan and visited its primitive caves which are teeming with life and activity, I was again and again impressed by the striking contrast between this rustic place and the role it claims for itself in China.

How could this little Yenan vie with Chungking as capital of the other half of patriotic China, as the other directing center of the war against Japan, as model for a new China?

Here was Yenan—with only 40,000 people, of whom 12,000 were soldiers, government and party officials and students; without electricity and modern machinery; with no other motor traffic than four or five ancient trucks; with practically no roads, and without a navigable river; without any planes bringing in supplies from the outside world; with the bulk of the large territories and the 80,000,000 people under its control scattered deep in the enemy's rear between innumerable Japanese fortification lines; and with the semibarren Border Region of 1,500,000 people, its only rear base outside the war areas, fenced in on three sides by the rigid blockade of Chungking's armies and on most of the fourth by strong Japanese forces along the Yellow River.

And there was Chungking—with almost 1,000,000 people; with power plants, factories, and modern machinery; with thousands of trucks and motorcars, thousands of miles of motor roads and navigable rivers; with hundreds of Allied planes flying in supplies every day; and with some of the most fertile parts of China and about 150,000,000 people as its huge, compact rear.

This Is Yenan

Viewed at a distance in comparison with Yenan, Chungking's physical handicaps seemed to me even less grave than I had considered them at close quarters. And its potential strength—which forceful democratic government policies could long have mobilized—appeared even more formidable than I had always been convinced it was.

The steadily deteriorating picture of Chungking kept coming back to me like a nightmare. I saw it during the last few years—getting more war-weary, lax, and helpless; its gray, bomb-damaged, patched-up buildings and its new bamboo structures sprawling over more and more of the green, fertile rice terraces of the Yangtsze hills, growing bigger yet more inert; its ever-increasing crowds looking strained and purposeless in the stale and futile commercial atmosphere of dirty streets—people who have so long been ready not only to endure but to be mobilized for action; its officials sitting year after year in clogged, overstaffed government offices—more undernourished and dejected as time went on, yet in spite of everything as willing as ever to see the war through and ready to help an inactive government overcome all difficulties in well-directed reforms; Chungking as it is—in reality, not in its own propaganda—a pathetic city of passive war suffering rather than of active war effort, of frustrated tenacity rather than inspirited exertion.

Would I find it true that little Yenan was able to vie with big Chungking—because the Communists really knew better how to use the great power of hand and mind of the ordinary Chinese people on which they said they depended so much?

It was still too early after the first six weeks or so to judge this question and many others that came up during my first round of investigation. But I felt able already to summarize some preliminary conclusions about evident atmospheric differences between the two cities.

This is what I wrote in my diary at that time.

First, there is no war weariness here, but the steady fighting enthusiasm of a primitive pioneer community. Although most of the leading people and thousands of the others have had seventeen years of war—ten years of Civil War with the Kuomintang, then, after a few months'

88

IMMIGRANTS FIND NEW HOMES IN THE BORDER REGION

break early in 1937, seven years of grim struggle with the Japanese—and since 1941 in addition to the war with Japan something like near-war with Chungking. War, apparently, became their profession.

Second, there is no reliance on outside help. They would like to get it but do not count on it. During most of those seventeen years the Communists have been living and fighting in an almost watertight blockade, so that self-reliance seems to have become second nature to them.

Third, people seem surprisingly young here, whatever their age, and full of refreshing optimism and confidence. They repeat all the time that they have lived through much greater difficulties than those of today, and that they always overcame them. They seem to feel, whether we believe it or not, that the future is theirs.

Fourth, they never seem to speak badly about each other in private. There is no gossip or backbiting here as in Chungking, where, after a few days, people will take a newcomer into a corner and whisper about the defects of certain colleagues and superiors. But there is much public criticism of the remaining shortcomings of their system in Yenan, which would not be tolerated in Chungking.

Fifth, their shortcomings, mainly in the category of an inefficiency corresponding to the rustic background of men and life and to the remnants of an ancient past, seem somewhat less irritating than those of the Kuomintang people in Chungking. For their defects are accompanied by a veritable passion for self-criticism and a genuine readiness to correct mistakes as far as possible, if necessary by scrapping policies that had for some time been cherished as final answers.

Sixth, the leaders in Yenan know the Kuomintang and conditions in its territories much better than Chungking seems to know the Communists and their areas; and they differentiate much more in their critical estimate of personalities and policies on the other side because their approach is analytical rather than emotional.

The Kuomintang members of our party returned to Chungking after six weeks in the Border Region. The newspapermen said their editors had more important work for them than studying the Communist situation. And our government guides felt they were of no use since we had made ourselves independent of them and went our own way.

They suggested taking us back to Chungking. But we reminded them of the written promise every member of the party had to give the Generalissimo as his condition for letting us go—that we would stay for at least three months in the Communist regions.

"Never mind that promise to the Generalissimo," we were told. "Haven't you seen and heard enough in Yenan?"

Only Father Shanahan, the American priest, left with them, having made a satisfactory arrangement with the Communists for the reopening of Catholic missions in the Border Region, an arrangement which might be valueless if Chungking continued its refusal to let missionaries follow the invitation of Yenan to return.

Our three main Kuomintang guides were in a bad mood when they left. From our messages which they precensored before they were sent on to Chungking for final censorship, and from frank talks we had with them, they knew that all of us were on the whole favorably impressed with what we had seen and heard so far. Two of them admitted frankly to me that the Generalissimo had made a grave mistake in letting us go to Yenan, and an even greater one if he had believed that a prolonged stay would convince us that the Communists' administrative work was no more than a farce and their war effort against Japan a hoax.

They must have realized, as most of the Kuomintang newspapermen did, how badly the Generalissimo seemed to have been misinformed. His yes men in Chungking evidently told him what they surmised he wanted to hear about Yenan. And the semi-Fascist demagogues in Sian, who have always been eager to push him into another civil war, apparently provided him with the kind of information which might make him consider such a venture necessary as well as comparatively easy.

We had all been together on a visit to the office of Yenan's party newspaper, the *Liberation Daily*, where the editor gave us proof that the Generalissimo's own information about Yenan is actually censored by his anti-Communist crusaders in Sian. Official notices of the Sian postal censorship authorities informed the *Liberation Daily* that copies of the paper sent from Yenan to the following persons had been confiscated on the way to Chungking: Generalissimo Chiang Kai-shek, Marshal Feng Yu-hsiang (the famous "Christian General"), General Cheng Chen (at present, 1945, Minister of War), General Chou En-lai (at that time Communist representative in Chungking), and many others. Sometime later, a letter arrived at the *Liberation Daily* from the Generalissimo's headquarters in Chungking, complaining that no copies of the paper had been received for several months.

In talks with some of the Kuomintang men in our party I noticed that a good number in the group were suffering from a conflict of loyalties when they saw in Yenan what ordinary Chinese people of all strata were able to do under the most difficult circumstances, once their dormant energies were set free and stimulated. Their patriotic loyalty to China made these men inclined to acknowledge many of Yenan's achievements and on account of them to be more hopeful for the future of their country. Bashfully, and sometimes in terms of conventional Chinese politeness, they showed definite signs of national pride in some of the men and institutions we saw together in Yenan.

On the other hand, their party loyalty toward the Kuomintang seemed to make them hate and fear the Communists even more bitterly when they recognized that Yenan was much stronger and more successful and stable than they had expected to find it. Keeping themselves isolated within their own group and being to some extent under the influence of a few cynical reactionaries among them, they breathed even in Yenan the stagnant air of Chungking. In order to balance their favorable findings on matters which left little room for doubt—like the surprising progress of production in the Border Region, the unusually good state of health and morale of the troops, and the refreshing pioneer spirit that animated the people in this part of China—they stressed their grave doubts in the genuine character of Yenan's New Democracy.

I, too, was still doubtful. But before I went on to investigate in more detail, I had to sort out the impressions of all the manifold aspects of Yenan's new political, economic, and social life which rushed in on me during those first six weeks, and to see whether they fitted into a plausible whole.

Part Three

NEW DEMOCRACY IN THEORY AND PRACTICE

VILLAGE ELECTION

Chapter Eleven

YENAN'S POLITICAL A B C

YENAN has a special political idiom, as our interpreters used to say when a government leader, a peasant, or a worker referred to one of those many new terms and slogans of which even our Kuomintang colleagues were ignorant. I spent a few days compiling for myself a Communist dictionary from what I heard and saw. It proved to give a fairly complete survey of the ideas and practices of the people in the Communist-controlled regions.

ACTIVE ELEMENTS are people anywhere in villages, factories, or army units, in schools, shops, cooperatives, mule caravans, hospitals, and anywhere else, who take a special interest in the tasks of war and social progress and show spontaneous enthusiasm and initiative. They seem to be the basic factor in this new society, its reservoir of strength and growth. The next step from being an Active Element is often popular election to public office or to the title and duties of a Model Worker or a Labor Hero. A small part of them may eventually become members of the Communist party of China.

ANTI-JAPANESE WAR BASES are the eighteen regions in the enemy's rear—eight in North China, eight in Central China, two in South China—with a total population of about 88,000,000 at the end of 1944. By March, 1945, the total was claimed to be 94,000,-000. Those territories were liberated from the Japanese by the Communist-controlled armies in cooperation with the local people and consolidated into self-governing territorial units for defensive and offensive operations against the Japanese in the occupied cities and along railroad lines and motor roads.

BIG REAR is the name for Kuomintang-ruled Free China, in contrast to the small rear base of the Communists in Free China, the Border Region.

THE BORDER REGION is the Communist-controlled area around Yenan composed of parts of the northwestern provinces Shensi, Kansu, and Ningshia, with 1,500,000 people. Most of it is the former Northwestern Soviet Region established by local Communist partisans who led an agrarian revolution during the Civil War in the early 1930's. It is surrounded on three sides by a strict Kuomintang blockade and on most of the fourth by the Japanese on the opposite bank of the Yellow River. A ferry service across the river connects it with the adjoining Anti-Japanese War Base in Shansi province and through it across many fortified Japanese lines, with all the other Communist-controlled territories behind the enemy's rear.

CADRES, high, medium and low, are responsible workers in the army, party, and governments, in schools, factories, cooperatives, and other institutions. Terms like "officer" are scoffed at; no badges of rank are worn and no titles used. Everybody, including non-Communists, is addressed as "Comrade." But grades of position, denoting only responsibility, are strictly observed on duty.

CHEE LAI ("Arise") is the partisan song of the Chinese Communists, most popular among the armies and people in the Yenan-controlled areas, of which there is an American recording sung by Paul Robeson:

> Arise,
> Ye who refuse to be bond slaves:
> With our very flesh and blood
> Let us build our new Great Wall.
> China's masses have met the day of danger,
> Indignation fills the hearts of all our countrymen.
> Arise! Arise! Arise!
> Many hearts with one mind
> Brave the enemy's gunfire.

March on!
Brave the enemy's gunfire!
March on! March on! March on, on!

Don'ts at present propagandized are along these lines: Don't be dogmatic, subjective, formalistic, bureaucratic, cliquish (addressed especially to party members); don't write for yourself, write for the masses (to writers); don't separate from the masses but rely upon them and adopt a thoroughly democratic style of work (to all cadres).

Eighth Route Army was the name the National Government gave the Red Army of the Civil War when a new United Front between the Kuomintang and the Communists was established at the beginning of the war against Japan. It became so popular that Chungking's later change of it to Eighteenth Group Army remained unrecognized in the speech of the rank and file and the people all over the Communist-controlled areas. Soldiers and officers wear arm badges with *18.G.A.*, in English lettering, but are always referred to as Eighth Routers, in Chinese "Pa Luchün." The Eighth Route Army had 321,000 men in the spring of 1944 but is growing steadily from its militia reserves and was claimed to be almost 600,000 strong in the spring of 1945.

Families of Anti-Japanese Fighters, listed in rolls of honor everywhere, are helped by their villages or towns in a manner that creates no tax burden and no bureaucratic organization. Special aid groups are voluntarily formed in every community to assist them in field work, spinning, and weaving and to take care of their children. These families are guaranteed the minimum living standards of "middle peasants."

The Great Three Tasks of the Army are to fight the enemy; to help the people in raising production; and to mobilize, organize, and educate the masses of the people for war and social progress.

Guerrilla Areas, by contrast to consolidated, self-governing Anti-Japanese War Bases, are territories in which Communist-controlled troops and political workers have organized sufficient popular sup-

99

port to frustrate the attempts of the Japanese and their puppets at pacification, and to carry out military operations. Guerrilla areas lie all along the thin lines of enemy occupation. They link up the Anti-Japanese War Bases.

HOME SPIES, distinct from traitors and puppets in the employ of the enemy, are secret agents of the Kuomintang in Communist-controlled areas, whom the popular Be Frank movement induces to confess against a guarantee of impunity and tries to convert into loyal supporters of the New Democracy.

IMPROVE THE ARMY AND SIMPLIFY THE GOVERNMENT is the much-propagated slogan for a thorough rationalization policy, introduced three years ago at the suggestion of a non-Communist landlord elected to a high government office by the people. It is still used although its main aims have since been fulfilled.

THE JAPANESE PEOPLE'S EMANCIPATION LEAGUE with seat in Yenan and secret contacts in the Japanese-occupied areas and apparently in Japan proper is a political organization of Japanese antimilitarists, consisting mainly of former war prisoners who were converted to anti-Fascist ideas. It aims at undermining the Japanese Army and government during the war and at the creation of a new postwar Japan, roughly along the lines of the New Democracy practiced in Communist-controlled China.

KUNGCHANTANG is the Chinese name of the Communist party, as KUOMINTANG is that of the Nationalist party at present in sole control of the National Government in Chungking.

KUOMINTANG AND COMMUNIST PARTIES, COOPERATE! is the slogan for national unity addressed to Chungking. It is widely propagandized by the Communists and recurs in all political speeches.

LABOR CREATES EVERYTHING is the motto most frequently found on walls. It was stressed to stimulate the impulse of self-help in view of the isolation of the Communist-controlled areas from the outside world.

LAO-BAI-SHING, or "The Old Hundred Names," the Standard Chinese term for "common people," is probably the most used word in the Yenan areas; for the furtherance of their interests and their awakening to political consciousness and initiative are the main substance of Yenan's policies in every field.

LEARN FROM THE MASSES AND THEIR EXPERIENCES is Mao Tse-tung's favorite phrase, based on the belief that the common-sense judgment and knowledge and the accumulated experiences of the ordinary people on all matters must be taken into account by intellectuals and professionals.

LIBERATED CHINA is the only term comprising the Communist-controlled regions behind the enemy's lines in North and Central China which, while individually self-governing and administratively independent of each other and of the local government of the Yenan Border Region, are under the general political guidance of the Communist party.

LOVE THE PEOPLE—AND SUPPORT THE ARMY is one of the most popular slogans. The first half is addressed to the army, the second to the people. Practical cooperation between the two in all their respective tasks is basic to Yenan's general policies.

MAGNANIMITY has taken on a new, popular meaning as the central idea of the three-year-old policy "Convert Them and Win Them Over," which is applied to all antisocial elements, from loafers, drunkards, and other backward elements to Japanese war prisoners, puppets, national traitors, home spies, and political opponents of the New Democracy within the Communist-controlled regions. This new policy replaced the revolutionary methods of punishment of Civil War days.

MASS MOVEMENTS, under the general guidance of a special department in the Central Committee of the Communist party of China, in Yenan, are carried out by Active Elements in the villages, towns, and organizations, mainly by means of discussion meetings, visits to individual families, theatricals, and study groups. Their aim is to explain and popularize the manifold slogans in which the goals of government policies are expressed.

The MASS VIEWPOINT must be taken by cadres in party, government, army, and other organizations. To find out about the opinions and needs of the masses and take them into full account in the formulation and execution of decisions is the supreme law for all.

The MILITIA, or MIN BING, in the Communist-controlled war areas numbered some 2,200,000 at the end of 1944. They are selected from the much larger Self-defense Corps of villages and towns in North and Central China. They are mobilized in case of defensive or offensive operations in or near their own districts and are the auxiliaries, as well as the recruiting reserve, of the regular Communist-led armies.

NEW DEMOCRACY is the programmatic name of the permanent political system introduced by the Communists in 1940, and the title of one of the most read books of the party leader, Mao Tse-tung, which was translated into English.

The NEW FOURTH ARMY comprises all the Communist-controlled forces in Central China. It was officially "disbanded" by the National Government in Chungking and its denomination was abolished in January, 1941, after a surprise attack on its headquarters by Government troops. But since then it has grown from 110,000 to about 300,000 men, early in 1945.

OLIGARCHY, "government by the few," is the standard term by which Generalissimo Chiang Kai-shek's one-party Kuomintang government in Chungking is censured.

The PARTY SCHOOL in Yenan is a school without teachers and curriculum in which high and medium cadres, army officers, government and party officials, factory managers, intellectuals, and other responsible Communist workers improve their education through self-study, exchange of opinion, and self-criticism of their work.

PEOPLE'S POLITICAL COUNCILS, democratically elected by all strata of the population, elect and control the governments of boroughs, towns, districts, and regions—different from those in the Kuomintang areas which are appointed and have only advisory capacity.

QUACKS, or "witch doctors," are the main target of a strong mass movement against superstition and for the popularization of modern medicine and hygiene.

RAISE ALL PROBLEMS TO A THEORETICAL LEVEL is Marxist slang for another standing order of the Chinese Communist party to all responsible workers, that is, to study any given problem thoroughly from a factual, scientific viewpoint before making decisions, instead of using hit-and-miss methods or being guided by wishful thinking.

REDUCTION OF RENT AND INTEREST—AND GUARANTEE OF THEIR PAYMENT TO LANDLORDS AND CREDITORS is the fundamental policy of solving the problems of tenant farmers and of those who are heavily indebted. This new policy which aims at reducing land rents to 40 per cent of the tenants' crops replaced the Communists' Civil War practice of confiscating the landholdings of landlords and canceling the peasants' debts. It fulfills a programmatic demand of Dr. Sun Yat-sen, the late Kuomintang and United Front leader, and enforces in the Communist-controlled areas a ten-year-old decree of the National Government of the Kuomintang which has never been observed anywhere in the regions under its own control.

SLOGANS play an even greater role in Communist China than in Communist Russia as a realistic means of mobilizing and educating a primitive society on a low level of literacy and political understanding.

STRUGGLE MEETINGS are occasionally called in various party and government organizations, army units, schools, factories, etc., to achieve improvements, adjust differences, and deal with misdeeds of individuals, whatever their position, by means of free, public discussion between all ranks. Mutual criticism and self-criticism characterize these meetings.

The THREE-ALL POLICIES OF THE JAPANESE, a daily reality in all the war areas of North and Central China with their continuous struggle for food, supplies, and positions, in which the people participate actively are Kill All, Burn All, Loot All.

The THREE-THIRDS SYSTEM OF POPULAR REPRESENTATION is the functional basis of the New Democracy under which the Chinese Communist party voluntarily restricts its own power and encourages the cooperation of other political elements. Voters cannot elect Communists to any more than one-third of the seats in any People's Political Council; representatives of other parties can be elected to another one-third of the seats; and at least one-third goes to nonparty candidates.

THREE YEARS' HARVESTS IN TWO YEARS is the slogan under which a drive for the further increase of agricultural production is carried on in 1944 and 1945 in order to build up stocks against the possibility of crop failures and for the counteroffensive against Japan.

USE YOUR OWN HANDS AND PRODUCE YOURSELF WHAT YOU NEED, originally Mao Tse-tung's instruction to all Communist party members during a critical economic situation in 1940, has become the standing order of all the armies, governments, and educational institutions to their members. Everybody, from the highest to the lowest ranking, must do agricultural or other production work outside duty hours, with the aim of increasing production and keeping the tax burden of the people as low as possible.

VILLAGE MEETINGS, in which every adult has an equal vote, elect the village head and control his activities, and discuss measures for the increase of production and other improvements. They are the basis of China's first effort at self-government.

WELL-FED AND WELL-CLAD was the first slogan of the New Democracy, devised as the aim and promise of the production movement during a period of widespread poverty in 1940. It has since become a fact in the Border Region and in part of the war areas but remains an important propaganda stimulus in some of the worst suffering Anti-Japanese War Bases behind the enemy lines.

WORK WHILE YOU LEARN AND LEARN WHILE YOU WORK is a slogan designed to make the educational policies of schools and colleges more practical and more immediately useful to the people, and to raise the educational standards of farmers and workers.

YANGKO, an ancient folk dance of Northwest China, revived and politicized by the Communists, has spread over all their areas like wildfire. It is a combination of dance and drama, used in an artistic,

104

entertaining manner to popularize the various mass-movement slogans.

Zamen Bienchu, Chinese for "Our Border Region," is affectionately used in the people's talk and in the songs they sing. These words sum up their pride in the progress which one of China's most backward areas has made in spite of the war with Japan and the blockade of the Chungking government against the Border Region.

Chapter Twelve

THE CREDO OF MAO TSE-TUNG

"CAN'T you do without that awful name Communist?" Allied diplomats and military officers who were inclined to think well of Yenan's war effort and its wish for democracy and national unity have recently been asking the Chinese Communists.

"You do not seem to be Communists in the generally accepted sense of the word," their argument used to run, "but simply social reformers, and you even call your political system New Democracy. An appropriate change of name of the Communist party of China would make it much easier for our people at home, of whom many are suspicious of the mere word 'Communist,' to understand your real aims and your intentions for the future. This would facilitate Allied cooperation with your forces in the war against Japan."

The leaders in Yenan and their representatives in Chungking would point out in reply that they cannot change their name—because they are and intend to remain Communists. They would explain that being Communist means no more than to accept the Marxist methods of thinking and of solving social problems; while it depends entirely upon basic conditions in the country to which any specific Communist party belongs, in what manner and at what time the introduction of a Communist system of social life has to be sought. For Marxism, the Communist doctrine, categorically demands from its adherents a correct political approach to the specific conditions prevailing in a given society. It condemns the application of identical revolutionary policies to countries in dissimilar conditions of social maturity.

China, they would continue, being predominantly agricultural in the economic respect and largely semifeudal politically, is far from ripe for Communism or even for its preparatory, socialistic stage which is being developed in the USSR.

106

China will first have to pass through a prolonged period of economic, social, and political evolution in which democracy and capitalism are equally needed to lay the foundations for later progress toward the next phase of socialism.

The Chinese Communists believe that the transition first from the present semifeudal system of Kuomintang dictatorship to democracy, then from democracy to socialism, and eventually from socialism to communism can be made a peaceful and painless progress. The only condition is that genuine democratic rule must be realized without delay, while the Chinese social system still remains sufficiently pliable for capitalism to develop without some of those harmful social by-products that tainted it in other countries.

If the Communist party shares power with other political groups all over the country, as it does already in Yenan's Liberated China with its ninety million people, the class struggle will never have to express itself in the manner it did in some other countries, but it will continue to act purely as a stimulus to progress in the evolutionary way.

The Communist leaders would sum up their argument in words like these: We are convinced democrats because we are convinced Communists who realize what China's concrete needs are for the present and for a long period to come. We have already gained sufficient influence and popular support in large parts of the country to fight together with other progressive elements for the peaceful introduction of such a democracy and its gradual evolution to a higher stage of perfection.

Mao Tse-tung gave me as much time as was needed for detailed answers to all the questions I asked him. No victim of my journalistic inquisitiveness has ever been so patient as he.

Our first interview began at 3 p.m. and ended at 3 a.m. We talked in the reception room of his four-cave "apartment" outside the town. It was a small high-vaulted cave, whitewashed and sparsely furnished, looking out on a pleasant old orchard. Mao Tse-tung sat on a rickety chair, lighting one cigarette after another and sucking in the smoke with the strange noise characteristic of peasants in certain parts of China. I perched on a low sofa spiked with fiendish springs, my notebook on a shaky miniature table, writing down everything he said as the American-trained subeditor of the *Liberation Daily* interpreted. From time to time Mao Tse-tung paced up and down the cave and then stood tall and massive over me for a while, his eyes fixed on mine for minutes on end, while he talked slowly and systematically with quiet emphasis.

After a short dinner under an old apple tree we carried on inside. Two candles were put between us which threw Mao Tse-tung's huge shadow on the high vault of the cave. He noticed my struggle with the rocky little table in front of me, went out into the garden, brought back a flat stone, and stuck it under one of its legs. From time to time we had a glass of grape wine, and one pack of local cigarettes after another was exhausted as we talked on and on.

During the night I made several moves to leave, although I was anxious to ask more questions. But he would not hear of it. He was going to give me more interviews, he said, but why not continue tonight and get done as much as possible? At three in the morning, when I finally got up to go, with a bad conscience, aching limbs, and burning eyes, he was still as fresh and animated and systematic in his talk as in the afternoon.

Mao Tse-tung evaded none of my questions. His convictions impressed me as honest. And the logic of his arguments stood out forcefully against the background of the social and political life I watched every day during my five months in the Border Region.

My notes of the interview were retranslated for him to make sure that no mistakes had slipped in. I did not get them back for almost a week, and when I happened to meet Mao Tse-tung during those days he apologized for the delay and said, "I had to consult Comrades Chu Teh and Chou En-lai about all I told you. They approved." My notes were returned without changes.

I give the following account of the main points of the interview which are pertinent to this chapter, without adding any comment of my own, in order to preserve its documentary character.

The Credo of Mao Tse-tung

"Communists in all countries have only one thing in common," Mao Tse-tung said in reply to my question whether there was really no possibility of a change of "that awful word Communist" in the name of the party. "What they have in common is their method of political thinking along the lines of Marxism.

"Communists everywhere have to distinguish between this system of thought and an entirely different matter: the Communist system of social organization which is the final political aim of their system of thought.

"Especially we in China must strictly distinguish between the Communist method of observing, studying, and solving social problems on the one hand, and the practical policies of our New Democracy on the other, which during the present stage of China's social development must constitute our immediate aim. Without the Communist method of thinking we would be unable to direct the present, democratic stage of our social revolution. And without the political system of the New Democracy we would not apply our Communist philosophy correctly to the realities of China.

"Our present New Democracy will have to be continued under any conditions and for a long period to come. For the concrete conditions existing in China dictate to us the continuation of that policy.

"What China needs now is democracy and not socialism. To be more precise, China's needs at present are three: (1) to drive the Japanese out; (2) to realize democracy on a nationwide scale by giving the people all the forms of modern liberty and a system of national and local governments elected by them in genuinely free and general elections, which we have already done in the areas under our control; and (3) to solve the agrarian question, so that capitalism of a progressive character can develop in China and improve the standard of living of the people through the introduction of modern methods of production.

"These, for the present, are the tasks of the Chinese revolution. To speak of the realization of socialism before these tasks are accomplished would merely be empty talk. This is what I told our party members in 1940 in my book *The New Democracy*. I said already then that this first democratic phase of our revolution would by no means be short.

109

We are not Utopians and we cannot isolate ourselves from the actual conditions right before our eyes."

He added with a smile, "It is quite possible that China may reach the stages of socialism and communism considerably later than your countries in the West which are so much more highly developed economically."

Mao Tse-tung gave me his views on the question of the future Communist attitude toward the landlords when I asked him what he considered the principal economic and social contents of the New Democracy.

"The central economic feature of the New Democracy," he said, "is the agrarian revolution. This holds good even during the present period when the fight against Japan is our main task. For our peasantry is the chief object of exploitation—not only of Chinese reactionaries but also of the Japanese imperialists in the occupied territories. Only the introduction of the New Democracy in our war regions has enabled us from the beginning to resist the Japanese as successfully as we do, because of its reforms in the interest of the peasant masses who constitute the very basis of our war effort.

"The present unreformed agrarian system in the rest of China, with its scattered, individual peasant economy—in which the farmers are not free but bound to the land, in which they have little contact even with one another and live a stagnant cultural life—has been the foundation of our ancient feudalism and despotism. The New Democracy of the future cannot rest on such a foundation. For the progress of Chinese society will mainly depend upon the development of industry.

"Industry must therefore be the main economic foundation of the New Democracy. Only an industrial society can be a fully democratic society. But to develop industry, the land problem must first be solved. Without a revolution against the feudal landlord system it is impossible to develop capitalism, as the course of events in Western countries many years ago has shown quite clearly.

"Our agrarian revolution until 1937, during the period of the Civil

110

War, was fundamentally of the same social character as the great agrarian revolutions which took place in the past in all progressive countries of the West and cleared away the feudal obstacles to the growth of the capitalistic democratic system."

I asked whether the radical Civil War policy of confiscating land from the landlords and distributing it to the peasants would not be resumed after the present war with Japan, since Mao Tse-tung had still emphasized the need for a continued agrarian revolution.

He explained, "During the Civil War period we had no reason to prevent the farmers from confiscating land, because the landlord class not only suppressed them but actually led the fight against them. Our party only followed the opinion of the farmers on the subject, formulated their demands into slogans, and then put them into practice as policy. Land confiscation as such was not a bad policy under Chinese conditions. The basic demand of the rural masses has always been concentrated on their desire for land ownership. Dr. Sun Yat-sen, the late leader of the Kuomintang, recognized it and advocated the ownership of the land by the tillers. This was one of the main points in his program for the improvement of the livelihood of the people.

"During a period of national war against a foreign aggressor things are of course different. A national war makes it possible to persuade the masses not to confiscate the land of the landlords, because the masses realize that, while the landlords are also willing to resist the enemy, a policy of land confiscation might drive them into the Japanese-held cities and make them return to their villages together with Japanese troops in order to recover their land.

"In this way, the peasants understood soon after the beginning of the war with Japan that our new policy of reducing land rents instead of continuing confiscation of land had the twofold advantage of improving the peasants' livelihood and of inducing the landlords to stay on in the villages and join in the fight against Japan. The general reduction of land rents in favor of the tenants and the guarantee we gave the landlords for the actual payment of the reduced rents resulted in

111

improved relations between tenants and landlords; so that the Japanese found practically nobody to cooperate with in our areas."

I wanted to know how this change in the land policy of the Communist party had been decided at the time.

"This is a characteristic example of the democratic ways in which our party devises policies," Mao Tse-tung said. "This fundamental change from land confiscation to a general reduction of land rents and the guarantee for their payment to the landlords was first suggested by comrades in lower party organizations. Our Central Committee took up their suggestion, which was clearly based on the wishes of the masses. We studied and formulated these demands and put them into effect as general policy.

"If the whole of China becomes a genuine democracy on the basis of cooperation between all political parties, it will be possible to practice our rent-reduction policy on a nationwide scale. This would be a great reform indeed, although it would still be inferior to Dr. Sun Yat-sen's idea of ownership of the land by those who till it, which will have to be the final solution of the land problem. But it is conceivable that even the gradual transfer to the tillers of all the land now under feudal exploitation may be brought about peacefully all over China if a genuinely democratic system of government is introduced everywhere.

"The way of bringing about such a gradual transfer of all land to the tillers would be to encourage the investment of the landlords' capital in industrial enterprises and to devise other measures of economic and fiscal policy that would be beneficial to the landlords, the tenants, and the development of Chinese economy as a whole.

"But such a solution depends upon genuine internal peace and genuine democracy in China. The possible need in the future for outright confiscation and distribution of land to the tenants can therefore not be ruled out entirely. For in the postwar period there may again be civil war if the Kuomintang insists on attacking us.

"Yet," Mao Tse-tung said with emphasis, "no matter whether we shall have internal peace or civil war, we prefer not to resume land confiscation but to continue our present policy of reduction of rents and guarantee of rent payment to the landlords; because that would reduce the obstacles to progress and reform in general.

"I want to remind you," Mao Tse-tung said, "that in 1930 the Kuomintang government in Nanking issued an agrarian law restricting land rents to 37.5 per cent of the tenant's main crops while no rent was to be paid from secondary crops. But the Kuomintang has proved unable and unwilling to carry it out in practice. The law was never enforced. Therefore only the Communist party has proved really able to realize agrarian reform, even in the shape of a mere reduction of rents."

I asked about the postwar attitude the Communist party intended to take toward commercial and industrial capital in China.

"We are firmly convinced that private capital, Chinese as well as foreign, must be given liberal opportunities for broad development in postwar China; for China needs industrial growth," Mao Tse-tung replied.

"In China's postwar commercial relations with the outside world we want to replace Japan's principle of colonizing China by the principle of free and equal trade with all nations. In the internal sphere we want to replace the policies of the Kuomintang government, which depress the living standards of the people and thereby restrict industrial development in the country, by the policies we are already practicing in Liberated China, that is, of fostering the productive forces of the people, raising their purchasing power, and thus achieving the main prerequisites for the most rapid and most solid growth of modern industries.

"There will have to be three forms of industrialization, according to the ideas of Dr. Sun Yat-sen, which we consider justified by the conditions prevailing in China. Key industries in a position to control national economy, like railroads and mines, can best be developed and run by the state. Other industries will have to be developed by private capital. And for the exploitation of our great potentialities in handicraft and rural small-scale manufacture we shall have to depend upon strong, democratically run cooperatives."

The Credo of Mao Tse-tung

What political role did the Communist party plan to play in post-war China, I asked.

"The membership of our party is necessarily a small portion of the Chinese people," he said. "Only if that small portion reflects the opinions of the majority of the people and only if it works for their interest can the relationship between the people and the party be healthy.

"Today the Communist party reflects the opinions not only of the peasants and workers but also of many anti-Japanese landlords, merchants, intellectuals, etc., that is, of all anti-Japanese people in our regions. The Communist party is willing and will always be ready to cooperate closely with all people in China who are prepared to cooperate with it.

"This willingness is expressed in our 'Three-thirds' system of democratic representation which restricts the seats of Communist party members in all elected bodies to a maximum of one-third of the whole and gives two-thirds of the seats to members of other parties and non-party elements.

"Yes," Mao Tse-tung replied to my question about relations with the Kuomintang, "we are also willing to cooperate with the Kuomintang: not only while the war lasts but afterward. That is to say, if the Kuomintang lets us do so.

"And we are willing to practice in the future, as we do today, the four promises we made to the Kuomintang in 1937."

I asked him about the contents of those promises to which I had often heard vague reference in Chungking, and about the conditions that had been attached to them.

"We promised (1) not to continue the kind of agrarian revolution we had practiced in the past; (2) not to overthrow the Kuomintang government by force; (3) to reorganize our Soviet government in the Border Region as a democratic, local government; and (4) to reorganize our Red Army as part of a National Revolutionary Army.

"These promises, we stated at that time, we would carry out if the Kuomintang on its part (1) stopped the Civil War; (2) fought against Japan; (3) adopted a system of democratic government, and granted

114

the people freedom of speech, publication, assembly, and association; and (4) took measures to improve the livelihood of the people."

"Is there any opposition within the Communist party to your present policies?" I went on, "or to your interpretation of the long-term requirements of China?" I was referring to the frequent rumors in Chungking about dissension within the Communist ranks.

"No," he said, "there is no opposition in our party now. In earlier periods there were two deviations. One was of a Trotskyite nature, identified with Chen Tu-hsiu, who died in 1942, years after his opposition had ceased to have any influence. The other was that of Chang Kuo-tao, who had for some time set himself against our party's correct policy and left it, practically alone. He is now working in the Special Service of the Kuomintang.* Both deviations never influenced the solidarity of our party and have left no trace."

I interrupted, "Do you mean to say that none of your policies are ever questioned or opposed?"

"Naturally, from time to time there may be certain differences of opinion within our ranks. But they are always solved in a democratic way, by discussion and analysis of the problems in question. If a minority is still not convinced of the correctness of a majority decision, it submits to it after thorough debates in party meetings. The decisive factor in our work is that we always find out which of our policies the masses of the people accept and which they criticize or reject. Only policies which prove popular with the masses become and remain the policies of our party.

"At the time of the introduction of a new measure there may be people inside and outside the party who do not quite understand it. But in the course of the execution of any measure a united opinion of an overwhelming majority inside and outside the party is invariably formed, because our party organizations are all the time watching out for popu-

* During the Long March, in 1935, Chang Kuo-tao opposed the Communist party's decision to move to the present Border Region in preparation for its intended fight against the Japanese. He advocated the withdrawal of the Communist forces into the province of Sinkiang (Chinese Turkestan), in order to get direct contact with, and support from, the USSR.

lar reaction, and because we modify our measures continuously according to the actual needs and opinions of the people. All party organizations from the top down are held to observe our vital principle of not separating ourselves from the masses of the people but of being in closest harmony with their needs and wishes.

"The correctness of any of our policies has always to be tested and is always being tested by the masses themselves. We ourselves constantly examine our own decisions and policies. We correct our mistakes whenever we find them. We draw conclusions from all positive and negative experiences and apply those conclusions as widely as possible. In these ways relations between the Communist party and the masses of the people are constantly being improved."

Mao Tse-tung had arrived at his favorite topic, his constant demand on all party members to observe what he calls the "mass viewpoint" in all their decisions and actions. He spoke with enthusiasm.

"This is the most fundamental point. If the leading elements of a political party are really working for the interests of the broad masses of the people, and if they are sincere in this endeavor, they have unlimited opportunities of listening to the opinions of the people.

"We listen to the people. Through the media of popular meetings in villages, towns, districts, regions, and everywhere in our territories; through individual conversations between party members and men and women of all strata of the population; through special conferences, newspapers, and the telegrams and letters we receive from the people— through all this we can, and do, always find out the real, undisguised opinion of the masses.

"Apart from that, our method is to find typical samples both of satisfactory and unsatisfactory work in every field of activity. We study those samples thoroughly, learn from them, and sum up our experiences on the subject in order to draw concrete conclusions for the necessary improvements. The period of such observation of reality and of studying samples of good and bad work may in one case be a few weeks, in another several months, and sometimes even a few years. But in this way we always keep in close touch with actual developments, discover

116

what the people want and need, and learn from those among the people inside and outside the party who do the best work.

"Some of our cadres may sometimes fail to understand our policies thoroughly and make mistakes in their execution, so that such comrades have to be criticized and taught. For this purpose, too, the thorough study and analysis of a specimen of good work is of great importance."

Mao Tse-tung showed me a copy of the *Liberation Daily*. "Take the example in tonight's newspaper. Here is a long article covering a whole page which describes in detail the ways in which one of the companies of the Eighth Route Army got rid of its shortcomings and became one of the best units. The cadres and fighters of every company in our armies will read and study and discuss this article. This is the simple way in which the positive experiences of one company will be taught as policy to five thousand companies. On other days you may find similar articles about a cooperative, a school, a hospital, or a local administrative unit.

"To come back to the vital matter of close understanding and cooperation between party comrades and nonparty people. There has been a very great and steady improvement; but mistakes are still being made by some of our comrades.

"Some incidents and misunderstandings still occur. Here and there we still have some Communists who tend to monopolize affairs.

"We are therefore all the time calling everybody's attention to the importance of giving nonparty people actual power under our democratic 'Three-thirds' system. In the course of the practical execution of our policies we show all our comrades concretely how genuine cooperation between us and nonparty people helps not only the masses but ourselves. In consequence, mutual trust between party and nonparty people is growing in the process of all the practical work they have to do together."

I asked Mao Tse-tung whether he considered that the Communist party had made any major mistakes in its policies.

"On all basic points our policies have proved correct from the very beginning. This is true first of all of our fundamental policies under the New Democracy—of letting the masses of the people organize themselves for a revolution aiming at national independence, democracy, and the improvement of the people's livelihood on the basis of private property.

"It is only with regard to the application of these basic policies to concrete conditions that certain deviations are liable to appear from time to time, deviations partly to the left and partly to the right. They are, however, not deviations of the party as a whole or of groups in the party, but of certain people in our ranks. From all those mistakes the party as a whole has learned.

"Yes, in certain periods there have been a few individuals in our party who believed that Communism is feasible in China at this time. But the party as such has never held that view. Even the existence within our party of a group advocating the immediate practice of a Communist social system is impossible on account of the concrete conditions in China which make Communism unfeasible for a very long time to come.

"The Kuomintang allegation that there are groups with diverging views within our party is completely unfounded. The Kuomintang, which is itself so badly split by cliques, cannot conceive of a really united political party, and that is probably why such rumors are believed by some in Chungking."

"Did you ever find yourself in a minority so that your own ideas on a subject were not carried out?"

"Yes. I have been in the minority myself. The only thing for me to do at such times was to wait. But there have been very few examples of that in recent years."

I had been asked by Chinese friends in Chungking to find out whether the Communists were "Chinese first" or "Communist first" and put the question to Mao Tse-tung.

He smiled. "Without a Chinese nation there could be no Chinese Communist party. You might just as well ask, What is first, children or parents? This is not a question of theory but of practice; like the other question people put to you in the Kuomintang regions, Whether we are working for our party or for the people. Go and ask our people, anywhere you want. They know well enough that the Chinese Communist party serves them. They have had their experience with us during the most difficult times.

"As to our method of thinking, I told you already that we, like Communists in any other country, are convinced of the correctness of Marxism. This is probably what people refer to when they ask whether we are 'Communist first' or 'Chinese first.' But our belief in Marxism as a correct method of thinking does not mean that we negate the Chinese cultural heritage or the value of non-Marxist foreign thought.

"It is certainly true that much is good in what Chinese history has handed down to us. And this heritage we must make our own. There are, however, certain people in China who worship the obsolete ideas of ancient times which are not suitable for our nation today but on the contrary harmful. Those things must be discarded.

"In foreign cultures, too, there is much that is good and progressive which we must accept; and, on the other hand, much that is rotten, like Fascism, which must be destroyed.

"To accept ideas from the Chinese past or from abroad does not mean to take them over unconditionally. They must be coordinated with actual conditions in China and practiced in accordance with them. Our attitude is that of critical acceptance of our own historical heritage and of foreign thought. We are against blind acceptance as well as blind rejection of any ideas. We Chinese must think with our own brains and must decide for ourselves what can grow on our own soil."

"I want to summarize what China needs today," Mao Tse-tung took the initiative. "China needs internal peace and democracy. Without internal peace China will not be able to win the war against Japan or win the peace. Our failure to achieve internal peace after the war with Japan might actually disturb peaceful international relations. For if there were to be another civil war in China, it would last for a long period and would influence foreign countries as well.

"Among people abroad there are still many who have not fully understood that during the last twenty-three years of China's political development the key problem has always been the relationship between the Kuomintang and Communist parties. And the same will be true in the future.

"In the first stage of that important twenty-three-year period of our history, from 1924 to 1927, there would have been no national revolution in China without cooperation between the Kuomintang and Communist parties.

"In the latter part of the second stage, from 1931 to 1936, China's inability to resist Japan resulted from the fact that the National Government of the Kuomintang used all its strength, the proceeds of its foreign loans, the services of its foreign military advisers, and other foreign assistance for the campaigns it waged against the Chinese Communists.

"In the third stage, from 1937 to the present, our war against Japan might not have been possible, or at least China would not have been able to hold out as long as she did if it had not been for what Kuomintang-Communist cooperation there was.

"Conversely, China's war effort against Japan today would be infinitely stronger than it is if the Kuomintang had continued to cooperate with the Communist party at least to the extent that characterized the first short phase of the war."

Chapter Thirteen

LABORATORIES OF SELF-GOVERNMENT

IN THE bare little assembly room of Yenan Municipality, fourteen people were sitting around the mayor and his secretary at a table and on benches along the walls. They were surprised at my unexpected entry, made polite bows, and continued their business without paying any further attention to me.

It was the joint meeting of the executive and legislative committees of the People's Political Council of the municipality which is elected by the townspeople and villagers within the wide limits of Greater Yenan.

Some of the members were peasants, barefoot, in old-fashioned cotton jackets, smoking their native pipes, cracking melon seeds, and listening eagerly. Some were typical old-style merchants, shrewd looking and better dressed than the others, puffing local-made cigarettes. One was an old scholar in a long robe, with a thin, white beard and a wise smile, who accompanied the proceedings with frequent nods and occasional gestures of disagreement. A few were young local Communists in blue uniforms, with stern, energetic faces. And two were girls—a gay, robust village lass, and the other a pale, bespectacled intellectual, the subeditor of a small newspaper.

The mayor, a blue-uniformed man in his middle forties, reported to the assembly. He was in the midst of giving examples of good work that had been done in the municipality during the last few months.

This was one of the cases he recounted in detail: A disabled soldier came to settle down somewhere at the fringe of the town. The people in the neighborhood on their own initiative held a meeting to decide how they could help him and drew up a cooperative plan to get his new farm going. Within two hours they had collected a supply of millet,

121

cooking pans, crockery, tools, and whatever else he needed immediately. Several people volunteered to assist him in the reclamation of wasteland. The soldier was much impressed and grateful and is now very active in production.

"This is the way to do things," the mayor said. "Take cooperative action. Don't rely on the government where self-help is possible." An old peasant solemnly whispered approval.

The mayor came to examples of bad work. One of the officials of a lower administrative unit was to launch a new phase of the Support-the-Army movement, but he never gave the people practical directions on what to do and they complained about his bureaucratic attitude. Another official talked a great deal about the new tree-planting movement, but he did not go to the hills and help the people, so that they were indignant at his hypocrisy.

Most of the assembly laughed, and an old landlord near me proudly remarked to his neighbor that in his own village everybody without exception planted more trees than had originally been planned.

The mayor then gave a long general report about the administration. The schools had been much improved, he said, and the new policy of giving parents an influence on the curriculum in order to make it more practical had caused a considerable increase in the number of pupils. The idea of persuading difficult children through good example to improve their "bad attitudes" instead of beating them was now generally established in Yenan families in consequence of some surprisingly successful "conversions." Night schools to teach adults the reading of newspapers were increasingly popular. There was still much avoidable sickness in the municipality because the people did not yet pay sufficient attention to sanitation, although they had begun to realize that it is harmful to drink unboiled water.

A peasant interrupted: "We have long practiced all the new regulations and are now very sanitary. For two years not one child has died. This is something new in our village. In the old days several children died every single year."

The mayor gave figures about the progress of land reclamation be-

122

yond the plan, and several members, full of interest and enthusiasm, made detailed comments. He went on to particulars about the large numbers of families in towns and villages who were mobilized for spinning and other household industries through the production movement.

There was a general expression of satisfaction when he reported that the staff of the municipality were now covering 60 per cent of their salaries and office expenses from their own agricultural production and that taxes could therefore remain what they had been before, in spite of increasing expenditure on public works.

He then explained in detail the importance of the latest mass movement which was to bring about the realization of the Program of Ten Small Points in every community of the Border Region.

Each family must dig one well; plant so and so many trees; keep more pigs; and build one new latrine. Each administrative village unit must have a "mutual aid granary," a producers' and consumers' cooperative, one midwife, at least one blacksmith shop, a school run by the people, and a folk-dance group. Every one of these points must be discussed in detail with the people, the mayor said, so that they could understand the meaning of these demands and the ways of fulfilling them.

The discussion began. One of the non-Communist members, a merchant, called the mayor's report very concrete (which is the highest praise in the Border Region) and said that, in spite of some continuing defects in the municipal administration, its work in general was now very good, so that the people had no severe criticism. Especially the new Ten Small Points Program was very popular. But the municipality must do something to repair the roads more thoroughly or, better, to pave them; a dike along the small river must be built; and it should be made clear to merchants where new shops could best be put up in the growing city, to fit in with future development plans.

The old scholar gave a long and fluent speech. He also talked about the bad roads and the lack of a dike and then went on to criticize the

123

schools. "We have never had so many and such good and practical schools," he said. "But we must still improve them. The schoolrooms are in many cases too small and crowded and are bad for the children's health. Our curricula are not yet complete enough and parents have further wishes for their improvement. Kuomintang textbooks would of course never be suitable for the people, and our own are much better. But they are not good enough yet. Our methods of teaching the children to write Chinese characters are sloppy. What the people want is to have their children learn the regular type of classical script and not that sloppy writing they are taught. I must ask the administration to provide better writing teachers."

The discussion had only started. It would go on in much detail for a number of days, I was told. And I heard later that the members of the Joint Committee made the mayor correct his proposed program for the next six months on a number of points.

Another meeting on which I dropped in unannounced consisted only of non-Communist members of the People's Political Council of one of the Border Region's highest administrative units, a subregion comprising half a dozen counties.

It has recently become the practice in various elected self-government organs to call special meetings exclusively for non-Communist members, apart from the normal full sessions in which all nonparty and Communist members participate. The aim is to activate that fundamentally unpolitical element which represents the great majority of the common people and to make the nonparty delegates more articulate in the expression of the wishes of the masses, outside any possible influence of better trained Communist speakers.

"It may seem strange to you," one of the party leaders told me later, "but we consider it one of our main tasks to give the nonparty people opportunities for the independent development of their political abilities, not only within the elected bodies of which they are members together with Communists, but also among themselves."

Some sixty people crowded a large assembly room with crude tables

124

and benches: peasants, landlords, merchants, and scholar gentry, the same kind of old-style Chinese people I saw at other meetings. It was a disciplined, animated meeting of men and women who until a few years ago had probably never thought of something as unheard-of as active participation in genuine local self-government. They seemed to enjoy their new opportunity immensely, made themselves comfortable, sipped tea, chewed melon seeds, smoked, and did not mind interrupting a speaker with unconventional remarks of agreement or disapproval.

They were all elected by the people, but probably more for their personal reputations than because of any political efforts on their own part. Such meetings, one of them told me, were a great education for them and they were gradually getting used to their unaccustomed political tasks.

In their whole attitude these men and women gave the impression of being eager pupils of self-government. What they said was sound and practical. They spoke about achievements and shortcomings and made all kinds of demands on higher organs of the government. One wanted more initiative in the development of cottage industries, another advocated the introduction of a greater variety of vegetables in the villages with the help of the Border Region government's model farms. An old peasant complained bitterly about the harm done by wolves and boars in the wintertime and asked the government to help the villagers in killing them. A merchant suggested that mulberry plantations and silk reeling should be introduced into his region. And an old scholar speaking about the continuing lack of certain medicines suggested that this might be partly overcome by the production of some particular herbs which normally came from Kuomintang regions.

There was a surprising note of unanimity among the speakers in their appreciation of the great progress that was being made everywhere under the new political system and of all fundamental policies of the government in Yenan. These individual expressions of opinion were supported by practical examples which men obviously unused to public speaking brought forward in a manner as simple as it was evidently honest.

Laboratories of Self-Government

The meeting had one special theme I had not encountered before, a matter of particular importance to the counties on the fringe of the Border Region facing the grim blockade belt of the Kuomintang: almost every speech contained bitter accusations against the neighboring Kuomintang troops.

There were many long tales of kidnapings and killings, of robbery and rape, reported with a good deal of gruesome detail. Every speaker asked the Yenan government to bring those things to the attention of Chungking and to protest against the continuation of the blockade of the Border Region and its peaceful citizens, most of whom were not even Communists themselves. In the county of Fuhsien alone, one of the speakers said, there had been eighty-nine raids of Kuomintang troops against small villages during the last six months: sixty-four people had been kidnaped, one buried alive, four injured, and much property had been taken away from merchants and farmers.

General Chu Teh, the Commander in Chief of the Eighth Route Army, told me later that raids of individual units of the National Government Army on the fringes of the Communist-controlled Border Region were indeed happening all the time and that his garrison forces were not strong enough to protect the people in outlying villages. He did not blame Generalissimo Chiang Kai-shek or even Lieutenant General Hu Chung-nan for ordering such raids but regarded them as inevitable consequences of conditions in the National Government Army.

"Even inside the Kuomintang areas, National Government troops often rob and maltreat the people," he said. "One of the reasons is that the Kuomintang troops and their officers are not properly fed and cared for; and another that good relations between the army and the population are not promoted by the general policies of Chungking. In Honan province, for example, the common people were so much antagonized by their own soldiers that they felt almost relieved when the Japanese invaded the province this spring." (Foreign observers in Sian had told me the same.)

"If things are so bad in Chungking's own territories, what can we expect from Kuomintang soldiers in the blockade belt against our Border Region?" Chu Teh said. "Their intensive anti-Communist

126

education makes many of them forget completely that the people in our areas whom they rob, rape, kidnap, and kill are Chinese like themselves."

I also watched several joint meetings of the executive and legislative committees of the Border Region government itself in the large, barn-like auditorium of the People's Political Council. The elected heads of the various government departments, all popular figures in the Border Region, made detailed reports to the Standing Committee of the People's Political Council of the Border Region.

There was considerable discussion on a higher political plane than in the other meetings I attended, although the subjects were more or less of the same practical nature: agriculture, industry, and afforestation; manifold measures for the intensification of the war effort; the improvement of education and hygiene; complaints about the Kuomintang; and criticism of the Border Region government in matters of detail, but apparently without any disagreement on fundamental policies.

Among the non-Communists, who were in a two-thirds majority as everywhere else, there were a number of prominent landlords, scholars, and former Kuomintang officials of considerable education. They gave long and able speeches, praising and criticizing and making practical proposals.

A well-to-do merchant who had once been head of Yenan's Public Safety Department under the Kuomintang regime, expressed his conviction that the Border Region government was the first administration in China to carry out the Three Principles of the People of Dr. Sun Yat-sen. The mutual help that had developed between the people and the Eighth Route Army, he said, was an achievement of which every patriot, no matter what political conviction he held, must heartily approve. He praised the progress of irrigation work in which he had long been interested and the new ways in which it was made to benefit not only the rich, as before, but also the poor.

He criticized certain lower officials, Communists and others, for lack of experience and occasional deviation from the policies laid down by

127

the popularly elected governments and asked the authorities to give more training to such officials. He also expressed dissatisfaction with the comparatively slow tempo of the liquidation of illiteracy.

At last he reproached the Kuomintang for its constant attacks on the Border Region. "If we had more territories in China like this Border Region . . ." the former Kuomintang official summed up, ". . . if all the people in China were enabled to work and fight as we do here, China would really become one of the Big Four of the world."

Pointing to the Generalissimo's picture on the wall, he concluded: "And you, General Chiang Kai-shek, would get more real fame and honor."

Were all those meetings staged for our benefit? Were all those non-Communists on the various elected councils no more than puppets in the hands of the powerful party of Mao Tse-tung? Was the praise-of-general-policies-cum-criticism-of-details pattern of their speeches, which is so characteristic of both Chinese and Russian Communists, imposed on them from above?

I became less skeptical about the primitive manifestations of Yenan's New Democracy the more I saw, not only of such meetings, but of realities in the Border Region. It seemed to me that the common people of all social strata were really responding to their new opportunities for self-government in a businesslike manner, with increasing enthusiasm, and with a surprisingly intelligent understanding of rights and duties they had not known before.

Yet I would still hesitate to dismiss all skepticism about the performances of those laboratories of a primitive New Democracy if I had not convinced myself of the compelling reasons for the Communist party and the people to work together on the development of self-government.

The Communist party has a vital interest in making its leadership in one-half of China a success, both for winning the war and for the sake of its influence in China after victory. It must therefore try to overcome the backwardness of those regions which were liberated from the Japanese. This requires development work in every field. Produc-

128

tion must be increased, educational and health standards must be raised, the administration of justice must be improved, the interest of the people in public affairs must be awakened.

All this has to be done with two aims in view: to strengthen the war effort of the poor and backward areas in which the power of a well-organized and enthusiastic population has to overcompensate the lack of armed strength; and to make the people at the same time more prosperous and more satisfied with their lot than they have been in centuries of squalor and misery.

Theoretically, such development work can be promoted either from above or from below. If it is to be done from above, as the Kuomintang government has attempted to do it in its own regions, the administrative machinery has to be increased to an enormous extent. But very few good administrators are available anywhere in China; and the capacity and willingness of the people to finance a large bureaucracy is strictly limited by their poverty and their traditional skepticism of bureaucratic blessings. As a result, the bureaucratic-authoritarian approach must lead to endless delay, friction, discouragement, and eventually failure. This is precisely what happened to the attempted reform policies of the Kuomintang. It is one of the main reasons why Chungking's war effort waned from year to year and why the people in the Kuomintang regions have come to blame their government, rather than the inevitable consequences of the war, for the pathetic lack of social progress.

The Communists chose the approach from below. They realized that reform and development work can be based only on the effort of the masses themselves, on the activization of the greatest possible numbers of common people. The only way of mobilizing them is to win their confidence, enthusiasm, and voluntary cooperation. And this can be done only through giving them a maximum measure of rights and duties by way of the development of self-government.

This is what the Communist party was forced to do if it was to achieve success. This is what it did. And this is how its own interests and those of the people met and merged.

But the Communist party did not only permit the people to participate in all kinds of administrative efforts, giving them rights and leaving it to them to make use of those rights. That would not have been sufficient to mobilize the backward, apathetic masses and to overcome the distrust of the Communists on the part of the landlord, merchant, and old-style scholar gentry. What the Communists did was to launch vast awakening campaigns and virtually press on the people the use of their new democratic rights.

Instead of the former class struggle, the need for cooperation between all strata of the population was stressed everywhere: in the one-half of the small Border Region where the agrarian revolution of the Civil War days had radically done away with large-scale landlordism and gentry privileges; in the other half of the Border Region which came under Communist control after the agrarian revolution had already been stopped in 1937, and where a peaceful government-sponsored reduction of land rents was the only change from the old social system; and in the vast areas in the enemy's rear liberated by the Communists from the Japanese, where the same mild reform policies were applied.

The people were mobilized against only two enemies—the Japanese invaders and their own age-old political and social backwardness. Simple, practical slogans were propagated all over the country by primitive but often ingenious mass movements. Raise production. Foster cooperatives. Aim at the goal of being well fed and well clad. Support the army. Improve your standards of health. Discard superstition and acquire knowledge. Learn to read and write. Help the backward people in your community.

Hundreds of thousands of Communist party members saw to it that those slogans were explained and understood in a concrete, practical way. They aimed first at newly awakened activists who would help the Communists in carrying on the mass movements; then at the average people; and last at the most backward and actually or potentially hostile elements. Special efforts were made to overcome the initial suspicions of some of the old gentry, landlords, merchants, and Kuomintang members and to make them realize that they were not to be excluded from the New Democracy but could play a role in it to their own advantage and that of the country.

To get more prosperous, you must produce more, the people were told. To produce more, you must improve your technique. To improve your technique, you must learn. To make use of your great reserves of strength, you must develop new methods of mutual help among yourselves. To get things done in the way you want, you must take part in social activities. You must participate in elections and choose those you trust, no matter what their political views are, if only they support the war against Japan and work for social progress. You will have to rely more upon yourselves; for Communists are allowed no more than one-third of the seats in any assembly or government.

This was the general lesson which ran through all the various mass movements and eventually merged them into one: the mass movement for the realization of the New Democracy through the effort of the people themselves.

There can be no doubt of its success. From all I have seen and heard, more and more of the common people and the gentry are responding and taking the initiative in criticism and suggestions and practical experiments of their own.

The oft-expressed opinion that China's ability to survive periods of disaster lay in the common sense and ingenuity of her people and their fundamentally democratic approach to social life took on a new meaning. Given their first opportunity to practice these great qualities in an atmosphere of encouragement rather than of restraint, the common people themselves became the creators of a new society.

For the first time in China's history, self-government has begun to work in part of the country, although still in a primitive form. It is the main reason for the military successes of the Anti-Japanese War Bases behind the enemy's lines and for the social progress of the areas under Yenan.

Self-government is now so implanted in the thinking and habits of the common people and the majority of the gentry that the Communists could no longer stop the steady growth of its inherent strength, even if they chose to do so at the cost of destroying their own mass support.

The Communists are committed to the continuance and development of political democracy, not so much by their own promises as by the new political conditions they have helped the people to create.

Chapter Fourteen

OFFICIALS PAY THEIR OWN WAY

ONE of my first surprises in the Border Region was the casual remark of a county magistrate that he and his staff would this year achieve complete independence from the taxpayer's money. They would actually contribute about one thousand pounds of grain each to public funds.

"You mean to say that an official in the Communist areas, instead of drawing a salary, pays for the honor of working for the government?"

"If you want to put it that way, yes. This is one of the results of our production drive. Comrade Mao Tse-tung demands that all government and party officials, all ranks in the garrison forces, all teachers and pupils use their own hands, produce as much as possible of their own needs. This is to lighten the burden of the people and at the same time to set examples for them in production."

I found later that these instructions to the "nonproductive elements" of society had indeed been carried out to a remarkable extent. There are about 100,000 such people in the Border Region with its 1,500,000 people.

In 1944 they were expected to produce with their own hands about two-thirds of all they needed, so that only one-third of their food, clothing, miscellaneous, and even office expenses had to be financed out of the taxpayer's money. The rate of their self-sufficiency is rising from year to year, while their standard of living is steadily being improved.

"The expenses of our city government last year were covered to the extent of 50 per cent from tax money while 50 per cent came from our own production," the mayor of Yenan had told me, "and in 1944 we ourselves shall produce at least 60 per cent."

133

"But how can you do your office work and at the same time produce for your own upkeep?" I asked.

"We even manage to do our two hours' daily studies which are expected of everybody, as well as our production work. Our daily schedule changes from season to season. Now, for example, our office time is three and a half hours in the morning and three in the afternoon. Two early morning hours are devoted to studies, and later in the afternoon we do on an average about three hours' production work. During agricultural rush seasons we spend more time on production, and our offices are open only a few hours a day. That is in tune with the requirements of the people, who are too busy during those weeks to want much attendance. Part of the production work is done individually in our own gardens and on the fields we ourselves reclaimed on the hills, although we often help each other to save labor. Another part is done collectively on the large farm we developed for the municipality."

"Is nobody free from those duties?"

"No," said the mayor. "I am doing them as well as my responsible colleagues, the clerks, and the policemen. And we also do some of our building work ourselves. We don't really consider production work duty. We enjoy it. With daily studies and manual work our ordinary routine becomes less tiresome and our physical condition is better than before. We also get much closer to the people we serve; for we know now what manual work means and respect it more than we used to. I confess that our total hours are sometimes very long. I, for example, often have to do some extra office work at home in the night. But we all like to do as much as we can."

The little mayor certainly looked happy and well, and he had chosen this kind of pioneer work of his own free will. He was the son of a fairly well-to-do landlord who was able to send him to one of the best modern universities in Peking. He himself was county magistrate in the neighboring province of Kansu under the old regime and in 1927 was the last Kuomintang magistrate of Yenan. He did not know much about Communism at that time but felt dissatisfied with the methods of the Kuomintang, worked with the Communists when the United

Front was established, and after some time became a party member. In 1943 he was elected mayor by the people.

"The circumstances under which you practice your new policies here are of course much more primitive than in any of the large Chinese cities," I said. "Do you believe any of those methods could be applied to them, too?"

"Yes, of course. Naturally they would have to be modified. But the fundamental ideas of our policies are valid anywhere. Democracy and unity, with the aim of getting all classes to cooperate in every respect: those are our only secrets. The officials must help the people and adapt themselves to circumstances. They must not ask more of the people in return for what they do than the people can easily provide. They must have some imagination. That is all. And with that we can do a good job wherever it is required of us. The Kuomintang could do the same as we do and be popular and successful. They are, in fact, very stupid not to do so. We have our minds bent toward learning and adapting ourselves to circumstances, although we still make many mistakes. With this and with our aim of working for the real interest of the people, we can also master greater problems."

It seemed to me that the Communists owed their success largely to the manner in which they approached the fundamental Chinese problem of creating an administration cheap enough for the people to finance without difficulty, and large and enthusiastic enough to take on much greater responsibilities than in the past—an administration rising out of the people themselves and responsible to them through democratically elected governments.

I had a long talk about the subject with Lo Mai, the secretary-general of the Border Region government. When we first met that large, hefty man who looked like the personification of "Chinese Bolshevism," some of my Kuomintang colleagues seemed to shiver mentally, and one of them said, "This must be a dangerous fellow." Many a slender intellectual hand hurt when Lo Mai had shaken it for a little while in his own huge, muscular paw. His apparently irremovable cap, old and faded and worn at a rakish angle, looked much more provocative than anyone else's. His arguments, his voice, and diction resembled that overpowering handshake.

I had quite an argument with him at our first meeting, during which both of us got somewhat hot. But I came to respect him as one of the ablest men in Yenan and to like him as a straightforward and warm-hearted fellow.

In the last and longest talk I had with Lo Mai, shortly before my departure, he kept on for hours discussing the deficiencies of administration in the Border Region. To discover and overcome them is his main job, and he takes it seriously. There is no trace of Oriental self-depreciation in the manner in which he talks about the shortcomings of the Yenan government.

"For years we have been fighting against bureaucratic attitudes among our officials, for greater efficiency and thrift. We have been cutting down the numbers of our staff considerably. This rationalization movement, originally proposed by the non-Communist vice-chairman of our government, has been very successful.

"With the rapid development of our system of self-government, which was not sufficiently understood by all at the beginning, we lacked clear delimitations of authority in our administration. Too many people were responsible for overlapping duties.

"We had too many meetings. Last year we found that in our small Border Region altogether 300,000 people spent on an average a total of one month on meetings. Meetings are certainly necessary and useful. They keep our social activities alive. But imagine, 9,000,000 working days a year for meetings in a region with 1,500,000 people. In some respects we actually had too much democracy, in the sense of too much discussion, and that kept responsible workers too busy and caused the postponement of too many matters which, although small in themselves, were important enough to be done more quickly.

"Some of our higher officials still failed to understand the true character of our policies. For example, the head of the Border Region Bank tried to follow the methods of other countries, methods unsuited to our tasks. He aimed at making money for the government through

136

the bank instead of assisting the people in every possible way. It took us too long to discover his mistakes and correct them."

"What became of the bank manager? Was he punished?"

"Of course not. He was heavily criticized and defended his policies. Then he was sent to the Party School. He is a good and honest man and will be very useful in the future. But he has to learn more about the fundamentals of our policies and unlearn some of his wrong notions. We, too, have to keep on learning and getting a better understanding of our problems. All of us."

Lo Mai reminded me of the report on improvements in the Border Region administration, submitted by its chairman Lin Pai-chu to the People's Political Council in January, 1944, which showed the great progress that had been made in all respects. Lo Mai smiled when I told him that I had heard much about that report in Chungking because it had made a strong impression on the Generalissimo. Chiang Kai-shek had called a meeting of high officials, showed them the document, and said that the Communists were "doing many things we could do, too, and should have done a long time ago."

"It is true," Lo Mai said. "We have overcome many of our deficiencies and our system is running quite well now. The bureaucratic attitude of most of our officials has definitely been liquidated. Delimitations of responsibility have been clarified. We don't have too many meetings any more. Work has been speeded up. Our struggle for rationalization has achieved a great deal. The people notice how our administration is constantly being improved and how sincere our officials are in serving them. But we still have deficiencies. We continue to be hard with ourselves in our self-criticism. We have to be."

The methods of recruiting and training administrative workers are characteristic of Communist policies. To draw upon "talent among the masses" is the unwritten law.

Practically all the 2,000 officials in the 1,250 lowest administrative units in the Border Region are former peasants who gained the confidence of their communities as active elements and were elected by them. A great part of the 1,000 functionaries in the 210 boroughs orig-

137

inated from the lowest strata of the administration. Many of them have already been promoted into the next higher categories and are playing increasingly important roles among the 1,200 officials in the 31 counties and 5 subregions, and now even among the 300 men and women who run the highest administrative unit, the government of the Border Region itself.

Most of those 4,500 government officials who cooperate with the People's Political Councils of various strata were illiterate a few years ago. But all have had ample education in practice as well as in theory. There are few above the village level now who have not learned the 1,000 to 2,000 complicated Chinese characters necessary to read either the *Mass Newspaper* or the party organ *Liberation Daily*. Every month more village functionaries achieve this level of literacy.

Each subregion has special middle-school classes for officials in which attendance is largest during the agricultural off seasons. The hundreds of students of the Administrative College of Yenan University are practically all officials with considerable practical experience whose progress is much quicker than that of ordinary middle-school graduates. These students spend part of their university time continuing practical work, according to the Border Region's supreme educational principle that theory and practice must always go hand in hand.

The greatest single achievement in the administrative field is the virtual disappearance of corruption. Among all the people I asked during my four months in the Border Region, there was not one voice of disagreement with the claim of the Communists that the administration was absolutely clean and that it was the democratic participation of the people in their government as well as the selection of officials from below which disproved the belief of generations of Chinese and foreign skeptics that the uprooting of "squeeze" and the implanting of honest administration was an impossibility in China for a very long time to come.

The new officials in the Border Region are guaranteed a living standard which is comparatively low but in harmony with that of the population. Like the army and party functionaries, the officials can always rely on having enough to eat, sufficient clothing, fairly decent shelter, and a minimum of luxuries like cigarettes, etc.

They get practically no cash wages, and their living standards are almost the same, no matter how small or great their responsibilities. Having risen mostly from the ranks of activists whose characteristics include a marked devotion to the public good, and enjoying an altogether new popular respect if their work is satisfactory, these new officials seem to see nothing extraordinary in the fact that the improvement of their own living conditions depends entirely upon the progress toward greater prosperity of the general public for which they work.

I came to know some of the high-ranking officials who belong to the old landlord-scholar gentry of the Yenan areas but seem to cooperate closely with the activists of the new generation.

Old Li Ting-ming, the Vice-Chairman of the Border Region government, is one of them. Kuomintang people somewhere in the blockade belt had told me that he was "the only decent person in the Yenan government."

At first, when we met the toothless, fragile little man at parties and meetings, he did not make an impression on us. In fact, I suspected the Communists had picked the mild and somewhat decrepit-looking man who was said to be so popular in his home district as a harmless puppet to adorn their New Democracy.

But I had to change my view about Li Ting-ming—not because I heard him praised by farmers and landlords and Communists of all ranks; but mainly because in long conversations with him I found that he was genuine in every respect, intelligent, and active, a man with a firm and clear mind who evidently supports the New Democracy of his own free will.

"I kept away from politics all my life," he said after having told me the story of his life which was devoted to education and social-reform work in his little town. "I did not agree with the Communist party. And I am old. But during those critical days in 1941 there were three compelling reasons why I accepted the election of the people of my district

139

to the People's Political Council and then the election of my colleagues to the vice-chairmanship of the Border Region government."

"First, my old objections to the Communist party were overcome by the introduction of the New Democracy. It coincides fully with what I have always considered the needs of the Chinese people in war and peace.

"Second, when I compared the elections under the Communist party with the so-called elections we had in our parts under the Kuomintang —including those of delegates to the National Assembly whom Chiang Kai-shek now promises to call together after all those years since their dubiously conducted 'election'—I found our elections absolutely genuine, free, and equal in actual practice, without any bribery, compulsion, or violence as in the old days. The people elected me although everybody knew that I disagreed with the Communists on their doctrine and on some of their former practices.

"Third, the action in 1941 of the Kuomintang against this Border Region and against the brave anti-Japanese armies under Communist control convinced me of the need of helping to keep up the war effort and to save the people through participation in the government, in spite of my advanced age.

"When the Kuomintang ceased to give payment and supplies to the Eighth Route Army and used hundreds of thousands of troops to surround the Border Region and some ten thousand blockhouses to make the blockade watertight, the following thoughts were in my mind: Among all the armies in China the Eighth Route Army was probably fighting the Japanese most actively, and if those good troops were not well treated by the government in Chungking and had to suffer cold and hunger, it certainly indicated a deep national crisis. Further: the Communist party is strong and well organized, a minority among the people. It cannot be starved to death in spite of all the difficulties it may have to face. Those who will have to suffer most from the crisis will be the common people. The blockade and the stoppage of pay and supplies was therefore really directed against our people. I felt I had to help overcome this crisis.

"My belief in the New Democracy has proved correct during those

140

four years I have worked in the government. Really, I think Mao Tse-tung is a genius. He sees every problem very concretely and without any prejudice. What Mao thinks is not just his personal opinion but is what the masses of the people think. And what he does is what the masses want and can do. It is strange to remember now those Kuomintang rumors which I first heard in 1927, that Mao Tse-tung and Chu Teh, the Commander in Chief of the Eighth Route Army, were bandits who kill and burn and rob."

"But do you feel you have any real influence on the government, as a non-Communist and landlord?" I asked him.

His wrinkled old face with its parchmentlike skin and sunken, toothless mouth, became all smiles, and he looked proud for the first time. He spoke even more slowly and emphatically than before.

"After my election," he said, "when on a visit to his cave I met Mao Tse-tung for the first time, I told him at once that I had a proposal to make, a very grave and sweeping proposal. Mao Tse-tung was very much interested. I told him frankly that a thorough rationalization not only of the government but also of the army seemed necessary now because of the crisis. I said we must cut down the number of troops and officials and increase efficiency everywhere.

"Mao Tse-tung agreed. I brought up my suggestion before the People's Political Council, and it was adopted.

"You can hear from my colleagues in the government how thoroughly that rationalization and efficiency program was carried out everywhere in the army as in all other organizations, and how enthusiastically the Communists enforced it although it originated from a non-Communist and landlord.

"I continue being active in the government, working as hard as I can, and I have never been so happy in my life. For this is the first time since I began to take an interest in reform work, long before the Revolution in 1911, that I see real progress in China. You have not been here before and you cannot judge how much things have improved. Believe me, if the Kuomintang adopted policies like ours and carried

141

them out with that new type of honest administration we have developed, China would indeed be a strong and happy country.

"I wish Chungking realized why men of the old gentry like myself really identify themselves with the New Democracy of the Communists and are proud of our Border Region."

But people who have lived in the Anti-Japanese War Bases, like Michael Lindsay, look upon the administrative achievements of the Border Region as no more than a dim reflection of what they saw in the pioneer communities behind the Japanese lines.

Those front regions, they say, are in most cases far ahead of Yenan's small rear base. They started out somewhat earlier along the same road toward an entirely new administrative system. They benefited from the stimulus of constant fighting with the Japanese. And their government officials today equal the best fighters of the army in their efficiency and devotion to the war effort and social progress.

Chapter Fifteen

CHINA'S OWN COMMUNISTS

I FOUND very little in Yenan that reminded me of Moscow. Pictures of Marx and Engels, Lenin and Stalin are quite rare in comparison with those of Mao Tse-tung and Chu Teh; and even the portraits of the two leading Chinese Communists are crowded out by those of Labor Heroes and other leaders of the New Democracy, non-Communists as well as Communists.

The Communist classics are in every library; but so are Chinese translations of the "bourgeois" standard works of the West which seem to be studied with great interest. Reference to Lincoln and Jefferson, Roosevelt and Wallace and other progressives of the past and present is frequent in books and articles published in Yenan.

Marxism is frankly called the "correct method of thinking" on which the Chinese Communists rely as a matter of course; and the simple essence of Marxism, the materialistic approach to all social phenomena, seems to have penetrated deeply into the minds even of poorly educated party members.

But I did not find the Chinese Communists engrossed in dogma. Their insistence on the importance of Marxism does not seem to arise from a passion for theorizing but from their firm conviction that that philosophy was fundamentally responsible for the success of their various policies. They prove that whatever failures they suffered in the past were due to its neglect.

During eighteen years of civil and national wars the Chinese Communists had little time for anything but urgent practical work, although Mao Tse-tung and other leaders always considered it their main task to check practice by theory and theory by practice. "Most of our cadres are much too busy to read more than a few theoretical books," I was

143

told, "and they must learn from their practical work. But we always stress the need for close connection between correct theory and practice. Problems of work must be raised to a theoretical level to find the correct answer, unless examples of successful solutions in the same line already provide a sufficient lesson."

I heard this phrase about "raising practical problems to a theoretical level" in many different contexts, as in a statement about the cursing and beating of soldiers the head of the Political Education department of the Eighth Route Army made during an explanation of his policies. "It is strictly forbidden to our cadres to curse and beat their men," he said, "but to ban cursing and beating is not enough. Those who do not understand the meaning of that order must be taught to regard cursing and beating as a matter of wrong ideology, of wrong theory, instead of thinking of it simply as a bad habit. Our few officers who still occasionally curse and swear and even beat their soldiers are mostly men with an old Kuomintang background. We have to make them understand that their old ideology is to blame for their faults and to teach them correct theory. Once that is done, the cursing and beating habit disappears automatically with their other shortcomings."

I found Chinese nationalism a more characteristic trait of Yenan's ideology than Marxism. In some details Soviet Russian institutions and habits might seem to have been copied. The Labor Hero movement, the great role of the cooperatives, the wide use of slogans, and the habit of Chinese Communist speakers and writers of leading up to an important argument by asking themselves appropriate rhetorical questions are all reminiscent of the USSR. But these "un-Chinese" features, which impressed our Kuomintang colleagues, do not take away from the prevalent nationalism of Yenan. They seem to be less a matter of mere imitation than of expediency or rediscovery.

Just as Leninism and especially Stalinism are largely developments of Marxism on the basis of specific Russian conditions, the ideas and practices of Mao Tse-tung and his party are the application of Marxism to Chinese reality.

Yenan condemns Trotskyism as Moscow does, although with less

144

emphasis because the Communist party of China was affected much less than any other by that "deviation." And Yenan is proud that its fundamental theories remain in tune with international Communist thought and therefore with Stalinism. But there is no tendency to follow Moscow, and certainly not the slightest indication that Comrade Mao Tsetung may from time to time ask Comrade Stalin for directions.

Marxism has been made Chinese. The thorough Sinification of Communist practices in their application to Chinese society impressed me as an undeniable fact, not as a propaganda front.

Its steady course can be traced back through the years to 1927, when Chinese Communism became isolated from the outside world through the split of the national-revolutionary movement and through Chiang Kai-shek's break with its Russian advisers who had wielded so much influence over both the Kuomintang and Communist parties.

The absorption of Yenan's former Marx-Lenin Institute into the new Party School; the eclipse of Gorki and other Russian playwrights on the stage in the Chinese Communist regions; the thorough Sinification of the contents and forms of literature and art; the absence of special emphasis on the Russian war effort in the Yenan press; and especially the great revival of all that is considered valuable in Chinese traditions—all these random indications confirmed my general impression that the Chinese Communists have become self-contained and self-confident in their nationalism. They keep their ears to the ground—to Chinese ground, not to Radio Moscow.

They feel as grown-up, after eighteen years of continuous responsibility for the conduct of armies and administrations, as the Soviet Union does after twenty-eight years. They regard the conditions under which Marxism has to be applied to China as utterly different from those prevailing in Russia. And they consider themselves as little in need of advice from any foreign Communist party as Moscow does.

The policies of the Communist party have certainly become much less radical since the end of the Civil War and the beginning of the war against Japan in 1937.

145

China's Own Communists

No matter whether or not Mao Tse-tung's explanation of his change of policy, as expressed in a previous chapter, can be considered convincing, or how plausible his assurance may sound that the New Democracy in which this change culminated must logically continue to be the platform of the Communist party after the war—there is one objective factor in favor of his arguments: The social composition of the Communist party's membership has undergone a deep change, away from radicalism.

Ninety-three per cent of its present numbers, about 1,200,000 at the end of 1944, joined only after 1937. The new members themselves are to the extent of almost nine-tenths peasants. And the great bulk of them are "middle peasants" with a pronounced petty-bourgeois, nationalistic background.

These new members came to the party, not after having read and agreed with the theories of Marx, Lenin, Stalin, and Mao Tse-tung, but in the course of liberating their homes from the Japanese and reforming the social life of their villages. It was in the practice of grim fighting and hard work for freedom and social progress that they found themselves in agreement with the new Communist policies that made this twofold fight possible.

These nine-tenths of all party members became Communists; but Communists in the sense of the New Democracy, not in the old sense of the period of the Civil War and the Communist International.

Many of them have in the meantime risen to posts of vital importance, especially in the Anti-Japanese War Bases in the enemy's rear. Everywhere but in the very highest ranks of the party, they have come to outnumber the intellectual, proletarian, and poor-peasant revolutionaries of the Civil War days before 1937.

Many of those new men and women have made great progress in the political theory of the New Democracy as well as in practical work. They are young and vigorous. They know what they want and make their influence felt at party headquarters.

They are evidently in harmony with the leadership of Mao Tse-tung—not in spite of the mild policies of the New Democracy, but be-

146

cause of them. For these new party elements are in close cooperation with the nonparty people of all classes in those vast war areas of North and Central China where sympathies with the formerly almost unknown Communist party seem to have developed merely for two reasons—the Communists' fight against the Japanese and their mild but effective reform policies. It would seem that continued adherence to the general principles of the New Democracy will indeed be necessary for the Communist party in order to retain the cooperation of the people after the war.

The function of members of the Communist party of China seems to be everywhere: in the armies, local governments, villages, factories, cooperatives, hospitals, schools, theatrical groups, and wherever else it is considered necessary to push important work.

They are expected to show greater daring and initiative than nonparty men in the Communist-controlled armies; to work harder and more efficiently than their nonparty colleagues at their various professional tasks; to devote more of their off-duty time to voluntary social and educational work and to their own studies; to be models to others in performance and behavior; and to establish relations of trust, harmony, and equality with nonparty people without whom their work could not be successful. These are the criteria by which the qualities of individual party members are judged.

To be a member of the Communist party of China is an entirely different matter from belonging to a political party in the United States or Britain and from being a member of the loosely knit Chinese Government party, the Kuomintang. As in the case of the Russian Communist party, it means devoting one's life without reserve to a duty which overrules every personal interest. It means being under party orders in one's professional work and choice of domicile; and having to adhere to party decisions, whether they are handed down from above or taken by a majority in a lower party organ to which one is directly attached. Being a Communist party member is like being a professional soldier.

It was naturally one of my greatest difficulties to judge the inner workings of the Communist party and to draw comparisons with what I had learned years ago in Russia of the Bolshevik party.

My impression was that the mellow character of the New Democracy and of the primitive agricultural society in which it grows without acute class struggle is to some extent reflected in the comparatively placid relationship that seems to exist between various ranks within the Chinese Communist party.

The party members I met in various organizations seemed in tune with the responsibilities entrusted to them and with the men who direct their work. I had no reason to doubt their full confidence in the party leadership.

Like ideal human material for an elite army, those unsophisticated men and women appeared to have that particularly reliable kind of discipline which is basically self-imposed. This is probably the reason why the party leadership, while evidently forceful and in many respects absolute, can afford to direct its members with a light and almost gentle hand and often in an almost imperceptible manner.

I failed to discover any signs of political dissension among the leaders or the rank and file. The deeper I probed, the more likely I found it that relations inside the party were largely determined by mutual frankness and a good measure of democratic procedure which led to a harmonization of views.

Every functionary seems to be freely elected by members, from the lowest organizations up. It is true that the highest organ, the Central Committee of the party and its chairman Mao Tse-tung have been in power for a long time without the prescribed elections. This may or may not be due to the consequences of the war which have scattered party members over wide areas behind the enemy lines; yet a party congress took place early in 1945 and re-elected the Central Committee. Meanwhile, the Central Committee seems to have given the lower party organs opportunities for criticism of its policies.

There is certainly no disagreement on the way the war against Japan is being fought. There seems to be none on the party's avowed intention to come to an understanding with the Kuomintang, or on its demand that the basis of such an understanding has to be the establishment of a truly democratic regime in China as a whole. There is definitely no difference of opinion on the fact that the Communist International had long outlived its usefulness and had been without any practical or even ideological importance to the Communist party of China when it was dissolved in 1943. And the need of a prolonged stage of New Democracy for China seemed to be generally recognized.

I did not discover in the Border Region any parallel to Generalissimo Chiang Kai-shek's demand on his troops to put the party first in the loyalties they have to observe: "Soldiers of our country should manifest their loyalty to the Kuomintang and to the nation." *

The Chinese Communists are naturally unwilling to impose on their armies loyalty to a rival political party, the Kuomintang; and Chiang Kai-shek's identification of the Kuomintang with the National Government and the National Army is one of the greatest hindrances to an understanding between Yenan and Chungking. But the Communists demand from their troops and even from their party members loyalty to the nation and the people as their first duty.

The Communist party seems to mean what it says when it orders its members to get close to the masses of the people and to "identify themselves with the people"—because the successes it has had in its military and other policies are mainly due to the cooperation between party and people.

To take the "mass viewpoint" was evidently the serious endeavor of the party members whom I came to know fairly well. "It is their religion, that's all," one of the Kuomintang men in our party once said to me.

The movement within the Communist party for the "Remolding of Ideology" which has been going on for some time aims at overcoming all ideological deviations, and with them the practical shortcomings of

* From an address to 500 student volunteers on January 11, 1944, as quoted by the Bulletin of the China Information Committee of the Ministry of Information, Chungking, January 13, 1944.

party members, through a thorough understanding and acceptance of the mass viewpoint.

The three main deviations in theory and practice, as analyzed in detail in a recent book of Mao Tse-tung, sound more abstract and difficult to grasp in their English equivalents than they are supposed to be in Chinese.

The first taboo may be called Subjectivism. It covers the two extremes of blind adherence to doctrinaire ideas and of experimentalism in the sense of thoughtless trial-and-error methods.

The second can be translated as Sectarianism. It brands the attitude of people who confine their thoughts into watertight little compartments, within narrow local or departmental limits, barring the wider prospects they should take into account, and showing superiority, condescension, or lack of cooperation toward people outside the party.

The third is Schematism or Pedantry in thinking as well as in the style of writing, in the couching of orders, in education, and in art. For cliché is a disease to which Communists in all countries seem particularly susceptible, and Chinese Communists are no exception.

The translation of the term "Remolding of Ideology" is poor and may easily be misunderstood as aiming at a change of fundamental ideas. It really means the mastery of the lessons the Communists have, or feel they should have, learned from their experiences; and the clear understanding of Marxist theory as applied to the present phase of China's social revolution—the New Democracy.

Having worked and fought so many years without sufficient leisure time for examining their ideology, and having grown from little more than 80,000 old guards in 1937 to about 1,200,000 in 1944, the members of the Communist party are now to be given an opportunity to examine themselves, to learn from their past experiences, and to overcome the deficiencies in the practice of their work by recognizing the shortcomings of their theoretical thinking on which those deficiencies are supposed to be based.

It was in connection with this movement, which is thoroughly practical in its aims in spite of its highly theoretical-sounding terminology, that the Party School in Yenan developed into the largest and most important educational institution in all the Communist-controlled areas.

It is the strangest school I have ever seen: a school without teachers and without textbooks, without lectures, and without that discipline from above which is normally regarded as essential to any school. I spent one of my most interesting days in Yenan in one of its five departments which, like the average of the others, has about one thousand pupils.

It covers a large area with innumerable caves and little houses in which men and women live and work, some alone, others in twos, threes, or fours; with large, pleasant dining rooms where food is somewhat richer than elsewhere; with a huge theater-cum-auditorium, a library, and reading rooms; with playing grounds, gardens, fields, and workshops.

Pang Chen, a tall, muscular man of forty-two, one of those in Yenan of whom it is difficult to tell whether the peasant or the intellectual element is the main characteristic of his personality, is the director of the school. He is one of the veterans of the Communist party and, from the impression I got of his intellect and energy, may be one of its most important coming men.

On our tour through the campus I met pupils from the various Anti-Japanese War Bases in North and Central China and from all walks of life. Almost all of them were higher and medium cadres, people who had held responsible positions: commanders of brigades, regiments, battalions; political commissars in the army, party functionaries, and government officials; factory managers and teachers, writers, and artists; Labor Heroes and model workers from factories, farms, and cooperatives. A good part of them were women.

These people are organized in self-governing groups of forty or fifty, composed in such a way that all occupations are represented and that there are "strong" as well as "weak" members in each.

Individual studies, to fill in whatever gaps they may have in their general education, and even in their knowledge of reading and writing the necessary number of Chinese characters, are only a minor part of their work. Their main task is to learn from one another's experiences:

151

for everyone to supplement his special knowledge of one field of activity by an all-round understanding of the concrete problems that have to be faced and the ways in which they have to be solved in other fields.

A military commander above junior rank is not considered fully qualified unless he knows the answers to economic, social, and educational questions he may have to help the people solve under the peculiar conditions in the war regions. An official holding a responsible position in those areas has to be versed in certain concrete aspects of warfare, apart from the essentials of all important policies. Every Communist, whatever his profession, has to take an active interest in all matters concerning the New Democracy and to have an all-round knowledge of its main problems in order to fulfill his task of guiding the people wherever guidance is needed. The aim of the Party School is to train all-round proficient pioneers for the requirements of the war and the New Democracy.

Life on the campus impressed me as being stimulating and vivid, free and pleasant. Individual reading and group discussion of practical problems take up a good part of the day. But there seems to be plenty of time for quiet thinking and physical exercise, for amateur theatricals, music, and personal contacts.

To most of the men and women who have had scarcely a free hour for years, their one or two years in the Party School are a vacation as well as that great opportunity for undisturbed studies and self-assessment which so many busy professionals crave in every kind of society. Whether it was for positive or negative reasons that they were selected for a course in the Party School, these veterans of practical work seem to appreciate it very much indeed.

Some of those who are at the school in order to correct shortcomings made grave mistakes in their work, which arose from insufficient understanding of the political system—like the former manager of the Border Region Bank who aimed at making money for the government instead of expanding credit facilities for the people. Others were handicapped by their narrow expert knowledge, so that they had to widen their horizons. Still others were hampered in their practical work by a lack of general education. All are considered promising enough by the party to be given the opportunity of prolonged study.

But the majority of students are men and women of particular talent, achievement, and character who are to be groomed for higher responsibilities while teaching and influencing others. The strangely mixed crowd at the school seemed to lead a happy community life and to be enthusiastic to learn and unlearn and acquire a more universal knowledge of the manifold aspects of the fight for national independence and social progress.

Nothing could be more original and practical, freer of regimentation and dogmatism, than this peculiar staff college of the Communist party.

Part Four

"LABOR CREATES EVERYTHING"

A Forge

Chapter Sixteen

GROWN FROM THE SOIL

NO PERSON except Generalissimo Chiang Kai-shek himself has such fame in the Chungking areas as Wu Men-yu, a plain peasant, has in the Yenan regions.

Wu Men-yu's name is everywhere. Farmers and soldiers praise him for the help he gave them in the reclamation of wasteland and the increase of agricultural production. Magistrates, doctors, teachers, and artists speak of the services he rendered them in making the policies of the New Democracy successful and popular in the villages. Mao Tsetung refers to him with respectful affection as one of the individuals who have contributed most to the great expansion of agricultural crops, which made the Border Region safe against the Kuomintang's attempts to starve it out by blockade.

Wu Men-yu is the first of the Labor Heroes of whom so much is made in the Border Region.

I had no sympathy at first with everybody's enthusiasm for Labor Heroes. The idea itself, so alien to China, seemed to me artificial and purely propagandistic.

Wu Men-yu came to visit us in his working clothes, the customary cotton towel wound turbanlike around his bald head. He is a sturdy man in his middle fifties with a strong-willed, honest face and a twinkle of good humor and kindliness in his intelligent eyes—the type of Chinese farmer whom nobody could coach and use for a role not entirely his own. His straight and factual answers to our questions and the simple logical manner in which he spoke about agricultural and general progress in the Border Region impressed all of us.

I saw much more of him later, noticed the real influence he has on practically every kind of activity in Yenan's New Democracy, and came

157

to the conclusion that his popular fame is as genuine as the man Wu Men-yu himself.

It is evidently not only his personality that makes him rank with Mao Tse-tung and Chu Teh in the people's feelings. He has become a symbol of all that is good and sound and progressive in the Chinese farmer—the pride and model of a recently awakened peasantry which is still somewhat astonished at its own successes in overcoming age-old backwardness and at its satisfaction with a new political and social system.

Wu Men-yu is modest and was hesitant when we asked him to tell us his own life story first. He thought it quite unimportant and wanted to start with facts and figures on the great agricultural progress in his village and the Border Region as a whole. Eventually he consented to tell us about himself.

"I used to live much farther north in this province," he began, "and had to leave my native village in 1928 because of a bad famine. We had nothing to eat. I sold my three-year-old daughter for five pounds of grain to keep the others alive a little while longer. Two more daughters I had to give away as girl brides to well-to-do families so that they, too, could eat. You know, such things still happen in the Kuomintang areas even now."

When he came to a valley near Yenan, he said, he reclaimed one acre of poor land in the hills, dug a primitive cave as a dwelling, and cut firewood for the market to pay for a few tools and some food because his new landlord gave him neither tools nor credit. On the contrary, Wu Men-yu had to surrender a good part of his crops to him as rent. It took a long time and much hard reclamation work to build up a little farm again. By the time the Communists came to this area during the Civil War in 1935, he was a tenant on ten acres of poor hill land which yielded his family barely enough food to survive. And he had to keep on cutting firewood to pay his rent and buy clothing.

"How was it when the Red Army came?"

"There had already been an agrarian revolution going on for years in neighboring counties," Wu Men-yu said, "and I had heard that the

158

Communists were quite good to poor people. But we knew very little about them and were a bit doubtful. At first, some eighty or ninety Red partisans came from near by, while Yenan was still held by Kuomintang troops, and began distributing some of the landlords' land and cattle to the poor peasants. I was the head of our little village then. I called our people for a secret meeting with some partisans to find out what the Communists were like. The main point they discussed at that meeting was the exploitation and oppression of the Kuomintang. You know, the Kuomintang never called any meetings with us and never told the people anything. All we knew of them was that they always wanted money and grain from us."

"What became of your landlord?"

"He is still here and is well off. Only his hill lands were taken away from him and distributed to his fifteen tenant families. They left him some good land in the valley where he grows vegetables now. He had not been so very rich and always worked himself, too. His own son was in sympathy with the revolution and took part in it."

We wanted to know how Wu Men-yu had become a Labor Hero.

"In 1941 Comrade Mao Tse-tung asked the people to find out who among the peasants were model farmers and could be regarded as candidates for the first Labor Hero elections. The people investigated everywhere and picked me out as one of the candidates. The magistrate also found out about my work and my political loyalty to the New Democracy. One day in 1942 there was a big meeting and the people of my district elected me. They gave several reasons. My methods of cultivation were more intensive than those of the others. I weeded more and did more work on every one of the twenty or twenty-five acres I had by then. I had also raised two head of cattle, which was then quite unusual for poor farmers.

"My attitude toward the government and the war was considered better than that of others—I always responded well to the calls for all kinds of voluntary mobilization work. And maybe the main thing was that I had a good name with the other farmers because I used to help them with advice and showed them with my hands how to improve things."

He laughed when we asked him whether he was better off at present than before.

"I have almost one hundred acres of land now, all my own, and good savings. I eat much better now than my former landlord did be-

HOMECOMING OF A LABOR HERO

fore the Communists came. I will show you everything when you visit me."

"Brigadier Wang Chen in Nanniwan said you helped him so much. What did you do for him?"

Wu Men-yu became very enthusiastic. Neither the fact that he was made a Labor Hero nor that his little village was now a "model village" and he himself a rich owner-farmer made him as proud, evidently, as his cooperation with the Eighth Route Army.

"I gave the brigade much practical advice at meetings in which the soldiers planned their agricultural work. I also helped them with the work itself. Last year, for example, I worked with them eleven days, showing them how to sow in the best way on the steep slopes they had reclaimed; and another seventeen days on land reclamation, teaching them better methods from my own experience.

"You know, the army and the people are now really helping each other wherever they can. The Eighth Routers don't treat the people like the Kuomintang soldiers and are not rough. In the busy seasons, altogether about ten days in the year, the soldiers everywhere help the farmers in their work. But the Eighth Routers never demand food from us. They don't even accept any when we offer it to them. And the army doctors come and cure the people when they are sick. My personal relations with Comrade Wang Chen are very good. When he asked me to help his brigade develop its agricultural production work, I felt it was a great honor to have personal relations with him. Because he leads his troops himself in all their work, and because it is all done to lighten the burden of the people. I love him very much."

He began talking about Mao Tse-tung and we mentioned Chiang Kai-shek's name, asking him what he thought of the Generalissimo.

"I know Chiang Kai-shek is the leader of the whole nation. But . . ." He sighed, and thought for a little while. "Let me put it this way: Can simple people in Chungking shake hands with him as we do with Mao Tse-tung? I had meetings with Comrade Mao Tse-tung and we also had long talks alone, and I ate with him several times."

"Why did you sigh when you talked about Chiang Kai-shek?"

"When I first fled here from the famine in the North, nobody helped me. The government did not care. There are still many refugees coming here from Kuomintang areas in the North and also from Honan province in the South, and under our New Democracy the Border Region government and the people are helping those refugees. You can see some refugees right in my village. It is more like heaven here in our Border Region now; and under the Kuomintang it was like hell."

161

"Don't many people disagree with you on your views about the new government?"

"No, we have no really backward people here any more. They have all learned and many followed my own example, because they understood why I received such great honor. They also came to know that they get personal advantages from accepting the new ideas. The backward people in my village found that they could do the same as I and also get richer. And now, all people answer my call when I try to introduce further improvements of one kind or another."

"You must be quite tired now," I said to the old man, for we had talked for many hours after his busy morning in the fields.

"A farmer does not get tired from talking," Wu Men-yu laughed. "There is much more I want to tell you, and much you should see. I hope you will come to the village."

My observations proved that Wu Men-yu's claims about the improvements in village life in the Border Region were well founded. I talked with many people about the changes that had taken place during the last few years: with peasants and officials; with doctors who judged from their experiences in hospitals and outpatients' departments; and with shopkeepers whose yardstick is the rising purchasing power of their rural customers. Their accounts all checked.

I found some interesting statistics at one of the popular exhibitions which are frequently held in Yenan in connection with the unremitting production drive. Many farmers, workers, and local officials were there, and students of Yenan University explained to them the various exhibits, especially the statistical graphs on the walls. It seems that figures like the following must be correct if the authorities expose them to the critical eyes of their own people, who know conditions well enough to judge for themselves.

The increase of popular food consumption, shown district by district, ranged from a minimum of 33 per cent to fully 100 per cent, comparing the last year of Kuomintang rule with 1943. It averaged about 50 per cent, while the total production of foodstuffs in the Border Region increased even more.

The increase of per capita grain reserves held by the peasants of typical villages increased two and a half times from the period immediately before the 1940 harvest to that of the 1943 harvest, when the great drive for the accumulation of food stocks by individual families began.

The improvement in the "class composition" in the villages was shown by a number of examples. I copied the figures of one which seemed typical. From 1936 to 1942 the number of families of landless laborers decreased from 14 to 1; the number of "poor" peasant families fell from 48 to 15; that of "middle" peasant families rose from 44 to 94; and that of "rich" peasant families from 2 to 15; while the total number of households in the village increased from 108 to 125, mainly through the separation of large families and the settlement of disabled soldiers and refugees. The village had more than twice as many head of cattle as before.

In 1943 alone, more than 25,000 famine refugees from Honan province and other Kuomintang areas were settled in the Border Region. More than 5,000 persons from the poorest and overcrowded parts of the Border Region itself were resettled on reclaimed land elsewhere. And from 1938 to 1943 more than 9,625 disabled soldiers with their families, mostly from other parts of the country, were helped to establish homesteads.

We visited Wu Men-yu at his village. His family lives in a row of three or four caves, simply but comfortably by Chinese standards. Some more caves serve as stables, chicken coops, and storerooms. We sat with him on a broad brick-built bed and enjoyed his talk at a pleasant meal. But the old man did not mean our visit to be wasted in entertainment. He wanted to take us around and show us his village, of which he is so proud.

His replies to our questions helped us to form a lively picture of the pioneer work that goes on in the villages of the Border Region.

I remarked that his village was called "The Date Garden of the Wu Family" and asked whether it had been renamed for him and where the trees were which bear that datelike fruit characteristic of North China.

It was another Wu family which gave the village its name many years ago, he said. One of the great famines drove them away. Most of the date trees were cut down by the people who remained. And the village was still a very miserable place when he arrived in 1928, with much of the formerly cultivated land gone to waste. "But now," he said, "we take no more chances with famines. Crop failures from drought are always a danger in these parts. But the government has shown us the way to put up reserves. This is why the production movement, in 1943, launched the slogan, 'Produce three crops in two years.' We should all have one year's requirements in reserve. And each farmer already has larger stocks than ever before."

Wu Men-yu took us out to the little farmyard in front of his caves. "Buried here I have sufficient millet to last my whole family for eighteen months, apart from what we shall need until this coming harvest," he said, stamping on the ground. "After this new crop which promises to be the largest I ever had, because of the new land we reclaimed since last year and the good weather, I shall have enough millet for all of us for more than five years. For I shall harvest about eighteen tons this year from almost one hundred acres."

"Does the government let people keep their own reserves?"

"Certainly. The government builds up stocks of its own against crop failure and for the counteroffensive—partly from the production of the garrison troops and partly from the 'National Salvation Grain Levy.' This is the only tax on the farmers, and it amounts to no more than 10 or 12 per cent of the average crop. All the rest we can keep."

He got hold of me somewhere on a leisurely walk through the fields in order to make this point quite clear to me; for he had heard that I was especially interested in economic matters. "You will find out anywhere you ask," he said, "that the tax burden of the people has never been so small. And the reason is that the army, the government officials, and the students are using their own hands in production work, as Comrade Mao Tse-tung told them."

164

"And here you see a Labor Exchange Brigade at work," he said, pointing to a group of eight or nine men in a row who were hoeing and singing as they worked.

Everybody in the Border Region was very proud of the Labor Exchange Brigades. It had been an ancient custom in some parts of China for peasants to get together and do certain jobs for each other collectively; but it had never played a great role and gradually faded out. The Communists learned about it from old peasants, refined the ancient method and handed it back to the people, together with the necessary propaganda stimulus. The Labor Exchange Brigades, in which 50 per cent of all peasants in the Border Region are already voluntarily organized, have thus become the outstanding example of the success of Mao Tse-tung's rule, "Learn from the masses and then teach them."

The movement started some four years ago when the increasing requirements of the army, of industries, cooperatives, and new administrative organizations began to make the lack of labor in the fields more and more acute. That was at a time when special stress had to be laid on land reclamation and on more intensive farming methods. There are different forms of Labor Exchange Brigades which the people everywhere organize under their own free will. In some cases whole villages work together on various tasks. In others small individual groups are formed for a long period to deal with special jobs like land reclamation and dike building. Sometimes they get together for short periods during rush seasons. They use each other's tools and draft animals, which greatly increases their working capacity.

Even where all the work is done collectively, the fields and implements and crops remain private property, so that the incentives of both collectivism and unrestricted private ownership are used to the fullest possible extent. Special methods have been worked out by which individual brigade members who work more on the fields of others than on their own, or those who contribute more than their share through the loan of their tools and draft animals, get adequate payment in kind.

"The farmers show great inventiveness and enthusiasm in applying this old method in new ways," Wu Men-yu said. "They feel that it is

165

their own method and was not imposed on them from above. This is why we expect to achieve our goal of getting altogether about 90 per cent of all farmers to organize themselves in voluntary Labor Exchange Brigades."

The Labor Exchange Brigades lend every three of their members the productive capacity of four or five farmers working in family groups or individually. They make work more pleasant and more efficient. And in creating a new community spirit they do much to overcome the proverbial individualism and clannishness of the farmers.

Wu Men-yu pointed to the hills all around his little village, on which even the steepest slopes were covered with green fields.

"All this land could never have been reclaimed if we had not succeeded in our propaganda for the Labor Exchange Brigades. This shows you that propaganda is necessary. Before the Communists came we had only about 100 acres under cultivation in the whole village. In 1942 we had 150 acres, in 1943, 200 acres, and this year we have 325 acres."

During the last five years reclamation has added 1,000,000 acres to the 1,500,000 acres of land that had formerly been under cultivation in the entire Border Region. The army alone with its 40,000 to 50,000 garrison troops has contributed about one-third to this new source of food and wealth.

It is all marginal land, bound to become useless from erosion in the course of years. The greater part of the land at present under cultivation in the Border Region will probably have to be abandoned as unprofitable once the economy of a united China develops freely and fully. But the determination of the Communists and the methods with which they won the voluntary support of the people have made the wasteland in this poorest corner of China the basis for their great social experiment and for a considerable war effort.

Wu Men-yu had some work to do, and I visited the village head, one of those who had come from the Kuomintang areas after the Border Region was established. He had then fought the Japanese with the

166

Eighth Route Army, was wounded several times and eventually discharged.

I asked him about the class composition of the little village.

Yes, Wu Men-yu was by far the richest man, he said, but nobody grudged him his wealth. He and his family worked their land themselves and he gave away much to refugees who came as new settlers. He was always ready to help anybody, and the people felt that in time they could do as well as he, for he had already shown them the way to much greater prosperity than they had ever known. Even the latest settlers were now getting more than one-tenth of what Wu Men-yu harvested after so many years of effort, and quite a few villagers had incomes about one quarter as large as his, while the next richest farmer had about half his income and would probably get as much this year as Wu Men-yu had two years ago.

A group of singing men passed us out of sight behind a hillock. Their pleasant song sounded new to me and I asked the village head to call them. They were members of a Labor Exchange Brigade who had arrived only a few months ago from one of the overcrowded districts in the northeast of the Border Region which has no wasteland to reclaim and where the landlords still owned most of the cultivated fields, because no agrarian revolution had taken place there before the war.

"Life is good here," said one of the singers, "and after the harvest we go home to bring others to this district. Where we live there is not enough land and we still have landlords although our rents have been reduced by the government. We are poorer than people here, but not nearly so badly off as we were under the Kuomintang. At that time we always had to give the village head and the soldiers whatever they demanded, or they would beat us. And there were many taxes, taxes on everything. But now the government helps us.

To make conditions better in our district, people are asked to go and settle in other parts to make room in the old villages. There are many farmers in the Kuomintang areas around the Border Region who would also like to come here. Some do, every year, but it is very difficult for them because it is forbidden on the other side."

167

I asked him about the song I had heard.

He said the Labor Exchange Brigade had "made" it themselves. They had first thought of the tune and then discussed the words and dictated them to a man who could write, and the words had been read out loud so many times that everyone had learned them. "But it is not only one song. We have many such songs."

They sat down and sang a few for me. These are some of the lines:

> The red sun rises from ,the East.
> In China we have Mao Tse-tung.
> He plans production work for us.
> Comrade Mao saves the Chinese people.
>
> The hills are high and the rivers green.
> Our Border Region is a good place to live in.
> Let us produce more food this year.
> Comrade Mao called the refugees to come.
> And the refugees came and will be prosperous soon.
> Let us produce more food
> While the Eighth Route Army fights the enemy.
> We have a peaceful life
> Because we have our Eighth Route Army.

Every week I spent in the Border Region I found new traces of Wu Men-yu's work and influence. For agricultural progress is only one of the aims of this practical farmer, and his village is now no more than a kind of laboratory for him.

He works with the director of a well-run scientific model farm near Yenan on the selection of better seeds and the introduction of new varieties of grain, vegetables, potatoes, cotton, and hemp, giving the learned botanist practical advice on local conditions and working out methods of introducing the new seeds to conservative farmers.

If Wu Men-yu lends his name to something new and tries it on his own farm, they will accept it more easily. He is one of the moving spirits behind the new drive for education and, although he cannot read and write himself, he tries hard to make the school in his village a model for others.

He goes to meetings in Yenan at which modern hygiene is taught and propagandizes the new methods in the villages. He is a great enthusiast for the development of cooperatives and has done much to make them popular.

He meets writers and artists and tells them whether or not their work appeals to the taste of the people. One of the famous poets, an old revolutionary intellectual, once published a poem about Wu Men-yu in which he said the old man had been fortunate to become so rich and famous. Wu Men-yu went to see him and said it was not luck but hard work which was responsible for his success and would the poet please cut out that wrong passage, "For what we need is hard-working people and not fortunate people."

He is a member of the People's Political Council of his county and a strict and outspoken critic of whatever is still unsatisfactory in the administration.

As the first Labor Hero of the Border Region he consults frequently with the other 180 Labor Heroes who were elected after him from farmers, factory workers, soldiers, and staffs of hospitals and other organizations. These Labor Heroes, among whom I later found other impressive men and women, occasionally meet to discuss the various methods by which the elite corps of the masses can help progress in every field.

Wu Men-yu has grown to the stature of a popular statesman in the New Democracy; just as during virile periods of China's ancient history farmers of outstanding personality sometimes rose to high rank and fame in the imperial dynasties.

There have always been Wu Men-yus in China. Even now there must be many all over the country, in the Kuomintang areas as well as in the Communist territories. To have allowed this man to develop, to work for the people, and to make tens of thousands of them into "active elements" is one of the merits of Yenan's New Democracy.

Conversations with Wu Men-yu about the manifold problems and "drives" of this pioneer region seemed to prove to me that the mass viewpoint of the Communists and of their nonparty collaborators is not just talk. The old man's vocabulary is full of those new terms of the Communist A B C, but to him everything has a concrete meaning and purpose and he made several of the slogans clearer to me than other men of infinitely greater learning.

He is now a member of the Communist party, one of that vast and influential new majority in its ranks who have a definite petty-bourgeois background and are fond of their new prosperity.

Men of this type would seem to offer the best guarantee that, whatever may happen in China and the world, Yenan's New Democracy will have to adhere to the conviction that the Chinese peasantry needs on the one hand a maximum of collectivism in order to break down its hampering traditions of family separatism, but on the other the incentive of private property as a stimulus to self-interest and progress.

The Labor Hero Wu Men-yu, the ardent believer both in popular cooperation and private property, member of the Communist party and at the same time the richest man in his model village, seemed to me to personify Yenan's New Democracy. . . .

Chapter Seventeen

BEFORE THE INDUSTRIAL REVOLUTION

E VERYWHERE I went in the Border Region, in government offices, schools, shops, farms, and dwelling caves, there were crude wooden spinning wheels. Almost everybody, high and low, seemed to put some spare energy into the spinning of wool or cotton yarn.

People set themselves monthly tasks and standards of quality and I met men and women in important positions who took pride in the progress they made in their spinning. At an exhibition I saw an animated crowd examine prize specimens of hand-spun yarn with the name tags of those who had produced them: school children, peasants, workers, government and party officials, and military men, including some well-known leaders.

There is no doctrine like Gandhism behind the mass movement which revived spinning in the villages, introduced it into towns, government offices, schools, and armies—and eventually made it the virtually universal spare-time occupation and the main manufacturing industry all over the Communist-controlled areas.

The leaders of the Communist party who launched the movement and the people who responded to it are at least as machine minded and as eager for modern industrialization as the Chinese anywhere else in the country.

The return to primitive hand spinning, which the competition of machine-made goods had almost destroyed by the time the war broke out, was to them a practical answer to part of a serious problem: soldiers and civilians suffered a serious lack of clothing, especially since Chungking blockaded the Border Region, which had neither cotton cultivation, on account of its short growing season, nor more than a trifling number of antiquated spindles and looms.

SPINNING COMPETITION

Farmers were taught to plant cotton and were stimulated by tax exemption to give part of their fields to that newfangled, risky crop. The customary wool exports from the Border Region were reduced and the flocks of sheep increased.

Weaving was dealt with on a semiindustrial basis: simple wooden looms were designed for production by industrial cooperatives, army workshops, and village carpenters; hand weaving by farmers was encouraged; and large, primitive weaving mills were set up in towns.

But spinning had to be arranged without tying up more full-time labor in factories and without intensifying the transportation problem by making it necessary to bring raw cotton and wool from widely scattered villages to manufacturing centers. This is why the population was mobilized to use part of its spare time spinning yarn on hand spindles which were produced locally on patterns provided by the government and industrial cooperatives.

As a result, the Border Region, which had almost no production of raw cotton and cotton goods in 1937, covered three-quarters of its needs in 1944—on a higher level of per capita consumption than had ever before been known. The production of woolen yarn and cloth was considerably increased. And it is expected that complete self-sufficiency in clothing materials will be achieved in 1946.

The mass movements that popularized these production policies seem to have proved equally successful in those Anti-Japanese War Bases behind the enemy lines which also had a clothing problem.

The armament industry in the Border Region and the war areas grew mainly in similar ways—on the basis of primitive handwork. Blacksmiths were mobilized everywhere. They had to train ever-increasing numbers of apprentices. Army units in the rear and at the front had soldiers trained, and established their own blacksmith shops. No iron deposits in the hills and plains were considered too poor for use. Farmers were asked to help exploit them. And new forges were set up next to primitive mines.

It seems that wherever some ore or scrap is available in the war areas, the two main weapons of the Communist-controlled armies and militia are being produced on the spot. One is the hand grenade and the other the land mine. Both are charged either with a fairly effective "yellow powder," which is also said to be made in most areas now, or with the old-fashioned "black powder," in the production of which the Chinese once were far ahead of a bow-and-arrow-using world.

The production of hand grenades and land mines in the war areas would seem to be quite considerable, judging from what I was told in Yenan and especially from what was implied in Japanese and puppet newspapers that I saw. The Japanese-controlled press explains from time to time why no supplies of food and raw materials are coming into the Japanese-occupied cities from their "bandit" hinterland and why the frequent Japanese mopping-up campaigns fail to pacify those areas. They always refer to the widespread land-mine and hand-grenade warfare of the Red Bandits as one of the main obstacles to their fight against the Communists.

The Communist-controlled territories also have small arsenals and factories. I saw a number of them within a hundred-mile radius of Yenan. "We cannot make steel in our regions," the director of an arsenal said as he took us through his plant. "Wherever possible, we are using steel rails which our troops tear up from Japanese-occupied railroads. But transportation across the enemy lines to Yenan is difficult and we must as a rule be satisfied with local-made iron, which is plentiful. We even make quite good trench mortars from iron."

The little arsenal where 330 men are working has about a dozen low buildings with the strangest assortment of machinery I ever saw in use: ancient lathes, planing, drilling, rolling, and stamping machines made in China, the United States, England, and Germany which were bought second-, third-, or probably tenth-hand in Sian before the Kuomintang blockade; and simple new machines of various kinds made in the arsenal itself or in one of the Border Region's new engineering workshops. All the machines are well kept. And they run—driven by an old truck engine with a home-produced charcoal-burning attachment.

The various departments of the arsenal make cast iron, neat-looking trench mortars, cartridges, bayonets, Very pistols, and—since the farmer

174

enjoys a high priority everywhere—copper syringes for veterinary use in the campaign against cattle epidemics. Other shops repair rifles and light and heavy machine guns and refill Chinese and Japanese rifle cartridges.

All the copper used in the plant is from copper cash or odd pieces of old dragons and Buddhas, collected by the peasants on scrap drives. In its courtyard under a thatched roof, the arsenal keeps a precious supply of wire captured from the Japanese. Steel screws and files are made from rails torn up in the war areas. And there seem to be primitive substitutes for every essential that is lacking in its conventional shape.

The arsenals of the Border Region, I was told, are not the pioneers of arms production in the Communist-controlled regions. On the contrary, the older and more experienced arsenals in the Anti-Japanese War Bases are in the lead. A number of them are larger and better equipped because they have accumulated much machinery that was taken from the enemy's rear repair shops and the puppets' factories. The production of trench mortars, for example, was learned from arsenals in the war areas which are still turning out much larger quantities of them than the Border Region.

One of the engineers in the plant near Yenan told me of his participation, two years ago, in a large raid by thousands of Communist troops on a strong Japanese position. The raid was made for the sole purpose of getting urgently needed machinery for an important arsenal.

Other people I met in Yenan related stories of Japanese attacks on Communist arsenals in the war areas, which are always in danger. If the arsenals cannot be defended against superior forces, the most vital instruments are carried away by units of the local self-defense corps and the bulky machinery is buried according to a prearranged plan. When the enemy has been made to withdraw by the customary Communist strategy of flank and rear attacks, little time is required to reassemble the arsenal and get it going once more.

A privately owned weaving mill I visited appeared modern enough from the outside with its large, new, well-designed buildings in nicely laid out grounds. Inside, however, it seemed like a reproduction of a big medieval manufacturing enterprise. Its large halls were crowded with hundreds of noisily clattering looms, entirely of wood with scarcely a piece of iron visible, driven by a large water wheel over woolen transmitter belts. In a carpenter's shop, wooden machinery for the constant expansion of the mill is made by hand with the most primitive tools. The few old lathes in the small mechanical workshop are kept in motion by an old mule trotting in a circle in the courtyard and turning a big wheel.

I saw a good-sized paper mill standing over a stream. Large wooden water wheels drove giant grindstones set in a complicated-looking wooden superstructure, milling grass from the near-by hillsides into pulp. This factory, within the few years of its existence, has become the parent of more than a dozen other paper mills which were set up all over the Border Region with a few of its experienced hands as the *nuclei* of their new, farm-recruited personnel.

I visited a small oil field, once the property of Socony before it was taken over by the Kuomintang government of China before the war, and now one of the most precious possessions of the Border Region. It produces several hundred thousand gallons of oil a year—very little indeed, but enough for the limited needs of the almost motorless Border Region and for some exports to the Kuomintang areas.

The workers have a hard time keeping in operation the stingy, erratic wells and the ancient machinery of the primitive refinery. But they seem to be successful: the present production is ten times larger than it was before the outbreak of the Sino-Japanese War in 1937.

The Border Region's nonhandicraft industry includes machine spinning and weaving, iron and coal mining, and engineering; the production of ceramics and glass, salt, oil, soap, matches, and of a number of chemicals; the manufacture of paper, cigarettes, vegetable dyes; and tanning and printing. It is infinitesimal even by comparison with the industry of the Chungking regions. But its development in recent years, against the almost incredible odds of the lack of machinery, mechanical power, and technical skill under the twofold Japanese and Kuomintang blockade is no small achievement and testifies to the organizing ability of the Communists which may one day be applied to much greater tasks.

In the total area with its 1,500,000 people the number of industrial workers other than artisans was only 270 before the beginning of the war in 1937 and 700 before the beginning of the Kuomintang blockade in 1939. It rose to 7,000 in 1942 and to 12,000 in 1944.

Industrial production seems to have increased more than the number of workers. Handicraft production, which still outweighs the total industrial output, has also been raised considerably in consequence of the efforts of the Border Region government to expand it as much as possible.

The further growth of industry planned until 1946 is expected to make the Border Region self-sufficient in almost all essential products.

Industrial development in some of the Anti-Japanese War Bases is said to be even more successful than in the Border Region. Some of these bases are richer in coal, iron, and other raw materials, and the Communist troops have been able to procure for them a good deal of machinery in their fight against the Japanese. The Japanese blockade is nowhere so effective as that of the Kuomintang against the Border Region, because the people in the war areas have been trained to co-operate in the Communists' active economic warfare against the enemy, so that in occupied cities purchases of key materials are not so difficult as might be thought. And considerable numbers of skilled workers from Shanghai and other Japanese-held industrial centers have constantly come over to the Communist forces and are helping them in the development of mobile as well as stationary plants.

The workers in the industries of the Communist-controlled regions apparently do not claim a right to greater influence on public affairs than other classes. The class consciousness that is clearly developing among them seems to follow occupational rather than political lines. Their professed solidarity with the peasantry from which they come has nothing artificial about it. None of the factory workers to whom I spoke about labor problems referred to their class as "proletarian."

Workers seem really free to change their jobs, as trade-union and government officials claimed. In each case I found, their colleagues had exerted strong social pressure on the men, and after a short venture into another job one at least returned, drawn by a sense of duty and by bonds of group solidarity which appear to be almost as strong in factories as in army units.

Working hours are more or less standardized. A ten-hour day is normal, except in mines, where eight is the rule. But one to two hours of daily studies are semi-obligatory, and various social duties connected with mass movements for the war effort and general progress probably fill up what leisure time there is.

Yet there seems to be no dissatisfaction among the workers. Most of the men and women I saw in the factories gave the same impression as the soldiers of being devoted to their jobs, keen on their education, and aware of the fact that they have already a better life than under the old regime on their farms.

"I never had three catties [3.3 pounds] * of meat per month in the past, which is what I get now," a worker told me. "Formerly I got meat only a few times a year."

Wages, too, scarcely differ from one factory to another. Men and women of average qualification have roughly the same standard of living as soldiers and officers in the army and government and party officials.

Like them, factory workers get virtually all they need in kind— on an average 1.1 pounds of millet, ½ pound of wheat flour, and 1.1 pounds of vegetables per day; 3.3 pounds of meat, 1.1 pounds of vegetable oil, and 1.1 pounds of salt per month; and two cotton summer suits, one cotton-padded winter suit, three pairs of strong cloth shoes, two towels, and twelve cakes of soap per year. Similar rations are provided for dependents, with special allowances for young children. Living quarters, mostly in individual caves, are free. The money wages in addition to those rations are fixed in terms of millet but paid out in

* The "official" catty in the Communist-controlled regions is the "new catty" of ½ *kilogram* or 1.1 pound, which the National Government adopted as the new weight standard before the war but failed to introduce in most of its areas.

cash. They decrease from about 100 pounds of millet per month for highly skilled workers and heads of departments to 10 to 20 pounds of millet per month for apprentices.

The near standardization of hours and wages restricts the professional functions of the trade unions to the protection of their members in minor regards, like the inspection of their food and living quarters, the supervision of safety devices, and the prevention of individual injustices.

But the trade unions play an important organizational part in Yenan's industrial policies. They have to help the workers raise their technical qualification and their general educational level; to maintain labor discipline; and, together with the management, to solve many kinds of factory problems—all in order to increase production.

The unions support the existing regime and its production policies frankly and unequivocally and have a strong Communist party element in all parts of their organization. But it would be wrong to put them on the same level with the trade unions of the National Government in Chungking. Union membership in the Communist-controlled areas is not compulsory, as it is in the Kuomintang territories. I met workers in Yenan who were not union members and seemed to suffer no disadvantage.

In the Yenan unions functionaries are elected by members, which is not the case in the Chungking unions. The union officials I met in the factories, both Communists and non-Communists, all seemed to be in the category of active elements who take a positive or even enthusiastic attitude toward the raising of production, the war effort, and the aims of the New Democracy and are not in any way militant in their attitude toward the management.

But this need not mean that the choice of such men and women is imposed on the union members; for the majority of workers might well be in agreement with government and union policies which have brought them educational facilities and better living standards than they ever had before and which have given them a strong sense of being important to the war effort.

Before the Industrial Revolution

In the factories I saw in the Chungking areas, where the rigid domination of the especially reactionary Ministry of Social Affairs prevents the unions from having any real life, the workers seemed completely apathetic toward them. In the Border Region, however, the unions were evidently full of animation, and most of the members seemed to participate with personal interest in their many-sided activities.

The Chungking unions seem unable to contribute anything to the war effort; while the Yenan unions are no doubt one of the chief factors in the increase of production in the Border Region and the Anti-Japanese War Bases.

At a general trade-union conference in Yenan in the spring of 1945 it was claimed that the total number of organized workers, including agricultural and handicraft workers, in all the Communist-controlled regions was 925,000—of which 60,000 were in the Border Region, 665,000 in the Anti-Japanese War Bases in North China, and 200,000 in those of Central China.

Of the "modern" factories in the Border Region, 78 per cent are owned by the government, 20 per cent by cooperatives, and only 2 per cent by private capital. This distribution of industrial ownership is not regarded as satisfactory by the Yenan authorities. For their New Democracy aims at giving private and cooperative capital the exclusive right, and the task, of engaging in enterprises other than railroads, mining, armament, and other heavy industries, which are to be wholly or partly owned by the government because of their key importance in the shaping of the national economy.

The present government predominance in the industrial field is explained as a temporary phenomenon which is due solely to the abnormal conditions under which factories had to be developed in the blockaded Border Region.

The capitalists of Yenan, the merchants and landlords, are not opposed to the major role the government now plays in industry. I found them surprisingly industry-minded—aware of the benefits they will derive one day by expanding or leaving the narrow limits of their semifeudal occupations and engaging in manufacture. And they

180

seemed satisfied that the political and economic system of the New Democracy provided the two prerequisites for such a change—security of private property and good prospects for profit.

To make the change to a more modern form of capitalistic enterprise is evidently the aim of most of them. But they saw no possibility of doing it now.

"It is impossible for us to establish any factories until the Kuomintang blockade comes to an end," I was told, "because the difficulties of getting machinery and certain key materials from the outside, and their cost if they can be obtained, are too great for individuals or private companies. For the time being we have to leave the initiative to the government. And we are glad that it is laying the foundations for industrial development."

Yet even now the capitalists of the Border Region are not wholly inactive in industrial enterprise. Curiously enough, many of those merchants and landlords who used to be the traditional enemies of cooperatives have been investing considerable amounts of capital in industrial cooperatives of a primitive semi-handicraft character which can be developed more easily.

"This should prove to you the confidence we have in the existing political and economic system," a well-to-do, progressive landlord said to me, "and our eagerness to engage in industry under the New Democracy."

Chapter Eighteen

THIS IS HOW THEY TRADE

I N MY continued "opium hunt" I made a real discovery: Yenan
has developed remarkable trade policies, characterized by a positive attitude toward private enterprise which is to be continued
after the war.

Yieh Shih-chiang, the head of the Trading Company in Yenan, was
another type of Communist new to me. In spite of his blue cotton tunic
and army-style cap, he looked somewhat like one of those liberal elderly merchants, lawyers, or journalists one meets anywhere in the big
cities of China. He had, in fact, been in each of those professions—but
very much in his own way. As a young man he learned all about commerce in his father's prosperous firm in Hong Kong and Canton,
against his own will and because his real interest was already the Chinese Revolution. He then studied law and practiced it mainly for the
sake of the poor. He edited a leftist newspaper in Hong Kong during
the Great Strike and fled to the Red Army when an order for his arrest
was issued by the British authorities. After the Long March, of which
his weak heart still reminds him every day, he was for years at the head
of the supply department of the Communist Army. And he is now the
reorganizer of trade in the Border Region.

"A National Government official in Ichuan gave me this certificate
for the export of 5.4 ounces of opium from the Border Region," I said.
"It is supposed to have been issued by your Local Products' Trading
Company." And I handed him a dirty little scrap of packing paper with
a red seal and a few scribbled Chinese characters.

He laughed: "And you were told that the company was suspended
by us for the time of your visit to Yenan?"

"Precisely."

"Well, the company was really suspended. It was merged with other commercial agencies into the Trading Company of which these caves are the headquarters. I think I need not tell you that that had nothing to do with opium or with your visit but only with the reorganization of our trade mechanism."

In the meantime, Yieh had sent for a file with the seals of the affiliated companies. None of them resembled the seal on my scrap of paper.

"When I first heard of the rumor about our so-called opium trade, I thought some of our employees might have connections with smugglers. I made a thorough investigation because since the earliest Red Army days we have always enforced a strict ban on the production, use, and smuggling of opium. It proved to be nothing but a malicious rumor. I cannot do any more than assure you that no opium is grown in the Border Region and that there is no trade in opium. Our police guards closely against any smuggling of opium through our areas. You will have to decide for yourself, after studying affairs in the Border Region, whether to believe us or those who are spreading such rumors."

I asked Yieh about trade between the Border Region and Japanese-occupied areas. For it was another of the standard accusations in Chungking that Yenan was trading with the enemy.

"There is no direct trade between here and the occupied areas. We do not even have any trade with our own Anti-Japanese Bases in the enemy's rear. The only point of contact between the Border Region and the adjoining Anti-Japanese Base in Shansi province is a precarious crossing over the Yellow River, and that is strictly reserved for military and passenger traffic. No trade is allowed there.

"Whatever goods we get from the Japanese-occupied areas—and you can see in our shops and cooperative stores that there are rather few—come in through Kuomintang-controlled areas: either from the direction of Sian in the south or from Yulin in the north of this province, or from the region of Marshal Yen Hsi-shan, which you visited."

I found it true that Japanese goods were much less in evidence in the Border Region than in Chungking, Sian, and other cities under Kuomintang control—where especially enemy goods of a luxury character are plentiful.

"In fact," he continued, "all our outside trade is with Kuomintang territories."

"Does this mean that the blockade of the Border Region is not complete?"

"It is very strict but not complete. In 1943 we imported from Kuomintang territories 4,455 million Border Region dollars' worth of goods and exported to them 3,581 million Border Region dollars' worth." (This corresponds roughly to $US4,400,000 and $US3,500,-000, respectively.)

Trade between the blockaded Border Region and the blockading Kuomintang territories is probably one of the most curious forms of internal commerce in history. In theory it does not exist; and in practice it is a grim struggle that costs lives.

The fundamental factor in these unofficial trade relations with the "friendly areas," as Yieh called the Kuomintang territories without meaning to be ironical, is that the blockaders are in need of certain Border Region products. They want salt from the Border Region's famous salt fields; kerosene and paraffin for which the Border Region with its miniature oil wells has a virtual monopoly in these parts of China; and in the case of Marshal Yen Hsi-shan's areas also some foodstuffs.

The second factor is that merchants and peddlers in the surrounding Kuomintang areas are as keen on trade as anywhere else in China—whatever the risk. And many low Kuomintang officials in the army and the civilian administration who have to try to survive on very meager wages condone it for the sake of profit or even participate actively in the traffic.

Against this background there is a constant struggle of wits between the authorities on either side of the line for the greatest possible advantage. Both attempt to influence the blockade-running in their own interests—the Communists to strengthen their economic basis and to improve the livelihood of the people; and the Kuomintang to obtain

184

what their adjoining areas need and at the same time to exert the strongest possible economic pressure on the Border Region.

"The Kuomintang try to let us get as few goods as possible in exchange for our exports," Yieh said, "and to sell us only nonessentials or even luxuries. They often confiscate goods that have been purchased for us in their regions, fine the merchants, keep them in steady fear of arrest, and occasionally even kill some. As a result of the risks and the bribes involved in our import trade, the merchants in the Kuomintang areas are forced to raise their margin of profit considerably. Moreover, all possible means are employed on the other side to keep the prices of our export goods down and raise the prices of our import goods. There have been cases when salt and other of our export goods yielded us only one-half of the prices at which they were sold a few miles inside Kuomintang territory. On the other hand, we often had to pay almost twice as much for our import goods as the prices at which they were originally bought across the line. This is the reason why our balance of trade last year was so unfavorable that the Bank of the Border Region had to spend large amounts of its national currency reserves to cover the deficit."

The imports of the Border Region in 1943 amounted to almost 70 per cent of raw cotton, yarn, and cloth. But by the middle of 1944 Yenan's production drive was already so successful that the Border Region needed much less from the Kuomintang areas for its clothing, although the average people seemed really better clad than on the other side. The peculiarities of the smuggling trade virtually forced Yenan to import wine, tobacco, and cigarettes to the extent of 8 per cent of the total purchases; but production of these minor luxuries in the Border Region has increased in the meantime and such imports are now prohibited. There is also a new ban on canned goods, which mostly originate from Japanese-controlled areas, and firecrackers and incense, on which about 5 per cent of the total import bill had to be spent in 1943.

The Kuomintang's purposeful political blockade control is comparatively effective on articles the Border Region needs most urgently.

185

Metals and metal goods made up only 3 per cent of all imports; and medicines only one-third of 1 per cent, although the Sian shops are well stocked with drugs from Japanese-controlled areas.

Yenan's methods of trade with the Kuomintang areas have been developed into an elaborate system. "We have definite regulations," Yieh said, "which our merchants have learned to observe. We give them specified orders for their purchases: either on behalf of the army, the administration, and educational and health institutions which then get delivery direct from the merchants; or for popular consumption, in which case the goods are allowed to be sold freely in the market when they come in. As a rule we have to advance the purchasing money to the merchants, who are allowed very liberal profits so that they can cover their risks.

"We have been rather inexperienced in this form of economic struggle against the blockade of the Kuomintang, made mistakes, and suffered for them. But we have learned. Things are getting much better now. And we are determined to balance our imports and exports from 1944 on."

I wanted to find out about the extent of freedom that was left to commerce in wartime and, if possible, to draw conclusions as to the future attitude of the Communists toward internal trade. I asked therefore about Yenan's domestic-trade policy.

"We follow two fundamental aims in all our economic policies," Yieh said. "To increase production in all possible ways, and to serve the interests of the people with all our trade measures. As a matter of principle, trade within the Border Region is free. But this Trading Company exerts a beneficial influence on it by indirect methods.

"This is an example of the indirect control the government wields over private economy: The Salt Company, which is one of the subordinate concerns of the Trading Company, buys up not only all the salt that is needed for export but also any that is offered to it by merchants or individual producers at a price fixed by the company. The salt fields are privately owned and their owners might suffer from pressure on the part of the merchants if it were not for this arrangement which

186

guarantees producers an easy sale and a fair profit. But the merchants have no reason for complaint, either, since the margin between the cost of production and the buying price of the Salt Company is always large enough to permit them a reasonable profit. In this way, everybody's interests are protected and there is a sufficient stimulus for the increase of production. This method, too, has been developed on the basis of lessons we have learned from mistakes."

I asked what measures were taken against hoarding, a problem that proved practically insoluble in the Kuomintang areas and plays a prominent role in Chungking's economic crisis.

"Our first task was to persuade people to make proper use of surplus capital in production enterprises," Yieh said, "and to give them practical incentives for doing so. We stimulated in many ways the development of production through private projects, especially in cooperatives and home industries, and also through the reclamation of wasteland and cattle breeding.

"Second, we made it unprofitable for merchants to hold hoarded goods for undue profits. This was done in a very simple way. Government enterprises like the Trading Company participate in free competition with private merchants in the buying and selling of important commodities, just as in the case of salt. This policy follows the same aim of giving an equally fair deal to producers, merchants, and consumers and of raising both production and consumption. Government enterprises are always ready to buy from those who might not find a buyer at a fair price and to sell to others who might not find a reasonable seller. The cooperatives play a similar role in keeping supplies plentiful and in making hoarding unprofitable.

"In these ways we do not merely struggle with private enterprise but also cooperate with it, and we certainly do not suppress it. In fact, private trade in the Border Region has developed considerably in recent years.

"Finally, our Chambers of Commerce contribute much to the prevention of hoarding and of an undue rise of prices through the manipulations of unscrupulous profit makers. Our Chambers of Commerce have lost their old character of restrictive merchant guilds and are now constituted along the lines of our political 'Three-thirds System.' That means, merchants and manufacturers are classified as 'large,' 'medium,' and 'small,' and each category has the right to elect its own candidates to one-third of the seats of the board. This simple system introduces the basic principles of democracy into the economic sphere. It works very well, because the various groups are in a much better position than the government to check each other on unfair practices and thus to work for the common good."

I asked Yieh whether these general trade policies were only an *ad hoc* answer to the peculiar situation in which both the blockaded Border Region and the Anti-Japanese War Bases in the enemy's rear find themselves today or whether they foreshadowed the attitude the Communists would take toward trade problems in postwar days.

Yieh replied, "These underlying ideas of our present trade practices will continue to guide our commercial policies after the war, wherever we may have responsibilities; for they developed logically from our experiences in laying the permanent foundations for our New Democracy.

"Our main aim in matters of trade is, and will be in the future, to stimulate production in every possible way. Private enterprise has definitely proved to be essential to the achievement of this aim and will remain vital in the future. Those who may doubt the sincerity of our intention of maintaining and helping private enterprise should judge by the needs of China and not by speculation about the alleged possibilities of future changes in our political ideology.

"This refers not only to private enterprise on the part of Chinese capitalists. We need foreign enterprise, too, and we shall give it full scope. We realize fully that American and other Allied capitalists will not be willing to invest their capital in China unless our country is politically and economically in a position to use it properly and to assure the safety of such investments. To create such conditions is our first task."

188

Chapter Nineteen

THE MERCHANTS APPROVE

IN THE New Market of Yenan, the shopping district in a little side valley with several hundred primitive stores, I asked a blacksmith with whom I became friendly to introduce me to a typical shopkeeper for a private talk. He came one evening to visit me with the merchant Chu Tsang-shou, a man of thirty, who is a native of Yenan and the son of a poor farmer.

Chu looks more prosperous than any of the high cadres of the Communist party, and he is more prosperous. I did not have to ask him many questions. He was a great talker and full of good spirit. Once I had told him that I was interested in his own life story and his little business, he went ahead without restraint.

"Before the Communists came to Yenan, my shop was only a table in the market," he began. "I sold cigarettes and oil and wine. Business was not so bad. I made over 120 silver dollars per year. That was much money, you know. Prices were so low then and they are very high now. But I had to pay almost 80 dollars in all those taxes they imposed on us. And once there was a fellow, a company commander, Sun, who bought more than 30 dollars' worth of wine and cigarettes from me and never paid. After six months he still had not paid. And then he went to Yulin and said he would pay when he came back. But he never came back. That son of a ———"

"Were there any more cases like that?"

"Many," he said furiously. "Officers and even soldiers came and we had to sell to them on credit. You simply could not refuse. They were strong. Most of them paid later, though, at least something. But the trouble was that when they came and paid we always had to invite them to an expensive feast. Even when they paid only half."

189

"And how are things under the Communists? What is your profit now?"

"You know prices are very high. It sounds much more than it is. My net profit is 300,000 dollars a month, but all the taxes I pay every half year amount to only 20,000 per month. I have a shop now. It is a solid house, not just a table any more. We sell cloth and household goods and many other things. And all last year and so far this year I have saved half of my profits."

Together we brought the astronomical figure down to earth, calculating both his prewar and present net incomes in terms of plain millet, the popular standard of value in the Border Region.

He made ten times as much actual profit in 1943 as in 1936 before the Communists came.

"And we eat very much better," he said, patting his paunch. "Before the Revolution we ate millet, and wheat only three times a month. Now we eat wheat a number of times every week. Every week we have several pounds of meat and every day plenty of good vegetables for the family. I have my own vegetable field. You know we all do some production work."

We figured the growth of his capital since the time before the Communists came, in American dollars at the free market rate. In the old days he had about $30, and now he had $375.

"But I also own the house with the shop and living rooms which I did not have before. That is not included in this amount. And don't forget that when the Japanese planes came in 1938 and destroyed everything, I was down to nothing. But the government helped me to start again."

I wondered how well off the other merchants were; whether he was an exception.

"The fellow opposite me had only about one-third as much capital as I had before the Communists came. He has twice as much now as I. But we are not among the rich ones. All the merchants in the New Market have a much better life now. Formerly there were 60 shops, and now there are over 300. No, the cooperatives are not doing us any harm. They have their customers and we have ours."

Had he also made progress in his education? I asked.

"I had been in school for a while when I was a child. But I learned nothing. Accounts I have learned only recently, in the Chamber of Commerce. I have also learned to read much better. Those students of Yenan University you saw in the New Market teach anybody who wants to learn, blacksmiths and merchants and clerks and all. They have newspaper-reading groups for us every evening in our New Market. I am a member of one. I listen to them and follow the printed characters as well as I can in my own paper. And I learn more characters that way.

"Yes, I am a member of the Chamber of Commerce. What do they teach us? Well, I have learned accounts, as I said. And they tell us about the production drive, to be polite to our customers, not to raise prices for greater profit, and to be honest. Yes, I am quite busy with my shop and all those new things. I am also platoon commander in the Self-defense Corps.

"No, I am not a Communist, just a merchant. None in my family are Communists. But my fourth brother is a sympathizer. We all have a much better time now. My father is not a poor peasant any more. He has reclaimed ten acres of land, and has now over thirty acres, although it is all only hill land. After the war I want to go into production. I want to make stockings and blankets. I could have got unused machines in Yulin and I had the money to buy them. But up there in Yulin the Kuomintang people did not allow the machines to be brought to Yenan, although they are not using them. I shall have to wait now. When the war is over many of the merchants want to put up little plants, at least as a sideline."

The next merchant I interviewed was "the richest man in Yenan," Wang Keh-wan, a dignified-looking man of about forty who would have cut a good figure in prewar Shanghai but did not seem to feel out of place in the frugal pioneer atmosphere of Yenan. His two big dwelling caves to which he invited me looked prosperous, with good Chinese carpets on the brick bed, a gold-framed picture of the commercial center of Shanghai, and some good household utensils. His large shop in

191

the New Market was filled with textile goods and everything else that makes a general store. "But this is nothing," he said proudly, "my wholesale stocks are in bombproof caves up the hill."

In 1935 he came to Yenan as a peddler, with a capital of twenty silver dollars. Business in Marshal Yen Hsi-shan's "model province" Shansi had become too difficult because of very heavy taxes. When the Communists settled down in Yenan, Wang Keh-wan began to buy goods for them in Sian, in the Kuomintang regions. And by the time the blockade was organized and trade had become an art as well as a matter of adventure, he was an old-timer and an expert in the business. It is still his main interest, although he now sends his clerks on those dangerous journeys while he looks after his retail store.

"I earn lots of money by our standards here. From January to June I earned . . ." and we calculated. It was almost $US6,000. He did not care to give an estimate of his fortune but said that it was quite considerable. Nobody grudged him his wealth, because it came from useful work and he did not charge much more than 10 per cent net profit on sales in his shop, although the government did not control prices.

"Yes, there is of course the competitive influence of the cooperative stores," he said, "but that is healthy and does not kill private business."

I asked him who had been his predecessor as the richest man of Yenan before the Communists came and whether he knew what had become of the man.

"He is called Tsai Fang-chang," he said, "a merchant and landlord who was worth about 10,000 silver dollars (about $US3,000) in land and cash before the war. He still has one of the big stores here with a capital of something like . . ." This time our calculation resulted in the figure of about $US3,000, roughly the same as his prewar wealth. "He was elected a member of the Municipal Government Committee and you must have seen him, since you say you attended their meeting."

Wang Keh-wan returned to the subject of business under the new government in Yenan.

Things looked bright for businessmen, he felt, because the govern-

192

ment realized their usefulness for economic development. Taxes were low and one could count on government loans for the financing of useful trade or production. Yes, he beamed, production was the future. He was giving it much thought, especially for the time after the war. But he would actually start this year setting up one or two small plants in cooperation with six other store owners.

One day this man may be one of the private promoters of new enterprise, whose plans for profit would work in well with the plans for progress of the more politically minded people in the New Democracy. He seemed to have little doubt about it and mentioned proudly that government and party men were often consulting him on matters of economic policy.

"And my business colleagues have elected me chairman of the Yenan Chamber of Commerce," he said, "on which representatives of big, medium, and small business are equally represented. None of us are Communists but the Communists in the party and the government are not looking down on us. They help us, as we help them. Otherwise we could not develop so much in the Border Region."

Some of the peculiar tasks of the new Chambers of Commerce are to stimulate frank discussions on the ethics of price policies, on the merchants' share of responsibility for the increase of production, for the improvement of the standard of living and therefore the purchasing power of the people, for class unity, and for the war effort. But their voice, according to Wang, is also heard by the government when they make suggestions for the benefit of the business community.

From all I saw in the Border Region it seems that these small-town business parliaments have done much to make the merchants realize the new character and the importance of their role in Yenan's New Democracy and to benefit both them and the community.

Finally, I met a "real capitalist," An Wen-ching, a man of sixty-nine, big, very tall, and with a deep, authoritarian voice. His good clothes, Western-style straw hat, painted fan, and ornamented walking stick gave him the appearance of a genuine old-timer.

He came of an ancient-gentry family and was himself an old-style

Imperial scholar and merchant-landlord. His home town Suiteh in the northwest of the Border Region had not been touched by the agrarian revolution of the Civil War days, so that he retained together with his rich general store and town mansion 400 acres of fertile valley land. During the days of the war lords and the Kuomintang he had consistently declined official posts and fought against corruption, nepotism, opium, and gambling.

"It is my opinion," he said, "that politics in China have always been very bad. The responsible officials did not know what the people wanted. They were too selfish. They killed their own people in civil wars. Because of this, the Japanese were able to invade our country. Before the war, our soldiers in China were also bad. They beat the people and did not pay for their purchases. I knew little about the Chinese Communists before the war and had heard many bad rumors about them. But eventually Wang Chen came to Suiteh when the town was incorporated into the Border Region."

Like everybody else who referred to Wang Chen, the railroad worker, brigadier general, and production enthusiast of Nanniwan, the solemn Mr. An pronounced the name with appreciation. He put his hand over his heart and said, "He is a military man, but he has a good heart and is very kind and humble to the common people. His troops were very good. We were frightened when they came. But we were reassured by their behavior and soon lost all suspicion of them.

"After the policy of reducing all land rents was introduced, my income from the 400 acres of land which my family has owned for the last thousand years became, of course, smaller. But we can live very well even now. And for the tenants it makes a great difference. It is for the people's sake and we have to be considerate. Instead of my former twenty-four tons, or so, of annual rent income in grain I get now about thirteen tons in an average harvest year. But the taxes are only half as much now as they used to be, because the army supports itself from its own production.

"On my store in Suiteh I also pay less tax than before. I cannot remember exactly how much. I have a manager to run it for me. Business is very good. Some of the landlords in Yulin, in the Kuomintang area

194

north of Suiteh, want to come here because the burdens are so much greater there. But, of course, they are not allowed by the Kuomintang to leave."

I asked An Wen-ching whether he found it difficult to work with the Communists.

"No. We are all like members of the same family. They never oppose or ignore suggestions I make, like on this visit to Yenan when I told them our people in Suiteh want certain improvements in education. They always respect the opinion of others and do what they can.

"There was too much bureaucracy before. Even a respectable landlord and shop owner could not go to the Kuomintang magistrate without formality, and nobody's interests but their own were considered by the high officials. These new people here are practical and realistic and not bureaucratic. They really work for the people. Anybody can go at any time to talk to the highest official—an ordinary farmer with a towel around his head, a merchant, a worker, or anybody else. Even Mao Tse-tung is very simple and willing to receive anybody. People feel at home with their officials now. That makes a great difference. . . ."

Mr. An rambled on, discussing his family. His grandson had become a Communist when he was quite young, to the old gentleman's great displeasure. But he does not mind any more, because he is now in full agreement with the New Democracy, as a merchant, a landlord—and a grandfather.

Chapter Twenty

"BANDIT MONEY"

O NE of the Kuomintang newspapermen of our party bought
something in a shop in Yenan and put a national-currency
note on the counter. The salesman told him politely that he
could not accept the note; but the Border Region Bank would exchange
it into local currency.

Our friend got angry. "Don't you know that this is national currency
and that the National Government issues it?"

"I know it is national money," the salesman said quietly. "I know
also that the National Government issues these notes—to you, but not
to us. We have to use our own notes."

This little incident summarizes the essentials of the Kuomintang-
Communist currency controversy. The National Government in Chungking does not pay anything to the administrations of the Border Region
around Yenan and of Liberated China behind the enemy lines or to the
large Communist-led armies. When the National Government tried to
force Yenan to its knees and stopped all payments early in 1941 in
connection with its attack on the Communist-led New Fourth Army in
Central China, the Communists had to introduce their own currency
and to establish their own financial systems. They are now self-contained financially as in every other respect.

Yenan's "refusal to recognize the financial sovereignty of the
National Government" is one of Chungking's main accusations against
the Communists, whose currency the Kuomintang extremists call
"bandit money."

Before I left for Yenan a cabinet member showed me a complete
collection of Border Region bank notes pasted on a large sheet of paper

by years of issue. "Would it be possible in any other country," he asked, "for a political party to use its own bank notes? Does not that in itself prove their insincerity when they say that they recognize the supremacy of the National Government? They will tell you they introduced their own currency only in 1941, after we stopped all payments to them. But here you see notes that were printed from 1938 onward. Ask them about that. They won't be able to deny it. I wonder what they will tell you."

I met the new manager of the Border Region Bank, a former Kuomintang member, fortyish, modest, and keen. He gave me a complete set of the same kind of notes which I had been shown in Chungking. I did not tell him at first about the talk with the minister but asked him to give me the history of the Communist note issuance.

"When the United Front was formed at the beginning of the war," he said, "we withdrew all our former 'Soviet' notes from circulation and replaced them with the national currency we received from the National Government for part of the upkeep of the Eighth Route Army. From 1937 to 1941 the official medium of circulation in our areas was national currency.

"Already early in the war we had very great difficulties in obtaining coins and subsidiary notes of small denomination which were of course most urgently needed in these poor areas. We made many attempts to exchange coins and subsidiary notes at National Government banks in Sian and requested the government in Chungking to help us out of our difficulties, but without success. This is why these token notes of denominations from 2 to 75 cents were at last issued by us in 1938. The total amount was trifling. It was no more than 90,000 dollars Chinese National currency (about $US25,000) in 1938 and was never increased to more than $CN300,000." Those subsidiary notes were the early issues the Minister had shown me in Chungking.

"Only the stoppage in January, 1941, of all payments to the Eighth Route Army made us issue proper bank notes of our own. Naturally, the circulation of national currency had then to be stopped in our areas, although it remained exchangeable into Border Region notes."

"Bandit Money"

At the same time, the strict blockade of the National Government cut off all military and most other supplies to the Communists. "We were faced with the alternative of being starved out and stopping our fight against Japan, or, on the other hand, of aiming at self-sufficiency. Production therefore became our main task. We had to issue notes to develop production in every possible way. And we did. These first issues of our own bank notes were used mainly as capital funds for new enterprises like the army farm project you saw in Nanniwan. We gave our army units and our various government and educational institutions capital in the form of notes and ordered them to provide for their future needs out of their own production. As a rule, they were given the equivalent of two years' current expenditure to finance their new production enterprises. You will admit that these advances were very small. This shows you how anxious we were to prevent inflation and that our new currency was used to save our fighting power against Japan.

"The process of readjustment was extremely painful and difficult. Our armies and government organs, our schools and all public institutions had to struggle through a long period of semistarvation to achieve that degree of self-sufficiency and comparative prosperity you see today in the Border Region. We suffered great hardships. All of us. But we succeeded; in spite of our lack of experience and the mistakes we made; in spite of the extreme natural poverty of our regions. And we learned a great deal."

In May, 1944, the value of the total note issue of the Border Region Bank of 1,600,000,000 Border Region dollars amounted to the equivalent of 200,000,000 dollars Chinese National currency, or about $US1,300,000. In other words, the Communist note issue, which some people in Chungking tried to blame as one of the important secondary reasons of Kuomintang China's acute monetary crisis, was equal to no more than one-tenth of 1 per cent of the total circulation of national currency!

I had just found out at the counter of the Border Region Bank that 1,350 Border Region dollars were paid for one United States dollar,

198

while the last black-market quotation I had heard in Chungking valued the United States dollar at "only" 170 dollars Chinese National currency (about fifty times its prewar price). I asked, therefore, how it was that the value of the Border Region currency was even lower than that of the national currency.

"This is the only important problem we have not yet solved in the Border Region," the bank manager replied frankly. "It will soon be settled. But the low exchange rate is no indication of maladjustment in public finance. What it indicates is nothing more than the peculiarity of our trade situation under the Kuomintang blockade. You know that we have not yet achieved complete self-sufficiency in our own production of clothing and other manufactured goods. Since we do not want to restrict our army and population to the low total of our own supplies, we have to import a considerable quantity of important commodities from the Kuomintang areas. You may also know that we have to pay enormous smuggling premiums on what we buy in that way. All these imports through the blockade lines have in the last analysis to be financed against the issue of notes. This upsets our own price level, in spite of the fact that the finances of our administration have long been in good shape.

"But things have already improved considerably, because our import needs have diminished with the steady increase of our own production. The exchange rate is moving in our favor. In February, 1944, 1 dollar Chinese National currency was worth 11 dollars Border Region currency; but in June, 1944, our official exchange rate was only 8.50 dollars Border Region currency for 1 dollar Chinese National currency. And in the black market the rate was even lower—6 Border Region dollars for 1 dollar Chinese National currency.

"Yes, it was a strange phenomenon that the black market should value our Border Region currency higher than our own Border Region Bank did. The reason was that we restricted the purchase of national currency to our import needs, at a time when the people in the Border Region who still had national currency in their possession began to lose confidence in it and wanted to sell. For we must be careful not to do harm to our private holders of national currency, and this is why we

199

do not want to raise the exchange rate too rapidly in favor of the Border Region currency. We even abolished the restriction on our purchases of national dollars and are now buying more of them than we actually need, at the overvalued rate of 8.50 Border Region dollars."

Prices in the Border Region rose rapidly until their course was steadied during the summer of 1944. They are still extremely high in terms of Border Region currency. But I found that the excessive cost of smuggled imports from Kuomintang territories was evidently the only cause of this unsatisfactory state of affairs. The price problem in itself plays an infinitely smaller role in the peculiar and fundamentally well-ordered economy of Yenan's New Democracy than it does in the completely unreformed and increasingly chaotic economy of Chungking.

In the Kuomintang regions under the Chungking government the incessant rise of prices pauperizes and demoralizes the armies, officials, teachers, and students more and more. All the government does for them is to provide in kind their minimum requirements of rice or wheat and also, in the case of soldiers and certain officials, some clothing. But all those categories of people must try to cover their other needs in the open markets, from money salaries which follow the incessantly rising price level at an ever-widening distance, so that their living standards are falling all the time.

In the Yenan regions things are different: all the essentials and small luxuries required by the troops, officials, teachers, and students are provided in kind, either from their own production or directly by the government. They have no real need for money salaries and are entirely outside the market economy and therefore completely unaffected by its vicissitudes.

The comparative situation of wage earners in the Chungking and Yenan areas is about the same as that of the dependants of their respective governments. In the Chungking areas workers are usually provided with rice and, in the case of some factories, with all their food. But that does not prevent the workers, and especially their families, who, as a rule, do not get food supplies in kind, from suffering an increasingly severe depression of their living standards. For the additional money wages are falling further and further behind the price level. In the Yenan areas this is prevented: the cash wages which workers receive in addition to much fuller supplies in kind are fixed in terms of millet, the local staple food, so that they keep pace with the rise of prices. And dependants, like the workers themselves, are supplied with all essentials.

In the Kuomintang areas, even the farmers suffer from the rise of prices. For they are still in the grip of profiteering merchants. Being at the same time their landlords, moneylenders, magistrates, and local Kuomintang functionaries, the merchants are able to monopolize the bulk of the farmers' sales and purchases. They are therefore in a position to underpay the farmers on their crops and to overcharge them on the goods they have to buy. And they manipulate the markets still more to their own advantage by hoarding and speculation which the government is unable to prevent.

In the Communist-controlled regions, however, the farmers are protected against all those age-old scourges of village feudalism. Numerous well-run cooperatives allow them to sell their own products at normal market prices and to buy whatever they need at the cheapest rates. Farmers who continue to deal with ordinary merchants do not have to grant them high and rising profit margins, because of the free competition between the merchants and the cooperatives. Moreover, there is still much simple barter trade in the Border Region.

I found it true, for all these reasons, that the people of the Border Region do not suffer much, if at all, from the unsolved price problem. The average standard of living of the common people in the Border Region—already higher than that of the Kuomintang soldiers and the officials, teachers, students, workers, and farmers in the Chungking territories—is under no pressure from the inflation, but in spite of high prices shows in fact a rising tendency on account of increasing production and just distribution.

Until recently the opinion was widespread in Chungking that the Communists found themselves in a weak and deteriorating financial situation and that their plight was even worse than that of the Kuomintang territories. This view was due partly to wishful thinking and partly to ignorance of the peculiar economic structure of the Border Region, where high price figures mean little to that vast majority of people who either live altogether outside the market economy or whose trade is virtually barter.

Critics who used to judge the strength and the rate of progress of the USSR from the development of black-market prices were proved shortsighted and undiscriminating by the magnitude and consistency of the Russian war effort.

There are scarcely any similarities between the socialistic economy of the USSR and the cooperative, petty-bourgeois pioneer economy of Yenan's New Democracy. But they have this in common: the livelihood of practically the entire population does not depend upon harmony between supply and demand in the free market, which is a symptom of "normalcy" only in well-developed capitalistic countries with an economic system of free competition. It depends almost exclusively upon the output of the most essential consumers' goods, in the distribution of which the free market plays a comparatively small role.

The economic development of the Border Region can be appreciated more correctly from the state of its public finances—a yardstick equally applicable to societies of any type yet devised.

Chapter Twenty-one

SOMETHING NEW TO CHINA:
A BALANCED BUDGET

YENAN'S financial experts have never been to Harvard, Yale, or Oberlin, to Oxford or Cambridge, nor have they attended any international monetary conferences. They have not been in charge of big banks and trading concerns and probably never owned a bank account. Wall Street and Lombard Street have never heard their names. Yet their record of achievement is incomparably better than that of Chungking's internationally trained and known financial leaders.

Those men in Yenan have for the first time in China's modern history solved the basic problems of public finance. They. found ways of obtaining true income declarations from all strata of the population and of distributing the financial burden of war and reconstruction equitably among the poor and the well-to-do—matters in which Chungking has failed in spite of the clamor of the common people in the Kuomintang territories and of Generalissimo Chiang Kai-shek himself.

They have made certain that all the taxes collected from the people reach the public treasuries—a precondition for healthy public finance which the Kuomintang government has been unable to create in wartime Chungking or even in prewar Nanking.

They have reduced the tax burden of the peasantry and at the same time increased revenues sufficiently to draw from them considerable funds for investment in productive enterprises—while developments in Chungking went in the opposite direction.

Finally, they have recently balanced their budgets without further borrowing—an achievement which the Kuomintang government has not even tried any longer to bring about in its own areas since the early stages of the war.

Something New to China: A Balanced Budget

There is nothing fortuitous or uncanny in Yenan's accomplishments. They cannot be explained by any fundamental difference between conditions in the Communist- and Kuomintang-controlled regions which might have made it easier for Yenan to succeed where Chungking failed. I became convinced that the same methods could at any time be applied in the other half of China where the financial crisis is going unchecked. The adoption of Yenan's methods would not require any change in Chungking's avowed political principles. On the contrary, it would only be in full accordance with them. And Yenan's methods would be even more successful in the Kuomintang territories, which are so much richer than the Communist-controlled areas.

Nor did I find any financial genius in Yenan to whom those achievements could be ascribed. What I found among the men responsible for the financial policies of the New Democracy, from Mao Tse-tung himself to low-ranking officials, was this: a clear understanding of the specific Chinese economy with which they have to deal; a strong determination to make the best of it financially as otherwise, no matter how primitive and unorthodox their methods may have to be; and the realization that the masses of the people must be given a square new deal if they are to support the regime under which they live.

I never heard in Yenan the word "impossible," which occurred so often in Chungking when liberal government officials confided to me how they tried in vain to convince their superiors of the urgent need for financial reform, and especially of the fact that political reform was its prerequisite.

The system of the New Democracy does not hamper financial reform work, as does the existing Kuomintang regime, but stimulates it.

Nan Hang-ching, the director of the Department of Finance of the Border Region government, is an unpretentious, hard-working man who seems competent, practical, and enthusiastic. He has been a revolutionary for thirty-three of his forty-nine years, took part in the overthrow of the Manchu Dynasty in 1911, and worked in Dr. Sun Yat-sen's national-revolutionary movement. At one time he had to flee to Japan when his life was threatened by his former Kuomintang associates. His last ten years have been devoted to matters of finance, in a hard school of theoretical self-education and administrative practice.

I tested Nan's financial knowledge on my own ground, asking him for his views on Chungking's financial problems, with which I was acquainted. His sober and penetrating analysis was probably the best I heard in years of discussion on the subject. It provided a good background for his equally sober account of Yenan's financial policies.

"Our first problem was to get true income declarations from all the people," he said. "Chungking explains its inability to obtain proper assessments, and therefore to introduce a workable income tax, by the undeniable insufficiency of modern-trained finance officials in China. We could not afford to accept that excuse for ourselves.

"We realized that China could not approach the problem of assessment in the same manner as the highly developed nations of the West. It would take any government in our country much too long to establish a modern financial administration of sufficient size, and such an administration would be much too expensive under existing conditions. We had to use what may appear to you as rather crude democratic methods and to make them yield the required results.

"We solved the problem in a simple way, with a staff of financial officials which was proportionately even smaller than that of Chungking. Each administrative village unit was ordered to hold a special meeting once a year at which all the people—owner-farmers, tenants, and landlords—have to state their incomes in public. The people know each other's affairs intimately and if anybody made a false statement he would be corrected at once.

"Yes, it did happen in the beginning that whole villages tried to deceive us; but practically every locality now has 'active elements' who have been educating the people successfully on matters of civic consciousness, so that such cases are extremely rare. And we know from sample investigations that we are getting correct returns, practically without a bureaucratic machinery."

"How can you possibly apply such methods in the towns?" I asked.

"Just as easily," Nan said. "As you know, we replaced the old, corrupt merchants' guilds with democratically organized Chambers of

Commerce. In separate annual meetings of the small, medium, and big merchants' groups of each chamber, everybody states publicly how much profit he has made during the year. The merchants themselves check each other, as the village people do, and the elected chamber councils check them again. The merchants are well acquainted with each other's business and have an interest in the equitable distribution of their total tax burden, so that the method works with equal success in the commercial sphere.

"Chungking could easily have adopted the same system and avoided its financial crisis. It may be primitive; but so are conditions in China. We have to adapt our methods to them."

"How are manufacturing enterprises assessed?" I asked.

"We do not tax them at all. The most important permanent aim of all our financial and economic policies for the sake of the war and of reconstruction must be to increase the production of manufactured goods by every possible stimulus. That helps our financial situation indirectly; much more than if we taxed manufacture."

The progressive taxation scales of the Border Region, according to farmers, landlords, and merchants I asked, are moderate and just. For all but the well-to-do the rates are much lower than they have ever been. Even many landlords—that is, all those who were not influential enough under the old regime to evade most of their tax payments—are now paying less than they did before.

The only direct tax on agriculture—the National Salvation Grain Levy—leaves one-fifth of the population exempt: new settlers, the poorest of the peasants, farmers who are willing to introduce cotton on their fields, and the families of anti-Japanese fighters. For other producers and landlords the rates range from 3 to 35 per cent, according to their incomes and the number of their dependants.

"We had to take a very high grain levy from the people in 1941 when the stoppage on National Government payments, the strict blockade against our regions, and the danger of an attack on us by the Kuomintang armies created such a serious situation. In 1941 the tax collection amounted to over 20 per cent of the comparatively small total crop. In consequence of the concentration of all our efforts on the increase of production, the percentage of the total crop we had to take for the National Salvation Grain Levy fell to 10.3 per cent in 1943 and it will be only 8 or 9 per cent of the total crop this year."

The only other direct tax lexy, the business tax, ranged in 1943 from 4 to 19.6 per cent of the merchants' net profits. Other taxes are levied on salt (between 5 and 7 per cent of its sales value); and on imports and exports (mainly designed to control the smuggling trade with the Kuomintang areas in the interest of the development of the Border Region). There is also a transaction fee on the trade in grain and cattle, but this is not really a tax because it is charged only on transactions in government commission houses which have been set up to compete with private commission merchants who used to charge the farmers exorbitant rates.

During the first two years of the Kuomintang blockade the Border Region government had to borrow considerably from the Border Region Bank, which printed notes to finance part of the government's venture of laying the foundations for economic self-sufficiency. Even in 1943, 18 per cent of the government's total revenue still came from this source; while 20 per cent originated from taxes other than the National Salvation Grain Levy, which is not contained in the revenue figures; and 62 per cent of the total was income derived from productive enterprises of the army and various government institutions.

Since 1944 all borrowing has been stopped. The 1944 budget of 7,800,000,000 Border Region dollars (about $US5,700,000) was to be covered exclusively by revenue from taxes and productive enterprises. It is due only to the peculiar budgeting methods of the Border Region government that its financial accounts during the last few years did not already appear to be fully balanced with nonborrowed revenue and that the budgets of 1943 and 1944 failed to show considerable surpluses.

The hidden surpluses of the last two years are partly contained in the fast-expanding grain reserve which the government has accumulated in order to provide against the possibility of a crop failure and the special needs of the final counteroffensive. For the all-out attack on

Something New to China: A Balanced Budget

Japan in the last stage of the war will necessitate the withdrawal of troops at present engaged in production, as well as the mobilization of many militiamen in the villages where lack of labor power may then affect production.

In order to lighten the burden of the people the National Salvation Grain Levy was reduced from over 30,000 tons of wheat and millet in 1941 to 24,000 tons in 1944. But the army and government institutions have in the meantime achieved such a high degree of self-sufficiency in their own food production that only part of this levy is needed to cover their remaining requirements.

For military and political reasons the size of the grain reserve is kept secret. This is why revenue in kind from the National Salvation Grain Levy on farmers and landlords and from the surpluses of a number of army units and government institutions is not included in the published budgets. The other part of the undeclared surpluses consists of the income of portions of army and government enterprises which are being reinvested for the purpose of expanding production. This, too, seems to be a considerable amount which in itself would easily have offset the borrowing that still took place in 1943.

In contrast to the budgets of the National Government in Chungking, which have been running up astronomical deficits during the last five years, the balanced budgets of Yenan are an important indication of what a genuinely democratic effort at financial reform can achieve even in the poorest parts of China, in spite of war, lack of personnel, and isolation from the outside world.

I remembered that a high-ranking Chungking official had sadly told me some time ago that in his estimate at least one-third if not one-half of all the tax money and tax grain collected from the people in the Kuomintang regions failed to find its way into the coffers of the national, provincial, and local governments, but went into the pockets of corrupt gentry and financial officials.

Was there really no graft in the Border Region? I asked Mr. Nan.

"Fraud simply cannot develop under our system," he said.

"First of all, we pay our financial officials a living wage; their fami-

208

lies get all they need in food, shelter, clothing, and simple luxuries, like our fighters, party functionaries, and all officials. The Kuomintang government pays so little to its financial administrators and other officials that graft and squeeze are simply inevitable on the other side.

"Second, our staff is imbued with the desire to help the people, and our methods of self-government enable the people to supervise its work.

"It happens from time to time that some fellow steals from public funds the equivalent of a few packages of cigarettes or a pair of shoes. But that is all. And we are extremely strict in enforcing absolute honesty. If you stayed until the Chinese New Year, when 'struggle meetings' are held everywhere for two weeks, you could see how frankly people who have committed mistakes or thefts speak up, or how they are openly criticized by those who know about their failures."

I asked scores of people—Communists who discussed freely the defects of the administration, nonparty people with long and bitter memories of the Kuomintang regime and with keen eyes for bureaucratic faults, and foreigners who had lived too long in Communist-controlled regions to be unaware of corruption if it existed. Everyone gave me the same reply, which sounds almost incredible anywhere in the Orient.

"There is no corruption, no squeeze."

Chapter Twenty-two

COOPERATIVES WITH A MISSION

I T WAS the last day of the Conference of Cooperatives. Mao Tse-tung was to give a short closing speech. The large assembly hall at Communist party headquarters was packed with hundreds of delegates, sitting on rows of wooden benches. Mostly peasants and peasant women; some factory workers, mule drivers, soldiers, and schoolteachers—all administrators of cooperatives. For several days they had discussed their problems and the Yenan newspapers were full of detailed accounts of what went on in the conference.

Mao Tse-tung stood on the big stage in baggy brown pants and a homespun tunic with the collar open. Around him men and women were squatting on the boards and looking up attentively at his tall, slightly stooping figure. He spoke without manuscript, slowly and in a simple, homely manner, like peasant to peasants, seeming more at ease than I had seen him on other occasions.

"Two or three years ago," he began, "few of our cooperative societies were really good. None were examples to others. Most of them were very weak. But now, many are much better.

"Why are so many of them better now?" he asked, looking around the audience. When he saw the familiar face of Comrade Liu Chien-chang, the popular Labor Hero who made the South District Cooperative of Yenan the universal model for cooperatives everywhere, he nodded and smiled at him.

"Because we have learned," he answered himself in his characteristic manner, which is reminiscent of Stalin. "It is not from books that we have learned; but from the South District Cooperative, which showed us the proper way through practical work. I, too, have learned, not from theories, but from Comrade Liu. And now, at least a few dozen of our 420 cooperative societies with more than 200,000 member families are very good. Only a few are still really bad."

The audience applauded.

"The bad cooperatives and those which are not so good don't know yet how to work properly for the interest of the masses of the people. That is their trouble. Many of you have realized that during the last few days, as shown in your self-criticism at this conference.

"To understand the needs of the masses properly and to put them first is what gives us success in any kind of work, whether in the cooperatives or anywhere else. To overlook this always means failure."

Mao Tse-tung does not mind repeating himself on this point. It recurs in all his speeches. As usual, he gave a number of positive and negative examples to illustrate his favorite theory.

"We are developing an entirely new type of really universal cooperatives," he continued. "In our New Democracy all the cooperative societies must be many-sided. They must help in the development of our economic life, our social life, our education, as some of them already do, using the initiative of the masses of the people to supplement the activities of the government.

"We can develop great strength from the cooperative effort of our people. It is your task to mobilize it further. We must plan those new activities of the cooperative societies. You have already discussed these new tasks in detail. I want to mention only a few which are especially urgent."

He spoke about the producers', consumers', and sellers' sections of the agricultural cooperatives, which had made greater progress than any other cooperatives. Their main task now was to introduce to the farmers the seeds produced by the experimental model farms and to see to it that their use was gradually extended to all fields.

The transport cooperatives also had made satisfactory progress, reducing the cost of transportation by draft animals and at the same time improving the living standards of transport workers.

"From now on," Mao Tse-tung continued, "the industrial units of our cooperative societies should get first attention. They have many important tasks, but the most immediate one is for each of our 210 boroughs to establish a cooperative workshop for the production of agricultural implements. And each cooperative must have blacksmiths who go regularly to the villages to repair tools for the peasants. Cattle breeding and afforestation units must be developed in more of our co-operative societies. Our tree planting has not been successful. We must learn more from peasants who know well how to do it.

"The new medical and sanitary sections of some cooperative societies are most important. We must develop them everywhere so that we will eventually have one in every township. We have to use the organizing ability of the masses of the people to solve our medical and sanitation problems in a cooperative effort. In that way we can overcome our present difficult situation, which the government alone cannot solve.

"For we want all old comrades to live longer, don't we? and all babies to grow up healthy and strong."

The people showed hearty approval.

"You all know of the initiative of a village midwife who worked through a local cooperative and organized a training group to provide midwives for other villages." Mao Tse-tung thought for a while. "I cannot remember her name. I am sorry."

The audience laughed and some people shouted the name of the woman.

"Yes, that's right. I should have known it. We have to learn from her. She helped the people a great deal.

"The educational units of a good number of cooperative societies have done very well. They can also fill in a gap left in spite of all the efforts of our government. If they are well run, such cooperative schools, with the help of our educational organizations in Yenan, can teach the children in the villages what they need. And they can raise the literacy of the grown-up people. Every township without ordinary elementary or adult schools should have a cooperative school unit, run by the people according to their needs."

Somebody from the audience remarked in a loud voice that many people in his district had learned to read several hundred Chinese char-

212

acters in a few months since the cooperative had opened an evening school with its manager as teacher. Others spoke up, giving their experiences about the successes of cooperative schools. There was a minor uproar of eager response.

Mao Tse-tung paused, smiling and chatting with a few people around him until the crowd quieted down.

"Wherever there are cooperative societies, their staff and organization and active membership can develop many new activities without much extra cost. And the government is always willing to help them in any possible way."

Mao Tse-tung came to the financial activities of the cooperatives. They, too, had to become more many-sided. The extension of cheap credit with the help of government funds was not enough.

"Insurance sections, already developed by a number of cooperative societies, should be generally introduced. For example, if the people regularly put some money into the cooperatives to insure their families for the cost of a funeral, such an event will not make them bankrupt any more. It is the law of nature that everybody must die. Even those legendary men in the past who are supposed to have lived to 800 years or so had to die eventually. Some of our people still get deeply into debt paying for large funeral expenses. They have no reserves for such occasions. And, as you know, everybody eats so much at those big funeral feasts. . . ."

Whispers of approval among the audience. A man next to me says, "Yes, those crowds of guests at burial feasts can eat up a man's house and fields like nothing."

"But this is not only a matter of insurance," Mao Tse-tung continued. "We must also change our attitude toward such matters: nobody should take advantage of old customs any longer. In our new society the people must help each other. If they do that, they'll feel better. Even better than if they eat as much as they can put away at funeral feasts of poor farmers."

More approval, whispering, and laughter.

"Modern attitudes will help people to be happier in many respects.

213

For example, if young people invest as much as they can in the productive enterprises of cooperative societies which give such good profits, they can all marry. . . ." He had to stop again for the wave of joyful agreement to die down. "And they won't have worries in their old age.

"Investments in cooperatives are very important for our economic progress. All people should invest in the cooperatives whatever they can spare—money, the draft animals and implements they do not use all the time, or what land they cannot cultivate themselves. Everything can be used and made profitable in the cooperatives.

"And nobody should mind if the landlords, too, make use of those good investment opportunities. It is to the general good if they do. For example, a rich landlord with over 250 acres of land invested 20 acres of his land in a cooperative for the members to cultivate, and that investment made the small cooperative grow to everybody's advantage."

Mao Tse-tung raised his voice.

"Comrades, our people should not be afraid of landlords and capitalists any longer. You, too, must make the people understand that under our new system there is no reason any longer to fear them. On the contrary, landlords' investments in cooperatives should be welcomed. The people should know that the cooperatives, under our law, are always the collective property of all who belong to them; and all members benefit when the cooperatives grow."

He paused awhile and then spoke even more emphatically. "Now that you have solved many of your concrete problems at this conference and are going home, keep this in mind: the most important economic organizations in our areas are not the few factories we have, but our many small cooperative enterprises. The Border Region is not like Shanghai. In all our regions we must rank the importance of the cooperatives very high in every respect. We must also mobilize more people for organization work in cooperatives.

"I know that some of our cadres still consider cooperative work beneath their dignity and prefer government or party work. They are wrong and must correct their mistaken idea.

"More of our writers and intellectuals, too, should go into the co-

214

operatives to study and help them, as some have already done. The cooperatives belong to those real, living things in our society which writers have to know from their own experience before they can write well about our new life and its future."

The meeting came to a close. Mao Tse-tung mentioned half a dozen names of outstanding cooperative workers he wanted to see for private talks, congratulated others on the introduction of new ideas into the cooperative movement, and bade the delegates farewell "in the name of the Central Committee of the Communist party."

The applause was of the same informal and cheerful kind which had from time to time interrupted the meeting.

On the way back to the Guest House, Labor Hero Liu, a quiet, modest man of about forty, was on our truck. When he was introduced to our *Tass* colleague, he asked him, "I wonder, comrade, do you also have cooperatives in your Soviet Union?"

We suppressed our amusement and the *Tass* correspondent did not enlarge on his positive reply. Liu's naïve question did not seem entirely unjustified.

I thought of the modern machinery I had seen in Soviet cooperatives, supplied by giant factories; of the political power behind the collectivized farms which had purged landlords and kulaks from the villages and was able to enlist all other parts of the population in their cooperative effort; and of the manifold aid all the Russian cooperatives received from a thoroughly revolutionized state in which they never played a greater role than that of important auxiliaries to a rapidly developing structure of large-scale modern enterprise.

Neither the Soviet Union nor any other country ever had cooperatives like those of the Border Region and the Anti-Japanese War Bases in North and Central China—which have to be prime movers in the economic and political development of a primitive society and in the organization of an all-out war effort.

For these are the main achievements of the cooperatives in the Communist-controlled regions:

They have helped to raise agricultural production and the output of clothing sufficiently to contribute in a decisive manner to the growth of the anti-Japanese fighting forces.

They have helped to develop industrial enterprise, instead of first getting aid from it.

They have done much to overcome the class struggle and to promote democratic activities in the villages, instead of being enabled to rely upon the results of an accomplished rural revolution.

They are spreading out into other fields, doing some pioneer work for the social and educational policies of government organizations which are still too young to be the only agencies for the execution of progressive measures.

The cooperatives of the Border Region and the Anti-Japanese War Bases are necessarily of a very primitive character, like the country and the people from which they sprang. But they are steadily developing.

Their mission in Yenan's scheme of reform is becoming meaningful and desirable to increasing numbers of peasants. That mission is to mobilize popular initiative for the development of an elementary economic, social, and political democracy at the "grass roots" of China's society.

216

Part Five

MOVING THE MASSES

WINTER SCHOOL FOR FARMERS

Chapter Twenty-three

POLITICAL SWING

AN ANCIENT dramatic folk dance of Northwest China, almost forgotten until the Communists revived and politicized it a year or two ago, has taken the Border Region by storm.

I did not have to ask why the *yangko* has become the craze of young and old in villages and towns and why it is the most effective means of popularizing the various policies of the New Democracy. Each time I saw it performed I was under its spell like everybody around me.

More and more frequently *yangko* evenings are arranged in villages, on the market places of towns or the drill grounds of army units, in schoolyards or meeting halls.

A band of motley instruments plays a tuneful, marchlike air in a vigorous seven-beat rhythm; slowly at first, while the crowd forms a wide-open circle. A score or two of trained amateurs with a suggestion of costuming—lustily singing a ballad which sets the particular theme of the performance—start dancing around the circle, singly in loose formation, as in a conga, with their hands on their hips, swinging their bodies, kicking out their legs, improvising flourishes. A few long steps forward, a few short steps back.

As the band gains tempo the crowd falls in, singing and dancing. After a while everybody steps and swings around the circle in an exhilarating free-for-all. Quicker and quicker. The singing peters out as the music grows louder and faster and drives on to a breath-taking climax.

Laughing, panting people once again form a circle and chat, waiting for the one-act play that follows—a simple, stimulating drama of ever-varying specific content, performed by a few men and women of the amateur *yangko* group who need no props to give reality to the show.

219

Political Swing

The villains are either Japanese soldiers and Chinese traitors or witch doctors, loafers, and other antisocial elements who hamper the war effort, the increase of production, or the march of political and social progress. The heroes and heroines are Eighth Route Army soldiers, militiamen, or simple pioneers of class unity and mutual aid; fighters against superstition, illiteracy, dirt, and disease; or model workers in villages, factories, cooperatives, and government offices whose individual action has aroused the initiative of the masses.

The leitmotiv seems invariable, no matter what the subject and plot of the particular play may be. It is the overcoming of material and human difficulties in the way of victory over Japan and of a more complete realization of the New Democracy.

The play always ends on a cheerful note of success while the dance leaders, representing the masses of the people in the play, take over with another song and dance which summarizes its moral.

The audience joins once more, stepping and swinging faster and faster around the circle and bringing the *yangko* to an exultant end.

A good *yangko* party goes on for hours with several shows, in a gay and happy community atmosphere such as I have never seen elsewhere in the Orient.

Nobody among those unsophisticated people seems to object to the undisguised sales talk of the songs and plays, as American radio listeners do to advertising skits in artistic broadcasting programs. For the *yangko* is real, living folk art, natural, dramatic, full of comic relief, and evidently in tune with the feelings of the people. It is certainly tendentious, but not as crudely black-and-white as it might be. For the basic stories are usually taken from topical events somewhere in the Communist-controlled regions. And many of the texts are written by the best among Yenan's authors who have been made to understand in recent years that realism is not achieved by exaggeration.

The people themselves are not merely the audience and chorus of the *yangko* but are increasingly becoming its initiators.

When they decided to revive the old folk dance, the Communists were determined to make it once more the people's own, in accordance with Mao Tse-tung's general policy of "learning from the people, re-fining their practices, and handing the new methods back to them as theirs." To achieve this, the drama department of the Yenan College of Art and Literature has trained hundreds of *yangko* dancers, actors, musicians, and writers who created model folk-dance plays and traveled through villages and towns, performing them and teaching the revived art to all who showed an interest.

The spontaneous popular response surprised even the enthusiastic sponsors of the *yangko* mass movement. Peasants, workers, and soldiers, students and schoolchildren began to organize *yangko* groups every-where, showing the people how to dance and sing better, creating little bands of amateur musicians, consulting the people on new topics, and writing their own texts on the basis of specific local problems and inci-dents.

In many villages the *yangko* has already become a regular weekly event, and the new "Program of Ten Small Points" for the improve-ment of village life includes the creation of a *yangko* group in every community.

The Chinese country and small-town folk love entertainment and are starved for it. The *yangko* has acted on them like rain on parched earth. It has brought them not only theater, but theater they can easily understand. For it deals with matters close to their own lives—instead of putting before them the kings, queens, and concubines, the feudal warriors, courtiers, ghosts, and jesters which dominated their ancestors' imagination in ages long gone by when Chinese art became formal and stagnant.

The *yangko*, more than any other experience, impressed me with the significance of those manifold mass movements to which everybody in Yenan was referring all the time, no matter what subject I brought up —mass movements for the correct practice of the new democratic rights and duties of the people; for the increase of production; for popular aid to the fighting forces and assistance to the people on the part of the armies; for education, modern hygiene, and many other practical aims of the New Democracy.

"The mass movements are of central importance to us; all our policies are carried out through them," said Teng Fa, who is in charge of a special mass-movement committee at Communist party headquarters.

"To carry on a prolonged war and to achieve progress in every field, we have to rely on the masses of the people. We could not rely on bureaucratic methods or on dictatorship if we did not want to fail as the Kuomintang did. We had to mobilize the masses, to awaken, educate, and guide them to the goal of self-help. This is the purpose of the mass movements we launch for so many specific purposes."

Teng Fa, a slim, sprightly Cantonese of thirty-nine, is a veteran revolutionary. He worked once on the coasters of a British shipping company, and his party has used him for years in positions that require a real firebrand with drive, imagination, and practical experience.

He paced up and down the room, shouting at me in an aggressive kind of good humor as though he were addressing a mass audience.

"No, our party has no special mass organization of its own to carry out its tasks," he protested against my question, which apparently proved to him that I did not understand the really popular character of the mass movements, the real crux of the matter.

"No, we don't give orders either, in the sense you mean," he laughed. "We work mainly through the newspapers all over the Border Region and the Anti-Japanese War Bases. In newspaper articles we launch practical suggestions for the popularization of particular phases of fundamental government policies, and criticize whatever serious mistakes may have been made in the work of the mass movements.

"Our suggestions come up for discussion everywhere—in local government, party, and trade-union organizations; in army units, schools, and factories; and in the Anti-Japanese People's Associations, which are the basic mass organizations that have grown from below in every village and town. They adapt our ideas to local conditions, call mass meetings, and mobilize the Active Elements to interest the people around them by talking in a concrete and helpful manner to groups, families, and individuals who need explanation or encouragement.

"This is how the mass movements organize themselves everywhere, right among the people. We do direct them, that is certainly true, although our directions are often based on ideas and experiences we get from villagers and townspeople. But the initiative in adapting those directions to the specific circumstances of various places and in putting them into practice is always left to local organs and in fact to the people themselves."

Teng Fa made clear to me what I had already begun to realize from my own observations—that the mass movements in the Communist-controlled areas have nothing to do with benevolent educational endeavors of the placid Sunday-school type, like the much-advertised but pathetically abstract, unpopular, and futile New Life Movement of Generalissimo and Mme. Chiang Kai-shek in the Kuomintang territories.

He analyzed the New Life Movement in scathing terms. He criticized the way its organizers talk down to the people, telling them not to spit and smoke, to be clean, healthy, and honest, to be observant of filial piety and obedient toward their superiors in society and government; without doing anything to help the people use their own initiative in bringing about that improvement of their fundamental political and economic conditions upon which all aspects of a genuine new life must depend. What he said was different only in diction from opinions I had heard many Chinese liberals and foreigners express in Chungking—especially on the annual occasion of the anniversary of the New Life Movement when its normally ignored taboos are grimly enforced in the streets by policemen who stop and reprimand anybody who smokes, spits, or does not keep to the sidewalk.

"The fundamental difference between the New Life Movement and our New Democracy is this," he summed up. "The Kuomintang and its shallow reform talk have no connection with the masses; the Kuomintang people try to do things by order from above, in a bureaucratic manner. But we realize that the people's economic and political problems must be solved first to enable them to be clean, healthy, and honest. We mobilize the people in every possible way and help them to solve their problems on the basis of their own free will and initiative."

223

Political Swing

I found it true that the educational endeavor of the Communist-sponsored mass movements is thoroughly practical and in a primitive sense democratic. Far from being wishy-washy and repressive in the political respect, it gives realistic emphasis to the element of struggle by which alone the masses of the people in a backward society can mobilize themselves, increase their usefulness in the war, and achieve real social progress.

The mass movements arouse a spirit of struggle. Yet this struggle does not seem to contain any elements of class conflict. For class friction has been reduced by the political and economic reforms of the New Democracy—like the introduction of general franchise, the reduction of the landlords' rent charges to tenants, and the government's guarantee of rent payments to the landlords—and even more by the practical co-operation in the fight against the Japanese in the Communist-controlled war areas to which all classes have been educated and mobilized.

On the contrary, the mass movements themselves stress the need for democratic unity as one of their most important aims; and so do the *yangko* plays, with whatever specific subject they·may deal.

The struggle which the mass movements stimulate is directed against all those—in any social class, in any local government or party organization, in any army unit, school, or factory—who are slow in awakening to a full understanding of their duties and rights under the new society.

The methods and aims of this struggle are most actively propagandized through a special mass movement concerned with the correct treatment of backward and antisocial elements. This movement condemns the "old ways" of either ignoring or ostracizing such people and demands, "Convert Them and Win Them Over."

This idea of conversion—the Policy of Magnanimity—dominates all the *yangko* plays. It has much to do with their success in creating an atmosphere that helps all the other educational efforts of the New Democracy to swing the masses in the direction of progress.

Chapter Twenty-four

RESTRICTIONS OF FREE PRESS AND SPEECH

THE main tasks of our newspapers are to help in the war, to foster the New Democracy, and to reflect the views of all its social strata," we were told by Bo Ku, the man in command of Yenan's press headquarters, when we first visited him at the Caves of the Ten Thousand Buddhas. "You will see for yourselves that our press is no more exclusively Communist in character than our governments. Read our papers and form your own opinion."

"But are you free from Communist party censorship?" one of the Kuomintang newspapermen asked his Communist colleague. The intelligence, honesty, and wit of Bo Ku had won him a reputation in liberal Kuomintang circles when he was Yenan's representative with the National Government early in the war.

"Are you enjoying freedom of the press like, say, the New York or London *Times?*" another Kuomintang correspondent elaborated the question. It was obviously meant to be ironical since Bo Ku himself as member of the Politburo of the Communist party is one of its prominent leaders, while both the *Liberation Daily* and the *New China News Agency*, of which he is the head, are Communist party organs.

Bo Ku could not possibly answer the questions with a simple yes. He did not try to get away so easily. However, he seemed to have a good deal to say in reply, and the Kuomintang and Communist newspapermen, huddling over their teacups, had a pleasant time discussing the relative merits of newspaper work under their respective regimes and pelting each other with anecdotes—to the booming of Bo Ku's laughter, which is as characteristic of him as the brilliance of his talk and writing.

Feeling that I would have to make my own observations about the freedom of the press in Communist China, I was satisfied to leave the group to itself.

Restrictions of Free Press and Speech

Press headquarters in the cave-punctured hill of the Caves of the Ten Thousand Buddhas is one of Yenan's three political commanding heights. Like the headquarters of the Communist party and the Communist-led armies, it is one of the coordinating centers by which the Border Region and the Anti-Japanese War Bases in North, Central, and South China, whose locally elected administrations depend upon no over-all government, are unified into a well-integrated whole.

The *Liberation Daily*, the soul of press headquarters, is more than a newspaper in the ordinary sense. It is the official gazette and the authoritative tutor of the cadres in government, party, and army organizations all over Communist-controlled China. It is, in fact, something like the daily installment of an endless serial textbook on all the policies of the New Democracy.

The paper's news, or that portion of it which does not originate in Yenan itself, is received in the numerous caves of the *New China News Agency*, where dozens of radio operators are busy day and night at the primitive Yenan-made sets they work with locally produced hand generators. They keep in touch with the agency's eight branches, and through them with eleven substations, in the widely scattered Anti-Japanese War Bases, picking up military and general news reports and a good deal of locally collected inside information about conditions in the Japanese and puppet camps. And they take down the broadcasts of radio stations in Kuomintang and puppet China.

They monitor verbatim the news broadcasts from America, England, the USSR, and Japan. For the "commercial air" is Yenan's only contact with the outside world.

The men and women in the editorial caves of the *Liberation Daily* look like any other workers in Yenan—nondescript people in cotton pants and tunics of various shades and with the usual soldiers' caps. But they are picked specialists, and when I came to know several of them more closely their sound knowledge of Chinese affairs and foreign countries and languages surprised me.

Decisions on the paper's policy are made in regular editorial conferences. Without difficulty or friction, it seemed to me, because every staff member has to be attuned to the general and specific aims of the

New Democracy, so that special advice from party or army headquarters is required only on rare occasions.

Their difficulties are of another, purely technical kind. The special character of the paper makes it necessary for them to compress into its four pages an astonishing variety of news, editorials, and analytical articles on Communist- and Kuomintang-controlled China, on the enemy camp, and the outside world.

Every one of those vertical lines in which Chinese newspapers are printed is of importance, and the struggle for the best possible use of space which is so familiar to editors everywhere in the world is especially grim in the *Liberation Daily*. The only time I encountered envy in Yenan was when I mentioned to one of the editors, by way of apology for the comparatively small space given to China news in America, that the paper shortage had reduced the size even of the biggest metropolitan newspapers to a mere thirty-two pages or so.

The *Liberation Daily*'s selected news, its editorials, and analytical articles are the basis of the stream of messages which flows back to the radio operators of the *New China News Agency,* who in turn hammer them out to the branch stations for use all over the Anti-Japanese War Bases. The little paper is therefore the main source of basic information for 90,000,000 people, although the actual radius of distribution of its total edition of 7,600 copies is restricted by the pace of pack animals which make only some twenty miles a day.

The editors of the only other Yenan daily, the *Mass Newspaper,* have the task of producing a two-page sheet for readers on a low level of literacy and knowledge. For the *Liberation Daily,* which prides itself on a simpler and clearer style than is customary in the Chinese press and manages with the use of "only" 2,000 or 2,500 of those complicated word pictures called Chinese characters, is still much too difficult for most of the newly literate people of Communist-controlled China to understand.

The *Mass Newspaper* prints its elementary news and editorials with 1,000 of the simplest Chinese characters and their combinations and is even more truly than the *Liberation Daily* the textbook of tens of thousands of people. It is widely used in primary and adult schools and in the ever-increasing newspaper-reading groups which university students and other voluntary workers hold in their leisure time for villagers and townspeople who want to inform themselves about current affairs and at the same time to learn more script signs.

The primitive printing shops at press headquarters are safely housed in the beautiful, thousand-year-old Caves of the Ten Thousand Buddhas at the bottom of the hill. Long rows of carved Buddhas on the walls of the tall, ancient caves and some huge statues look down on an odd assortment of busy machinery—old-fashioned pedal-driven printing presses, some of which were made in Yenan with remodeled Japanese "dud" bombs as rollers, and all kinds of improvised equipment of which even men who once worked in Shanghai's modern printing plants are extremely proud.

The two newspapers are not the only products of those shops. They print also a large variety of books and pamphlets; woodcuts which bring modern Chinese art into the peasants' homes; the various educational posters and black-and-white portraits of the leaders of Yenan's New Democracy, of Roosevelt, Churchill, Stalin, and Chiang Kai-shek, and those fairly detailed, well-made maps of the Communist-controlled war areas and the different World War theaters which are displayed everywhere in the Border Region.

I followed the *Liberation Daily* regularly with the help of translators and referred to its back numbers to satisfy myself that its editorial policy was uninfluenced by the presence of critical visitors in Yenan. I compared in detail full translations of an old copy of the Kuomintang-owned government newspaper, *Central Daily News*, which I had brought from Chungking, and of the *Liberation Daily* of the same date.

The *Liberation Daily* seems to me an incomparably better and more factual paper than any of the dozen dailies in Chungking which are so dependent upon the material of the government-owned *Central News Agency* and so strictly censored in their editorials and their individual reporting that they are almost uniform in their insipid contents and their colorless character.

228

These are the main differences between the Yenan and Chungking press:

The *Liberation Daily* devotes much more attention to the war in China than any of the Chungking papers can do. It makes the war a live issue of popular concern and fascination, giving firsthand accounts from the fronts, which are practically absent from the Chungking press because the Kuomintang Army discourages the presence of war correspondents on the scene of action and censors reporters most unreasonably even in rear areas.

The Yenan paper does not restrict itself to coverage of the warfare at the Communist fighting fronts but makes fairly full use of Chungking's war communiqués, although the Chinese Communists are as skeptical of their reliability as American military critics. By contrast, the Chungking newspapers have not been permitted for five years to print any reports about the war in the Communist-controlled front areas.

The *Liberation Daily* analyzes the Chinese, Pacific, and World War situations in a much more scientific and realistic manner, without any of the vague wishful thinking about China's own military position or the naïve reproaches against her Allies which characterize the Kuomintang-inspired cliché editorials of the Chungking papers. Detailed reports and critical comments on the civilian war effort in the Communist-controlled areas deal in a concrete and practical manner with all phases of political, economic, social, and cultural developments and take up at least one-quarter to one-third of each issue. A whole page is often devoted to the painstaking description of typical examples of good or bad units of the army, of schools, cooperatives, factories, hospitals, village or district governments, and party organizations—for others to learn from and for the encouragement of popular interest and criticism.

All this reporting about domestic affairs has no parallel in the Chungking papers, which are not permitted to take a factual approach to any important subject of internal policy; for all issues of interest to Chungking readers are also elements in the growing crisis of the Kuomintang regime and therefore more or less under the taboo of a rigid censorship.

The entertainment matter of the *Liberation Daily* is on a higher literary level and is more serious and purposeful, yet of a more truly popular kind than that of the Kuomintang press.

Advertisements, upon which even the heavily subsidized Kuomintang papers have to rely to such a large extent that they fill a good part of their four to six pages, play only a small role in the Yenan paper.

The *Liberation Daily* is frankly a crusading organ. Its manifold campaigns are of a thoroughly positive character, designed to support, explain, and popularize the policies of the New Democracy for the war against Japan and for general progress. Criticism of the Kuomintang regime in Chungking occurs, as a rule, more by implication than as a main subject.

I did not find the paper boring, in spite of its preoccupation with many matters of practical, didactic detail, and came to understand the enthusiasm with which the unsophisticated pioneers in all strata of the Border Region seem to rely upon it as their guide and teacher. Wherever I was able to compare its writings with reality, the *Liberation Daily* seemed to deserve its reputation for honesty and reliability.

I saw also front-line newspapers from the Anti-Japanese War Bases which seem to be original in character, although they apply the line set by the *Liberation Daily* to the specific conditions and tasks of their respective territories. They reflect the extreme difficulties in the war areas under which the fighting forces, the local governments, the people, and the newspapers themselves carry out the basic demands of Yenan's relentless crusade for victory and progress.

The press in Communist China is certainly not free in our sense. Censorship as such may really not exist, yet its essence and the element of guidance from above are inherent in two facts: The primary news organs are owned and run by organizations of the Communist party and local governments. And their staff members, both Communists and non-Communists, are selected for proved loyalty to the existing regime, which implies their willingness to conform to all official policies.

It is one of the aims of these policies under the New Democracy to develop the initiative and stimulate the criticism of non-Communists.

230

The newspapers evidently try to reflect the views of a coalition of progressive patriots among which the Communists are the leading group. Yet, it is of course impossible to judge how far this ideal is actually being accomplished.

The leaders in Yenan were not apologetic about the guidance they exert over the press. But they told me that they realized the need for additional independent newspapers in the future and that the New Democracy definitely provided for their free development, not as a mere concession to non-Communists but in the interest of strengthening the new regime.

The present restriction of the freedom of the press was motivated by three sets of compelling circumstances.

First, the peculiarities of the war situation in Communist-controlled China make the press an important instrument for mobilizing the people and fighting the enemy. The Japanese and their puppets are within a few dozen miles of almost any point in the war areas, and within one or two hundred miles of Yenan and all important towns in the Border Region itself. The struggle with them is incessant; it permeates all phases of life in the Communist-controlled regions and is fought as a combination of military, political, economic, and psychological warfare of a popular character; so that it is considered necessary to give the civilian population a maximum of clear guidance through a thoroughly responsible press which must work in close contact with the military and civilian authorities.

Second, the Sino-Japanese conflict in those areas is complicated by the war of nerves which Chungking carries on against the Communists. "Numerous secret agents of the Kuomintang try relentlessly to spread dissension and dissatisfaction in our areas," I was told by many Chinese and by the few foreigners who have lived for years in Yenan territories, "so that it is necessary that the press shall not play into their hands, even unwittingly."

Finally, material conditions are at present singularly unsuited to the development of independent newspapers. No private enterprise could hope to overcome the difficulties of obtaining machinery and newsprint,

231

of collecting other than local information, and of securing a worth-while number of readers among a scattered rural population which is only beginning to emerge from its illiteracy.

There are at present no Kuomintang newspapers in Communist-controlled China, although the Communist party is still able to publish its *New China Daily* in Chungking.

What are the reasons for this contradictory situation?

Chungking never took a serious interest in establishing a Kuomintang organ in Yenan and the Border Region because it could not have hoped to appeal to any group of consequence even if the Communists had given it full freedom to express its views. For the Kuomintang followers in the present Border Region have always belonged to the progressive wing of the party and never ceased to be critical of its right wing, which has dominated the National Government since 1927. Those progressive Kuomintang members of the old Sun Yat-sen school came to cooperate closely with the Communists, especially since the introduction of the New Democracy. I talked to several of them and found that no Kuomintang paper would interest them unless it took its critical stand on the basis of genuine United Front cooperation with other political parties—a policy Chungking would be unable to adopt on one side of the blockade wall while rejecting it on the other.

The former supporters of the right-wing Kuomintang in the present Border Region, however, were swept away by the agrarian revolution of the Communists before the Sino-Japanese War. They were corrupt local war lords who for several years paid nominal allegiance to the Kuomintang, in exchange for the right to continue their feudal rule over "their" people under an equally nominal overlordship of the National Government. Chiang Kai-shek's former cooperation with those local war lords is not forgotten and is responsible for the continuing distrust of Chungking among the old gentry in the Border Region.

Some copies of Chungking's newspapers still find their way to Yenan; but it seems from what some landlords and merchants told me that they have only one effect: to reinforce the critical views of non-

232

Communists in the Border Region about the policies of the Kuomintang and the National Government.

The surviving Kuomintang organization in Chin-cha-chi, the largest of the Communists' Anti-Japanese War Bases in North China, had its own newspaper until 1941. But that paper had to be closed down for lack of funds when Kuomintang headquarters in Chungking disowned the organization on account of its cooperation with the Communists and nonparty groups in the spirit of the United Front. Liberal Kuomintang elements in other Anti-Japanese War Bases were equally disowned by Chungking. Right-wing Kuomintang members are more numerous in the war areas than in the Border Region. But, being declared enemies of the United Front and accused of cooperation with Japan's puppets, they would never get permission from the Communists to maintain their own newspapers even if they were able to do so.

However, the National Government had no reason to suppress the Communists' *New China Daily* in Chungking. The special censorship of the paper has made it colorless and on the whole so uninteresting that it is regarded as innocuous. On the other hand, its continued publication is even useful to the National Government because it provides it with a worth-while argument for foreign and liberal home consumption about its tolerant attitude toward the Communists.

Freedom of speech in Communist-controlled China is also not of the same kind as in America and Britain, although Yenan seems to compare favorably with Chungking in this respect, too.

The saddest aspect of the suppression of free speech in the Chungking regions is that it is so ruthlessly applied to those, even inside the Kuomintang's party organization itself, who are anxious to make Chiang Kai-shek's regime survive by pressing for the urgently needed and popularly demanded democratic reforms which alone can prevent its eventual eclipse. A prominent member of the Kuomintang and the National Government in Chungking once told me he had discovered that one of his houseboys, acting for General Tai Li's Secret Police, wrote down the name of everyone who visited his villa, eavesdropped on conversations, and reported in detail about his master.

233

In one regard Yenan's suppression of free speech would seem more ruthless and effective than Chungking's—where defeatist and compromising attitudes toward the Chinese puppets of the Japanese are concerned. The Communists are proud that they never had any parallel cases to the treason of Wang Ching-wei, Generalissimo Chiang Kai-shek's deputy chief of the Kuomintang, who together with a large number of leading party officials went over to the Japanese.

What other restrictions of freedom of speech I found in the Border Region seemed less than in Chungking the consequence of coercion from above and of secret activities of party and government organs. They appeared to a large extent self-imposed or tacitly enforced by the specific social atmosphere which the popular war against Japan, the defense against Kuomintang underground activities, and the widespread pioneer enthusiasm for the New Democracy have created.

The great majority of the people under Yenan's active influence are certainly much more aware of their tasks in the war and in the promotion of social progress than the people under Chungking's authoritative yet lax and uninspired rule; just as a much larger number of the people on the Yenan side seem to be in fundamental agreement with their government than is the case on the Chungking side. And they are apparently more aware of the need of protecting their war effort and their new society by reticence toward strangers.

Basically, however, freedom of speech is not only unrestricted but actually encouraged, to bring about improvements of the existing regime of the New Democracy—inside as well as outside the Communist party.

"But what about dissenters—people who oppose the Yenan regime as such?" I asked Michael Lindsay, the progressive English liberal who has for years lived in Communist-controlled China. "What would happen if somebody said publicly at a meeting that the Kuomintang regime is better than the New Democracy of the Communists? Would he be arrested?"

"Of course not," Lindsay said. "The others would discuss the statement with him as a practical problem, in all detail. They might even call a special meeting at which both sides would talk as factually as possible. That is all. And such things have actually happened. The authorities don't take an interest in anything that is said openly, but the people do."

I heard of such a case from the president of Yenan University.

"Some of our students expressed the opinion that 'the kind of Fascism Chiang Kai-shek advocates in his book *China's Destiny* is good for China,'" he said, "arguing that 'the Chinese people are still too illiterate and ignorant for democracy.'"

I interrupted him: "Do you mean to say that Chiang Kai-shek's book was available to your students?"

"Naturally. The full text was reprinted in Yenan in a large edition, together with a critical article by one of our political theoreticians. It was sold everywhere and we have it in our library."

The students in Yenan were more fortunate than we foreign correspondents in Chungking who tried in vain to get permission from the Generalissimo to quote from his book in messages to our papers. More than a dozen draft translations of a committee of high-ranking government officials were torn up: it was evidently impossible, in spite of further improvements and cuts of the revised Chinese edition, to make *China's Destiny* into a book which would give American or British readers the impression that its author really held democratic views.

"And what happened to the students?" I asked.

"We had long, concrete discussions with them in large meetings of students and teachers. Their arguments were of course defeated and they realized their mistake. Everybody learned a great deal from that episode. We teachers found that we had not paid sufficient attention to practical political education and improved our methods.

"We are not afraid of freedom of speech on political matters. On the contrary, we need it because it helps us to clarify and popularize our policies."

Chapter Twenty-five

CHRIST, MOHAMMED, THE SAGES, AND THE FAMILY

FOREIGN missionaries had good reason to side with the Kuomintang against the Communists during the grim period of the Civil War. They found it impossible to continue their work in the embattled Soviet areas and their missions, as a rule, withdrew with the Kuomintang authorities before the advance of the Reds. The Communist scheme of social revolution evidently left no room for religion, while the Kuomintang, led by professing Christians like Generalissimo and Mme. Chiang Kai-shek, was eager for missionary aid.

I was greatly surprised, therefore, that the first favorable opinion about the Communists I heard on my arrival in wartime China in 1939 was from American, Canadian, and British Protestant missionaries who had visited Yenan early that year. They told me how well Yenan's efforts for victory and social progress compared with those of Chungking. They had found the Communists free from antireligious bias and inspired with apparently sincere morality. They believed that the change of Yenan's policies would prove to be permanent and hoped that Yenan's social reforms would raise China to a higher ethical level and make missionary work more effective than it had been in the past.

At the time I took no notes of what I heard from those missionaries. But five years later in Yenan I found the following entries in the visitors' book of the Guest House:

"When I returned recently to China from America I was disappointed to find so many students unconscious of the war and living the same kind of life that they had been used to before the war. This visit to Yenan has impressed me very much, for I have discovered here that a large body of the very best of Chinese youth are willing to live sim-

236

ply, work hard, suffer, and sacrifice everything for the sake of a new and free China and for world peace. Your cooperative spirit, your humor and creative ability, the entire absence of class distinction . . . and your thorough and sincere struggle for freedom appeal to me greatly." (Signed) Andrew T. Roy.

"I have seen what I did not think possible, namely, workers, students and officials all working unselfishly together in the task of freeing China, of creating social justice and of achieving world peace. In spite of poverty and the war of resistance you have created schools, hospitals, and new social institutions unlike anything in the world." (Signed) S. Lautenschlager.

"One of the most interesting, profitable, and happy experiences of my life." (Signed) George A. Fitch.

"I have been impressed with the friendly spirit of cooperation and your willingness to sacrifice for your country. . . . We as Christians sincerely wish your cause well and believe the inclusion of a religious faith and worship would greatly strengthen your many fine qualities and bring about . . . a relationship to the Supreme Being which makes life complete and helps us love all our fellow men." (Signed) Robt. E. Brown.

Since that time, various missions and other foreign-supported Christian organizations like the Y.M.C.A. have tried to get permission from Chungking to take up work in the Communist-controlled areas in accordance with repeated invitations from Yenan.

Generalissimo Chiang Kai-shek finally gave his approval in 1942. But various Kuomintang organizations, especially those at anti-Yenan headquarters in Sian, strongly "advised" the missionaries not to go to the Communist-controlled areas. At least one foreign Christian worker was black-listed by the Kuomintang authorities when he attempted to remit money to Yenan for Chinese Christians. And the Christian organizations, anxious not to endanger their work in Kuomintang-controlled territories, did not try to force the issue, although some of them seem to have quietly continued their efforts for admittance to Yenan.

Meanwhile, many of the missionaries had especially good opportunities of watching the trend of the Kuomintang's educational policies toward stricter and stricter thought control in schools and universities and Chungking's growing tendency toward intimidation of democratic elements in general. Progressive Chinese teachers and students in missionary institutions knew a good deal about developments in the Communist-controlled territories which seemed to continue in the opposite direction. The foreign missionary societies in China are continuing to cooperate closely with the National Government in Chungking and try to keep out of political controversy. But this has not prevented individual missionaries, especially on the Protestant side, from developing their own opinions about political trends in China.

The majority of the missionaries I met during five years in the Kuomintang territories, although becoming more outspoken about their disappointment in certain aspects of Chungking's policies which hinder their work by being either illiberal or inefficient, remain uninclined to revise their fundamentally negative views about the Chinese Communists or even to take an interest in their present ideas and practices. A comparatively large minority of liberal men and women in Protestant missions have come to think well of the Chinese Communists and do not hesitate to say so in their own circles. They are anxious to see Chinese national unity established on a democratic basis and to get an opportunity to work on the Communist side, too.

I have found only a few missionaries, however, who are actively supporting the Kuomintang in its condemnation of the Communists.

Shortly before going to Yenan, I met one of the foreign missionaries who worked in the present Border Region during the last phase of the Civil War until he had to follow the orders from his mission board to withdraw. I found him a religious man without political interest but with a passion for truth. This is what he told me, omitting the names of places and persons he mentioned.

"We never saw any religious persecution in the Red areas. During the fighting between Kuomintang and Communist troops in our district our mission station was occupied by a Red division headquarters while we were absent. But it was evacuated immediately on our return. The

238

commanding general who moved to the vicinity offered to pay for whatever damage our buildings might have suffered and was fair in his dealings with us.

"I know we would suffer no risk in returning to the Border Region and we are eager to do so. The Communists would certainly welcome us, for they realize our usefulness in educational and medical work.

"I found during my many years of work in China that one could be more frank with the Reds than with most officials here in the Kuomintang areas. I allowed myself all kinds of criticism there; yet I was free to go wherever I wanted and was never interfered with or spied upon.

"Yes, the Communists are of course good at propaganda," the missionary replied to my question whether they might not have tried to make a good impression on the few foreigners in their region. "But what methods are the Kuomintang authorities using to give foreign visitors like you an untrue picture of conditions in certain areas?

"The Communists, I believe, will let you go where you want to go. You will find them more open-minded than many of the officials on this side. And I think you will agree with me that, whatever their political beliefs, they have a conception of truth which is closer to ours."

In Yenan we asked for a statement about the official attitude of the Border Region government toward religion. "The New Democracy gives everybody freedom of belief and worship," Lo Mai, the secretary of the government, told us. "Before our law all are equal, no matter whether they are Buddhists, Moslems, Christians, or atheists, and we give religious organizations the right to own property."

Father Shanahan, the American priest who was said to have been included in our party at the personal wish of Generalissimo Chiang Kai-shek, obtained an agreement with the Communists about the reopening of Catholic missions before he left Yenan. General Chou Enlai, who had carried on the negotiations for the Communists, gave me the following account of his understanding with Father Shanahan.

"He asked me about our conditions for the reopening of Catholic missions and I said that they were these (which hold good for Protestant missions, too): Foreign missionaries must observe the laws of the

239

Border Region government. They must not oppose the political leadership of the Communist party. And they must not use religion as a means for political activities. Father Shanahan agreed with these points.

"I told him that the Catholic church near Yenan and the other mission buildings they need will be returned to the fathers when they resume their work. The Art College of Yenan University is at present housed in the Catholic mission station near Yenan and will evacuate as soon as the fathers arrive.

"We promised that the government would give the missionaries full freedom for their religious activities, that is, freedom of movement, ceremonies, meetings, and religious connections. He was satisfied with these points, too.

"Father Shanahan mentioned before he left that his mission would probably send Spanish fathers to Yenan. I told him frankly that in my own opinion Americans or missionaries of other nationalities would be more suited. For we are definitely opposing Franco in our publicity and this might unnecessarily strain relations in case Spanish fathers came to Yenan."

Chou En-lai added that he was anxious also to see Protestant missionaries return to Communist-controlled areas and that he was certain of harmonious cooperation with them. But he doubted, for the time being, whether Chungking would permit either Catholics or Protestants to come.

The number of Christians in China is probably under 1 per cent of the total population and their number is proportionately even smaller in the rural Border Region where prewar missionary activities were on a small scale. In the city limits of Yenan there may be about five hundred Christians. Part of them are still holding prayer meetings, although the withdrawal of the missions before the end of the Civil War left them without clergy.

I met a number of them. None seemed to have suffered in any way on account of their religious beliefs. Among them were students of Yenan University who said that nobody tried to convert them to atheism. Several Communists who had been believers in the past told me that they still adhered to Christian ethics and found no difficulty in reconciling them with their strong Communist convictions.

Dr. Fu Lien-chang, the elderly director of the Medical Department in Yenan, was one of them. He grew up in the orphanage of a British mission in Fukien province, studied in its medical college, worked in the mission hospital, and finally became its chief during the days of the Civil War when the Red Army occupied his town. He spoke with respect of the work his former missionary colleagues had been doing and with affection and admiration of "a British missionary lady from London, Miss Rainey, who had a good understanding of the character of the Red partisans and helped us devotedly to nurse them."

"My political beliefs changed at that time although I joined the Communist party only several years later," he said. "I am still convinced that Christianity and Communism have much in common. Christ helped the poor. And Christ was anti-Fascist. . . ."

The Reverend Comrade Pu Hua-jen, our chief interpreter in Yenan, was a special case: not only because he had been an ordained minister before he became an enthusiastic Communist, but because he still professes to an ardent faith in Christ.

"Bishop" Pu, as the old man was nicknamed many years ago by his fellow students because of his religious devotion, was baptized when his belief and a scholarship opened to him the door of St. John's University in Shanghai. He cut his queue off, as one of the first of the students to indicate his progressive political views, and delved into theological studies, being twice voted the most religious student in the school.

A pamphlet he wrote, "Christianity Can Save China," brought him in contact with one of the leading figures in the days of the war lords, Feng Yu-hsiang, who was then in the process of becoming China's famous "Christian General" and made the Reverend Pu Hua-jen his chaplain.

"The ordinary way of saving China by Christianity was too slow in my opinion," Pu said. "I thought it was better to use two weapons—the Bible and the rifle. This was my reason for joining General Feng Yu-hsiang, whom I still regard as a good man and a patriot."

241

Christ, Mohammed, the Sages, and the Family

The "Christian General," impressed by a visit to Moscow in 1926, sent Pu there to study certain social policies for him. "And when I saw the peasants and workers in Russia leading a happier and more promising life than our people in China, I realized that revolution was more effective than preaching. I saw the pictures of Communist martyrs and connected their fate with that of the crucified Christ and found that Christianity and Revolution are not in contradiction to each other. I joined the Communist party as soon as I returned.

"Even my old mother, who had developed from a Buddhist to one of the best Christians in our church, made her way to Communism and helped me much in dangerous underground work during the time of the Civil War. My son became an enthusiastic Communist at the age of twelve and served us as a fearless and clever courier in our dangerous illegal work. Three years ago, when the Japanese captured my boy in a mopping-up campaign in the Communist war areas and bayoneted him in the presence of some comrades who later escaped, he died with the words, 'Long live the Communist party, down with Japanese Imperialism.'

"I am still a Christian," Pu said. "The party knows of it and does not object. I have even converted a few Comrades. Jesus was the leader of the revolution of his time. His aim was to change society so that everybody would be free and happy. But his apostles failed in their attempt to create a simple Communism. Today we need not only Christ's ideas but also those of Marx and Lenin in order to establish a better society and permanent peace. Many Christians in China have helped the Communist party very much, and the United Front must include Communists as well as patriotic Christians."

There does not seem to be any conflict, either, between Mohammedanism and the New Democracy, although the Moslems in the Communist-controlled areas are as orthodox and fundamentally as suspicious of non-Moslems as those anywhere in Northwest China.

China has a Moslem problem. It is not nearly so great or so acute as that of India. But the Chinese Moslems, especially in the Northwest, have long been complaining about the oppressive intolerance of the

242

"Han" (Chinese) who rule them without much regard for their religious faith and rituals. Moslem risings of varying magnitude have been frequent: in the old days against the Manchu dynasty; later against local war lords; and recently against both the Kuomintang government and the survivors of those war lords of whom the Kuomintang still makes use.

Dr. Sun Yat-sen had promised the Moslems during the heyday of the National Revolution that they would henceforth be considered as a national minority and given local autonomy and equal treatment with the other national groups—Chinese, Mongols, Manchus, and Tibetans —in a virtually federated state. But his successors ignored his promise.

The Communists, in their effort to unite all parts of the population for the war against Japan, made Sun Yat-sen's promise their own. And Chungking complains today that Yenan is trying to gain the support of a numerous Moslem population in the adjoining Kuomintang territories by pampering the comparatively small number of Moslems in the areas under its control.

The various Mohammedan associations in the Border Region and the Anti-Japanese War Bases, which seem to contain very few if any Communists, stress the fight against "chauvinist Chinese oppression," for the freedom of the Moslems' religious and cultural life, and for Moslem autonomy within China along the lines of Dr. Sun Yat-sen's promise.

Whatever the motives of the Communists may be, it seems that the demands of the Moslems in their own regions are being satisfied. The *ahung* are free to perform their rites, new mosques have been built, Islamic schools have been established in areas with sufficient Moslem population, and Moslem refugees from adjoining Kuomintang territories have been helped to settle down. Where Moslems and other Chinese live together, mutual insults are supposed to have decreased under the educational influence of the Communists; and where they still occur, the community leaders of both sides consult and settle such incidents.

One of the brigades of the Communist-led Eighth Route Army, recruited in the Mohammedan areas of Suiyuan province, is constituted as a Moslem brigade in which all Islamic rituals are observed. Dr. Hans C. Mueller, a refugee from Germany, saw the brigade when after many years of fighting it was brought to the Border Region to recuperate and replenish its great battle losses. He told me that for lack of sufficient Moslem recruits in the Border Region its ranks had been filled with ordinary Chinese who have to live according to the rituals and habits of their comrades.

The Mongols, to whom Dr. Sun Yat-sen gave the same promise of local autonomy, have also found sympathy and support in Yenan and are given the rights of a national minority. Their number in the Communist-controlled regions is small, but their influence on their compatriots in the territories under the Kuomintang and especially in those at present under Japanese occupation may come to play a role after the war.

I met one of the Mongol leaders in the Communist-controlled regions, Wulanteleh, the grandson of a noble in the Tumite tribe of Inner Mongolia, a well-educated man who has fought all his life against the twofold suppression of the Mongol people by the chieftains of the feudal tribes and by the Chinese Government, whose policy of pushing Chinese settlers into the grasslands of Inner Mongolia reduced the pastures of the nomads and aroused their bitter opposition. Anti-Japanism brought him, like other Mongols, into closer cooperation with the Communists, and he became director of education in Yenan's Institute of National Minorities as well as one of the leaders of the Mongolian Culture Promotion Association.

"The Mongols everywhere," Wulanteleh said, "have gained much more understanding of the position of their nation during the last few years. Their bitter experiences of suppression by the Chinese as well as the Japanese have taught them much.

"They know from Chiang Kai-shek's book *China's Destiny* that he does not really recognize us as a national group, as Sun Yat-sen did. They demand national equality and local autonomy under a free and democratic Chinese government."

I asked Wulanteleh whether his people in Inner Mongolia wanted to be united with those of Outer Mongolia, at present under Soviet control, and what his idea was about the return of Outer Mongolia to Chinese suzerainty, which is now mere fiction.

"During a transitionary period," he said, "Inner Mongolia should have its own local government, apart from that of Outer Mongolia. Inner Mongolia is in a different position, having a much larger Chinese population and closer contacts with China than Outer Mongolia ever had. It is too early to predict whether the two may unite in the future.

"Outer Mongolia has a progressive government of the Mongolian people. It does not belong to the USSR, although the Russians support it. But Outer Mongolia does not want to belong to the Kuomintang either. Once the whole of China is no more under a chauvinistic one-party dictatorship but has a really democratic government which recognizes the rights of national minorities and the national character of the Mongols, the present nominal Chinese suzerainty over Outer Mongolia will once more become a fact. All the Mongols are willing to be part of China when their national minority rights are fully recognized."

Buddha is tolerated by the Communists, like Christ and Mohammed. The vague and loosely held superstitions which are all that remained of Buddhism among the Chinese peasantry are gradually waning in their contact with war and social progress. The religion from which they sprang is held by few and offers no problem to the New Democracy.

The ideological enemies of the Communists are Confucius and the other sages of China's distant past, or rather those of today who extol their ancient wisdom as the eternal truth by which the Chinese people should be ruled. The following, in short, is what Ai Sze-chi, professor of philosophy at Yenan University and editor of the bimonthly *Life of Learning*, told me about the subject. It was scarcely different from the opinion of my liberal Chinese friends in Chungking.

"Confucius was certainly a great progressive statesman at the time when slave society began to develop into feudalistic society; for he made himself the spokesman of the new forces of feudalism. But all

245

those who used his sayings in later phases of social development were fundamentally reactionaries who tried to maintain their power by keeping the people's mind in a feudalistic frame.

"The present Kuomintang government is no exception. It uses the sages for three purposes: (1) To reduce the interest of China's youth in modern, progressive thought and to make young people suspicious of the basic truths of new ideas; (2) to instill in the people the idea that the teachings of the sages about absolutism, obedience, and the classification of society into feudal groups are fundamentally as valid for the 'special conditions' of China as they ever were; (3) to reinterpret Dr. Sun Yat-sen's political philosophy and his political program in a Confucian light, with the intention of making his ideas serve as a modern disguise for the continuation of the traditional political ideology by which China has been suppressed for thousands of years.

"China's friends abroad would realize this immediately if Chiang Kai-shek permitted his book *China's Destiny* to be translated into English. For what he preaches in it is feudal, reactionary Confucianism in the role of an emasculated Sun Yat-senism."

I knew there was truth in what the professor said on this point, for I had seen a translation of *China's Destiny*. I had also seen English excerpts from a later book of the Generalissimo about economics in which the ideas of Confucius and other ancient Chinese sages, rather than the "alien" theories of foreigners like Adam Smith and Ricardo, are called the foundation on which China's economic thought and practice must be based. And I had heard liberal Kuomintang men in Chungking express their despair at the increasingly embarrassing manifestations of thought of the Generalissimo.

"The Japanese militarists use Confucianism in a similar way," the professor continued, "both at home and in occupied China, in order to suppress modern thought and to keep themselves in power. The New People's Association the Japanese are using in Manchuria and North China has much in common with Chiang Kai-shek's New Life Movement. Both stress the feudal morality of Confucius and both teach obedience as their main precept.

246

The leader of "Red" China—Mao Tse-tung

he leader of Kuomin-
g China—Chiang Kai-
ek

Generalissimo and M
dame Chiang Kai-shek

Communist party leader Mao Tse-
tung and wife

The commander of Yenan's Eighth
Route Army—General Chu Teh

he commander of Chung-
g's ground forces—General
o Ying-chin

Lt. Col. Joseph W. Stilwell, Jr., son of General Joseph W. Stilwell; Col. N.
Roshchin, Russian military attaché in Chungking; and General Chou En-lai,
of the Chinese Communist party leaders

Outstanding Communist generals, left to right: Peng Teh-huai, Chu Teh, Y
Chien-ying, Nieh Yung-chen, Chen Yi

enan, showing caves of the "Japanese Peasants' and Workers' School"

enan's only street

Some wards of Yenan's International Peace Hospital *Acme Ph*

Medical students in front of their dormitory cave *Acme Ph*

Acme Photo

Communist-led Eighth
Route Army men

Acme Photo

Japanese stronghold cap-
tured by Eighth Route
Army troops

Eighth Route Army men with Japanese booty

Communist-led militia men behind the Japanese lines

Christ, Mohammed, the Sages, and the Family

"The Western countries are not using the theories of men who lived at the dawn of their civilization as the basis of their modern political ideology and practice. Well, this is what Chiang Kai-shek is doing because he believes it helps him to keep down the desire of the Chinese people for a modern democratic life.

"We have to fight against the reactionary misuse of the ancient wisdom of the sages—not only in the policies of the Kuomintang but also in Chinese family life where Confucianist traditions are still so firmly entrenched that they are a handicap to democratic progress."

The Communists are eager to reform family life. But they do not try to do it by revolutionary methods or by any direct interference with the private affairs of the people. The outdated Confucian traditions of the Chinese family—discrimination against women, blind obedience of juniors to seniors, and the semiseclusion of the family unit from society—are gradually overcome in the course of carrying out the various economic, political, and social-reform policies of the New Democracy.

The new methods of agricultural production with their emphasis on village-wide cooperation in the fields are slowly breaking down the age-old family isolationism of the peasantry. General suffrage for men and women over the age of eighteen and the new custom of solving local problems in public discussion are also making for more equality among family members in their lives at home. And the general process of education and political awakening which was set in motion by the various mass movements is making the people increasingly aware of the need for the reform of their family lives and its great advantages to their own prosperity. The much-vaunted democratic spirit of the common Chinese people is thus finding opportunities for full expression.

The attitude of the Communists toward the family is positive. There is no tendency even within their own ranks to dissolve it or to minimize its importance in the society they are building up.

Peasants like the Labor Hero Wu Men-yu have a sharp eye for the private lives of Communist leaders and functionaries. From all I have seen and heard, the peasants' respect for the pioneers of the New

Democracy is to a great extent due to the simple, clean, and normal lives they live. I have been to the homes of many of them, met their wives, and noticed their affection for their children, who have a habit of coming in to look at visitors with a healthy, childish curiosity.

Few, if any, own more than a few suitcases could hold—simple clothes and books, bedding, and household utensils. Their furniture is mostly provided by the organizations for which they work, together with the caves in which they live. There is no restriction on private possessions. But those men get no money salaries and all of them were almost incredibly poor when they first came to Yenan: in tatters from the Long March; with a little bundle from years of underground life in the Kuomintang regions; without anything from enemy-occupied territories; or from their poor homes in the Border Region where comforts, even before the war, were only for the wealthiest.

Yet they would be surprised if one asked them whether they consider themselves poor. After years of acute need they now have enough to eat and to keep warm, and the rosy cheeks of their children show that they are not lacking anything, either. Neither men nor women seem to give any thought to the comforts they would certainly like to have some day. What most of them long for are books and magazines from the outside and good music.

But what about the relations between the sexes, marriage and morals?

George "Ma Hai-teh," the American doctor at the International Peace Hospital in Yenan, gave me the following replies which checked with whatever observations I was able to make myself.

Being a doctor, he began with the incidence of venereal disease. It averages only 2 per cent in the party and government organizations and is no higher in the army. All of them enforce strong rules against promiscuity. Extramarital relations are strictly forbidden in the army, while marriage is permitted to the soldiers wherever possible.

Economic considerations are no hindrance to marriage among government and party functionaries whose incomes are sufficient to maintain families, especially since most wives hold jobs and get two months' paid leave before and after childbirth and adequate allowances for children.

Parents and families play no role any more in matchmaking in these circles. There are no "overnight" marriages, nor "second wives" as in other parts of China where the old institution of concubines is still in existence. The monogamy law is strictly enforced in the Communist-controlled areas and there are no more prostitutes or sing-song girls.

Love and courtship, in spite of all pioneer obsession for work and study, are normal—"and I may say as intense and fiery as at home in America or anywhere else," George added.

"Premarital intercourse is not considered a sin, for the people here are not prudish; but it is against the unwritten moral code of party, army, and all other organizations, and people marry soon when they are in love.

"There are comparatively few matrimonial conflicts. The reasons may be that their professional work is mostly a matter of common interest to husband and wife and that people have a new and broader outlook on life, so that purely individual problems arise to a smaller extent than elsewhere in China. Divorce is neither frowned upon nor encouraged. Colleagues and friends of partners who are in trouble use the probation period before divorce to help them clarify and if possible overcome their marriage problems."

The new style of family life among the pioneers of the New Democracy seems to have as strong an influence on the peasantry as Yenan's general educational efforts and its enforcement of modern marriage law in the villages. The old-style large families in which whole generations live together are not breaking up yet. But there are more and more cases in which such families voluntarily agree to the democratic election of a family head once a year. Such "democratic model families," in which production plans for the family farm, money matters, and the complaints of individual members are freely discussed in family meetings, are propagandized in newspaper articles and *yangko* dramas.

Child betrothals are not yet made illegal, because old customs have not been sufficiently undermined to make the people realize their im-

249

moral character. But parents can no longer force their children into marriage, as in other parts of China, if either of the pair objects; the progressive elements in the villages influence old-fashioned families; and the number of such marriages seems to decrease all the time. But child slavery under the pretext of betrothal is now a criminal offense.

The meaning to children in Chinese villages of the issue New Democracy versus Confucian Tradition became clear to me when at my request a young Labor Heroine whom I had interviewed on factory problems told me her life story.

Her parents, poor farmers in need of a few silver dollars, sold her at the age of ten to a landlord family whose crippled son she was to marry. Year after year she was worked as hard as any of the grown-up servants, beaten and half-starved because she attempted to run away—against the Confucian principles of filial piety and obedience. When a Red Army unit came to her village during the last year of the Civil War, she joined up as a "little devil" orderly, working in a sewing group. That sewing group developed into a large uniform factory, and the "little devil" into a highly respected Labor Heroine.

Her own children, she said happily, are leading a better life. . . .

Chapter Twenty-six

THE WAY OF A WOMAN

TING LING was brilliant and famous. Her best-seller stories were read by hundreds of thousands of Chinese people to whom the revolutionary, anti-Japanese pathos of her heroes and heroines appealed in various ways. To some they were exciting entertainment of a new kind, fascinating because of their sincerity and art. To others they meant inspiration in their desire for Chinese freedom and progress. She was a truly emancipated woman, beautiful, radical, and courageous—an unusual figure in a country of convention.

That was in the old days in Shanghai, years before the Sino-Japanese War.

"Look what has become of her here in Yenan," one of the Kuomintang members of our party said to me at a tea we were given, pointing at a plump, cheerful little woman who no longer looked young. "She has not been writing for years. She must have been silenced by the party machine and disappointed with life here in Yenan. It is the same with other revolutionary writers who came to their paradise Yenan."

Ting Ling was asked why she and other well-known Communist novelists had written so little these last years.

She gave a short speech in reply. There was more urgent work for her to do, she said, than to write literature in the old sense. She had chosen to devote herself for the time being to practical tasks in journalism, education, and the various mass movements and was busy and happy in that work, especially since she realized how much she still had to learn about the men and women in this revolutionary society of the New Democracy before she could write literature for them as she had done for the people of the old society from which she came. Nothing else prevented her and other old revolutionary writers from resuming their literary work.

"The intellectual who does not fit into the world she has been preaching and fighting for," some of the Kuomintang people whispered, "the talented individualist whom the party machine cannot tolerate. Isn't it pitiful?"

When I inquired into popular education and art, the mass movements, and the position of women in the Communist-controlled areas, I often heard Ting Ling's name mentioned. Months later I asked her for an interview.

She came one morning, in striped, worn-out men's trousers, a faded blue cotton tunic, cloth shoes, and the inevitable soldier's cap.

Taking off her cap as she sat down, she shook her mane of long, straight hair, hunched over my desk, and looked at me questioningly with her extremely large and lively eyes: there was so much to say about this new life here; what did I want her to talk about?

I said I wanted to know the story of her life and work.

She thought for a little while and began, slowly at first, for it was so long since she had recalled the past; but soon she was in eloquent ardor, as though she were living it again. It was fascinating to watch her as she spoke. Her full face, plain and beautiful at the same time, seemed to have a wider range of expression than any face I knew. At one moment during those many hours she looked like a happy, vivacious girl, mischievous and emotional, and at another like an inspired Amazon; now the image of a mother, passionate in her protective instincts toward a family beyond her own; then the prototype of the cool, intellectual feminist or the picture of an elderly peasant woman, understanding and wise. But she seemed always herself, natural and genuine, never playing a part.

This is what she told me—to give me a bit of the social background of the time, as she put it, not to talk about herself as an individual.

"If you recall the old Chinese tale 'The Dream of the Red Chamber,' " she said, "you know exactly what my family was like. My grandfather had been a great landlord and high official in the Manchu dynasty. Father was extravagant, spent much money, and died young, and the family fortune began to dwindle. My mother hated the old society, left the family with me early in the century, and became a schoolteacher, which was a very unusual thing to do. She was not exactly a revolutionary at that time but was always very liberal-minded. Much later, when the National Revolution failed in 1927, mother joined the Communists.

"When I was small I lived with her at the school where she taught. Her reform ideas influenced me from my earliest years. I had just started Middle School in 1919 when intellectuals in Peking launched that great May Fourth reform movement against feudalism at home and imperialism from the outside, which really started the National Revolution and led to the formation of both the Kuomintang and Communist parties. That made me a revolutionary.

"Mother allowed me to go to a new, very progressive girls' school in Shanghai where a good number of the teachers were Communists. But I was still very young, had no knowledge of Chinese society, and the revolutionary ideas I developed were illusory, Utopian, and vague, as with many of my class. I was for a while in the anarchist movement but soon left the school and the anarchists.

"I had always read a great many ancient and modern novels and poems and began spending much time with the members of a new literary society which published Chinese and foreign revolutionary books, trying to push the deep ideological changes that were going on in China.

"This made me discover my first task. I decided to go back to my father's native place, to study my family, who were such typical representatives of the old Chinese society we had to overcome. This was to be the basis of critical literary work of my own. There was much material for stories there. But again I gave up. I thought of fleeing from everything to Europe, but I had no money; or of accepting a teaching job in Malaya, but I was only sixteen and was not allowed to go.

"I traveled in China for a while, trying to learn about our people and their lives, and studied literature at another progressive college in Shanghai. But I remained restless and my revolutionary ideas were still very abstract. I was afraid of party discipline. My main motive was to be a heroine and famous all over the world.

"In Peking I lived for three years at one of those strange boarding-houses where poor students, enjoying much freedom, used to discuss literature and revolution. I got nowhere. I felt too weak to wipe out injustice in the world, and without purpose in life. I drank and smoked a good deal. Sometimes I wept and sometimes I laughed. I tried to escape from myself, learning music and acting in movies for a short while. But nothing in life seemed right to me.

"Finally I locked my door and wrote. I poured out all that was in my mind, all my feelings against the old society, my despair that young people like myself could not find themselves and did not fit into the present life. I wrote very much, at first short stories and then also novels, mainly in Shanghai. Many publishers asked for my manuscripts, and friends and editors spoke well of my work. It was so easy to get famous because I expressed the feelings of so many in my social class. That satisfied my dreams of fame and heroism for a while. But it did me harm. It made me proud.

"At last, under the influence of the political events after the split in the national-revolutionary front, my revolutionary ideas crystallized. While I was working in the Left-wing Writers' Union, editing their magazine, making investigations into the living conditions of labor in the Shanghai factories, and helping the workers in their cultural activities, I joined the Communist party.

"I had to join secretly, like many others who awakened at that time. For those were the years of the White Terror of the Kuomintang against all left-wing intellectuals.

"Great numbers of writers and artists were arrested or kidnaped by the Kuomintang, many were tortured or killed. Even the readers of progressive magazines and students and workers suspected of leftist sympathies were persecuted and taken to jail by the thousands.

"The authorities of Shanghai's International Settlement and French Concession helped the Kuomintang suppress books and magazines."

Ting Ling hesitated a little before she continued.

"The man I loved, my husband, was arrested together with four other well-known writers. All of them, including a woman, were machine-gunned to death in Lunghua prison, near Shanghai—without trial. That was on February 7, 1931. The shooting became generally known, but the Kuomintang banned the news and even the foreign press did not mention it.

"They did not find me for a long time, for I worked underground. But at last, early in 1933, I too was detected. In broad daylight in Shanghai's International Settlement, Kuomintang plain-clothes men kidnaped me, covering me with guns hidden in their sleeves. On the same day they took me to a hotel in the city and a day later by train to Nanking, where I was held in one secret Kuomintang confinement place after another.

"There was no charge against me and no warrant for my arrest. I refused my jailers' demand to contradict Shanghai rumors that I had been killed by Kuomintang agents. I also refused to write for Kuomintang magazines, which were then trying to build up a popular reputation with the help of Leftist renegades. The terror against the progressive camp, to which almost all the talented writers of modern China belonged, had left very few who could impress the people in favor of the Kuomintang.

"For months my jailers tried to frighten me day and night, shutting me up in a dark room with horrible gangsters, making me believe that I would be executed, and inventing new methods of mental torture all the time. But I remained firm. I knew mother tried to appeal to the courts and Mme. Sun Yat-sen was supporting her through Yang Ching-fu, a progressive Kuomintang member who was later killed by his party."

The story of Ting Ling's three years' ordeal is too long to be told in detail. Renegades from the Communist party were sent to break down her resistance. A rightist Kuomintang playwright, Chang Tao-fan, whom I had in the meantime come to know as the most illiberal Minister of Publicity in Chungking, was sent to Ting Ling to make her work for his party. Her health broke down and she was eventually given into the private custody of one of the renegades and his wife, in a village near Shanghai, where she was always followed and watched by secret agents. At last, in the summer of 1936, a visitor to her "host," who was sent by the Communist party in Shanghai, made secret contact with her, and she escaped after three years of illegal detention.

"Late in 1936, I made my way to the Border Region. I was at first with the Red Army at the front, during the last stage of the Civil War, as vice-director of the political department of a regiment and wrote articles about my experiences. I felt very much at home in the army. It was probably the most joyful time of my life.

"When the war with Japan broke out, I organized a Battlefield Service Corps for the entertainment of the troops and we went to the front. At that time, for a short period, even Kuomintang Army units invited us to come to them and we visited them, propagating national unity with our own plays, songs, and pictures."

For a while Ting Ling tried to do literary work in Yenan, but she failed.

"My stimulus had formerly come from disagreement with the atmosphere of oppression around me, and later, after the Japanese marched into Manchuria, from my desire to make the country wake up and resist Japan.

"But what was there in Yenan to stimulate me by irritation—where democracy is alive and the fight against the enemy is being fought? I did not know how to appeal to readers who were not suppressed, dissatisfied, or apathetic—to those new people here for whom I wanted to write.

"I felt that if I were to continue my literary work in the Communist areas I had to describe the soldiers, peasants, workers, and all the others here in their life and work in this new society. But I did not know them well, not nearly so intimately as I had known the old people of my own set. And the same was true of other old writers.

"Comrade Mao Tse-tung saw what was wrong with those of us who after coming to Yenan continued writing in the old way. We judged

256

the value of one another's work by formal literary standards and ignored the new public for which we wrote. He said to us, 'Don't write for each other; write for the people.' "

She came to realize, as most of the intellectual Old Guard in Yenan seem to have done, that she had in fact more to learn and unlearn than the ordinary peasants in order to fit into the new life. For the peasants are by nature closer to the reality of Yenan's new system than city-bred writers who fanned the revolutionary movement, scarcely anticipating its eventual crystallization in this temperate, earth-bound New Democracy with its sober problems of hard work and slow progress.

Politically, too, Ting Ling found that she had much to learn in Yenan—more than many women less brilliant and famous than herself. The issue was the women's movement in the Border Region, in which she and other radical feminists played an important part until their demands for various special rights for women came up for severe public criticism in 1942. Their views were still based on attitudes formed in the man-centered, antifeminist society of old China, they were told. They ignored the fact that full sex equality had already been established here and that for the sake of victory and progress the problem for both men and women was now to get on with the practical tasks of improving cooperation between all social groups. Their continued emphasis on narrow feminism was outdated and harmful.

The problem merged with others of a similar character and it was solved in the process of the movement for the Remolding of Ideology by which old party members learned to adapt their political ideas to the changed conditions of the New Democracy.

Ting Ling realized her mistake, became interested in political theory, of which, she said, she had known much too little, and spent two years of study in the Party School—not grudgingly like a defeated prima donna, but with the same stubborn determination to find the right way which characterized her literary career.

She was enthusiastic about the teaching she did while she was learning in the Party School. "I helped young writers from the peasantry improve their style and I still consider this one of my most important tasks," she said. "Some of the boys and girls who have grown up here during the ten years since the agrarian revolution are probably more gifted than we old writers and they know the people and the problems which must become the subject of our literature. But most of them cannot write well and have much to learn. A fusion of their gifts and ours will make the new literature one day."

She was not certain which type of writer would win the future—the native talent, after overcoming the drawbacks of prolonged illiteracy, or the veteran intellectuals like herself, once they master the subject matter of the new society and have sufficiently remolded themselves to be really part of it.

Ting Ling's present work is to learn and teach new methods of journalistic reporting. "We still have to learn good reportage," she said. "Well-written, fascinating newspaper reports about the life and work and the problems of our people as they affect the New Democracy are more important at present than literature. We are still bad at that. The literary people don't like that kind of work, and the newspaper reporters don't have the necessary training to write well enough. I want to develop a new style of reporting on these matters and am learning and teaching it at the same time."

She spends months on end in factories or villages, living with the people, getting acquainted with their problems, helping them in their cultural work, teaching young factory and village "correspondents" to write worth-while reports for the wall newspapers and the county weeklies. From time to time the *Liberation Daily* publishes one of her articles, from which young writers learn all over the Communist-controlled areas. And some of her old colleagues are following her example.

Men and women and school children adore Ting Ling. They know of her past fame, but it matters little. They love her for what she is and for what she does to help them.

Most of the people of the New Democracy, struggling with the

258

handicap of acquiring fuller literacy in the world's most complicated script, are not ready yet for the reading of novels. Ting Ling, by her simple, lively newspaper records, her influence in all cultural fields, and the occasional stories she tells at village and factory meetings, gives them what they want.

Chapter Twenty-seven

A PEOPLE GOES TO SCHOOL

THE Border Region seems like a big elementary school in which almost everybody, young and old, is eager to learn and—if at all possible—to teach.

The system of primary and middle schools and universities is only a small part of the all-embracing educational network the Communists have spread over the areas under their control.

All those organizations they have established to push the war effort and social progress—army and militia units, party branches, self-governments and mass associations, factories and cooperatives, hospitals, theaters, and newspapers—have also educational functions. And all the policies of the New Democracy, no matter what their specific subjects may be, are primarily of an educational nature.

All those means of civic instruction, practical, concrete, and popular, reach more people and spread knowledge in a more effective way than the schools can do. The school system itself is less advanced and settled than that great system of political education. The Communists confess that they have made more mistakes in matters of school education than in any other field.

They were faced with an appalling problem when they began their work: about 90 per cent of the people of the Border Region were completely illiterate and their general standard of knowledge was extremely low, even by comparison with most other parts of China.

The Communists decided on a frontal offensive from two sides. As a short cut to literacy for young and old they replaced the complicated Chinese script by a simple system of phonetic Latinization, using the twenty-six letters of our alphabet and a few from the Russian to trans-

260

literate the monosyllabic sounds of the thousands of word pictures in which Chinese has been written since the dawn of civilization. And to lay the basis for quick advancement of the young generation, they prescribed compulsory education for children. Both revolutionary policies were pushed with characteristic energy.

But the Communists failed in both. They had been too radical, too much in advance of their time. And the people told them so, in no uncertain terms, although the New Democracy and its system of self-government had not begun to function then.

In village meetings and in talks with party officials, plain peasants said that they wanted the old Chinese script for their children and for themselves. If they were to learn reading and writing it must be in the script in which the officials, the landlords, and merchants read and wrote and in which all the books were printed. The gentry and many intellectuals spoke up: "You don't have the facilities to reprint all the necessary literature in the new script. You cannot reeducate overnight those who are already literate. You must first unify the dialects which pronounce the script signs in many different ways, or introduce standard Mandarin Chinese as a universal second language, and that would take you dozens of years, even in peacetime."

The phonetic Latinization of Chinese writing did not become popular. Those who learned it—quickly and efficiently enough—remained an isolated group, like people who speak Esperanto.

There was equally strong popular opposition to compulsory school education. "We want our children to learn," the peasants said, "but it is too early to force them to go to school. We are poor and short of labor and your new production drive sets us great tasks, so that we need most of our children in the fields. Our villages are so small and scattered that the way to the few schools would take them hours every day. You have too few teachers, and we are not sure that what our children learn in your new schools is really useful to them and us." And many of the peasants refused to send their children to school.

The Communists realized their mistakes and gave up both policies for the time being, although their final aims remained the same. Compulsory education would have to be postponed for a few years until

economic and school improvements had caught up. And the Latinization of the script would have to be shelved for a generation or so, until
the unification of the spoken language—an absolute necessity for a truly
modern China—was accomplished in years of peace and political unity.

A new offensive against illiteracy was launched with even greater
energy. This time by educational guerrilla tactics which use every possible way of infiltration, consider no means of attack too unorthodox
and primitive, and enlist everybody's initiative in order to push ahead.

The mass movements were used to make the learning of a selected
list of something like one thousand Chinese characters a popular
pastime and a matter of keen individual and group competition. All
potential instructors were stimulated to voluntary cooperation with the
slowly increasing numbers of professional teachers—local party and
government officials, members of the old rural scholar-gentry, and
especially the "small teachers," that is, school children who pass on
their newly acquired knowledge to other children or adults. "Character
learning" became the craze in the Border Region; and the first goal, to
be able to read the *Mass Newspaper* with its "only" 1,000 hieroglyphic
characters, became a kind of promised land to young and old who were
thirsty for knowledge.

Publicity secured many imitators for inventive pioneers who worked
out new approaches to the reading problem, like the farmer who had
single characters written on large boards which he put up at the end
of his field, memorizing them while he ploughed. As a result, 80 per
cent of the people of the Border Region are now supposed to know a
minimum of 3 to 400 characters. And many of the active elements in
villages, factories, and elsewhere who could not read and write a
year ago have surpassed the stage of literacy of the *Mass Newspaper*
and approached or even reached that of the normal newspaper, the
Liberation Daily.

New types of schools were created, especially in remote rural areas,
for both children and adults—"people-managed" schools in which local
volunteers teach from Yenan-provided textbooks, according to the
specific needs of the pupils; "cooperative-run" schools, which use the

staff of cooperative societies as teachers not only of reading and writing but also of other practical subjects for their members; and "mobile winter schools," staffed by normal-school and university students on leave who provide short, intense courses for children, adults, and local amateur teachers.

The regular primary schools were improved and parents were consulted on their curricula in order to make them more practical in general and to adapt them to the needs of particular regions. Great efforts were made to train new teachers and raise the qualifications of old-timers. Textbooks were revised and re-revised to incorporate the experiences of model schools as well as amateur schools.

In consequence of all those changes and of the simultaneous improvement in the economic situation in the villages, school attendance is now much greater than it was during the period of compulsory education. It increases more and more rapidly, and I met several primary-school teachers who were as happy about the inrush of new pupils as shopkeepers are about new customers. "Never mind if it means more work," one of them said, "it proves that we are on the right way and that the people realize it."

I visited one of the model primary schools—unannounced, to be certain that I would see it in its normal routine. It was clean and apparently well run, cheerful, and with a natural sort of discipline which had no trace of regimentation. The children "administer" themselves through elected students' committees, which also decide on whatever disciplinary measures may be necessary.

The age limits are extremely flexible, so that pupils from six to thirteen, seven to fifteen, eight to nineteen, and so on, sit together in various grades, according to the time they have spent in school and their knowledge. The teachers said that the competition between those age groups proves to be stimulating to all. The older pupils have additional lessons after school and usually pass quickly from one grade to another.

Apart from ordinary primary-school lessons, a number of special subjects are taught. New agricultural techniques are practiced in connection with the production work by which all schools contribute to the meals of the children and the maintenance of the schools. Much stress is laid on modern hygiene and sanitation and on *yangko* folk dances. Special writing lessons teach the children the type of letters they will have to compose for illiterate peasants in their home villages.

The teachers, like all cadres in the Communist-controlled regions, spend two hours every day on the "self-study" of general and specific subjects in which they lack knowledge, and I got the impression that they are keenly interested in reading all they can lay their hands on. Their little private libraries of Yenan-printed books cover a wide range, and the questions they put to me about the latest developments in the outside world showed considerable knowledge.

Yenda, Yenan University, is a primitive institution by Western standards. But it seemed much more in harmony with the needs of China than the more orthodox universities I saw in Kuomintang territories. My first and strongest impression at Yenda was of the uniformly robust health of students and teachers by contrast with the pitiful state of undernourishment of the teachers and almost all but the well-to-do students in universities on the Chungking side.

I did not see one person in Yenda who showed either of the two characteristics which I met so frequently in Kuomintang universities: that prevalent expression of frustration from physical weakness and intellectual regimentation of students and teachers whose work is a pathetic and often unsuccessful struggle against formidable odds; or that less frequent air of self-satisfaction and cockiness of the wealthy or politically well connected for whom life is easy and a good career certain.

The Yenda people seem more like the soldiers or factory workers of Yenan: men and women with a simple enthusiasm for their practical tasks, in many cases quite unintellectual and even primitive by the standards of China's sophisticated upper class.

The courses in Yenda's Administrative and Natural Science Colleges take three years and those in the Art and Literature College two. All devote much of their time to general education, not only because the basic knowledge of freshmen is on a rather low level, but mainly because it is felt that the specialists the New Democracy needs must be acquainted with all aspects of its life and must be trained in its political principles. "All their thought must be directed toward benefiting the masses of the people with what they do," the president of Yenda told me, "and they must be versed in the mental technique of taking a scientific approach to all practical problems. Democracy and science as methods of thinking and working, taught on the basis of the development of the modern world, are therefore the main subjects of our general education for all students. For our purpose is to produce cadres, responsible workers, for the New China we are building up."

The "practical work-and-study periods"—six months each year in the Natural Science College and three months in the others—are considered of special importance to keep the students in close contact with society and to accustom them to their future tasks. According to their particular subjects, the students spend that period at local government offices, law courts, banks, or schools; in arsenals, factories, and public works; in theatrical or folk-dance groups touring the countryside; in newspaper offices or wherever else they can combine their continued theoretical studies or special research work with instructive and useful practical work. About 20 per cent of their time at Yenda is spent in production work. This has the threefold purpose of achieving self-support for the university, acquainting the students with modern methods of agriculture, and preventing them from developing into the type of intellectuals who are out of touch with the reality of life in the society they are to serve.

But they have no vacations and work long hours, so that they seem to be able to acquire considerable knowledge during the two or three years of their intensive training.

Chiao Yang, president of Yenda at thirty-six, is a Communist intellectual of the Old Guard, well known as a writer. He was the son of a rich landlord, studied English literature in Shanghai, and came to Marxism by way of English philosophy. When he had to flee from the White Terror of the Kuomintang he went to Japan—and to jail—because he participated in the Japanese Marxist movement.

He did not deny that Marxism is the ideological basis of Yenda's educational policies, although part of the faculty and many of the students are not members of the Communist party. But he stressed the fact that the main aim of the university is to help in the realization of the New Democracy and that this has done away with narrow dogmatism.

Nor did he deny the rather primitive character of Yenda's present curricula and the need for aiming at higher scholastic standards for freshmen and especially for graduates. "Our educational system is developing with the general progress of our regions," he said, "and we must not rush too far ahead of it.

"We started on a much more primitive level. Until 1939 we had no means or time for anything but specialized short-term training courses to meet the most urgent needs of the army and of mass mobilization in general. They were naturally superficial.

"After 1939 we made the mistake of going to the other extreme. The separate colleges which were later merged into Yenda adopted regular university curricula of the kind Chungking is using. This isolated us from the people and their needs, in almost the same manner in which Chungking's universities are isolated from them. And we had to change. To bring education on all levels into harmony with the actual conditions of the people under the New Democracy was one of the main purposes of the movement for the Remolding of the Ideology within the party, and the reforms we carried out during the last three years have brought about great improvements.

"We have now achieved that state of synthesis between scientific and practical work which corresponds to the requirements of our regions at the present time and have linked our higher education with the needs of the masses of our people.

"Before we can raise the level of our higher education, we have to accomplish the double task at which our entire educational system is now working in Yenda, in the Party School, and in every organization —to give more practice and experience to our theorists, and to raise and refine the theoretical knowledge and understanding of our practical cadres. Especially the cadres who are natives of the Border Region and

266

the other areas under our control are still in need of summing up their practical experiences on a higher theoretical level."

The educators of Yenan have emerged from the experimental stage and have learned from their mistakes. The way ahead seems clear to them. But they are anxious to raise the educational level of the masses together with that of their university graduates and to prevent the development of an intellectual upper stratum which is far above the people for whom it is to work.

"This is the main difference between our educational policies and those the Kuomintang has taken over from old China," Chiao Yang said, "and the main reason why we are more successful with our seemingly primitive but realistic methods of education."

I doubt whether the purely scholastic standards of graduates from universities in Kuomintang China are much higher today than those of Yenda; for their advantages of better equipment and better trained teachers are probably offset by the low vitality from which most of the students and teachers suffer on account of undernourishment and intellectual suppression.

But I am certain that the men and women from Yenda have greater practical knowledge of the kind that is required in wartime China. They have a much better understanding of what the people need and how they can be made to cooperate. They get much better opportunities of helping in the war and in social progress.

They are luckier than the numerous idealists I met among university graduates on the Chungking side, who would gladly undergo another spell of undernourishment, in any of the local government organizations in little towns and villages where educated young people are so badly needed—if only they were enabled to do genuine reform work and help the people.

Chapter Twenty-eight

HOW THEY CHEAT DEATH

TO SAVE the wounded, cure the sick, and raise the standard of health of 90,000,000 people in the backward, isolated regions of the Communists is a constant struggle with material and human deficiencies scarcely imaginable to the American reader. Nowhere else in the world, it seems, have surgery, medicine, and public hygiene ever been improvised on such a large scale, so primitively, yet so effectively.

I remembered the advice of a Chinese missionary doctor in Chungking when I began to study the medical situation in Yenan. "Look first of all into the basic state of health of the people," he had said. "Their power of resistance to disease and of recovery is more important than anything else. In our part of China low rates of resistance and recuperation, due to malnutrition and insufficient winter clothing, are a greater cause of preventable death than our lack of medical supplies and personnel. I wonder how it is on the Communist side."

I asked the American doctor who has been working at the International Peace Hospital in Yenan for six years, George "Ma Hai-teh," who steadfastly refuses to give his American family name.

"Until some time ago," he said, "we saw terrible numbers of undernourished people in our hospitals and outpatient departments. But there have been no such cases during the last two years or so. Resistance to disease is now perfectly normal. Not by the low Chinese peacetime standards, but by American standards.

"Our mortality rates, post-operational and from disease, are now scarcely higher in the Border Region than they were back home in the States in 1936.

"I should think this is pretty good testimony of what has been done here for the basic health of the people. Especially if you consider the fundamental poverty and backwardness of these regions in the past and the primitive conditions in our hospitals. For we suffer from an infinitely greater shortage of personnel, equipment, and medicines than the Kuomintang areas, as you will be able to judge for yourself.

"The basis for the success of our difficult medical work is the realization of the economic goal set by Mao Tse-tung several years ago—first of all, soldiers and civilians must be well fed and well clad. The people are well fed and well clad now. You don't need expert medical opinion for that. Just look at them. And compare what you see here with what you saw in the Kuomintang regions."

The truth of George's statement was evident. Day after day I was amazed at the way the Communists had succeeded in this poorest part of China to make all the people so well fed, while Chungking's crowds looked pathetically undernourished against the background of all the natural and commercial wealth of Szechuan, one of China's richest provinces. . . .*

George took us to the Bethune Memorial International Peace Hospital, where he works together with Chinese doctors. It is the parent institution of the International Peace Hospitals.

Dr. Norman Bethune, the great Canadian surgeon and humanist of the American-Canadian League for Peace and Democracy to whom the hospital is dedicated, fought with the Spanish Republicans and the Chinese Communists and died at the China front in consequence of an infection received while operating on the wounded. His name is venerated like that of few others in the Communist areas.

The hospital is an unusual place. Rows of caves in a steep, yellow hillside are its wards, with over two hundred beds. The doctors' and nurses' caves at the bottom of the hill are surrounded by vegetable gardens where all the staff, and even patients who are well enough, do

* "A study of the Child Health Society of China of 5,486 pupils attending fourteen primary schools in Chungking in March, 1945, disclosed that only 3.03 per cent of all children were normally nourished; 59.6 per cent were undernourished; and 37.29 per cent were terribly in need of nutrition. The eyes of 64.98 per cent of all children were suffering from trachoma." (Chungking broadcast, April 4, 1945.)

269

their production work. Only the two operating theaters are in a building, small but almost luxurious in its solid brick structure, with real glass windows and cement floors, and in the gleaming whiteness of its interior.

The "corridors" and "elevators" of the hospital are steep, narrow paths, slippery with mud when it rains. The hospital has no electricity, no running water, and no pressure sterilizers. The only X-ray set is practically unserviceable for lack of spare parts and films. The two microscopes are of only restricted usefulness because there are no modern incubators for bacterial cultures and no essential dyestuffs for the preparation of slides.

The surgical, medical, and laboratory equipment—partly captured from the Japanese—would be considered insufficient for the poorest country hospitals anywhere in the United States, both in quality and quantity. Yet the hospital works and works well. It is a matter of envy to all those who come from the Anti-Japanese War Bases, where even the most primitive surgical equipment is lacking.

On my way through the various departments I saw instrument sterilizers made of old gasoline cans, catgut containers used as test tubes, cuticle scissors serving the ophthalmologists for eye operations, and strange contraptions of old dye cans and cardboard for eye testing. I heard of doctors who for days carried test tubes with bacterial cultures on their bodies to secure the even temperature which is needed for their growth. In the wards there were water drippers made by nurses as substitutes for watches; for only two or three people in the whole hospital own a watch. An old caretaker sitting in his cave had the task of ringing a gong whenever the punks burning on a little table in front of him showed that half an hour had passed—for there is no clock.

Wires with bells on them were extended outside each row of ward caves, with strings branching off to the patients' beds. Nurses were running into the caves when a bell tinkled.

The pharmacy, housed in several interconnected caves, was scrupulously clean and apparently well organized. "Look what the Kuomintang's strict medicine blockade means to us," George said, opening a little drawer with a few half-empty bottles and boxes. "These are all

270

the modern medicines we have. And here is our most precious treasure
—less than one hundred tablets of various sulfa drugs. Several doctors
have to agree in consultation that a few of them are needed as an absolute lifesaver before any may be used.

"But we help ourselves as well as we can. They can't prevent us from
that." He pointed at the large shelves along the walls, filled with jars
and bottles neatly marked in Chinese, English, and German. "All those
medicines we make ourselves."

This is how Yenan overcame part of its medicine problem. Every
item in the huge pharmacopoeia of traditional Chinese herb medicine
was clinically tested by modern medical standards through years of
hard scientific work. Many useful ingredients were found, new composi-
tions were devised, dosages were fixed, and hundreds of substitute
medicines, in pills, tablets, powders, and mixtures, are now produced on
a large scale from local raw materials, together with some simple
Western-style drugs.

The pharmaceutical factory outside Yenan is developing from year
to year and many smaller factories have sprung from it all over the
Communist-controlled war areas. Many of the old-fashioned herb
doctors are using these new drugs and doing less harm and more good
to their patients than they used to do with their traditional prescrip-
tions.

"We also make smallpox vaccines," George said, "and quite a number of injections, like sheep-liver extract on the basis of the Lilly
formula. Being economical, we use the guts of the sheep we kill for
their livers to make a substitute catgut for surgical sutures, and their
bones to make medical charcoal. We also produce our own glass am-
poules for injections. Quite an enterprise, as you see.

"As a substitute for certain essential drugs, or rather as a substitute
therapy, we use blood transfusion in cases where it would not normally
be necessary, and we often get good results. We have no facilities for
storing blood, so that doctors, nurses, medical students, and relatives
of patients have to serve as blood donors.

"But for many of our most urgent problems no makeshift solution is possible. For example, local anesthesia is becoming almost impossible, since the medical administration of the Border Region with all its military and civilian hospitals has only five grams of cocaine left."

The ward caves made an excellent impression. They were whitewashed, bright, and airy. Each had six to eight beds, as clean and well kept as the caves themselves. On the walls were temperature charts, woodcuts, and war maps. The patients looked well cared for and as comfortable as the apparently devoted nurses could make them under difficult conditions.

I had seen a good number of army, government, private, and mission hospitals in Kuomintang China, but none were so clean and efficient and seemed to breathe such a cheerful atmosphere of genuine service to the sick as this primitive cave hospital.

More than half of the patients were soldiers or members of their families; for the International Peace Hospitals are mainly for the army.

George showed us one wounded soldier after another. "And they dared tell you in Chungking that the Communist armies did not fight and you would not see any wounded here in Yenan? Of course, we get only very few cases from the front, only men who are in need of special treatment, for the journey takes weeks and even months. But you can see hundreds more, and thousands of disabled men, around Yenan."

In the medical section several wards were occupied by soldiers suffering from relapsing fever. "They take up thirty of our badly needed beds. They will have to stay for many weeks. A good number of them we may not be able to cure, and some of them will most probably die. All that because we don't have any Neosalvarsan, of which one single shot cures a patient almost immediately and for good."

I understood his feelings only too well, for I knew that Neosalvarsan, like almost any pharmaceutical product from the United States or Britain, can be bought freely in Chungking, Sian, and other cities in Kuomintang territory where the numerous private medicine shops are completely free from government control and surprisingly well stocked with hoarded and smuggled supplies and with goods stolen from Red

272

Cross consignments. Those shops sell to anybody who can afford their usurious prices—no matter whether he needs the medicine for treatment or wants to store it as a safe capital investment.

The International Peace Hospital in Yenan is well off by comparison with hospitals elsewhere in the Border Region and the Communist war areas.

We saw an army hospital serving a unit of about ten thousand men. Its surgical instruments, old and dull, could easily have been carried away in one hand. Half a dozen quinine pills and a little bottle with a watery solution of Mercurochrome were all its "modern-style" medicines. Every one of us, including most of our Kuomintang colleagues, was much impressed with the poverty of the little hospital and the brave way in which its staff seemed to be carrying on.

We were resting outside the hospital when somebody recalled the most notorious incident of the Kuomintang's medicine blockade against the Communist-controlled areas, well known to foreigners in Chungking. Years ago, American and British friends had sent the Communist armies four truckloads of the most urgently needed lifesaving drugs and precious surgical instruments. The Chungking authorities held them up for years in spite of semidiplomatic efforts to get them released. Mme. Sun Yat-sen, the widow of the founder of the Republic and the Kuomintang, interceded with Generalissimo Chiang Kai-shek, her brother-in-law. But the trucks were eventually confiscated and not one ounce of the supplies ever reached Yenan.

A young officer, Ma Han-ping, the son of a wealthy Chinese family in Burma who had joined the Eighth Route Army as a medical student, had listened with rising emotion. Suddenly he jumped up, shouting, "At the front, two years ago, I was with one of our commanders, a great fighter. The Japs wounded him in the head. The doctors knew his life would have been saved had we had only one of the special instruments which were on those trucks."

He turned to the Kuomintang members of our party, his voice trembling with hatred and his eyes flashing.

"Those instruments were ours. They were given to us by our American and British friends. Your government had no right to take them away."

And then to us, in fluent English: "This will explain to you who was responsible for the death of that brave commander, and for the deaths of many other fighters . . . who murdered them.

"I am sorry. . . . I lose my self-control when I think of all that. . . . I cannot help it. . . . I have seen too many die who could have been saved even with those few truckloads."

I heard much about the work of the Army Medical Service of the Eighth Route Army in the war areas from Dr. Hans C. Mueller, who had just returned to Yenan after almost five years at the front. He is a young, half-Jewish refugee from Germany who had studied medicine in Switzerland before he came to China early in 1939 to help in the fight against aggression.

I asked him to tell me in some detail about a hospital station where he had been working recently.

"It was in a little village at the front," he said. "As usual, there was no real hospital building of any kind because we have to be mobile all the time and cannot think of establishing permanent quarters.

"The peasants are always willing to let us have rooms for our wounded and sick, and we had rooms for a few men each in about fifty houses. In the best house of the village a medium-sized room was thoroughly cleaned and whitewashed for use as our operating theater.

"How many properly qualified doctors we had at the station?" Mueller laughed. "None. I was not on regular duty there. The army used me mainly as consultant for difficult cases and I always spent much time traveling from place to place in our military district which has nine base hospitals, twenty-seven hospital stations like the one I am describing, and *altogether* two properly qualified men, both fresh from medical school: myself and a Japanese captive, a fine fellow who soon responded to the antimilitaristic education of the Communists and after a year or two joined the party. He does excellent, responsible work and I trust him as much as the Eighth Route Army people do.

"The hospital station itself had four so-called doctors, men who had

274

been illiterate a comparatively short time ago, who never went to a medical college, and learned all they know as nurses and doctors' assistants. Two of them are quite good, one is bad, and the other very bad. Medically bad, I mean; for those men, like all the doctors I met at the front, are keen, devoted, courageous, and do their very best.

"The problem at the front, however, is not so much the deficiency of medical knowledge as the terrible lack of instruments and medicines. Under those circumstances better doctors could do little more than those men who have at least learned all about correct wound treatment, which in itself is of inestimable advantage in China. They are doing much better on wound treatment, I am told, than the army medical service on the Kuomintang side.

"Do you know anything about first aid in the Kuomintang army?" Mueller asked me.

I told him about a pathetic few hours I had spent with a British doctor in a Red Cross hospital in the Kuomintang part of Central China, at the end of 1943. Taking me through his surgical wards full of wounded soldiers, he kept on explaining to me at one bed after the other that this man would live . . . that another need not have had an amputation . . . that this one could be fighting again by now . . . if only the medical service people had taught their doctors and nurses the elements of first-aid wound treatment in the dressing stations. . . .

Mueller continued, "Apart from the four 'doctors,' our hospital station has about twenty-five nurses, mostly 'little devil' orderlies, local boys who joined voluntarily to do their bit. Some of them do the rough work. Having gone through that stage and got one hour's daily education for a while, they begin to do actual nursing duties. When they are experienced in that, they do dressings and injections and assist the doctors. They make first-class nurses. That is probably the main reason for the comparative success of the primitive medical service of the Communists. For those nurses really love their work and their patients and do their very best for them. The simple political education they get is excellent.

"The hospital stations and the medical service as a whole are not cluttered with auxiliary personnel, for everything has to be highly mobile. Apart from a few stretcher-bearers in the fighting units themselves, we rely for all services on the peasants. They act as stretcher-bearers and do our cooking for us, with the exception of special diets, which are taken care of by 'little devils.'

"But our hospital station, like every other, has three or four political workers. You may be surprised and suspicious, as I was at first. But those men are the busiest and in many respects the most essential of all the staff. They mobilize the people to help us and show them how to do it. They keep up the morale of the wounded and sick and of the staff when conditions are grim. They help carry wounded, do nursing and all sorts of odd jobs when we have a sudden inrush of casualties. They inspect the food; they organize efficient evacuation when we have to move before the enemy; they propagandize, organize, and work; but I have never found them arrogant, dogmatic, or rude to anybody. They are the spirit behind it all and a very good type of people.

"Our equipment in the hospital station is incredibly poor. Amputations have to be made with ordinary saws we borrow from the peasants. Scalpels are made locally in every war base, from rails our soldiers rip up from the Jap-occupied railroads. But they are not keen enough and rust. We get all sorts of medical odds and ends which our troops capture from Japanese first-aid stations and our guerrillas can still buy certain Japanese supplies from occupied cities. All those Jap-made materials, however, have become scarcer and worse in quality.

"Can you imagine that there is now not one complete set of surgical instruments any more in that whole region with its thirty-six hospitals and hospital stations? The only one we had was mine. I had brought it from Switzerland and lost it through an unfortunate accident during a Japanese surprise attack."

Mueller was furious when I told him about the allegations in Chungking and Sian that the Eighth Route Army had not been fighting the enemy since 1937. "What a malicious lie," he said. "From 1939 on I have always been at the front. There was always action. I have been in many fights myself. Some were really on a large scale. For instance,

I was right in the middle of one of the big battles of the widespread Communist offensive in 1940, called the Hundred Regiments Campaign; and then, the year after, in the thick of that terrible mopping-up campaign in which the enemy used 200,000 Japs and puppets against much smaller forces on our side. I have seen the Eighth Route Army fight year after year, always attacking wherever there was a chance. I have seen thousands and thousands of our own wounded."

"Give me an estimate of how many you think you have seen altogether," I asked him.

He calculated for some time. "Within my own inspection zone, traveling around during those years and not counting the many months I myself was laid up with typhus, typhoid, and dysentery, I must have seen at least 9,000 wounded. That means 9,000 major cases.

"Those people in Chungking don't know what the Communist troops are going through. But I do. I have starved with them for periods of more than a week at a time in territories the Japs had burned and pillaged clean. I have moved with the troops in actual fighting for several weeks at a stretch with barely any sleep. I have seen how they care for their wounded and for the stricken civilians in the most difficult circumstances. I have seen many Japanese prisoners and treated a good number of them. But I have never seen any sign of the Communists attacking Kuomintang troops.

"You can tell them in Chungking how this primitive medical service saves its wounded when the enemy comes and when no troops can be spared from the actual fighting lines to protect us. I wonder whether there is anything like that on the Kuomintang side.

"I worked once at a big branch of the International Peace Hospital near the front. We were suddenly surrounded by powerful enemy forces while our own units, which could not send any troops for our protection, were fighting a considerable distance away. What did our people do? The 600 patients were scattered and hidden in the hillsides in small natural caves, in holes that were quickly dug for them, and in bushes. And the nurses, those 'little devil' orderlies, were running all night from one hiding place to another with food, water, dressing materials, and medicines.

"The political workers of the hospital who organized all this outwitted the Japs, for they killed or captured only fifty-seven of the staff and the patients."

Mueller asked me, "Have you met General Peng Teh-huai, the vice-commander in chief of the Eighth Route Army?"

I said I had and thought he was a good man.

"A good man? He is a marvelous man, a wonderful man. He commanded the area where I worked. I got to know him very well. I want to tell you a story about him to show you the spirit of those people.

"He developed a serious stomach ailment and suffered badly, which is the reason why he is in Yenan now. The other doctors and I put him on a strict special diet. He would not make an exception for himself and continued eating the same coarse food as the men although he was in constant pain. The political commissars at our headquarters had to inform Yenan. Peng got his orders and obeyed us at last.

"I admire those Eighth Route Army people. That was the reason why I stayed on and lived on millet and wheat, without most of the things I like in life and without a chance to improve my medical education—although I am not a Communist and, with all my hatred for Fascism, not at all interested in politics."

In Yenan, Dr. Mueller met one of those "apprentice doctors" who are in the majority among the medical officers at the front, and brought him along one afternoon for an interview. This is the story twenty-two-year-old "Doctor" Chang Chih-hsien told me.

At the age of thirteen, he and five other boys in a village of Szechuan province joined the Red Army on the last leg of its Long March to the present Border Region. As a "little devil" orderly, he did nursing and simple pharmacy work for one or two years before he began assisting an old Red Army doctor at the front against the Japanese. In the meantime he had improved his trifling knowledge of Chinese writing and read the books which the Eighth Route Army's medical department prints especially for such "apprentice doctors": books on anatomy and physiology, medicine and surgery, which I was told are quite good and modern.

278

During the last few years he did a doctor's routine duties in cooperation with better qualified men, and he is now in charge of a small out-of-the-way hospital.

"I still feel rather weak in theory and in surgery," he said, "but I am not afraid of medical diagnosis and treatment. My death rate has been low; better than that of most other doctors. But I am now getting a really good opportunity to improve my knowledge. I was just told that I will be admitted to the China Medical College here in Yenan. I am very happy about it."

The young fellow made an excellent impression, intelligent, thoughtful, and modest. Dr. Mueller said in all seriousness that if he were to suffer from any internal trouble he would confidently entrust himself to Chang. "He actually beat me at a difficult diagnosis," Mueller grinned, "in the case of an infant with a severe case of pneumonia. Chang insisted the child's toxic state was the result not only of pneumonia but that there were definite symptoms of meningitis, too. I did not believe him. But he was right."

The China Medical College in Yenan with its teaching staff of 15 well-educated and experienced men trains at present 210 students in medicine and surgery of whom 65 had formerly been "apprentice doctors" in the army, while most of the others are middle- and primary-school graduates. Various other medical institutions turn out about 100 doctors each year.

Both teachers and students in the college give the impression of being people who ignore their appalling handicaps and push ahead enthusiastically with their work. Their mimeographed textbooks are translations from the few obsolescent American, British, German, and Japanese standard works which happened to find their way into the Border Region, or collections of lectures of the most experienced among the college teachers.

The walls of the various departments are covered with medical drawings made by students and teachers, charts analyzing hospital experiences, pictures of the leading scientists of all ages and countries, work records kept by the students, and encouraging slogans. The lack of equipment and working material is pathetic.

There is an almost solemn atmosphere of seriousness everywhere. The students know they have only three years for their theoretical studies; but they mean to use their time as well as possible.

The college has its own hospital, a well-run branch of the Bethune Memorial International Peace Hospital in which the students work already before their one year's internship so that they may make up in practical experience what they miss in theoretical training.

Over the platform of the college's large auditorium is a hand-written message of Mao Tse-tung: "Save the people from death; help the wounded; carry out revolutionary humanism."

By contrast with these demands, scores of boy and girl students were sitting on the floor of the hall, spinning cotton yarn when we looked in. It was their leisure time, we were told, and everyone in the Border Region was supposed to participate in the production movement, no matter how important his professional duties might be.

At the end of our visit the director of the college asked for our criticism. Some of us told him we thought that medical students, being so urgently needed and having only three years for their studies, should be free from production tasks. A few weeks later the suggestion had been accepted, and no more spinning and agricultural work is now done by the students and staff of the Medical College.

From all I heard and saw I have no doubt that the soldiers and the masses of the people are already getting better medical services in the Communist-controlled part of China than they do on the Kuomintang side where administrative shortcomings impede the full use of much greater human and material facilities. Whatever medical supplies there are on the Yenan side go to the people who need them most, not to the highest bidders. And the army comes first, not last.

The doctors in the Yenan territories serve where they are of most use, instead of continuing in overcommercialized private practices—like the experienced doctors in the Kuomintang areas who are not conscripted into the army and who can scarcely be expected to join voluntarily under the present condition of the medical service because that would mean condemning their families to virtual starvation and themselves to a futile bureaucratic routine.

"The most important factor in our medical work," one of the doctors in Yenan told me, "is the encouragement we get from the government, the party, and the army. Their policies are aimed at the full use of all available facilities for all who need them. They are always willing to listen to our suggestions. And they have inspired all our medical workers with an enthusiastic fighting spirit for victory and progress."

I thought of several friends in Chungking's medical profession— responsible men of liberal leanings in the medical administration and private and missionary doctors—how frustrated they are in their desire to make the best of the existing supplies and facilities for real service to the army and the people; how handicapped in their fight against corruption and inefficiency; and how disillusioned by the helpless indifference of the bureaucratic one-party dictatorship of the Kuomintang. . . .

Chapter Twenty-nine

MAN IS GOOD

D URING all the time I spent in the Border Region I was on the lookout for indications of secret-police activities of a terroristic nature. According to Kuomintang allegations they were an integral part of the Communist system.

The police is not much in evidence but seems on its guard. It consists of the uniformed policemen of Yenan and other municipalities, the people's militia in the rural areas, and a special organization along FBI lines under the Public Safety Department of the Border Region government.

The movement of all persons is controlled by a system of passes for overland travelers and for visitors to some important organs of the government and the party in Yenan. But those passes are apparently issued in a routine manner by the organizations in which people work, like government offices, factories, colleges, etc., or by local administrative authorities.

I got the impression that almost everybody is on the watch for spies —the police, the militia, the army, the government and party organs, and also the people themselves. For until recently spies seem to have been numerous in the Border Region—enemy spies from the near-by Japanese-occupied lines; and especially "home spies" of the three separate secret-police organizations of the Kuomintang army, party, and government which vie with one another for the best results of their anti-Communist work in the Border Region. But the constant vigilance against these underground forces seemed free from that element of hysteria which might lead to indiscriminate suspicion and to political terror against innocent people. Nor did I discover any tendency to use the need for protection against secret agents as a pretext for police control over the political thought of Communists and non-Communists.

On the contrary, I found a surprisingly lenient and sanguine attitude toward political offenders and other "antisocial elements" and toward crime in general, which seemed to indicate a break with the grim revolutionary methods the Communists practiced in the past. The conviction that man is not born evil and that most wrongdoers can be improved by proper social education apparently determines the judicial policies of Yenan. In recent years the Communists have come to believe that reform, rather than punishment, of offenders against the law is the proper basis of dealing with them under the New Democracy; just as mediation, rather than litigation, is the correct approach to the exercise of civil law. To "convert and win over" criminals and to "explain and arbitrate" quarrels between potential litigants are the main rules of their judicial practice.

I had my first lesson in the peculiarities of Yenan's judiciary system on a visit to the High Court of the Border Region, a compound of a few brick buildings and a number of caves high up on a hillside overlooking the fields of an experimental model farm.

Lei, meaning Thunder, is the name of the Chief Justice who is at the same time the head of the Border Region's judicial administration. But his name seems inappropriate, for he gives the impression of being a kindly humanist, has a great sense of humor, and is one of the most popular men of the Communist Old Guard.

After finishing his studies at a university in Shanghai, he joined the National Revolution and worked under Chiang Kai-shek in the Whampoa Military Academy. Having been "purged" from the Kuomintang at the time of Chiang Kai-shek's *coup d'état*, he organized a local Soviet in Kwangsi province and later took part in the Long March as a private soldier. Since 1937 he has been in charge of the administration of justice in the Border Region, and he is said to have helped Mao Tse-tung considerably in mellowing the Communists' judicial policies when the New Democracy was introduced.

Lei explained the simple structure of the judiciary. Each county has a judicial department and a lower court, both with the democratically elected county magistrate as their ex officio chief. Cases of appeal go to the High Court of the Border Region in Yenan or its branch high courts in the subregions, of which the elected subregional prefects are the ex officio heads.

"The main tasks of the law administration," he said, "are to defend the interests of the people, to maintain the new social order, and to assist the country in winning victory over Japan.

"Yet," he volunteered, "there are still defects in the practices of our judiciary. We are trying all the time to overcome them, and the criticism we get from the people is very helpful."

We asked him about the system of criminal-court procedure in the Border Region.

"Prosecution in the Western sense has been abolished for ordinary criminal cases," he said. "We gave the people themselves the right to act as prosecutors, although in certain cases, like those against spies, the Public Safety Bureau is entitled to lead the prosecution.

"I shall tell you in some detail of a criminal case which happened in this valley here, because it became important as a classic example for our dealings with such matters.

"There was a witch doctor, a wizard, as the people call them, who worked as a professional healer and had not come to the attention of the authorities before. He was asked by an uneducated woman, one of the many people in these regions still steeped in superstition, to treat her for bleeding after an abortion. He decided she was obsessed by a ghost which had to be driven out. So he applied red-hot irons to her face, tied her thumbs together, using chopsticks as tourniquets, stuck needles into her arms, beat her mercilessly, and eventually killed her."

A woman neighbor reported the death to the court, although most of the people in the little hamlet at first did not blame the wizard: he had not beaten the woman but only the ghost!

"Considering the case of great social importance, we decided on holding an open mass trial. A jury was formed from representatives of the borough's self-government and of the Women's, Workers', and Anti-Japanese People's Organizations. A friend of the accused was admitted as defense council. The session was attended by two thousand people.

284

"The wizard defended himself by saying that the woman was physically and mentally weak and that this was the reason why she died under his treatment. Peasants among the public spoke up and reported about former cases in which the man had killed people.

"The crowd was furious and demanded his execution. But the jury decided on manslaughter and the judge pronounced a sentence of five years' imprisonment, the highest term provided in the Criminal Code of the National Government."

"Do you mean to say that you base your judgments on the law codes of the National Government in Chungking?" we asked.

The chief judge smiled. "The fact is that we practice a good number of the national law codes which are not really applied in the Kuomintang territories. For example, the law for the prosecution of public officials is actually applied only in our areas. The same is true of the law against national traitors which the National Government promulgated shortly after the outbreak of war. It is true also of the marriage law, the factory law for the protection of workmen, and the law for the protection of tenant farmers which restricts rent payments to landlords to a maximum of 37.5 per cent of a tenant's crop. That important law was published by the National Government long before the war but never enforced.

"This does not mean that we apply every single paragraph of the National Government law. Certain features of it do not fit the conditions of our struggle against Japan and for genuine democracy. For example, national laws like that on censorship and details of other laws which contravene the real interests of the people and the requirements of the war are not being observed. But our judicial policies are based on the principles of the national law codes and their spirit.

"It has therefore become necessary for the Civil Affairs Department of the Border Region government and a special committee of the People's Political Council to draft certain specific laws, which were later approved by plenary meetings of the People's Political Council."

I asked him about the main differences between such new laws of the Border Region and the laws of the National Government.

"These are some examples," he said. "Life imprisonment has been abolished and prison terms in general have been shortened, the longest term now being five years. For we believe strongly in the possibility of reforming criminals. We have therefore also loosened the regulations on parole and release.

"Yes, capital punishment still exists. But we apply it only to that comparatively small number of political and other prisoners whom juries and judges consider unable to be converted into useful citizens. County courts can pronounce death sentences but the High Court has to try such cases again and the confirming sentence of the High Court has to be approved by the Political Affairs Committee of the Border Region government. From 1938 to the end of 1943 capital punishment has been imposed in 104 cases in the entire Border Region. Of these, 17 cases occurred in 1943. Execution is by shooting."

The judge continued his account of the changes in national law. "All procedure has been simplified for the convenience of the people. In the theoretically conceived Kuomintang codes it is often so complicated and causes so much expense that it goes against the interests of the people.

"In civil law, the principle of our revisions has been to subordinate the interest of individuals to that of the people as a whole and to subordinate temporary to long-term considerations."

The chief method of dispensation of civil law in the Communist-controlled areas at present is mediation. Court settlements are avoided wherever possible. The judicial workers of the government are available to the people for mediation, and the elected functionaries of various kinds of mass organizations, administrative officials, Labor Heroes, model workers, and other active elements who are respected by the people for their common sense and integrity are often called upon by the people to mediate for them.

"The system of mediation, having been popularized by educational campaigns, is spreading all the time and is highly successful. It is in consonance with the present stage of development of our society and our administration and helps us to promote a democratic spirit of reconciliation. But our emphasis on mediation does not rob the people of the right of having recourse to the courts. Mediation is always voluntary."

We asked Judge Thunder about the frequency of political cases before the courts and the ways they are dealt with. He gave us figures, most of which were displayed in the High Court room. The graphs on the walls looked faded and must have been there for considerable time.

"From 1938 to the end of 1943 altogether 769 political offenders were sentenced in the Border Region for activities detrimental to the war, while other sentences during the same period were 370 for the smuggling, sale, and use of opium, and 174 for manslaughter and murder. The 104 death sentences of which I spoke before concerned incorrigible enemy spies and other traitors, bandits, and murderers and a few cases of embezzlement and opium smuggling."

It appeared that the number of political trials had been decreasing from year to year because of the success of the Be Frank movement which induces people to confess and convert themselves, in which case they are not tried and punished. In 1943, only ninety political cases came before the courts.

"And how many persons are at present in jail in the entire Border Region?"

"Only about four hundred altogether, political cases and others. Fifty-one of them are in the jail next door."

There were several dozen men sitting in a little courtyard which was formed by a wall in front of a long row of caves. They were spinning cotton yarn. The men looked well fed and in normal health and wore faded, bluish cotton uniforms very much of the same type as those of their jailers and the chief judge who accompanied us.

We talked to them without any restriction. There was the wizard, a primitive-looking man whose conversion had made progress, according to the jail attendant, so that he would probably be released before his term expired. He seemed quite proud of himself when he told us that during his two or three years in jail he had for the first time in his adult life done honest work and that he wanted to make good as a farmer.

287

One of the political prisoners told us his story in the jail's club, a cave plastered with pictures and war maps, full of newspapers, magazines, books, parlor games, and primitive musical instruments.

"Soon after I had left the higher primary school, at the age of nineteen, my former principal offered to introduce me to the Blue Shirts (the secret Fascist organization of the Kuomintang), saying that I could get a good job through them. I was very poor, knew nothing about politics, and had no opportunity of getting a good start. So I accepted his offer. In the Blue Shirts they assigned me to an intelligence group which was just being organized. After some special education I was sent to the Border Region to report certain details about the Eighth Route Army.

"I had to disguise myself as a peddler and get information from the people. I communicated regularly by letter with an old man somewhere in the Border Region. For example, if I wanted to tell him that I had found out that there were so-and-so many Eighth Route Army men at a certain place, I would write that so-and-so many catties of pigs' bristles had been received and he understood and passed on that information.

"I also had the tasks of trying to make people antagonistic toward the Border Region government and to sabotage its effort to collect grain for the Eighth Route Army.

"Finally, I had to provide quarters for others who came with more dangerous assignments, like assassinating certain persons. In these ways I worked undetected for three years. I did not really like the work, but I continued because I needed the job and the money.

"One day a number of Kuomintang plain-clothes men came to my lodging. The Eighth Route Army was on their heels and I was arrested, while the others escaped. The court sentenced me to five years' imprisonment. I have now served two."

Inquiring in detail about the actual state of judicial affairs in the Border Region and the Anti-Japanese War Bases, I found the judge's statements confirmed by Communists, non-Communists, and the few foreigners in Yenan who had been living in those areas for several years.

Many of the modern laws promulgated by the National Government since 1928 but not applied in the Kuomintang areas really seem to be observed by the Communists. Their own supplementary laws are not of a revolutionary nature but in accordance with the general aims of the New Democracy.

Court procedure still lacks legal perfection, especially in the lower courts. But there are important compensating factors. It seems free from corruption and probably suffers less from bureaucratic red tape than is the case in other parts of China. The presiding judges in the county courts are popularly elected. Juries composed of fairly well-experienced representatives of mass organizations play a considerable role. And public opinion, being at the same time educated to a new awareness of the law, is taken into account in a primitive but apparently effective manner.

The mediation of most civil law cases is genuinely popular and seems to be handled with due consideration for common sense and the law. It is not a new method but has revived and improved the ancient custom of mediation which had fallen into disrepute, so that the common people seem to have a sense of being protected in their private interests which they have not had for centuries.

The mass movement which propagandizes mediation has given rise to another popular figure, the Mediation Labor Hero Ma Hsi-wu who, like the Farm Labor Hero Wu Men-yu, has done more than government orders can do to make the people enthusiastic about new ideas. This rustic Solomon is affectionately called the "Blue Sky" for the clarity and justice of his exemplary reconciliations.

The Policy of Magnanimity, with its aim of winning over and converting as many political and other offenders as possible, is no mere façade. It has indeed replaced the stern policies of punishment of the Civil War period.

This break with the past seems due to the conviction of the Communists that their new political order can no longer be overthrown by political enemies since the large majority of the non-Communist population is now definitely considered to be firmly on its side. The change of legal beliefs it implies would therefore seem to have a sounder basis than if it were merely the result of ideological experiment.

It must be genuine; for the slogan "Convert them and win them over," applying to all antisocial elements from loafers, thieves, and other "backward people" to Japanese war prisoners, "puppets," and "home spies," figures so prominently in the political propaganda campaigns of the mass movements that the Communists could not afford to counteract it in their judicial policies.

Chapter Thirty

LIGHT ON THE CRIME MYSTERIES

AT A tea party given us by writers, artists, and other cultural workers in Yenan shortly after our arrival, a nationally known publicist got up to make "a few remarks on a personal matter."

"I am Wu Pei-hsiao," he said, "and I protest against the announcement in Chungking and Sian newspapers that I was killed by the Communists. I protest against the so-called 'memorial meeting' held for me and twenty-three other 'cultural leaders with Kuomintang sympathies' by the Kuomintang authorities in Sian on March 29, 1944."

There was embarrassed silence among our Kuomintang colleagues as Wu turned to them, one by one. . . .

"You know me, don't you? And you know me. . . . And you know me. . . . As you see, I am alive and well. And I may add that I am happy here, living with my wife and children, writing what I like without being restricted by censorship.

"The Kuomintang slanders our Border Region in many ways. The allegation that I and many of my twenty-three colleagues were killed by the Communists is one of their slanders."

A few days later we met another of the "Living Corpses," as we came to call them, the former Trotskyite Wang Shi-wei, who came to the Guest House at our request. This was Wang's account.

"I joined the Communist party in 1936 without admitting my former Trotskyite affiliations and came to Yenan the year after. I expressed dissatisfaction with conditions in Yenan during the difficult period in 1941 when the Kuomintang blockade became so strict that we had a very critical time. I published a series of articles in the Communist *Liberation Daily* here in Yenan early that year in which I accused the Communist party of deterioration. After many discussion meetings I convinced myself that I had once more been under the influence of Trotskyite ideas.

"But my problems have all been solved. I was never detained or tried. The progress of the Border Region since that difficult period has proved to me even more strikingly than theoretical arguments did before that I was wrong and defeatist during our most critical period. However, the party treated me with its new Policy of Magnanimity and I was again accepted in its ranks soon after my resignation.

"You see that I am very much alive in spite of the 'memorial meeting' that was held in Sian for me and all those others who are equally alive. I have also talked to your Kuomintang colleagues, who know me personally."

The ghost of this man later crossed my path in the United States. One of the most widely read American magazines was led to believe and print a badly distorted story about Wang, projecting his past political opposition into the present and alleging his mysterious disappearance.

I met in Yenan more and more of the "Living Corpses," and brought pictures of them back to Chungking. Two of them told me that the entire group had planned to present itself to us soon after our arrival. But they had been asked to keep in the background since negotiations for an understanding between the Kuomintang and Communist parties were going on in Chungking, and Yenan did not want to disturb them through a demonstrative exposure of malicious Kuomintang allegations.

I was also anxious to follow up the grim stories about Yenan we had heard from inmates of the Kuomintang concentration camp at Sian. Nobody I asked seemed to know anything about those men and women in the Sian camp who had given us details about the places at which they said they had lived and worked in Yenan before they fled, disgusted with the traitorous practices of the Communists and anxious to get political reeducation in the camp in Sian.

One night, on leaving the director of the Party School after an interview, I asked him, as I had asked almost everybody I met, whether he could throw any light on the mysteries of that camp which were still occupying my mind. He thought for a while and said vaguely that he seemed to have heard somewhere that two men had escaped from the camp and arrived in Yenan recently. I requested him to make certain that we could see them.

Two boys appeared unescorted at our Guest House one afternoon. We five foreigners interviewed them together. The Kuomintang newspapermen had already left Yenan. "Do you remember me?" one of them greeted us, grinning with delight. And strangely enough, we remembered having seen him in the Sian camp. He described in detail the place in the camp where we had met. Both of them related a number of little incidents of our visit which nobody in Yenan could possibly have known: how some of us were dressed, where we took photos, what questions we asked such and such a person, and how one of my colleagues burst into a classroom which our guides seemed to avoid.

There was no doubt that the two boys were genuine. "Some of us were determined to get to you somewhere in the camp and tell you the truth about it, at any risk," said the boy we remembered, twenty-two-year-old Lo Tso-yung. "But our plan became known and one of the companies was not allowed to show up at all when you came. The few of those boys who were present while you were in the camp found no opportunity of getting near you. We were very disappointed, for many of us had hoped you would find out about our hardships and we might somehow get help through you."

"Were things in the Labor Camp different from normal when we were there?" we asked.

The boys laughed. "Of course they were. Very different. Preparations for your visit had been going on for a long time."

They recounted in much detail, causing us no end of amusement, how the camp and its atmosphere had been changed to suit the taste of correspondents from democratic countries.

"You remember the nice blankets on our beds and the good uniforms we wore? On the day of your arrival they were borrowed from the Military Academy, and the blankets were taken back the same night.

"You remember the large pictures of Roosevelt, Churchill, and Stalin together with that of Chiang Kai-shek in the auditorium? They were all new. Churchill and Roosevelt remained after your visit, but Stalin was there only from the morning until the night of your visit.

"You remember the big, nicely ploughed field in the compound? It had been wasteland for years and was quickly ploughed up to give you the impression that productive work was done in the camp.

"You remember the English wall newspaper in one of the rooms? It was marked Volume 2, No. 5. But we had had only one before that and it contained nothing but anti-Communist propaganda.

"You remember that when we replied to your questions we always talked like you about the 'Communists,' the 'Border Region,' the 'Eighth Route Army,' etc. . . . We had been given special orders not to use the terms in which we have to talk normally: 'Traitors,' 'Traitor Region,' 'Traitor Army,' etc. . . .

"What you may not have noticed is that we were much less stiff than usual and not standing at attention all the time. For we were ordered to relax very much during your visit and show freedom and activity, as they instructed us at morning drills every day before you came. And the classes you saw, as well as the ball games, were all held especially for you."

The two boys were getting more and more excited while they talked, but everything sounded plausible. We cross-examined them thoroughly and found no contradiction in their accounts, but much that confirmed our experiences and impressions in the camp. For the sake of those who are still there not all they said can be reported.

"Some time before you came, mimeographed sheets with the questions you were expected to ask and the replies we were to give had been distributed to the Political Commissars of each company. They were rehearsed at morning drills. The company commander read out the questions and we had to answer."

"Do you recall some of them?"

"Yes, of course. Maybe not in the proper order. Just wait a while,

294

we shall remember them all." We waited patiently as they recounted one set of questions and answers after another.

" 'Why did you come here?'—'Voluntarily.'

" 'How is life here?'—'Very good.'

" 'Have you any freedom?'—'Yes, we are as free as the students in the Military Academy.'

" 'Are the Kuomintang's Three Principles of the People good?'—'Yes, they are good, because they are the theory of national salvation for China.'

" 'Why did you leave the Communist Border Region?'—'Because the Communists don't fight the Japanese and attack only the friendly armies of the National Government; because the Communists plant opium; because of the hungry life in the Border Region; and because of the hardships we had to suffer there.'

" 'Did you study Marxism in Yenan?'—'Yes, but we did not understand it because it is too hard.' ("This," one of the boys said, "was to prevent all those who were only progressive patriots and had never seen either Marxist books or the Border Region from getting into trouble over theoretical discussions with you.")

" 'Is Communism good?'—'No, it is not good, because what China needs is the same industrial development as the United States and Britain, without class struggle.'

" 'Why did you originally go to the Border Region?'—'Because the Communists said in their propaganda that they were fighting the Japanese.'

"We were told by our company commanders that our proper replies to your questions would have a great influence on relations between the National Government and Allied countries and that it was our duty to render good services to the Kuomintang on the occasion of your visit. We knew of course what we were to say about the Communists because propaganda against them was the main part of all our training."

We asked the boys about the life stories we had been told by some of the inmates, at the memorable tea party in the camp.

"All of us were taught individual life stories to tell you in case you might ask. Especially the boys and girls who were picked as reliable enough to be with you at the tea party.

"You remember the girl you talked to?" one of the boys asked a colleague. "The girl who had to tell you that her wealthy parents lived in the Border Region and were beheaded with big swords by the Communists?" He remembered. "Well," the boy said, "neither her parents nor the girl herself ever were in the Border Region. She is in the camp because she was accused in Kuomintang territory of being a Communist."

I asked whether they knew the two girls whom I had interviewed. Both said they knew them and their real life stories.

"One of the girls was never in the Border Region, either. She was a primary-school teacher in Paochi and was arrested when it was found out that her husband was in the Border Region. The other one was here in Yenan under a different name and ran away with her lover because she was dissatisfied with her husband.

"Most of the inmates of the camp never were in Communist regions, nor were they Communists before being brought to the camp. About 70 per cent were progressive patriots who were arrested all over Free China in high schools, universities, or their homes—for advanced political ideas. Another 15 per cent or so were wrongly accused of being Communist party members, like myself. And the few others were caught on their way to the Border Region or really left Yenan of their own will. Those who left, as a rule, were homesick and wanted to visit their people, had complicated love affairs, or were involved in cases of embezzlement.

"The majority of the boys and girls in the camp have remained faithful in their hearts to their political ideas. But most of them don't discuss politics. You never know who of us are spies. There are many among us and most people don't trust one another. One of those you interviewed as a pupil—you remember the one who said he had been an officer under the famous Communist General Ho Lung—was really a camp official, and another was a student of the Military Academy."

"How is the treatment in the camp?"

"They pretend to be comparatively kind to us. But every order has to be obeyed strictly. Otherwise we are sent to the Inner Detention Room and often beaten. That is for minor offenses of discipline. But those who commit political offenses are sent to the Outer Detention Room where they are very badly treated and sometimes tortured."

"How did you come to the Labor Camp?" we asked young Lo.

"I am a Manchurian. I joined the Fifth Manchurian Volunteer Army during the Japanese occupation ten years ago, when I was little more than twelve. When the war between China and Japan broke out in 1937, a group of us went to North China and joined up with the Eighth Route Army. I became platoon commander in the 115th Division under General Lin Piao and was in several battles. When I fell sick in 1938, I was sent to Yenan for treatment. After a while I was ordered to accompany General Cheng, the chief of staff of my division, who was very ill himself, to Chinese Turkestan. We were to have a long rest and good food there, since living conditions were then very hard in the Border Region. By 1940 General Cheng had recovered from his serious lung and mental troubles, had married his nurse, and we were all returning to the Border Region. On the way, in Kansu province, we were arrested by the Kuomintang authorities."

The boy, who had been an active fighter against Japan half of his life, then told a story of over three years' detention without trial in several Kuomintang jails, of torture, hardship, hunger, and constant, steadfast denial that he was a Communist.

"For I really wasn't a Communist. I was much too young to join the party. I was just a patriotic anti-Japanese fighter, like my father in Manchuria."

He spoke of the sufferings of General Cheng, who died in jail; of Mrs. Cheng, who was refused release or even the slightest assistance when she gave birth to a child in her cell; of the death of the baby; of the general's repeated hunger strikes by which he tried to force the prison authorities to have him unchained; and of the broken physical state in which he himself was released to the Sian Labor Camp in June, 1943.

297

"I myself was taken there blindfolded," he said. "That was the way I became one of its 'voluntary students.' "

The story of the other boy, twenty-three-year-old Wang Erh-ming, was not less grim.

"I was a radio operator in a Kuomintang military headquarters in Kansu province," he said. "One evening early in 1941 two strangers came into my room, told me that there was somebody to see me, and then forced me with their pistols to follow them.

"With a cloth wrapped around my head I was taken somewhere in the same town and spent two months in a dark room, chained and without being questioned or accused of anything. The next place to which they took me was the Detention Room of the Eighth War Zone in Lanchow, and I remember the exact address of the place." (He gave it to us.)

"After a few weeks I was questioned as to why I had studied the constitution of the Soviet Union. This made it clear to me why I had been arrested: I had replied to a letter of a friend who asked me to get for him copies of *La Marseillaise* and the Soviet Constitution and a picture of Maxim Gorki. My letter was read by the censor, they told me later.

"I was asked why I had a copy of the Soviet Constitution and replied, 'This is supposed to be the time for China to begin practicing constitutional government; we must therefore study the constitutions of other countries.' The retort was, 'You must be a Communist, then.' I denied it. I was not a Communist and knew little about Communism although I wanted to learn about it. I was then tied to a stool and bricks were forced between my legs and the stool legs, a torture which they called 'airplane.' I was tortured in even worse ways afterwards, but kept on denying.

"In March of this year, fourteen of us were chained together in pairs, loaded into a motor van with eight armed guards, and driven to the Labor Camp in Sian. For some time I was confined to that little courtyard you saw, and then I had drill and classes like the others and had to spend my spare time rubbing bricks to dust for wall plaster."

298

"What were you taught in the camp?" we asked.

"We had classes on the 'Three Principles of the People,' on the speeches of Chiang Kai-shek, and on history and military arms. We were told that we had to have that training because of our wrong ideology. They did not say when we would be released and some had already been in the camp for three or four years; but we would eventually be sent to work against the 'Traitor Region.' From time to time they released individuals who were willing to work against the Communists for the Special Service, but only if they were able to procure good guarantors. When there were 'graduations' in the camp, one of the slogans at the farewell parades used to be 'Fight for the annihilation of the traitors.' "

We asked the other boy, who had been longer in the camp, "Were there any preparations when the Chinese writer Dr. Lin Yutang visited the camp earlier this year?"

"Yes, of course. They were similar to those they made for you, but not quite so elaborate. Such visits always gave us trouble."

"Has the Generalissimo or General Hu Chung-nan ever visited the camp?"

"No."

"How were things in the camp after our visit?"

"Conditions became still worse, and supervision was even stricter. For we learned the day after you left us that the Chairman of the Border Region government, Lin Pei-chu, had gone to Chungking for fresh negotiations between the Communist and Kuomintang parties, and the camp authorities feared we might start trouble."

Part Six

3,000,000 FIGHTING ALLIES

STRUGGLE FOR GRAIN WITH THE ENEMY

Chapter Thirty-one

AN OFFER OF HELP

GENERAL CHU TEH, the Commander in Chief of the Eighth Route Army, gave me several interviews on the practical possibilities of military cooperation with the Allies. We sat for many hours in the one-room building that serves his headquarters' staff for conferences—poring over maps, reports, and military statistics.

Chu Teh was in the badgeless blue cotton uniform of the ordinary soldier in which I had seen him on social occasions. But the man himself seemed different. Instead of the famous big smile, there was an expression of firmness and concentration on his broad peasant face. His eyes were even keener than usual. The popular figure of the mellow, paternal man had changed to that of a cool and forceful commander of troops. He was as sparing of words as I had known him to be at parties and meetings, and just as completely unconventional. But he showed a military precision of thinking which surprised me. For the first time I understood why the Kuomintang armies during the Civil War and the Japanese in the present war regarded the kindly, easygoing Chu Teh as a dangerous adversary and brilliant strategist.

He spoke to me as concretely as though I were a military man myself and left it to my own discretion to omit from my writings whatever might be of use to the enemy, which was the greater part of the many interesting details he told me.

It was his first opportunity of letting the Allies know how much more the Communist forces could do on the basis of inter-Allied collaboration against Japan than they have been doing singlehandedly. Naturally, I had no means of checking the information General Chu Teh gave me; but all his suggestions impressed me as straightforward

303

and practicable. They made me see even more clearly than I had realized before how much we had already lost by the lack of timely coordination with the Communist forces and how much we could still gain by close contact with them during the last stages of the war against Japan.

"Our armies and our Anti-Japanese War Bases in the enemy's rear are unreservedly at the disposal of the Allies for every possible assistance," Chu Teh said. "Any Allied representatives are welcome to collect on the spot whatever proof they may want of the strength of our troops and our war bases and of our ability to help the Allies even more than we did during our seven years of struggle with the Japanese.

"There are many ways in which we can start immediately increasing our usefulness to the Allied cause—if only we are given an opportunity."

Chu Teh spoke at first about the possibilities of ground cooperation with the Allied air forces. "We can contribute substantially to the success of Allied bombing missions," he said, "for our Anti-Japanese War Bases in the enemy's rear surround almost every conceivable target in North and Central China, the large Japanese-held cities, industrial plants, and communication lines. And we have our underground workers in every center of Japanese occupation.

"Our areas extend over much of the way from Allied air bases in China to Manchuria, Korea, and Japan. A number of your plane crews who were forced down have already been brought to safety by our forces. Incidentally, this must have enabled them to report to the United States Army about the war bases they saw and the units of our armies which helped them cross the Japanese lines. With close coordination, rescue work can be systematized and improved."

Another important matter on which assistance could easily be given to the Allies is the supply of intelligence about the enemy. Chu Teh might well have claimed that his forces have the best information about developments in the enemy's camp. For the Communists have to depend upon it; the quick collection of intelligence is one of the main reasons why their forces deep in the Japanese rear have been able for

304

seven years to outwit a foe with greatly superior armaments and communications.

Many front-line officers told me, and Chu Teh confirmed it, that the Communists always have the great advantage over the enemy in defensive or offensive operations of knowing well in advance the intentions of the Japanese and their troop dispositions and movements. "For the Chinese people everywhere are on our side," Chu Teh said, "and we have taught them the technique of practical cooperation."

From what I was told on various occasions I found that military headquarters in Yenan are exceptionally well informed about the Japanese situation. A number of concrete items of intelligence Chu Teh and his officers told me in a casual way during the first two months of my stay would, I believe, have been of considerable practical value to the Allies had there been contacts to pass them on as quickly as they were received in Yenan. I had no doubt that by the supply of intelligence alone the Chinese Communists could render great assistance to the Allies. Chu Teh assured me of his willingness to share all the information of the Eighth Route and New Fourth Armies with the American and British forces and to cooperate fully in obtaining any additional material of special importance to them which would not normally interest Yenan.

The Communists believe that China will have to play an important role in the last phase of the Allied struggle against Japan, no matter how successful the Allied navies and air forces will be in pushing farther and farther toward the Japanese islands. For the bulk of Japan's land power in China and Manchuria will survive Allied victories in the Pacific and must be destroyed to make victory complete and secure.

The weakening of the military forces of the Chinese National Government in their resistance against fresh Japanese offensives cannot be considered a reason for the Allies to abandon hope of using the China theater for major operations, the Communists maintained. On the contrary, this weakening makes it even more important for the Allies to attack the Japanese in China, too.

"In this, we can help greatly with our 475,000 regulars," Chu Teh said, "with almost 2,130,000 militiamen and with those stable war bases we hold everywhere in the enemy's rear.* Their strategic value cannot be overestimated.

"We can also facilitate Allied landings in various parts of China. We control considerable stretches of coast line, especially in Hopeh and Shantung provinces in North China and in Kiangsu and Chekiang provinces in Central China. Most sections of Japanese-occupied coast line in those areas are close to one or the other of our consolidated inland bases and are already the hunting ground of our guerrillas.

"We can even give the Allies some cooperation in coastal waters. For when our forces, years ago, reached the sea at various places they succeeded in suppressing the old-established pirates and in converting them by political education to good anti-Japanese fighters. Those formerly antisocial elements which disturbed the China coast for generations have found new tasks as sea guerrillas and know how to carry them out in collaboration with our land guerrillas and regular forces. Some Allied friends have already been saved by them.

"What is even more important, we can assist Allied expeditionary forces everywhere in their progress through Chinese territory. We can effectively protect the flanks of Allied troops and are especially well prepared for all those tasks. Our men know the terrain like a book, not only where they are at present but also in our former Soviet areas in strategic parts of Central China which the Kuomintang took from us during the Civil War and later lost to the Japanese. We have not penetrated into the former Soviet regions because Chungking troops between our forces and the Japanese are objecting to the expansion of our activities and prefer having the enemy, rather than us, in those areas.

"Our troops are expert at harassing the enemy most effectively and at preventing him from quickly concentrating reinforcements where his main lines are in danger. They have great experience in organizing the masses of the people to a mighty cooperative effort with all forces of liberation. This particular point will be of greater importance than you might think. For the Allies would have to cross territories where roads

* See p. 328 for later figures.

are so few and bad that they could not rely on motorized transport and where the local people must be not only enthusiastic but well organized and experienced in order to do their utmost in helping to carry arms and supplies, to procure basic foodstuffs, and to assist in collecting intelligence about the enemy.

"The recent failures of National Government troops in Honan, Hunan, and Kwangsi provinces were largely due to the complete lack of cooperation between them and the masses of the people; while during all those years of war our successes in creating and expanding our war bases in the enemy's rear were mainly due to the fact that our democratic methods of awakening and mobilizing the people have virtually merged them with our fighting units. This may sound rather theoretical to you, but if any Allied officers with experience of the fronts on the Kuomintang side came to our war areas they would quickly realize what strength that close cooperation with the people gives us and how much help it would mean for Allied forces."

All this assistance to the Allies would, however, be secondary to the direct use of the Communists' great military strength against the Japanese. The generals in Yenan are certain of their ability to contribute very much in fighting the enemy on their own, either independently, as they have been doing for seven years, or in regular units directly attached to Allied forces.

"Our experienced regular and militia fighters, our consolidated Anti-Japanese War Bases with their surrounding guerrilla areas, and the anti-Japanese struggle of the well-organized population in all those territories have already helped the Allies a great deal during all those years of our isolation from the outside world. The day will come when this will be realized in spite of Chungking's attempts to disguise and deny the truth.

". . . We can do much more. We can fight in a new manner if our own war effort is at last coordinated with yours.

"In order to show you where we can help and where we cannot," Chu Teh said, "I want to make it clear that in the final campaign in

307

China Allied strategy will need three categories of forces: first, specialized and mechanized forces like heavy artillery, tanks, aircraft, and so on; second, regular ground forces, infantry, and some cavalry for use at the main front lines; and third, large numbers of well-organized and experienced guerrillas, which under the conditions existing in our country must play an important strategic role.

"We are certainly able to do very well in the last category. But better light equipment than we have at present and larger supplies of cartridges and modern demolition materials would be of very great use in increasing our striking power. Furthermore, it would be in the interest of the Allies to give us rifles and special arms like bazookas, which are at the same time light enough to be carried and powerful enough to deal with those thousands and thousands of brick-built blockhouses and fortifications guarding all the main Japanese communication lines and the enemy's inner defenses around the large occupied cities.

"Given some such simple supplies which would not amount to much in bulk, and given some occasional air support for specific tasks, our guerrillas and regulars would be able to do very much more harm to the enemy than they are doing with their present equipment. With such support we could on our own recover some important towns. We could paralyze all the vital communication lines of the Japanese in the whole of North China and in our parts of Central China; for we are already besieging all the enemy's communication lines and occasionally interrupt them wherever our strategy requires such action. We could rob the enemy completely of whatever economic bases he still has in the so-called "occupied" areas. And we could so thoroughly exhaust him, at least in the whole of North China, that the net results of those operations would become a very important factor in the Allied campaign as a whole.

"Strategically, therefore, our role in the counteroffensive will be to fight the Japanese in our own ways in their vast rear. Tactically, however, it is absolutely possible for us to help Allied ground forces at the main assault fronts. A good part of our armies could operate together with those of the Allies, or at least with their specialized and mechanized units, in the frontal offensive. For our armies have already sufficient experience and military education, apart from having the necessary physique, to become very good regular troops for operation in larger units than we normally employ. All that is required for this purpose is to reequip a number of our divisions with arms such as modern American and British infantry divisions use, and to give them comparatively short training courses in the handling of those new arms.

"Even in this case nothing more elaborate and bulky would be required than rifles, light automatic weapons, and infantry guns. Such supplies would give the Allies a strong first-line field force for cooperation with their own more heavily armed units.

"This would not reduce the scale of our guerrilla warfare in the enemy's rear. For we do not lack trained men. Our militia, over two million strong and constantly expanding, provides a great reservoir of experienced fighters with excellent spirit who could immediately take the place of any of our regular troops which would be employed together with Allied armies at the regular fronts. Apart from that, the militia could greatly increase their own activities to the extent to which ammunition would be made available for their guerrilla warfare.

"Under such conditions, our regular Eighth Route Army with its vast guerrilla support would soon become an entire Allied wing in North China. It would be able to reoccupy some of the large cities.

"The fighting power of the New Fourth Army in Central China is the same, unit by unit, as that of the Eighth Route Army in North China. As soon as the New Fourth Army and its militia auxiliaries could be supplied in a similar way—which at first might be somewhat more difficult because of greater transport difficulties—it would gain equal strategic importance as an aid to specialized Allied forces in that part of the country."

Chu Teh smiled when I asked him whether the Communists would ask the Allies to let them have tanks and heavy equipment for their own use. "Of course not; we know our limitations. And there are two other things we won't ask for. Because we make them ourselves, almost everywhere in the enemy's rear: hand grenades and land mines, our main weapons. They are most successful. Our men have mastered their use completely." He corrected himself. "As a matter of fact, we shall

309

ask the Allies for more potent explosives to be used in our hand grenades and land mines. That would make a very great difference. This one example shows you how much more we could do with comparatively small quantities of Allied supplies."

Chu Teh came at last to the important question of command. "For the counteroffensive against Japan in the China theater," he said with emphasis, "an Allied High Command over all Chinese forces will be necessary. Only an Allied commander in chief can guarantee equal treatment for the various Chinese forces—the armies of the National Government; the troops with close provincial affiliations, mistrusted and neglected by Chungking; and our own regular and militia forces, which Chungking tries to starve and handicap in every possible way. Only an Allied commander in chief can assure the full use of all those forces against the enemy and overcome all the handicaps to unified control which have hampered our war of resistance so much in the past. In no other way can coordination of the armies of China with those of the Allies be achieved.

"No, the question of 'losing face' by having, say, an American commander over all Chinese troops would play no role in the minds of the Chinese people or with our officers and men. The common people, like ourselves, would greatly welcome an Allied High Command. For they have come to realize that Chiang Kai-shek's command is as bankrupt militarily as politically. Moreover, were not the British forces and the British people willing to submit to an American commander in chief for the invasion of Europe and the final assault on Germany?

"All the Communist-controlled forces would submit wholeheartedly to an Allied commander, for the only thing that matters to them is that victory be won as completely and as quickly as possible. And victory would best be assured by an Allied Supreme Command over all Chinese forces.

"Beyond that, an Allied Supreme Command, by unifying all Chinese forces for the greatest possible war effort, would indirectly lay the foundation for true national unity after the war. And national unity on a democratic basis is most essential for China after victory.

310

"I can assure you," he summed up his offer to help the Allies, "that cooperation would develop smoothly and successfully, for every one of our fighters is imbued with a spirit of unrestricted inter-Allied solidarity and our sole purpose is to defeat the Japanese militarists."

I found enthusiasm for unqualified cooperation with the Allies expressed by many other military and political leaders, by officers of all grades, and a number of simple fighters of the Eighth Route Army. Their willingness to make whatever sacrifice might be demanded of them to win the war sooner, and at the same time to help save Allied lives, impressed me as genuine and dependable. For it seemed to me that cooperation with the Allies during and after the war was the very foundation of the realistic scheme of things devised for China by the Communists.

The Communists and their nonparty collaborators do not want the decisive last round of the war against Japan to be won for China exclusively by the Allies. They consider their strength great enough to make an important contribution to victory. And they are convinced that even in the areas under the control of the National Government a great revival of the war effort can still be achieved by carrying out the necessary political and military reforms which have so long been overdue.

They believe that only by the fullest use of China's total remaining strength in the last stage of the war can genuine unity and progress be achieved after the defeat of Japan. Only in this way would China be enabled to play the international role to which her patriots in all political camps have aspired for years.

The people in Yenan, unlike many in Chungking, have no illusions about the Allies' postwar attitude toward China. They expect the Allies to judge China by two standards when the war is over: by her real contribution to victory; and by the ability she will have shown during the war to prepare herself politically for partnership in a new, democratic, and progressive world order.

The Communists expect that when that time comes the most pathetic accounts of China's difficulties in eight or nine years of war and the most eloquent explanations of her failure in the last rounds of the fight

311

will avail her as little before the judgment of a sobered world as her protests that the Allies have no right to criticize the conduct of her internal affairs. This, and no false altruism, seems to me the basic motive for Yenan's offer to help us in every possible way.

But what about the help they would expect from us in case of collaboration against Japan? Might the Communists not hope to strengthen their postwar military power against the Kuomintang in this way? Chungking had used this argument already against the very first American suggestions that the Communists should be brought into the Allied fold.

I asked Chu Teh. He laughed and quoted the Chinese equivalent of the saying that people in glass houses shouldn't throw stones. "We shall accept any conditions the Allies may make for the use of whatever arms and materials they may supply us," he added, "provided of course that they are the same conditions under which arms and materials are given to the Kuomintang."

The Allies did not get the information General Chu Teh had given me for them. My message about the essence of the interview I had with him was suppressed by the Chungking censor.

But General Joseph W. Stilwell was always aware of the importance of the Communist forces and of the role Yenan might be able to play in the Allied war against Japan. He had long been endeavoring to obtain permission from Generalissimo Chiang Kai-shek for American Army officers to visit Communist headquarters. I knew he was continuing his efforts.

Now that we correspondents had succeeded in opening the door to Yenan, could the representatives of the United States Army still be kept out?

Chapter Thirty-two

THREE-CORNERED WARFARE

To *Trade Space for Time* has been the motto of Generalissimo Chiang Kai-shek's strategy from the beginning of the war with Japan in 1937.

We Advance When the Enemy Advances was the immediate answer of the Communist military leaders, the slogan which has determined their strategy ever since.

Early in the war, these strategies were equally correct for the respective forces of the Kuomintang and Communist parties. More than that, they were complementary and provided the basis for anti-Japanese cooperation between the former antagonists. Chiang Kai-shek's armies were too ill equipped to halt the avalanche of superior Japanese troops in frontal resistance. To retreat while fighting, to preserve as much of his strength as possible, and to gain time at the price of giving up territory was all he could aim at.

Meanwhile, it was urgently necessary to organize large-scale guerrilla warfare against the invaders in the hastily abandoned territories of North and Central China—in order to deny them the fruits of victory, to harass them, and eventually to wear them out.

But the Kuomintang armies were clearly unsuited to the purpose of carrying on guerrilla warfare in the Japanese rear. All their practical experience, acquired in ten years of civil war against the Communists, was the opposite of what they now needed. It had made them into *anti*-guerrilla fighters, used to relying upon superior armament and better lines of communication than their enemy had. It had educated them to mistrust the civilian population rather than to cooperate with it. And all their special training under Chiang Kai-shek's German advisers had followed the line of preparing them for modern-style warfare in large formations on regular front lines.

Three-cornered Warfare

The Communists, however, had the experience and training to fulfill the task of opening a second, popular war front in the enemy's rear. Chiang Kai-shek authorized them to penetrate into certain parts of the enemy's rear in which no Kuomintang troops had been left behind during the retreat. He did it hesitatingly—apparently more under the compelling influence of the United Front enthusiasm that pervaded the country at the time than from any other motive. Even during that initial period little or nothing was done to facilitate their work.

The Communists lived up to their strategic slogan. They advanced—backward, into the Japanese rear—the farther the enemy advanced in his frontal assaults on the regular fronts. The 70,000 or 80,000 men of the old Red Army of the Civil War days—reorganized into the Eighth Route Army under the National Government—penetrated farther and farther into North China, at the same time protecting the flanks of the withdrawing Kuomintang forces. Behind and between the enemy's positions the Communists systematically organized the population for resistance and recruited increasing numbers of militia auxiliaries.

As old hands at the guerrilla game, they harassed the enemy expertly in every possible way. In economic and political warfare they fought him with equal determination and experience—frustrating his desires to strengthen his home economy by an intensive exploitation of the rich resources of the conquered territories and to build up a large antiforeign puppet army in preparation of the eventual Japanese attack against the United States and Britain.

In this threefold military, economic, and political struggle and in the closest cooperation with the local population, the Eighth Route Army set up its Anti-Japanese War Bases in the enemy's rear and increased its regular forces to 156,000 in 1938, 270,000 in 1939, and 400,000 in 1940—not counting the steadily mounting numbers of militia fighters.

Similar developments took place in Central China. The Communist-controlled New Fourth Army—formed in 1937 with the consent of the National Government from 12,000 local Red Army remnants of the Civil War period—penetrated deeply into the enemy's rear, carrying on the same threefold warfare against the Japanese. With the help of the population, one Anti-Japanese War Base after another was set up in Central China, and the New Fourth Army grew to 30,000 in 1938, 50,000 in 1939, and 135,000 at the end of 1940. Everywhere the Communists and the masses of the people they had mobilized fulfilled their task efficiently, enthusiastically, and with surprising success.

Until 1939, many in the Kuomintang recognized and praised the achievements of the Communists. I found some enthusiastic entries of Kuomintang officers in the visitors' book of Yenan's Guest House of that time. This is one of them.

"The men of the Eighth Route Army are fighting heroically at the front. Their comrades in the rear are energetically carrying on construction work, thus turning enemy-occupied country and the barren areas of this Border Region into flourishing land enlivened with energy. Let us fulfill the great and hard tasks of armed resistance and national reconstruction in sincere unity.

"Yenan, June 6, 1939.
"(Signed) CHOU LI-WU
"Major General in the National Army."

The author of this entry was once more in Yenan when I was there— acting as Generalissimo Chiang Kai-shek's representative with the Eighth Route Army. I found his attitude toward the Communists in accordance with the hostile official line Chungking had begun to adopt later in 1939. He not only derided their present activities but also was unwilling to give the Communists any credit for what they had done in the past, probably forgetting that he had once gone on record with a different opinion.

On one of my journeys in China in 1940 I met a young Kuomintang liberal who told me in the presence of some of his reactionary party comrades about the favorable impression the 129th Division of the Eighth Route Army had made on him a short time before when he visited that famous unit as a member of a delegation from Chungking which Generalissimo Chiang Kai-shek sent to the Communist war areas with decorations for a great number of heroic Communist fighters. His

Kuomintang companions, I learned later, got the young man into serious trouble for having told a foreigner that Eighth Route Army men had ever been decorated by the Generalissimo for bravery.

While the Communists evidently succeeded with their strategy, We Advance When the Enemy Advances—what use did Chiang Kai-shek make of his strategy of Trading Space for Time? What brought the Japanese advance into Free China virtually to a halt from the end of 1938 to 1944?

It became increasingly clear to me during five years in Chungking that Chiang Kai-shek's plans for the use of "traded time" were never characterized by the clear-cut, single-minded purpose of a military strategist and that they developed more and more into the subtle, complex schemes of a shrewd though somewhat fanciful politician.

During the first year of the war, Chiang Kai-shek seemed to come fairly close to the realization that the time he had gained by retreat must be used to mobilize the whole nation for a virtually revolutionary war of the masses of the people against the invader. He seemed to acknowledge, too, that the prerequisites of a truly popular all-out war effort were (1) close United Front cooperation of all political groups in the country and suppression of all appeasers and traitors; (2) democratic reforms of the Kuomintang dictatorship and its administration; (3) facilities for the people to develop their own initiative in the war effort and in simultaneous social progress; and (4) the adoption of unorthodox methods of warfare in which the armed people would play a vital role side-by-side with the regular forces.

Most of those ideas were alien to his conservative, authoritative personality. But the famous progressive Program of Resistance and Reconstruction the Kuomintang adopted in April, 1938, seemed to indicate that he was overcoming his inherent prejudices in favor of less autocratic rule and less orthodox warfare. This Kuomintang program was strongly influenced by liberals within his own party who for a while came to the fore, and by suggestions of the Communists along the lines of their own war policies.

Chiang Kai-shek also accepted an early Communist suggestion to

316

help in the establishment of a guerrilla school which would retrain considerable numbers of Kuomintang troops—in order to use them as nuclei for the development of large, popular fighting forces in the enemy's rear, in the same way in which the Communists were using their own armies.

The reactionary elements in the Kuomintang's party, government, and army leadership were alarmed at these developments. They worked on Chiang Kai-shek's abiding fear of arming the population with any kind of democratic rights and any weapons of war, both of which they might eventually use against the fundamental vestige of power of an insufficiently liberalized Kuomintang dictatorship.

The reforms of the program were not enforced, and the United Front was not permitted to develop into a true partnership between the Kuomintang and all the other patriotic parties and groups. The liberals inside the Kuomintang suffered one setback after another, and the anti-Communist elements once more grew stronger.

The reactionaries warned Chiang Kai-shek against the use of Kuomintang troops as guerrillas, since it would necessarily bring them into close contact with the people, make them part of the United Front, and offset the effects of their anti-Communist indoctrination—so that their reliability as the armed support of the Kuomintang's one-party rule would suffer.

The plan for the guerrilla school was abandoned. The German military advisers retained their positions and influence although the Berlin-Tokyo Axis was already a reality. Nothing was done to change the strategy and tactics of the Kuomintang armies into those of a genuine people's war. The Generalissimo's *Handbook for the Extirpation of Bandits* of the time of the Civil War against the Communists remained one of the most important textbooks for military training.

The reactionaries stressed the possibilities, if not of peace, at least of some *modus vivendi* with Japan. For Japan was really out to attack Russia, America, and England, they said, and was only too willing to be lenient with a reasonable China. The organization of a virtual revolutionary mass war, however, would provoke Japan into continuing her all-out attack against the remainder of Free China. And they reminded the Generalissimo that it was really the United Front movement against Japan and the Kuomintang-Communist reconciliation after the Sian Incident in 1936 which had forced Japan into military action against China the year after and brought about the war.

A fair amount of attention was paid to those innumerable middlemen from the enemy-occupied areas who came to Chungking with all kinds of Japanese suggestions, conditional promises, and threats. Chungking seemed to distinguish less and less between the various categories of Chinese on both sides of the war fronts who were openly or clandestinely involved in the discussion of Japanese suggestions: sincere patriots who merely wanted to evaluate opinion in the enemy camp; weaklings and appeasers; dangerous defeatists; and outright traitors to China.

His reactionary advisers purposely nourished Chiang Kai-shek's sanguine expectations that Japan might any day embroil herself in war with Russia; that, in case of war, the United States and Britain would quickly defeat the Japanese, and that all these potential enemies of Japan would give decisive assistance to China if only they were sufficiently stimulated by clever Kuomintang publicity.

By the end of 1939, the time that had been traded for space was filled with little more than the wait for outside relief in one form or another. Efforts at self-help faded more and more into the background.

The Japanese, after their capture of Hankow and Canton at the end of 1938, gave up their effort to force China to her knees by means of military attack. Not only because the war in China had proved unexpectedly costly to them, but apparently because developments in the occupied areas under Communist control made it clear to Tokyo that the complete defeat of the Chinese National Government would not end the war, since it might be followed by country-wide popular guerrilla warfare on the Communist pattern—which would rob Japan of her fruits of victory and tie up more troops than she would be able to spare at the time of her intended attack on the Western powers.

From early 1939 until 1944—when the growing activities of the

318

Fourteenth U. S. Army Air Force made it necessary for the enemy to launch fairly large offensives against the American air bases in China— the Japanese-Kuomintang fronts were comparatively quiet, and often for long periods almost completely dormant.

The Japanese campaigns against Free China from 1939 to 1943, which gave an inattentive world the vague impression that China was still staving off unabated Japanese attempts to defeat her in the military field, were in fact comparatively small attacks—blatantly overadvertised by Chungking and Tokyo since for reasons of their respective domestic and foreign propaganda both were interested in exaggerating them.

Only a few of those campaigns had limited strategic objectives, like the cutting of the highway between China and French Indo-China or the rounding off of Japanese positions in various places. Almost all the other Japanese advances were followed by complete or partial withdrawals since they did not aim at territorial gains. The four main purposes that motivated them were of an entirely different nature.

First, they were to give a measure of realistic battle training to the Japanese Army in order to get it ready for action against the Western powers. This is why practically every Japanese division had a spell of duty in China at one time or another.

Second, those sudden stabs at the wealthy agricultural regions on the fringes of Free China were at the same time foraging expeditions designed to yield the Japanese large quantities of rice. For the military, economic, and political warfare of the Communist-controlled forces in his rear made it more and more difficult for the enemy to obtain the desired food supplies in the "occupied" regions.

Third, the Japanese aimed at breaking up as many Kuomintang army units as might be encountered in their quick, long thrusts. This is why Chungking was right, as a rule, to offer little resistance until the eventual Japanese withdrawal might give the Chinese troops an opportunity to challenge part of the enemy forces from the flanks or behind. And this type of action was the basis for a good number of much-publicized Chinese "comeback" victories during those years.

Fourth, those attacks, together with terror bombings, were to add weight to Japan's incessant intrigues for political settlements with

Chungking. For political pressure, supported by sporadic military action, became the essence of Tokyo's strategy toward China after the fall of Hankow and Canton had brought the Japanese into control of the last positions in China which were vital to their over-all plans for the conquest of Asia and the Pacific.

Tokyo's pressure for political compromise with Chungking increased as time went on, and never stopped. "Peace" was only one of the alternative objectives the Japanese endeavored to achieve at various periods.

The scope of the Japanese proposals received in Chungking ranged over a much larger field. The maximum aims—beyond a mere peace settlement—were a Sino-German-Japanese or Pan-Asiatic alliance against the Western powers. The minimum aims concerned different kinds of underhanded arrangements on such matters as the mutual limitation of hostilities by way of a secret, partial armistice, the regulation of trade between Japanese- and Kuomintang-controlled China, and cooperation against the Chinese Communists between the Japanese, their puppets, and the Kuomintang.

The Japanese motive for continuing the offensive for political compromise with Chungking appeared to be twofold. On the one side, they hoped that the strains and stresses in Free China's domestic situation and in Sino-foreign relations might make one or the other of their offers acceptable to Chiang Kai-shek. On the other, they seem to have calculated from the very beginning of the war that their incessant appeals to various groups in the Kuomintang camp would at least have the effect of undermining China's war effort.

It seems certain that Chiang Kai-shek himself never considered peace with the Japanese. But some around him did at various times— if only because they underrated the staying power of China, had a distaste for the necessary political and military reforms that would strengthen it, or thought that Sino-Japanese peace talk might induce the Western powers to lend China the desired assistance.

There is no means of knowing if members of the National Government have ever been party to arrangements on minor subjects of mutual accommodation with the puppets or the Japanese. But it was frequently alleged in Chungking by Chinese liberals and foreign observers that certain Kuomintang generals, party functionaries, and local government officials in regions adjoining the front lines had understandings with puppets and Japanese—concerning the smuggling trade across the line, the restriction of hostilities in their respective areas, and the common fight against the Communists.

Whatever may be revealed by history about the practical effect of Tokyo's political intrigues during the Sino-Japanese War and of the contacts between Japan's puppets and some of their former Kuomintang associates in the Kuomintang camp, there can be no doubt to anybody who spent the crucial years of the war in Chungking that both did much harm to China's morale and national unity.

The uninterrupted existence of these contacts was public knowledge. Not only Communists, but patriotic liberals inside as well as outside the Kuomintang, had good reason to believe that the authorities looked at them with greater suspicion and treated them less leniently than appeasers, defeatists, and people who maintained contacts with puppets.

The remarkable relaxation of Chungking's official propaganda against traitors like Wang Ching-wei and other puppets of former prominence in the Kuomintang—at a time when the propaganda campaign against the Chinese Communists was intensified—discouraged many patriots.

During all phases of the war, postal communications, the remittance of money, and actual travel between Japanese-held cities and Free China remained easy and only superficially controlled on the Chungking side—infinitely easier, in fact, than communication and travel between Kuomintang China and the Communist-controlled regions which were most effectively blockaded by Chungking since 1939.

It looked more and more as though Chungking's main domestic enemies were not the puppets of the Japanese, the traitors to China—but the Communists who fought the puppets as well as their masters. And the parallelism of Chungking's and Tokyo's pronouncements against the "bandits" at Yenan was an equally strange phenomenon.

Generalissimo Chiang Kai-shek has been without a strategy since the Japanese, at the end of 1938, gave up their original plan of forcing him to his knees by military means. There was no need any more to trade space for time. No practical use was found for year after year of time that passed. No means was devised to recover some of the space that had been lost.

As time went on the Kuomintang armies deteriorated. From under-nourishment, because their maintenance was not backed up by the necessary reforms of Chungking's economic and financial policies. From lack of military and especially offensive action, because the High Command did not change its strategy in such a way as to be able to make unorthodox use of the millions of brave soldiers who were always willing to fight. And from lack of arms and munitions, because the unreformed, undemocratic administration of Chungking was not able to exploit Free China's productive potentialities.

The short initial period of the Kuomintang's fighting war, which lasted somewhat beyond the heroic defense of Shanghai, was followed by year after year of a passive waiting war. . . . Chungking lost more and more of that spirit of counteroffensive which had once been implied in the motto, Trading Space for Time. . . . And the fight against the Communists seemed to gain greater importance in the minds of the Chungking leaders, who, in the midst of the stalemated war, came to think more and more in terms of their postwar problems than in terms of their fight against the Japanese.

Since late 1943, the enemy advanced again in various parts of the country—in Southeast China in order to occupy the advanced airfields and later the main bases of the U. S. Army Air Force, and in the Northwestern province Honan in order to capture the missing link in the railroad from North to Central China. But the Kuomintang armies —in spite of the heroic efforts of the rank and file at several places and in spite of American air support—were scarcely in a position to resist.

The Communists, too, suffered serious setbacks. In 1940 and 1941, while the Japanese-Kuomintang fronts were quiet, the enemy launched more powerful "mopping-up" campaigns than ever against all the Communist-controlled war bases in their rear, using large numbers of troops and much modern equipment and accompanying their military action with increasingly ruthless measures of economic warfare and terror against the population.

"The year before the Pacific War was the most difficult year we ever had," I was told in Yenan by military commanders, political workers, non-Communists, and foreign witnesses from the various war areas in the enemy's rear. "The enemy went all out, in great strength, to destroy our Anti-Japanese War Bases, and we know now that his main reason was to make his last preparations for the war with the Allies in which occupied China was to be a safe and productive rear. The Japanese realized that we would be able to render valuable help to the Allies if we survived."

The Communist-controlled areas shrank. Before the great Japanese offensives their population had numbered 100,000,000, and afterward they had little more than 50,000,000.

This was the time when the Chungking government attacked and "disbanded" the Communist-controlled New Fourth Army in Central China, when it stopped all payment and supplies for the Eighth Route Army in North China and made the blockade against the Yenan areas watertight.

However, this twofold Japanese-Kuomintang attack, which reactionaries in Chungking hopefully considered the beginning of the end of the Communists in China, did not find Yenan unprepared. For the Communists, in accordance with their materialistic creed, had just passed through a process of severe self-analysis and self-criticism. Summing up their military, political, economic, and general experiences during the first three years of war, their mistakes and achievements and the weak and strong points of their position, they had eventually brought the eminently practical system of the New Democracy to full maturity.

Instead of weakening the Communists, the pressure of the Japanese and the Kuomintang strengthened them in the long run. It brought the people in their war areas more closely behind the New Democracy. Before that time the Communists had already enjoyed the support of the masses of poor people and the loyalty of the steadily expanding armies. But the genuine cooperation of the majority of its former class

323

enemies—among the patriotic landlords, merchants, and the gentry in general, of which I found such surprising indications and impartial testimonies in Yenan—dates back to those critical days.

To the extent that the United Front was vanishing in Kuomintang China, the United Front of all social strata was consolidated in the Yenan areas which then ceased to be in the true sense of the word "Communist-controlled."

Most of the great economic effort in the Border Region and in the anti-Japanese bases, which strengthened the military power of the Communists, also took on its new intensity during those days. It was the time when Brigadier Wang Chen's Nanniwan production project was pushed and became the model on which all the garrison troops organized their self-support. It was the time when government and party officials without distinction of rank began producing most of their food and clothing in off-duty hours.

Because of heavy losses and an army rationalization scheme introduced in connection with the New Democracy, the numbers of the Eighth Route Army decreased from 400,000 in 1940 to 305,000 in 1941; and those of the New Fourth Army fell from 135,000 before its "disbandment" by Chungking early in 1941 to 111,000 in 1942. But the effectiveness of the armies is supposed to have been considerably improved during the crisis: through their fresh experience in extremely hard and prolonged large-scale fighting; and especially through the process of rationalization which weeded out weak elements, overhauled all branches of the armies' organization, and introduced improved methods of training.

From that time on, the military and political power of the Communists and the areas under their control have been steadily on the increase, in spite of the enemy's continued "mopping-up" campaigns against them.

The slogan of the Communists, We Advance When the Enemy Advances, continues to determine their warfare. Tactically, it is followed by a well-developed method of quick infiltration into the rear of the enemy's attacking forces and cutting off his supply lines. Strategically, it has been applied wherever there were no Kuomintang troops to prevent the Communist forces from penetrating into areas which Chungking had lost to the Japanese.

Soon after the Kuomintang armies were routed from Honan province in 1944, the Communists appeared behind the enemy lines, beginning to organize the population, to create militia units and to set up bases for guerrilla activities, which, in the meantime, have been consolidated into another Anti-Japanese War Base—to tie up as many enemy forces as possible.

Chapter Thirty-three

THE SETTING OF A UNIQUE WAR

T HE chief of staff of the Eighth Route Army, General Yeh Chien-ying, agreed at once when I asked him to let me see the inner sanctum of headquarters, the War Room.

"No stranger has ever been in our War Room," he said, "but we have nothing to hide. You can see it."

We walked up a steep mud path through nicely terraced vegetable plots where staff officers "use their hands" after duty, according to Mao Tse-tung's order that everybody without distinction of rank must do production work.

A sentry saluted and lifted a bamboo curtain, letting us into a one-room mud-built house. A number of keen-looking young officers sat working over the latest front reports at a cloth-covered conference table with several field telephones.

The walls were completely covered with a huge operational map of all China, in infinite detail. Colored strings demarcated the intricate mosaic of areas under the control of various forces—the Communists' stable Anti-Japanese War Bases in the enemy's rear; their guerrilla areas between those bases; the "pacified" regions under Japanese occupation; and the regular front lines between the most advanced enemy armies and the troops of the Kuomintang government in Chungking, indicating the shrinking borders of Free China.

A mass of little colored paper flags with unit numbers showed the exact dispositions of the four large forces that make up China's singularly complex war situation.*

* The following figures on the strength of the hostile forces in China apply to the situation in the spring of 1944. The over-all numbers of Japanese and puppet troops seem to have changed little since then. The Kuomintang-controlled forces were in the meantime considerably reduced through the disintegration of large armies in connection with further Japanese advances in Honan, Hunan, Kwangsi, and Kwangtung provinces

First, the *Japanese armies*.

In Manchuria, outside the Great Wall of China proper, the Japanese forces are estimated at twenty-five to thirty divisions totaling 450,000 to 600,000 men including their auxiliaries. They are outside the sphere of the present Sino-Japanese conflict—standing against the powerful Far Eastern Army of the USSR and more or less immobilized by them.

In North China, 84 per cent of the fourteen Japanese divisions with 220,000 men engage the Communist-led Eighth Route Army. Only 16 per cent face the remnants of the once very large Kuomintang-controlled armies at the fringes of this vast war theater which was over-run by the Japanese early in the war.

In Central China 59.5 per cent of the sixteen Japanese divisions with their 262,000 men are deployed against the Communist-led New Fourth Army, and 40.5 per cent against Kuomintang forces.

In South China, the Japanese have 4½ divisions with 80,000 men. Only 22 per cent of them are shown to oppose Communist-controlled partisans, while 78 per cent engage Kuomintang troops.

Second, the *Chinese puppet forces* of the Japanese.

Their total number in North, Central, and South China is 780,000. Originally 480,000 of them are supposed to have been Kuomintang troops which went over to the Japanese in the course of seven years of war, while the rest were locally recruited by the enemy and his political puppets. The Communists claim to engage over 90 per cent of all those puppet forces.

Third, the *Kuomintang armies* of the Chungking government.

The information on the map coincided roughly with the data I was given by one of the highest ranking Kuomintang generals in Chungking two months before, "between 310 and 340 divisions under their normal average strength of 10,000 each," and with the estimates of foreign

and the demobilization of troops unfit for fighting—about one-third of the entire Kuomintang army. The Communist-led forces increased as follows from the spring of 1944 to early 1945: the total of the regular Eighth Route and New Fourth Armies from 475,000 to 910,000, and the militia from 2,130,000 to over 2,200,000.

observers who put the total strength of the Kuomintang armies at somewhat more than 2,500,000 men.

Kuomintang guerrilla and militia forces seemed to play no role in the war situation, according to the map. The same general in Chungking had admitted to me that they were indeed "merely nominal," apart from some units in the general areas of Shanghai and Canton.

Fourth, the *Communist-led forces.*

The Eighth Route Army in North China had 321,000 men, although the National Government in Chungking never "authorized" it to have more than three divisions with a total of 45,000 men. Its total, early in 1945, had risen to about 600,000 men, through the incorporation of experienced militiamen into the regular army.

The New Fourth Army in Central China had 154,000 men, or about 40,000 more than at the time of the attack of Kuomintang troops on its headquarters units and the "official disbandment of the entire New Fourth Army" by the Chungking government early in 1941. By early 1945 it had been increased to about 300,000 men.

The main partisan detachments in South China are about 10,000 strong.

Those regular fighting units of the Communists are supported by strong militia forces: 1,580,000 in North China; 550,000 in Central China; and several tens of thousands in South China.

The fourteen large, stable regions under elected governments of the New Democracy, the core of Communist China, stand out clearly on the map. A few adjoin each other. Some are connected by large "guerrilla areas" less firmly controlled by the Communist armies than the stable regions. Some are completely isolated in territories under occupation of the Japanese and of Kuomintang armies. Early in 1945, these regions had grown to eighteen, with a total area of 331,000 square miles, with Communist-controlled coastlines measuring 535 miles and with an estimated population of 94,000,000.

The (Shensi-Kansu-Ninghsia) *Border Region* around Yenan, the westernmost of the eighteen main territories, is in a special position: it is the only one completely outside Japanese-occupied areas—the only rear base of Communist-controlled China.

Seven of those regions, the Anti-Japanese War Bases of the Eighth Route Army, are in North China.

The *Shansi-Suiyuan* Anti-Japanese War Base on the bank of the Yellow River protects the Border Region against frequent enemy attempts to attack Yenan itself. It is Yenan's connecting link with all the Communist-controlled regions in North China, and through them over devious routes along the China Sea coast with those in Central China.

The most important of all the Anti-Japanese War Bases is the *Shansi-Chahar-Hopei* ("Chin-cha-chi") region with a population of over 20,000,000. It is the model base of the Communists, the oldest, largest, most stable, and best developed, and the only one which was originally recognized by the National Government. It stretches 700 miles from east to west, from the Mongolian steppes past the outskirts of Peiping to the seacoast near Tientsin; and 600 miles from south to north, from the plains of Central Hopei right into the enemy's puppet state Manchukuo.

The map in the War Room showed that a large slice of the southern parts of Manchukuo has already been cut off by the Communists and made into small anti-Japanese war areas inside large guerrilla regions. These positions may one day be of great importance to the Allies as a spearhead against the enemy's semi-home base Manchuria. By early 1945 they had been organized into the *Hopei-Jehol-Liaoning* region.

The main coastal positions of the Communists are in the *Shantung* Anti-Japanese War Base where the expansion into Japanese- and puppet-held territories has made great progress recently. Its potential importance is equally great for Allied strategy and for the political postwar situation of the Communists in China.

The *Shansi-Hopei-Honan* and *Hopei-Shantung-Honan* bases, which have been expanding southward since the Kuomintang armies lost the long-preserved parts of Honan province to the Japanese in 1944 and the new *Honan Liberated Area*, round off the North China regions of the Eighth Route Army to the south.

The eight Anti-Japanese War Bases of the New Fourth Army in Central China, on both sides of the Yangtsze and Hwai Rivers and along the China Sea coast, are individually smaller than those of the Eighth Route Army in the north. They comprise over 30,000,000 of Central China's total population of about 70,000,000.

Along the coast—above, around, and below Shanghai—are the *North, Central,* and *South Kiangsu* bases and the *East Chekiang* base. In any of those bases, Allied invasion armies may for the first time come into contact with the forces of the Chinese Communists.

Loosely adjoining them to the west are the *North-of-the-Hwai-River, South-of-the-Hwai-River,* and *Central Anhwei* bases, of great importance as a perpetual threat to the most vital Japanese communication lines.

The southwesternmost base in Central China is that around the strategic Yangtsze city Hankow, the *Hupei-Hunan-Anhwei* region.

The map of the northern part of Central China is a confusing jigsaw puzzle of intermingled positions of all the four forces in the unique Chinese war situation. Fairly large units of Kuomintang troops stand between the Japanese and puppet forces on the one side and the Communist-controlled New Fourth Army on the other.

In the southern part of Central China and in Southeast China, the map shows still another picture. There are large, solid blocks of Japanese-occupied territory, free from Chinese forces inside the Japanese lines.

Not far from them, deeper in the Japanese rear, are Communist-controlled forces, eager to penetrate into those enemy-held regions in order to develop guerrilla areas and eventually to set up stable Anti-Japanese War Bases, as they have done everywhere else inside the Japanese lines. But adjoining them, or in their way, are strong regular Kuomintang armies which were left behind when the Japanese advanced. And they prevent the Communists from carrying out their intention.

These are the main scenes of that pathetic three-cornered conflict in which Chinese patriots—the troops under the respective control of the

330

Kuomintang and Communist parties—fight not only the national enemy but check, and often clash with, one another. . . .

Still farther to the south and east, red strings on the map mark the regular front lines between the Japanese and Kuomintang armies. They run out into great, menacing arrows, indicating the incessant advances the enemy made in 1944 into Chungking's Free China—into areas where the U. S. Army Air Force lost one important base after another because the Kuomintang armies were unable to defend them.

And hundreds of miles away from the New Fourth Army positions in Central China, in the very south of the country, completely isolated from Yenan and all the rest of Communist China, there are two small Communist positions, set up by native Communist partisans inside the enemy lines. One is the Pearl River delta in Kwangtung province, close to Canton and Hong Kong's mainland port Kowloon and along the railroad between the two cities. It claims control over a population of two million. The other is on Hainan Island, off the French Indo-China coast in the Gulf of Tongking, where a Soviet district of Civil War days was never cleared up by the Kuomintang and developed into an anti-Japanese war area when the enemy occupied the island.

The War Room map was an impressive sight, eloquent of the important role the Communists are playing in the Sino-Japanese War, in the enemy's rear.

Everywhere in North China and in half of Central China the dense forest of little green flags denoting Communist army units confines the enemy's position to thin strips of territory along railroads, highways, and stretches of seacoast or to small circles around the big cities—forming thousands of miles of front line.

There could be no doubt that the Communist positions as shown on the War Room map must be substantially correct. Not only because it is evidently the basis on which Yenan's military leaders do their strategic planning. Not only because Japanese war communiqués about fighting with the Communists confirm them to a very large extent. But because American pilots who came down over various regions of North and Central China and were rescued by Communist troops proved the justification of Communist claims in a good number of sample cases. And especially because the Communist leaders were hopeful that the United States Army might at any moment be able to follow their invitation and send parties of officers to the various war areas to find out the truth for themselves.

In consequence, three fundamental claims of the Communists seemed even more plausible to me than they had been from what I had learned before of the war situation in North and Central China.

First, the Communists with their comparatively small regular forces could never have established their vast war bases in the enemy's rear— over an area three and a half times the size of the British Isles—if they had not had the fullest cooperation of the armed and unarmed people in every village, a cooperation which must of necessity be voluntary and on an essentially democratic basis.

Second, the Japanese would not let the Communists continue for one day in those strategically and economically vital positions if they were able to dislodge them.

Third, the Communist war bases are so ideally situated for offensive operations that the Japanese have to retain the largest possible number of defenders in those rear areas and to counterattack the Communists at frequent intervals, in order to guard their own positions against increasingly dangerous losses.

Chapter Thirty-four

THE COMMUNIST FIGHTING FORCES

A SKIRMISH between Communist fighters and enemy troops somewhere in the Japanese rear. . . . Three Japanese killed or wounded. . . . Six or seven of their puppet troops killed, wounded, or taken prisoner. . . . Considerable damage done to a Japanese truck convoy, railroad, or blockhouse. . . . A haul of three rifles and sufficient rounds of small-arms ammunition for the cartridge-poor Communists to launch a similar attack at the next opportunity. . . . All at a cost to the Eighth Route or New Fourth Army of two fighters killed or wounded. . . .

. . . This is the average record of 23,000 engagements fought by the Communists in North and Central China during the twelve months from June, 1943, to May, 1944; and this is the type of miniature action on which Yenan has built up its plausible claim to an imposing seven years' battle record.

The Communists say they fought a total of 115,120 predominantly small engagements from the beginning of the war in 1937 to March, 1945. A considerable number of good-sized defensive battles took place in the 647 major mopping-up campaigns against the various Anti-Japanese War Bases in which the Japanese used an average of 4,000 and a maximum of 200,000 troops.

The Communists themselves launched several counteroffensives, like the famous Hundred Regiments Campaign in North China in 1940, and many medium-scale offensives.

These are the military results they claim from all their fighting with the enemy during almost eight years of war:

The Japanese lost 511,434 killed or wounded; 3,880 captured; and 222 deserters.

Of their puppet troops 458,225 were killed or wounded; 282,496 captured; and 104,620 deserted.

During the first six and a half years of the war, the Communists captured 313,487 rifles, 5,771 light and heavy machine guns, 589 mountain guns and other artillery pieces—altogether almost two-thirds of the equipment their regular troops and their best-armed militiamen had at their disposal early in 1944; and they seem to have captured much material since then.

They inflicted great damage on Japanese transport, supplies, and fortifications, on Japanese-occupied towns, mines, factories, and power plants, which cannot easily be summarized.

The casualties of the Communist-led armies were, from 1937 to March, 1945: in North China, 112,245 commanders and fighters of the Eighth Route Army killed and 211,381 wounded; in Central China, 47,993 commanders and fighters of the New Fourth Army killed and 73,886 wounded.

There is one sad addition to the battle record of the Communist-led armies which must be registered in parenthesis. Yenan claims that a further 60,000 of their commanders and fighters have so far been killed in the other conflict which has been going on since 1939, simultaneously with the war against Japan—in defensive actions against the Kuomintang troops of Chungking who have been attacking them in various parts of North and Central China.

On the Kuomintang side, 30,000 troops were killed in those battles with the Communists, according to one of the most prominent generals in the National Government in Chungking. "They killed many more of our men than of the enemy," the Kuomintang general said, briefing me for the journey to Yenan. "For they have not been fighting the enemy at all since they had a few engagements with him in 1937. They have been fighting only us. And all the casualties of the Communists at the hands of the enemy, during the entire war, cannot have been more than a *few thousand*. I wonder whether they will be able to show you even one or two wounded in their hospitals."

The Communist Fighting Forces

I studied the military system of the Communists as thoroughly as possible, questioning many commanders and men fresh from action, political workers and non-Communists just returned from the war areas, and Michael Lindsay and Dr. Hans C. Mueller, who have for years worked with the Eighth Route Army. I read a number of articles from the Japanese and puppet press which, apart from bitter complaints about the stubbornness and effectiveness of the Communists' fight, contained much valuable information about the tactics of Communist-Japanese warfare. From all the evidence I found I came to the conclusion that the battle records claimed by Yenan sounded very much more convincing than what I had been told in Chungking and Sian.

The main cause of the success of the Communists in expanding and consolidating their offensive positions in the Japanese rear seems to lie in the strength of their mass organizations. The Eighth Route and New Fourth Armies with their 910,000 men are merely the apex, and the People's Militia with its 2,200,000 men is only the middle stratum of the vast fighting forces which the Communists have developed for their closely connected military, economic, and political warfare against the Japanese.

The basic factor in all this warfare is the *Self-defense Corps* (also called People's Anti-Japanese Resistance Association) which embraces practically the entire population of Communist-controlled China and is supposed to have an active membership of 16,000,000 men and women.

The enemy, through his mere presence, his constant attacks on the Anti-Japanese War Bases, and his outrages against innocent farmers, did much to wield the Communist-led armies and the people of all classes into a close community of interest. But it was the Self-defense Corps—under the purposeful direction of democratically elected village, borough, county, and regional committees—which fashioned it into an active and effective community of resistance.

The Self-defense Corps committees seem to have attracted the most capable people of all social strata—peasants and landlords, workers, merchants, and former Kuomintang officials. They arouse and fan the patriotism and watchfulness of the population. They teach them in co-

335

operation with the armies primitive yet effective methods of active self-defense; for the complex warfare in the enemy's rear often makes it necessary for individual villages to take the initiative. They train them systematically for every possible assistance to the armed forces. And they make them the instrument of economic and political warfare against the enemy, often together with the patriotic people in the Japanese-held cities.

The men of the Self-defense Corps play a considerable role in military operations. They are part of the armies' intelligence organizations which function so well that the Communists can always rely on considerable advance knowledge of enemy moves. They do general rear service and transportation work and act as stretcher-bearers, water carriers, cooks, and couriers.

The fighters of the Communist-led armies and militia are therefore completely free for military action—different from the soldiers in the Kuomintang armies, of which large parts have to be used for auxiliary services; for Chungking failed to befriend the people in a democratic manner and to mobilize and organize them for maximum help to the armies.

The Self-defense Corps also provides actual fighters. Many of its members volunteer for service, and the strongest, most active, and otherwise best suited of those volunteers are taken into the Youth Vanguards and Model Detachments, the two organizations of which the People's Militia is composed.

The military education of the People's Militia seems to be taken very seriously. It is conducted by special training cadres of the regular armies who train them in rifle shooting, the throwing of hand grenades, the laying of land mines, and in guerrilla tactics in general. For the militia is not only the helpmate of the Eighth Route and New Fourth Armies but also their reserve, from which well-trained and experienced recruits must be available whenever and wherever the replenishment or expansion of a regular army unit becomes necessary.

Most militiamen seem anxious to joint the regular forces. The Eighth

Route and New Fourth Armies could be several times as large as they are today if all the qualified volunteers from the militia had been accepted.

It was one of the Communists' wisest decisions on general policy to resist the temptation of expanding their regular armies without too much consideration of economic factors. Taking many militiamen from their villages and making them into full-time soldiers would have meant reducing the labor power and the food production of the farmers and at the same time increasing the farmers' bill for the maintenance of the regular troops. It would have meant expanding the armies beyond the limits of their assured food supplies, endangering their standard of nutrition, and straining relations between the troops and the people.

Yenan always paid the greatest attention to economics as the basis of sound military policies. Chungking did not. Generalissimo Chiang Kai-shek apparently realized only in 1945—under the influence of repeated disastrous defeats in the Japanese campaign against American airfields—that an inflated, undernourished army is of infinitely lower value than a much smaller but well-fed army.

"Victory will be due 90 per cent to spiritual factors and only 10 per cent to material factors," * is Chiang Kai-shek's oft-expressed conviction. During all the years of war he seemed to rely more on moral suasion—on the spiritual exhortation of his soldiers and officials, of "selfish landlords," hoarders, speculators, and the people in general—than on the necessary material measures for an adequate economic war effort.

Yenan never failed to ascribe very great importance to spirit, in the sense of patriotism, devotion to duty, and self-sacrifice. That spirit plays a major role in the education and performance of the Communist-

* From *Central News*, Chungking, March 12, 1942, quoting the Generalissimo's speech on the Spiritual Mobilization Movement.—Mme. Chiang Kai-shek, in an address on the occasion of International Women's Day, expressed her own idea on the subject in a somewhat different manner: "I have recently become aware that in the history of human endeavor physical and material force has determined success and failure only in a proportion of 30 per cent, while spiritual force has amounted to 70 per cent of the total strength exerted." (*Central News*, Chungking, March 8, 1942.)

led armies and of all civilian cadres. The development of production and social progress was pushed by the Communists, not only in order to create the material prerequisites for enlarging its armies and participating with maximum strength in the final Allied land offensive against Japan, but also in order to raise the spirit of the soldiers and the people by satisfying their wants.

It is the increasing success of their energetic efforts in both the material and moral respects which now permits the Communists to launch out on a great expansion of the regular armies out of its militia reserves.

The total strength of the Eighth Route and New Fourth Armies has already risen from 475,000 in the spring of 1944 to 910,000 early in 1945, and military leaders in Yenan told me confidently that large parts of the militia—which itself grew from 2,130,000 to over 2,200,000 during the same time—will gradually be incorporated into the regular armies.

Characteristically, the growth of the Communist-controlled armies from its militia reserves coincides with the partial demobilization of unfit, undernourished, and demoralized troops of the Kuomintang-controlled National Government Army which became necessary in the course of belated military reform in 1945.

The Eighth Route and New Fourth Armies have two categories of fighters. In the spring of 1944, 131,000 out of their 475,000 men were organized in Special Guerrilla Detachments, while 344,000 were first-line troops in regular units. There is little difference between them: both are full-time, experienced fighters whom the command can use anywhere.

It seems that years of struggle have developed an economical and effective system of coordination between the two kinds of regular troops and their local auxiliaries, the militia and the Self-defense Corps—so that an Eighth Route or New Fourth Army unit, wherever it may have to fight in offensive or defensive operations, automatically acquires a strength several times its actual numbers.

In military operations of any size the regular troops, being the best armed, face the main enemy forces at the actual front. The somewhat

338

more lightly equipped Special Guerrilla Detachments are used as experts in the tactics of intercepting and deceiving the enemy and diverting his flanks. The militiamen harass and ambush small enemy units, plant land mines, do demolition work, help to maintain intelligence contacts, and guide the regular troops through their native terrain.

To intensify and improve cooperation between the armies, the militia, and the common people in the Self-defense Corps is one of the main purposes of political and military education in each of the three organizations everywhere in the war areas.

The regular soldiers are trained by their political commissars to be not only "model anti-Japanese fighters," examples to the militia and the Self-defense Corps, but also "model anti-Japanese citizens," examples to the civilian population as a whole.

The military qualities of army units and especially of the militia seem to vary a good deal, for their military training, which is to some extent coordinated, suffers from many handicaps.

First of all, there is comparatively little time for it, even during periods of lull in the fighting. The militia are primarily producers, and even the armies themselves are forced by the poverty of the war areas in which they fight and by Yenan's emphasis on lightening the tax burdens of the people, to do much production work.

Wherever regular troops are stationed for some time, they have to lead the farmers in the reclaiming of wasteland and to help them plough, sow, or harvest—in order to make good the losses of man power, animals, tools, and food which so many communities are suffering from enemy action. They have to spin yarn from which farmers or small weaving mills produce the cloth they need. They often have to help dig coal and iron from primitive native mines to supply the few small arsenals which produce hand grenades, land mines, and primitive cannon.

Training, therefore, has to take place during any odd hours, days, or weeks when there is neither military action nor urgent production work. Troops moving from one district to another, if not in a hurry, are usually given tactical practice on the way, and intervals in fighting or production work are used in the same manner. There seems to be a genuine spirit of competition for achievement in the armies which makes every unit eager to learn and practice as much as possible.

Another handicap is the scarcity of training equipment and especially of ammunition. The usual form of target practice is in actual combat with the enemy. "If you have ammunition and want to practice shooting," a young commander fresh from the front said to me, "you may just as well shoot at enemy troops. There are always plenty of them around."

The unified training of considerable formations of troops proves very difficult since regular army units are mostly scattered over wide areas, in constant readiness for defense or attack. Yet there is need for such training because joint operations of a number of separate units frequently develop in the course of the spread of local engagements over wider areas.

The method of "post-mortem" discussions immediately after such engagements is therefore used on the largest possible scale. Meetings are held in the various army units which took part in such an operation and criticism is free to any participants, officers, soldiers, and even militiamen.

Special efforts are made at regimental, brigade, and divisional headquarters to give advanced training to commanders, almost all of whom are promoted from the ranks. And the "Anti-Japanese University" in Suiteh in the Border Region gives training courses every year to thousands of commanders from the front. Some of them are particularly instructed for the education of militia troops, or even for leading them.

The commanders and the rank and file of the Eighth Route and New Fourth Armies have to devote a considerable part of their spare time to military, political, and cultural education and seem to learn with great enthusiasm. From what I have seen on both sides of the Kuomintang's blockade belt, it seems that the standards of literacy and general knowledge, of developed practical intelligence and keenness are definitely much higher among Yenan's troops than in the Chungking armies.

340

It is not easy to visualize the tremendous extent of the Japanese fortification system the Communist-led forces are facing. The enemy must try to protect his 4,640 miles of railroads and at least part of his 35,000 miles of highways in the Communist war areas; for the Communists are operating along every section of them. He realized the growing danger to his vital communication lines when the Eighth Route Army, during its three months' Hundred Regiments Campaign in 1940, destroyed 280 miles of railroad tracks and 880 miles of highways in various parts of North China.

Since that time, the Japanese have been using many hundreds of thousands of forced laborers under the "protection" of large numbers of troops, in order to extend and improve their fortifications. Even this was a matter of struggle with the Communists who attacked at many points, often liberated labor gangs, and together with them destroyed what had just been built.

This is the fortification system the Japanese have constructed along the Japanese-controlled railroads and highways and around the outposts of their main cities in the Communist war areas:

Almost 7,000 miles of wide, deep defense ditches. Over 10,000 elaborate brick-built strong points and blockhouses with surrounding ditches, underground shelters, and tunnel extensions. And hundreds of miles of blockade walls and barbed-wire barricades.

Yet the Communists continued their successful attacks. Between July, 1941, and May, 1944, they destroyed altogether 326 miles of railroad in various strategic sections of North and Central China. They captured and leveled several thousand blockhouses and strong points. And the Communists frustrated the enemy's intention of using this vast fortification system for offensive purposes, as a net which was to choke and exterminate them.

Instead of being able to reconquer the Communist-controlled areas, the Japanese and their puppets have virtually been imprisoned in narrow strips of territory along their communication lines and around the big cities. Almost every enemy strong point and blockhouse is under constant siege, and their garrisons often suffer acute supply difficulties.

341

Communist patrols watch every strategically situated mile of the defense ditches through which the Japanese try to rush reinforcements to endangered blockhouses. Their much-superior intelligence system gives the Communists advance information of all enemy movements. And the development of the local militia units, together with the mobility of their regular troops, has greatly improved their general defensive power.

Most of the enemy's fortifications—devised to protect him against attacks by hand grenades and rifle fire, and defended with no heavier weapons than machine guns—would become untenable the moment the Communists were to obtain from the Allies relatively small quantities of high explosives and bazookas.

But even without such supplies, the Communists will be able to do enormous harm to the enemy's communication lines when the final Allied land offensive against the Japanese begins. For when that time comes, it will be justifiable for them to sacrifice large numbers of men and what little reserves of ammunition they have, in order to keep strategic railroads and highways interrupted for more than a few days and in more than a few places.

It seems that the Communists are fighting continuously in the meantime—not only harassing the enemy where the cost is in proportion to results, and staving off his constant attacks, but also improving their assault positions by a steady expansion of the territories under their control, in preparation for the final counteroffensive.

The counteroffensive was apparently being planned in detail during the months I spent in Yenan. Most of the leading generals of the various war areas in North and Central China were there, reporting on their progress, consulting with Mao Tse-tung, Chu Teh, and the Yenan staff, polishing and coordinating their plans. I met among them men who struck me as personalities of unusual character, ability, and knowledge, and I found that they made equally favorable impressions on other foreigners.

Most of us felt that there was probably no abler general in all China than Nieh Yung-chen—the son of a wealthy landlord in Szechuan province, who studied chemical engineering in Belgium and France and military science in the USSR, taught at Chiang Kai-shek's Whampoa Academy, and was a political commissar in the Chinese Red Army during the Civil War.

Soon after the outbreak of the Sino-Japanese War he led 2,000 Eighth Route Army men into the enemy's rear in North China and thus became the founder of the largest, best consolidated, and strategically most important Anti-Japanese War Base—Chin-cha-chi, the Shansi-Chahar-Hopei region with a population of about 20,000,000.

General Nieh Yung-chen is tall and slim; he looks younger than his forty-six years and better groomed in his plain soldier's cotton uniform than anybody else I met in Yenan; his long, keenly intelligent face, like his entire person, expresses unusual will power, discipline, and drive. Yet he is intensely human and modest and has a good sense of humor. Chinese of all strata told me that no man in living memory has been so universally popular in North China as he—and Michael Lindsay confirmed it from personal experience.

In the course of wresting the vast territories of Chin-cha-chi from the Japanese and defending them against incessant attack, he became the initiator of many features of the strategic, tactical, and political policies which are now in force in the Anti-Japanese War Bases and the Border Region itself. "Neither we nor the Japanese knew how best to fight when we first faced each other for an entirely new kind of warfare," he said, and gave us a brilliant, systematic analysis of the process in which the strategy and tactics of military, political, and economic behind-the-front warfare have developed.

The Communists took the initiative with new practices, based on their Civil War experience. After a while, the enemy found means of countering them. The Communists developed new measures and the enemy followed with new countermeasures. And so on, through year after year of constant change and refinement of methods on both sides.

On the Japanese side, Nieh's counterparts, among the best known and most brilliant of Tokyo's generals, had the same task as he: to elaborate in the Chin-cha-chi area methods of warfare which would be applicable to all the regions of the Communist-Japanese struggle. But one Japanese general after another was recalled in disgrace. And Lieutenant General Abe, one of Tokyo's leading tacticians—trusting in the correctness of his tactics and anxious to prove it by directing the relief of a large body of troops the "bandits" had trapped—was killed in action in 1939. The Japanese never found an answer to the well-rounded, well-working Communist system of behind-the-line warfare. . . .

General Nieh Yung-chen would probably cut a better figure at inter-Allied military conferences than any Kuomintang officers of whom I know. And so, I believe, would General Peng Teh-huai, the Vice-Commander of the Eighth Route Army.

General Peng Teh-huai, who spent all his time at the front until sickness recently forced him to go to Yenan, is not only considered one of the best commanders but is also pioneer of the strong system of guerrilla economics which enabled the Anti-Japanese War Bases to survive and expand, to feed and supply large numbers of fighters, and to make economic warfare against the Japanese and their puppets the most essential and successful auxiliary to military warfare.

The economic, financial, and trade policies he helped to devise in the war areas of North China had considerable influence on the evolution of the present policies of Yenan's own Border Region and are fundamentally of the same nature.

He told me confidentially of the surprisingly large number of troops the Communists expected to be able to mobilize for the final Allied land offensive against Japan. "The reason why we can afford to expand the Eighth Route and New Fourth Armies to such an extent," he said, "is that our production of food and other essentials has been sufficiently increased to take all those militiamen out of their farm work and make them into full-time soldiers."

"And the necessary arms will have to be provided by your favorite munition carriers, the Japs?" I asked him.

"Surely." He laughed. "We shall capture much from them once we start our large offensive."

General Chen Yi, another outstanding military figure, acts as commander of the New Fourth Army in Central China while its famous founder and leader, General Yeh Ting, who was wounded and captured in the Kuomintang's attack on his headquarters units in 1941, is still the prisoner of Generalissimo Chiang Kai-shek. Chen Yi arrived in Yenan while I was there, after a "fast" three months' journey from Central China across some fifty or sixty of the strongest Japanese fortification lines.

His career has much in common with that of General Nieh Yung-chen of Chin-cha-chi. He, too, was the son of a wealthy landlord in Szechuan, studied chemistry in France, and taught at a military academy. During the Civil War he was commander of one of the Red army units which were left behind in the hills of small Soviet regions in Central China while the main body of the Communist forces went on the Long March to the Northwest. When the Kuomintang and the Communists united against Japan in 1937, he helped organize the New Fourth Army out of those remnants.

General Chen Yi spoke mainly about the good progress of preparations in the Anti-Japanese War Bases of Central China for the final Allied land offensive against the enemy. "We have been gaining much actual and even more potential strength recently," he said. "Our regular forces are only sixty miles from Shanghai, twenty miles from Nanking, and thirty miles from Hankow. Our guerrillas, in plain clothes, are operating very much closer to all those cities, almost within sight of their suburbs. Our organizations inside those cities are strong and getting ready. . . ."

What if the military leaders of Yenan had obeyed the orders of the National Government in Chungking . . . if the Eighth Route Army had kept its numbers restricted to the "authorized" three divisions with altogether 45,000 men and without any militia auxiliaries . . . if the New Fourth Army had "disbanded" itself . . . if the political and

345

economic reforms that were necessary to bring the population in the enemy's rear behind the war effort had not been carried out . . . ?

There would be no Anti-Japanese War Bases in North or Central China today. . . . The enemy would be in full control of enormous resources which the Communists are now largely denying him. . . . Hundreds of thousands of Japanese troops would be free to face the Allies. . . . There would be no armed support in those vast areas for the final Allied land offensive against Japan. . . . And 90,000,000 people would have had neither the protection against Japanese oppression nor the beginning of social progress they got in the Anti-Japanese War Bases. . . .

Somewhere in old Europe, I believe in the Austro-Hungarian monarchy, there was a high decoration for officers who through insubordination in the field achieved signal successes against the enemy. The leaders of the Eighth Route and New Fourth Armies—even *if* they were found guilty of insubordination—would still deserve to be decorated for it. . . .

Chapter Thirty-five

U. S. ARMY OBSERVER SECTION

JULY 22, 1944, was a historical date for Yenan—and it might have been for the Allies. Yenan's primitive airfield, unused during years of complete isolation from the outside world, had hurriedly been improved. A group of high-ranking Eighth Route Army officers and a small guard of honor stood expectantly in the hot noon sun. When the first sound of the long-expected aircraft became audible over the quiet Yenan valley we raced to the airfield on an old truck.

Three fighters with U. S. Army markings circled protectively overhead, skirting the tall pagoda while a C-47 transport plane landed. A number of American officers and enlisted men climbed out: Colonel David D. Barrett, rotund and jovial but soldierly, one of the most experienced Old China Hands of the U. S. Army; lank and lively John S. Service, an able, China-born young diplomat and language scholar who had for some time been attached to General Stilwell's China-Burma-India headquarters as political adviser; Major Ray Cromley, as keen on his hush-hush enemy intelligence job as he had been on his work for the American-owned *Japan Advertiser* when I met him in Tokyo years ago; Major Casberg, an army doctor, and some who were either Far Eastern experts or military specialists.

"We are mighty glad to be here—at last," Dave Barrett drawled in his broad Southern twang, with a smile to match.

The Yenan people, too, were mighty glad. Within two months the door to their blockaded, forbidden areas had opened for the second time. And with all due respect to us, these guests obviously carried more weight than the representatives of the world's most important newspapers. Evidently the United States Army realized that the Chinese Communists had a role to play in the war against Japan. And so, it seemed, did Generalissimo Chiang Kai-shek, who had at last given the American party permission to go to Yenan.

There could have been no better token of American sympathy for the Communist fighters than those few boxes the plane brought for them: precious medicines donated a long time ago by the American Red Cross to the International Peace Hospitals in the Red war areas which were suffering so badly from the Kuomintang's medicine block-ade.

At the government Guest House the national flag of the Chinese Republic, the same that flies in Chungking, greeted the first Allied officers to visit Yenan. And among those who received them was Major General Chou, the Generalissimo's resident representative with the Eighth Route Army in Yenan, smiling and apparently more pleased than embarrassed at the new phenomenon of Chungking-Washington solidarity with the Communist "bandits." It all seemed somewhat un-real, almost too good to be true.

"I want to make it quite clear from the beginning," Colonel Barrett told me in the evening, "that we are not a military mission in the ordi-nary, broad sense, as you seem to expect. We are only observers.

"O-b-s-e-r-v-e-r-s," he drawled with a quizzical smile. "Observers with some purely technical tasks. Those are the terms agreed upon with the Chinese government in Chungking. But we hope to do some good," he added seriously.

This limitation was a little disappointing in view of the great tasks of coordination that had to be tackled to make the best use of the large Communist forces and their invaluable strategic positions while the Allies were approaching the coasts of China.

But the technical duties of the U. S. Army Observer Section were in themselves important enough. They coincided with the two subjects General Chu Teh had put first in his interviews with me about possible Communist assistance to the Allies: ground-air cooperation for the U. S. Army Air Force, and enemy intelligence.

Both sides got busy without delay. The Communists made clear what

348

they thought they could do in order to help the Allies even more than they were already helping in their singlehanded fight. And the American observers stated clearly and simply what they wanted. Both approached their tasks in a practical, businesslike manner. There seemed little need for words. Experienced soldiers understand each other easily when they are faced with a common task.

"Whoever used the term 'lost Allies' for these 'Red' Chinese forces who operate behind the Japanese lines in North and Central China conveyed a totally erroneous impression," Colonel Barrett told me a few weeks later, referring to the title of an American magazine article which a second batch of observers had brought on the next plane.

"It would of course only help the enemy if I let you use in your dispatches any details about the first results of our work here. But you can say that the degree of wholehearted cooperation and of practical assistance rendered to the United States Army by the Eighth Route Army could scarcely be improved. From the Commander in Chief down, the entire Eighth Route Army placed its facilities at our disposal for the accomplishment of our various tasks. We are sometimes hard put to it keeping up with them."

This was as far as Dave Barrett would allow me to quote him in my cables. But to me it was confirmation that my own impressions about the abilities and the sincere cooperative spirit of the Yenan people had been correct.

A contagious enthusiasm soon prevailed among the American officers and G.I.'s as they got the feel of the Yenan atmosphere. Their quarters were like the camp of inspired pioneers. Week after week they worked at high pressure, digging into what they called unexpected gold mines of intelligence about the enemy; organizing the rich possibilities of ground-air cooperation; and grunting satisfaction at the wealth of general information, assistance, and impressions they got.

Dave Barrett had his officers and men up at six-thirty every morning, no matter whether they had been busy late into the night or even into the early morning. They worked and slept two, three, or four together in primitive, cavelike rooms in order to be all together in the same building. Even Dave and Jack Service shared a room. All lived in the same style as the Eighth Routers, officers, and enlisted men, eating their plain Chinese food with chopsticks at the same tables, with but one American addition—coffee and cream.

There was a most untraditional absence of griping in this strange little headquarters. Mac Fisher of the Office of War Information in Chungking, who came up on a visit between planes, said he had never seen anything like it. Every member of the plane crews agreed with him. They considered a trip to Yenan an invigorating experience, a pleasure second only to going home.

The active, natural Yenan atmosphere and those cheerful, warm-hearted, practical Eighth Route Army men seemed to charm all the American officers and G.I.'s. They enjoyed every bit of the Communists' simple, unsophisticated hospitality: the unconventional dinner parties at which famous Chinese generals and their wives—in cotton uniforms and pants, without lipstick and society manners, but gay and feminine—sat together with young American lieutenants and sergeants, talking with them about their homes and families back in the States; the theatricals in barnlike auditoriums crowded with animated spectators; and especially those rustic Saturday evening dances where everybody, party leader Mao Tse-tung and Commander in Chief Chu Teh, girls and boys from universities and factories, Eighth Route Army men, and, of course, the ever-ready Americans themselves joined in the breath-taking *yangko* folk dance and in waltzes and fox trots. "Gosh, what a difference from the other side," they used to say, thinking of the rigid prohibition of all dancing by the New Life Movement in the Chungking territories and of their stuffy, frustrated atmosphere.

The Communists were equally enthusiastic about the eager and natural Americans who seemed all so happy, informal, and young, whatever their age and rank, and who were so keenly devoted to their tasks.

There was much appreciative comment about the genuinely democratic attitude the Americans took toward one another and toward the Chinese. The Yenan people felt they had judged American democracy correctly. I had never seen large groups of Chinese and foreigners so unconventional and happy together, so completely unaware of differ-

350

ences of background, political creed, and race—so successful in cooperating with one another and so sincere in their mutual appreciation.

The Communists did not complain to the Americans about their unenviable position behind a twofold Japanese and Kuomintang blockade, although they made the facts clear, sometimes in grim seriousness but mostly in terms of good-humored jokes. They did not seem to worry about the strict limitations on the tasks of the U. S. Army Observer Section, relying on the logic of developments which must eventually break down all hindrances to inter-Allied cooperation—if only for the sake of saving many American lives.

There was no clamor for American assistance, although it was of course emphasized that mutual aid would greatly help the common war effort.

"What is wrong with these people?" one American asked me in real surprise a few weeks after his arrival. "They haven't asked me yet when we're finally going to send them tanks and planes and heavy artillery, and when we are going to hit the Japs harder, as everybody does on the other side."

Nor did anyone ever ask the plane crews which came and went between India, Chungking, and Yenan to bring them this or that from the well-stocked shops in the outside world—for themselves or their families. Their personal hardships were never mentioned.

One of the observers, an experienced Old China Hand, discussed with me the astonishing peculiarities of the Chinese Communists. "These Chinese ain't interested in money!" he burst out, as though a most paradoxical observation suddenly took shape and became so irresistible that he had to risk his reputation as a hard-boiled skeptic by confessing to it. "It sounds incredible, but I have convinced myself of it. They *really ain't* interested in money. I think this one strange fact sums up these people here better than any of those highfalutin arguments you guys probably use in your newspaper articles."

Another experience surprised practically every one of the American observers, week after week. "Face" did not seem to play a role in this

351

part of China, as it does everywhere else. All the irritating and often unconquerable handicaps to mutual understanding and practical cooperation which that fateful little word "face" still implies, as it has ever since foreigners made contact with China, simply did not exist in Yenan. It was not necessary to make certain that you were "giving face" to somebody from whom you wanted something or to avoid making a person "lose face" when you had to criticize something. You could deal with them more or less as though those strange Chinese were just ordinary Americans or Europeans.

And the Communists would smile with undisguised amusement when Colonel Barrett or someone else—having learned his Chinese on the conventional Mandarin Court pattern which still survives in all the rest of the country—would express his desires or his thanks for useful services in the best terms of exquisite politeness and flowery deference. The Communists are polite, too, but they want their "face" ignored, and formalities put aside, so as to get on better with practical cooperation and real understanding. They ask very often for criticism and advice. The Chinese do that habitually; it is polite. But the people in Yenan expect you to take such requests literally instead of answering them with a compliment, as in Chungking.

This is why seasoned, famous generals of the Eighth Route Army asked a very young American officer for a course of lectures about the best methods to be used on a certain detail of assistance to the United States Army; and why they did not consider it beneath their dignity to learn from him like eager schoolboys how to revise their own practices. In fact, they came back to him after a while with the confession that they might have misunderstood one of his instructions. "It seems incredible," he said to me, "how matter-of-fact these people are."

Their limited tasks could not prevent the American observers from forming certain personal opinions about matters concerning the work and fight of the Communists that were not formally included in their terms of reference. Their close contacts with all ranks of the Eighth Route and New Fourth Army people in Yenan, and later on in Communist-controlled war areas, were bound to give them a good idea of the veracity of the Communists' claims—about the strength of their forces and positions, the magnitude of their battle records, and their potentialities of helping the Allies.

They saw Eighth Route Army men perform in maneuvers and some of them later observed them in action at the front. I watched Dave Barrett's beaming face and heard his juicy exclamations when we witnessed Communist soldiers hit a target at seventy-five yards with their hand grenades. And he confirmed my impression of the splendid physique of the soldiers of Wang Chen's brigade at Nanniwan whom he had observed for days with his cool, expert eye.

American officers with open minds, trained in soldiers' jobs and with much experience of China, cannot work for months in close contact with the Communist army without gaining the impression that the military claims of the Chinese Communists, great as they are, seem essentially correct—and that the coordination of their fighters with the Allied forces would mean the saving of tens of thousands of American lives.

The war might soon be over—before the Communists or any Chinese forces could be used. But the war performance of the Communists was symptomatic for their character; and knowledge of their strength and qualities was politically of great importance.

Part Seven

WITNESSES OF THEIR WAR EFFORT

THE MEDICAL SECTION OF A COOPERATIVE SOCIETY

Chapter Thirty-six

WHAT AMERICAN OFFICERS SAW
AT THE FRONT

A N AMERICAN fighter pilot was strafing a Japanese-held railroad somewhere in North China when his plane was hit by antiaircraft fire. He bailed out close to the track. To escape the Japanese he hid in the daytime and walked short distances at night, away from the railroad. After two days he was confronted by a group of blue-uniformed soldiers. Were they Japs, he wondered, or did they belong to those "friendly troops" in part of the enemy's rear about whom he had heard vaguely?

The soldiers were more than friendly to the young lieutenant. They treated him like a long-lost brother, talked joyfully to him in a language he did not even expect to understand, fed him well, and got him a large quantity of cigarettes a day or two after he indicated to them that he wanted to smoke.

The first person he met who spoke a little English told him that he was with the Eighth Route Army of the Communists. Having arrived in China only a few weeks before, he had never heard of the Eighth Route Army. The name Communist, however, struck a familiar note with him. It was not so long ago that he used to harass Communist soapbox orators on Boston Common.

The men who rescued him were militiamen, peasant auxiliaries of the Eighth Route Army. They had been searching for him along the railroad track since the hour he bailed out. They wanted him to know how happy they were to have found him at last. And they apologized for having kept him waiting so long for the cigarettes: they had to get them from an enemy blockhouse garrisoned by puppet troops, and such things naturally took time.

Eventually he was on his way to Yenan, together with an Austrian-Jewish refugee doctor of the Eighth Route Army. He saw much of the Shansi-Chahar-Hopei Anti-Japanese War Base and spent some interesting days at local army headquarters. In many weeks on foot and horseback and during the exciting hours when Eighth Route Army men took him across various enemy lines, he had a good opportunity to observe conditions and activities in the Communist war areas.

I found the lieutenant full of enthusiasm for "those Chinese Reds" when I met him on his arrival in Yenan: not only because they had been so helpful to him, but mainly because he had come to admire them as genuine fighters. His testimony to the war effort in the Communist regions and to the close cooperation between the population and the army was especially valuable since he had a completely open mind on the Chinese situation as a whole.

The officers of the U. S. Army Observer Section questioned him in much detail and it seems that his factual replies confirmed the assertions of the Yenan leaders about the war effort in their areas behind the Japanese lines.

Comparison between the lieutenant's log and a map which the observers had received from the Eighth Route Army a short time before proved that the Communists actually controlled more territory in that area than they had claimed.

"If I were not in the army," the lieutenant said, "I would like to go on a lecture tour back home and tell our people the truth about the Chinese Communists."

Months later I met in New York bombardier Lieutenant Curtis Bush, who, together with the rest of the crew of his badly damaged plane, bailed out over another Anti-Japanese War Base in North China and spent two months there. He was equally impressed with what he saw. This is the main part of his own story, passed by U. S. Army censorship, as he told it to *PM* (April 8, 1945).

"The Communists have effectively organized the Chinese people within the areas controlled by them in an all-out war against the Japanese. Even in the remote, mountainous territory where I landed, the farmers, who might not be expected to know there was a war going on, knew just what to do when we appeared on the scene. They had been instructed to watch out for American fliers who might be forced down and told how to care for us.

"We were conducted to a near-by village, fed, clothed, and then guided to the area headquarters. It was here I saw convincing proof of the fight the Eighth Route Army and the People's Militia were putting up against the Japs.

"The Communists had gotten together a War Achievement Exhibit which had been attended by more than 10,000 natives scattered throughout the territory. On exhibit were weapons captured by the guerrillas from the Japanese. There were enemy carbines, machine guns, mortars, and even a few pieces of heavy artillery.

"But they do not depend solely on the enemy. They make their own rifles and even produce cannon by boring out sections of tree trunks. These are fired by low explosive charges using a charcoal powder base.

"In the production of grenades and land mines, the Chinese showed real ingenuity. They used iron castings, glass jars, crocks, and hollowed-out rocks as casings for the charges. Despite their simplicity, these grenades and mines are used with good effect against the Japanese.

"Compared with American equipment, the weapons were of a primitive type. But what impressed me was that these people are fighting as best they can with whatever they have at hand. I couldn't help wondering what results they might achieve with a few of our heavy machine guns and mortars.

"What amazed me is the progress they have made with the little they have. One part of the exhibit contained maps showing the progress made in various anti-Japanese bases. In one area alone, 1,899 square miles of territory had been recaptured from the enemy and more than 500,000 people liberated. The maps covered fifteen such areas and showed 300,000 square miles of liberated territory. There was no doubting the authenticity of these maps, as many persons receiving them had actually fought in the campaigns shown.

"I was particularly interested in the strides made in agricultural

359

production. Without a dependable and sufficient food supply, the resistance movement would collapse. Included within the exhibit were improved varieties of wheat, corn, and other products which were grown on an experimental farm run by the Communists. The Minister of Production, a graduate of the University of Minnesota, told me the seeds were derived from American-type crops and were being produced and distributed to the farmers throughout the area.

"Experiments were being carried out to raise new vegetables and fruit. Irrigation projects are being developed to reclaim arid land. In one area, 2,600 acres of formerly unused land are now producing. The experimental farm was well stocked with domestic animals and the farmers were being taught the proper care of them. The first glass of milk I tasted since leaving the States came from Holstein cows kept by the Communists.

"Eighth Army troops assist in the production drive. They help the farmers harvest the crops and even have small farms of their own. According to regulations, each soldier must reclaim three mow (one-half acre) of land and raise enough food to feed him for three months. The remainder is supplied by the army. So successful has the program been that in this area where famines were a regular occurrence, the Communists had stored up a two-year supply of grain against drought and emergencies.

"Since I've returned home, I've heard the charge that the Chinese Communists are not fighting the Japs. I can vouch for the fact that they are. The peasants are being taught by the Eighth Routers how to shoot and plant land mines. They also are being instructed in guerrilla tactics. People come from hundreds of miles around for training and then return to their homes where they participate in offensive operations with the regular troops.

"In the economic sphere, private enterprise is being encouraged. Cooperatives of all kinds, ranging from a two-man outfit to others where hundreds share the profits, are to be found everywhere. They produce leather goods, ammunition, blankets, uniforms, bandages, many types of simple tools, and other items not only for army use but for civilian consumption.

360

"Speaking with party leaders confirmed the impression of which you cannot help being conscious as you observe the people and their activities, namely, that nationalism is more important than Communism.

"It is interesting to note that in places where we were entertained by city and *hsien* [county] officials, the leaders were gentry—quite obviously gentry. Many of them were well-educated persons whose families had lived in the communities for several hundred years. They were landlords, merchants, as well as civic officials. They were exactly the type of civic leaders you would find in the U. S. A."

Raymond P. Ludden, a State Department official with long experience in China, who was a member of the U. S. Army Observer Section in Yenan, reported in Washington * after a prolonged journey through several Anti-Japanese War Bases during the fall and winter of 1944 "that these Communists are fighting the Japanese [and] that they have popular support in their area."

"Traveling mostly by muleback and afoot," the report continues, "the party went over mountain trails and forest tracks, crossing and recrossing the Japanese lines always accompanied by a strong escort of Chinese guerrillas. They wore the Chinese Communist uniforms on the trip. The party traversed Shansi and spent a long period in Hopei, and from there various sections of the party made side trips, one pushing as far as Peiping. [Where, according to what Chungking leaders had solemnly told me before we left for Yenan, "there were certainly no Communists any more."]

"He said the Chinese considered part of their forces as regulars and part as guerrillas, but that all were what we would call guerrillas, both for their way of life in fastness retreats and their raids and skirmishes with their enemies, the Japanese. One member of the party was killed during one of these skirmishes, and at another time the group was obliged to make a forced march of twenty-six hours without food or rest to escape being intercepted by the Japanese.

"He found a great admiration for the United States among the sol-

* *The New York Times*, March 23, 1945.

diers and the people whom he encountered in this area. He said the program supported by the peasants was not particularly Communist in character, but that it was indigenous to the peasantry of China. In its simplest terms the program preached by all these local leaders was in terms that everyone could understand: 'A full belly, a warm back, and nobody knocking them around.' In this period of continuous skirmishing he said the feeling is among these people that 'the man who has no gun gets pushed around.' "

Major Casberg, the American Army doctor who was a member of the U. S. Army Observer Section in Yenan and visited the war areas of the Communists during the summer of 1944, summarized a private report about his experiences as follows:

"I have found the medical personnel very much alive to the needs of the army and civilians in this section of China. When one considers the difficulties encountered, mostly attributable to the Kuomintang blockade, one cannot help being favorably impressed by the accomplishments of the medical profession.

"I have had numerous discussions with groups of the medical staffs of the local hospitals, medical schools, and military establishments of forward echelons, and have found them all very cognizant of their limitations in personnel and matériel. However, I have noted a definite lack of the 'begging for supplies' spirit.

"It does not fall in my domain to estimate the help these people are giving the Allied cause; however, if in the future ordnance is given these armies to carry on the war against Japan, we must by all means also supply them with their medical needs. Should medical supplies be sent there, I am sure that they will be used; not misappropriated or set aside for future periods.

"From my observations of the hospital clientele and the friendship existing between the soldiers and the local populace, I would say that the peasants as well as the army will benefit from any medical improvement in this section, and this would be a factor in improving the fighting qualities of the soldier; for the civilian, besides being his family, is also his rear echelon growing the food and making the supplies so essential to the army."

One day while I was in Yenan, a wireless message was received for the U. S. Army Observer Section from an American fighter pilot of Chinese ancestry who came down into the Anti-Japanese War Base near the Yangtsze city of Hankow in Central China and was rescued by the Communist-controlled New Fourth Army—which was officially "disbanded" by the Chungking government in 1941.

The American airman reported to the headquarters of General Claire L. Chennault's Fourteenth U. S. Army Air Force that he was safe and anxious to return to his base somewhere in China.

His rescuers were willing to escort him into National Government territory, but he could not get through since strong Chinese government forces were carrying on an offensive against the troops of the Communist-controlled New Fourth Army with whom he was.

The message ended with the airman's request of the American Army to ask the National Government in Chungking to stop the fight, so that he could rejoin his unit. . . .

Representative Mansfield, Democrat of Montana, reporting to Congress on his mission to China in December, 1944, dealt at length with the Kuomintang-Communist issue.

He stated that Major General Claire L. Chennault, old China expert and commander of the Fourteenth U. S. Army Air Force in China, "rates the Communists highly as fighters, and declares there is no connection between them and Russia, a conclusion which was borne out in my conversations during the rest of my stay in China.

"The Communists," Mansfield continued, "are a force to be reckoned with in China. They have approximately 90,000,000 people in the territories under their control and they seem to have evolved a system of government which is quite democratic. . . . The Communists are well disciplined. . . . They are not Communists in the sense that Russians are, as their interests seem to focus on primarily agrarian reforms. . . .

"They are organized effectively in the region under their control to

363

carry on the war and to maintain their own standing. . . . The Communists have gone into villages which they captured, told the people they were spreading democracy, asked how many were in favor of reducing land taxes, interest rates, and so forth, and then allowed them to vote. . . .

"Among their weak points is their spirit of sanctimoniousness. They look upon themselves as pious crusaders and do-gooders. Their knowledge of the outside world is primitive; there are social distinctions among them, and they are totalitarian and dictatorial in their own way.

"Their points of strength are they have a good military force, estimated at around 600,000, and there is more democracy in their territory than in the rest of China."

On Generalissimo Chiang Kai-shek's regime the Congressman reports, "The Kuomintang is disliked more every day and this is due to fear of the army and the attitude of tax collectors; and it is proved by the revolts of the peasantry, the party criticism by provincial leaders, and student revolts against conscription. It speaks democratically but acts dictatorially.

"The Kuomintang is afraid of the will of the people, has lost much of its popular support, and will not allow any of its power to be used in the way of agrarian reforms. However, the Kuomintang is still *the* party in China. It has its leader in the Generalissimo, who has the franchise in the war against Japan. It has a powerful army. The middle class leans toward it and it still has the support of America. . . .

"The disastrous results of this [Generalissimo Chiang Kai-shek's political] maneuvering have been manifested in many ways:

" '1. He has used something like sixteen divisions to blockade the Communists and has thus lost the use of large numbers of troops to fight Japan.

" '2. He has allowed Chinese military strength to deteriorate in other ways through his inability to mobilize China's resources; to conscript the college students and the rich men's sons; to see that his troops received food and medical supplies.

364

" '3. He has not checked hoarding; he has not stopped inflation; and he has allowed merchants and landlords to profit tremendously.

" '4. He has failed to improve the condition of the peasantry in regard to high rents and high rates of interest.'

"Under the present system, being conscripted into the Chinese [Kuomintang] army is like receiving a death sentence because the soldier receives little training, food, and equipment. They are starved and poorly equipped because of graft up above. The commanders hang on to much of the stuff they receive and then flood the black markets and enrich themselves. The administration of food supply on an equitable basis is necessary or the Chinese Army will not be able to fight as it should.

"When I started on this mission I thought that the Chinese problem was supply, but now I feel that the most important factor is cooperation among the Chinese themselves and that this has been the case for some time.

"Our military and diplomatic representatives are doing all that they can do to close this breach and to bring about greater cooperation among the Chinese.

"They realize that Chiang Kai-shek's position is a difficult one and that he fears giving in to the Communists because of the effect it might have on him and his party.

"They want the Chinese to get together so that we can win the war in Asia and they want to get the boys out of China as soon as victory is won.

"The main concern of all of them is the saving of American lives.

"They do not care whether a Chinese is an agrarian or not," Congressman Mansfield summed up, "just so he fights Japan and takes that much of the burden off our soldiers."

Chapter Thirty-seven

THE TESTIMONY OF AN OXFORD MAN

THIS is the testimony of a foreigner who has been with the Eighth Route Army in the war areas since the day of Pearl Harbor: Michael Lindsay, the son of the famous Master of Balliol College at Oxford, former press attaché at the British Embassy in Chungking, and lecturer in economics at Yenching University—an American missionary college in Peiping.

"Opinion in Allied countries quite underestimates the importance of the Communist forces in North China," Lindsay told me during our first talk in Yenan, which was followed by months of almost daily conversation.

"Both their actual and potential importance is far greater than people realize. They do not know what strength the competent leadership of the Communists and their true cooperation with the population give those forces.

"If the Eighth Route and New Fourth Armies had an adequate supply of no more than cartridges for the rifles and machine guns they have taken from the Japanese and an adequate number of light weapons capable of knocking out the enemy's blockhouses, I think it would be fairly safe to say that there would be a general collapse of the Japanese positions in North and Central China and it would be possible rapidly to extend guerrilla activities deeper into Manchuria. If the Japanese could not hold their little garrison points any longer, the whole Japanese fort system would become untenable. Even the railroads would continually be interrupted unless the Japanese very greatly increased their garrisons and supplied them with artillery—which they cannot afford to do. Under such conditions it should be quite practicable for the Communists to make effective raids on the main Japanese centers,

366

especially if the Americans could give them some occasional air support for such purposes.

"Having been with troops in active war areas for years, I had many opportunities of checking the published Communist claims on actions of which I had reliable firsthand knowledge. I always found them substantially accurate. I think that all the figures you have been given here on the strength of the Communists and their battle records are at least of the right order of magnitude."

Skeptics would probably call Michael Lindsay a "fellow traveler" of the Chinese Communists, especially if they saw him in his baggy Eighth Route Army uniform and the old soldier's cap he wears indoors and out; with his labor-hardened hands and his broken eyeglasses and pipe —looking more like the prototype of a guerrilla than anyone else I saw in Yenan.

In one sense he has been their fellow traveler ever since that December morning in Peiping when his wife Shao Li happened to tune in the radio a few minutes before the Japanese gendarmes did, and heard the news of Pearl Harbor. They fled in their car, succeeded in finding Eighth Route Army men in the hills a short distance outside the city, and went on a long trek with them to the headquarters of the Shansi-Chahar-Hopei Anti-Japanese War Base, wanting to go on to Chungking and eventually to England to help in the war against Japan. Michael and another Englishman, the physicist Professor William Band, who was with him, were so impressed with the war effort of the Communists that they decided to stay and help them with their knowledge of radio engineering. From then on, Michael worked with the Eighth Route Army. He and Shao Li ran with other noncombatants when the Japanese advanced in their great mopping-up campaigns, moved back to the war bases when the enemy was repulsed, always traveling with small army units and living with soldiers and officials, peasants and landlords.

But the Lindsays are not Communists. Michael retains the strict anti-authoritarian attitude of the typical progressive liberal, and with it a dry, almost fanatical objectivity toward the Chinese Communists—

367

although he does not deny his admiration for their war effort and their democratic achievements. He judges them with the same intellectual honesty that still makes him strongly critical of the Communist parties in his own country, in America, and in the USSR.

The opinions he gave were carefully weighed. His expressions of praise for the Chinese Communists were often examples of his typical English indulgence in cautious understatements, which I found characterized by his remark one evening when we heard over the radio that Hitler's fronts were cracking in France and Poland, that Allied bombers pulverized German cities, and that rebellious generals were after the Fuehrer's life. "Hitler must be rather annoyed," Michael said, completely serious, and he was somewhat shocked when I broke out into a roar of laughter.

His young wife, Shao Li, in spite of her present guerrilla appearance which is produced by the same kind of costume as Michael's, remains every inch the daughter of a once illustrious and wealthy mandarin-landlord family from Shansi province. Her brand of nationalism looks somewhat bourgeois in Yenan and she admits frankly to have no use for any political party or its doctrines. Her unqualified love and admiration for the fighters and the self-governments of the Communist war areas is that of a robust, unsophisticated woman who is part of the people and the soil of China and grateful to their defenders, no matter what their political label.

The Lindsays like Yenan, too. But they think it compares a little unfavorably with "their" Anti-Japanese War Base in the North, which they consider the "real thing."

I once had a long, systematical interview with Michael, reading to him for his comment what one of the highest-ranking Kuomintang generals in Chungking had told me about the Communist armies. This is the record as I wrote it down at the time:

"The Japanese have no reason to complain about the existence of the Shansi-Chahar-Hopei Anti-Japanese War Base in "occupied" North China, for conditions there are completely normal from the Japanese point of view," I read from my notes.

The Testimony of an Oxford Man

"The contrary is true," Michael replied. "There are very large areas where you can travel at the rate of about thirty miles per day without encountering any Japanese or puppets at all, for at least ten or twelve days from north to south and for two or three days from west to east. For these areas, conquered from the Japs, are strongly held by the Communists. Raids on Japanese-controlled railroad lines vary according to the strength of their fortifications. One of the lines in that area is not raided very much because it would be very costly and not worth while unless such raids were coordinated over large areas for the definite purpose of a large counteroffensive. But other railroads are mined fairly often and there have been frequent derailments. The Japanese-controlled highways are being attacked much more and Japanese trucks are very frequently ambushed, which does not cost the Communists much in men and munitions.

"But the main thing is that continual fighting for food supplies is going on around towns and cities wherever the enemy is. The Japanese go out to seize food since their plans of getting large quantities through the puppet governments do not work, a fact to be put down to the credit of the well-organized popular resistance and political warfare of the Communists. This type of fighting does great harm to the enemy and it is also one of the main reasons why the Eighth Route Army is so popular with the people."

I read the next statement I had been given in Chungking: "The Communist positions in Eastern Hopei near Peiping have been lost completely."

Imperturbable Michael got angry and used stronger words than I had ever heard from him.

"This is pure nonsense. Again, the contrary is the case. The East Hopei positions are expanding most rapidly. In 1943 eight county governments of the New Democracy type were started there in newly liberated regions, for the Communists gained control over 6,000 more villages during that year. In 1940 and 1941 the East Hopei area was very unstable so that guerrillas used to say, 'You can never sit down to get the lice out of your shirt because the Japanese are always coming.'

369

But now, East Hopei has developed a strong, stable base near the Great Wall. Around Peiping itself there are some less stable areas which survive in spite of incessant fighting. In 1943 the Japanese were on the offensive for more than 150 days in that region, but that did not change the situation."

Another statement made to me in Chungking was that "the militia plays no role in the defense of the country and causes only internal disturbances."

"That, too, is completely nonsense," said Michael. "The militiamen cooperate very well indeed with regulars and guerrillas. They are responsible for a great deal of scouting and play a very real role in active fighting and ambushing the Japanese wherever there is a good opportunity. Other people do their field work for them while the militiamen are on active duty. This system has been developed only during the past year and is already working smoothly in some places.

"The militiamen's military qualities vary greatly. Some are very good or excellent while others are not much good. There was one militiaman who with fifteen or twenty others killed about three hundred Japanese during the last big autumn campaign, mainly by laying land mines in an ingenious manner. The worst that ever happens, on the other hand, is that some militiamen may run away when the Japanese come, but that is not frequent. There was one such case. The men, thereafter, got some education from regular army men and in three further engagements they became very good.

"Last year I saw near our village some very clever mine laying done by the militia. In general, the Communists are very inventive and efficient in mine warfare, not only tactically but technically. I once told our local command what I had heard on the radio about 'leaping mines' used by the Germans. A month later I met a friend from the local munitions department who said they had started making leaping mines in their own primitive workshops and found them satisfactory. When the Japanese began using magnetic detectors against mines, the militia and the peasants began hollowing out stones and using them as mines most effectively.

"Land-mine warfare plays a great role and does the Japanese a lot of harm. The militia are pioneers of mine laying. During the last great offensive in our region the Japanese wanted to get into a big village but dared approach only the outskirts because of the good mining that had been done. They succeeded in burning only one house and never got into the village. Yet they lost thirty-six men."

"The people have lost their faith in the Communists," I continued my reading.

"I shall give you only a few examples from my own experiences," Michael said. "During the last Japanese offensive we were rushing around with small bodies of Eighth Route Army troops, covering considerable distance. Wherever we came the people were extremely helpful to the soldiers. The year before, when we crossed a Japanese blockade line, our guide went to talk to a scout of the militia. An old peasant of seventy, seeing us alone, thought we had nobody to guide us and volunteered to come along. This is typical. Everywhere people take the greatest trouble and risks to shelter and help the Eighth Route Army. They take it for granted that there is the closest cooperation between themselves and the fighters. We once passed through one of those areas where the Japanese destroy everything and shoot all the civilians they see, in order to create a 'depopulated belt' in which the Communist forces cannot survive. You should have seen how happy the remaining peasants were when the Eighth Route Army came. And the people do not get discouraged by war damage and hardship. Last year, after the big offensive, we passed through the village where we had lived before. Most of it was destroyed and much of the food had been looted by the Japanese. But the people were in very high spirits and said, 'We shall get rid of the Japanese all right with the help of the Eighth Route Army.'"

I quoted the next allegation: "There is no freedom of speech and democracy in Chin-cha-chi."

Michael smiled. "I wish you could see for yourself. There are heated debates in the People's Political Council and nobody feels restricted in

371

giving his views. Noncontroversial matters are passed easily. But questions of land rent and tax regulations are frankly and thoroughly discussed between peasants and landlords—in public, as never before. I went to a village meeting once in a place where we stayed. The tenants complained that a landlord had tried to evade the new law about the reduction of land rents. The landlord gave his own version. He looked like a rather nasty specimen and the meeting certainly did not approve of him, but he got his say all right. And he succeeded in having the matter referred to the next highest government organ. I know personally of a good number of cases where, according to merit, either landlords or tenants got their right after frank discussion."

"The Kuomintang has been suppressed in Chin-cha-chi," I read.

"No. It is untrue. The Kuomintang even had their own newspaper until 1941; it was closed down only for lack of funds. I knew a certain number of Kuomintang people there. Those elected to the government of the region are mostly of the liberal wing of the Kuomintang and they get on very well with the Communists. In that area, you must remember, the Kuomintang was a progressive organization in 1938 when the National Government recognized the right of the Communists to establish the Anti-Japanese War Base from parts of the provinces Shansi, Chahar, and Hopei which the Eighth Route Army had liberated by fighting the Japanese.

"The Kuomintang members of those areas sent a delegation to Chungking, requesting headquarters to let them set up a special branch of the Kuomintang for the base and to permit them to have its functionaries democratically elected through the local party organizations. But Chungking refused. No merger of the three separate provincial organizations in the base was permissible, it said, and the party functionaries could not be elected but must be directly appointed by Kuomintang party headquarters.

"The man who had revived the Kuomintang in the base, the prominent party member Liu Tien-chi, was edged out in due course by Chungking for being too progressive. Together with others he continued to criticize the increasingly reactionary appointees of Chungking.

372

But they got only rude replies to their requests for democratic procedure within the party and for permission to cooperate with the Communists."

I asked about allegations I had heard in Yenan that certain Kuomintang members in the base have been discovered cooperating with the Japanese.

"There is some evidence for that statement. It was admitted to me by a Kuomintang leader that the local party organizations were careless about membership and permitted people with Japanese affiliations to come in. It has been established that certain Kuomintang members helped the Japanese to find hidden Eighth Army supplies during their last offensive. Some were convicted in trial and shot. I also know of another case: Six staff members of the local Kuomintang office, having been captured with other Chinese by enemy troops, were singled out by the enemy for good treatment and accepted the puppet positions the Japanese offered them. On that I have direct evidence from peasants who were captured with them. A big popular meeting was held in the presence of Kuomintang representatives, and there was some argument. The matter was eventually referred to the local high court, which later published sworn affidavits of seven respectable witnesses, together with an order of arrest against the six Kuomintang officials who had indeed turned puppets."

"What did the local Kuomintang people say about it?"

"Their defense was that those men had just been scared and cowardly but not traitorous. There was still another, even worse case. I heard about it from a man in the Public Safety Department, whom I have known extremely well since 1938 and whom I trust fully. He said that he obtained the minutes of a meeting of the Tanghsien branch of the Kuomintang in the base, which explained certain recognition signals for contacting the Japanese during their offensive. In still another place a document was captured from the Japanese with an analysis of the best ways of eliminating Communist party organizations, identifying Communist militia organizers and discovering hidden supplies—in

373

which it was stated that assistance might be obtained from Kuomintang members."

I asked Lindsay if I should believe Yenan allegations that some of the puppet armies which had formerly been National Government troops and later went over to the enemy were still retaining connections with Chungking.

"It is said," he replied, "that that is true, and many people in the Eighth Route Army are positive that Chungking ordered certain of its armies to desert to the Japanese in order to have a Kuomintang force in North China for the time when Japan collapses, a force which could then be used by the Kuomintang against the Communists."

Finally I asked Michael Lindsay whether he believed that the Communists were sincere in saying that their activities in the Japanese rear were aimed only at defeating the enemy but not at preparing a position of postwar power for themselves, and I also wanted to know the opinion of the ordinary people on the subject.

"The best evidence is the very great length to which the Communists went in trying to cooperate with the Kuomintang," he said. "Until the summer of 1943 they gave no publicity to the numerous attacks by Kuomintang troops on the Communist-led forces, except for the New Fourth Army incident early in 1941. In many cases the Communists allowed Kuomintang troops to come and take over areas which the Eighth Route Army had reconquered from the Japanese in bitter fighting. For example, the Kuomintang general Lu Chung-lin came through a certain part of our base in August, 1938, and took over an area in South Hopei which had been liberated by the Eighth Route Army several months before. In all those cases the Kuomintang troops collapsed at the first serious Japanese attack. As a result, several important areas were twice lost by Kuomintang troops and twice reconquered by Communist troops."

Lindsay took the initiative in our talk now, bringing up some points he considered of special importance. "The Communists are always being accused by the Kuomintang of setting up new local governments," he

374

said, "and of issuing a new currency in the areas they liberate from the Japanese. But on the basis of my firsthand experience I have convinced myself fully that these two things were absolutely essential for carrying on the war. The reason why the Communist forces have been able to maintain themselves against continuous attacks of Japanese troops, which are much better equipped and often also more numerous, is that the Communists have 100-per-cent cooperation from the people. This full popular cooperation could be obtained only through the establishment of democratic and progressive local governments and through the growth of really active and popular mass organizations. Each Anti-Japanese War Base behind the enemy lines has to support its own armed forces, which is possible only with a new and honest taxation system that is regarded as equitable by the people, and with the organization of an efficient supply system for the armed forces. This, again, requires the existence of local governments willing and able to cooperate fully with the army. In other words, governments with higher standards of honesty and efficiency than the old-style local governments maintained by the Kuomintang were an absolute necessity for the war effort. If any Allied forces had operated in those areas, they would also have been forced by circumstances to try to set up such new local governments.

"In many of those areas the currency situation was chaotic. For example, in old Marshal Yen Hsi-shan's area of south Shansi, as late as the summer of 1939 most notes in circulation were those of local banks and pawnshops which were often valid only in one single county. Most of the war bases in the enemy's rear had practically no connection with Chungking's rear territories, and if they had continued to use national currency they would have been considerably handicapped in their continuous economic warfare with the Japanese—a very important phase of the war as a whole. In our base national currency was convertible into the new local currency issued by the Communists until after Pearl Harbor. At that time, huge quantities of national currency which had been used in the foreign concessions of Tientsin began to flood our base and made the continuance of that policy impossible."

The Testimony of an Oxford Man

"What do you consider the reason for the lack of Kuomintang-Communist cooperation against the Japanese?" I asked.

"You must not forget that there has been absolutely nothing to prevent the Kuomintang from having a large share in the war behind the regular front lines, that is, in the enemy's rear where the Communists reconquered one area after another from the Japanese. Let me put it this way: Nothing has prevented the Kuomintang from playing a role in that war in the enemy's rear but their dislike of any cooperation with the Communists and their equal dislike of any kind of popular, democratic organizations.

"In all those war areas the Communists made great efforts to get Kuomintang cooperation. There were still many Kuomintang members in important positions in those areas for considerable time. But the Kuomintang party organizations in the enemy's rear have developed more and more in a reactionary direction, toward secret-service and spy organizations—not against the Japanese but against the Chinese Communists.

"If the Kuomintang had been willing to learn a little from the Communists about guerrilla warfare and the use of popular mass organizations against the national enemy, their armies behind the regular fronts, which were very large at the beginning of the war in the southern half of North China, might have maintained themselves and expanded their areas once more at the expense of the Japanese. Instead, the Kuomintang preferred to keep their old-style tactics and their old-style authoritative methods of government and dissipated a large part of their efforts against the Chinese Communists rather than directing them against the Japanese.

"It seems indeed that the Kuomintang actually preferred to see those territories remain in Japanese hands rather than have them recovered by the Chinese Communists. For it was apparently felt that Japanese-occupied areas could be brought back under Kuomintang control when the Allies eventually drove the Japanese out, while things would be very difficult in areas previously liberated by the Communists where the people would in the meantime get used to democratic government and therefore after the war refuse to put up with a return to the pre-

376

war regime. Even where the alternative would have been to have Japanese-occupied territories recovered by Kuomintang troops—if this would necessitate the introduction of democratic reforms desired by the people—the Kuomintang seemed to prefer having them continue under Japanese rule.

"Apart from all the other evidence there is for that attitude of the Kuomintang, this policy can be seen quite clearly in the constant demands of the Kuomintang for the disbandment of the larger part of the Communist forces in the enemy's rear. You know that this demand again plays a considerable part in the present Kuomintang-Communist negotiations in Chungking. The disbandment of Communist forces would mean to abandon large parts of the liberated areas of North and Central China to Japanese control; for nothing but the presence of those forces prevents the enemy from reoccupying them.

"If the Kuomintang had adopted a progressive policy, if they had been willing to cooperate with the Communists, they could have helped a great deal in developing a democratic tradition in China. What China really needed during all those years of war was a two-party system, with the Kuomintang in opposition in Communist-controlled areas and the Communist party in opposition in Kuomintang-ruled territories. Two such parties which supported the Central Government on fundamental matters of resistance against the enemy and of democratic reform, but which criticized each other on details of policy, would have been a great help in developing a tradition of free discussion and of cooperation between different political groups.

"As things developed, however, the remaining Kuomintang organizations in North China have certainly acquired the popular reputation of being ultrareactionary, to put it mildly, and they have come under grave suspicion of actually working with the Japanese.

"On the other hand, the experience of liberal individuals among the membership of the Kuomintang in various local governments in the Communist-controlled parts of North China has shown clearly how well cooperation can develop between the Communists and other political parties which accept the fundamental demands of democracy. Most

377

people to whom I have talked in those areas, people on all sides, hope that this may be the line on which postwar China can achieve unity and progress."

I asked Michael Lindsay whether he found the Communists in the war areas of North China dogmatic in their Marxism and whether their ideology was in any way a handicap to cooperation with "bourgeois" elements.

He denied it. "I have often argued with Communists about Marxian economics and philosophy and especially about their criticism of certain features of British and American democracy. But this never made any difference to our friendship or to our ability to work together."

Chapter Thirty-eight

"I WAS A WEALTHY LANDLORD . . ."

YEN LI-HSUAN is a vigorous man of over sixty with a beautiful, strong-willed face; tall, slim, erect, and calmly dignified as only an old-style Chinese from the North can be. He wears his spotless, tidily fitting cotton uniform of the Eighth Route Army like a mandarin coat. His old-fashioned courtesy is simple but superb.

I met him by accident through Michael Lindsay, who had known him for years in the war areas of North China and had great respect for him. The Communists proved to be poor propagandists, or they would have presented old Yen to a full meeting of our group as one of their most plausible and impressive witnesses.

One day, having paid him a courtesy visit, I invited him to come to my room with Michael to tell me the story of his development from landlord to guerrilla, to "Vice-General" in the Eighth Route Army and to a supporter of the New Democracy.

He sat at my desk in an almost ceremonial manner, talking calmly and stroking his long gray beard with slow, measured movements of his fine hands, as they do in ancient Chinese plays.

"I was a wealthy landlord near Tientsin," he began, "and lived most comfortably. I had forty tenant families on 250 acres of fertile land and sixteen hired laborers on another 170 acres under my own management. When I was young I studied at the College of Law and Administration in Peking. I traveled much in China and Japan and was always interested in improving the lot of the Chinese farmers. For everything in our country was very bad and I was convinced that we needed great reforms. But I had no concrete ideas on the subject. From what I saw of it, it seemed no use to me to join the Kuomintang.

"I Was a Wealthy Landlord . . ."

"In this state of political helplessness I was surprised by the attack of the Japanese in July, 1937. My hope that the government armies would stop their hasty retreat in our easily defendable region and thus give us an opportunity to organize the people for armed resistance was badly disappointed. The armies, all the government authorities, and most of the Kuomintang leaders ran away and left the people to their fate, without organizing or helping us at all.

"I determined to act for myself," he said with a hard gleam in his eyes. "As commander of the local Self-defense Corps which we land-lords used as protection against bandits, I began to organize from my own tenants a small band of guerrillas which grew slowly to about 120 men."

In the place of military knowledge old Yen had only a deep hatred for the Japanese and a desire to help protect the people whom the government had abandoned. His men collected arms from the peasants, many of whom used to keep rifles and shotguns against bandits. They trained secretly in the spacious courtyards of his large mansion, and their number grew. All the men who joined were tenants and other poor peasants. Nobody else would have anything to do with such a dangerous venture; especially since the Japanese had already established a puppet magistrate in the county. That man would not allow Yen to endanger the 'peace' of the county and eventually Yen had to move away with his men.

Japanese planes frequently flew over the area and the people were very much afraid. Yen's amateur warriors used to shoot at them with their rifles, but of course in vain. The only result was that the enemy got to know about them before they were ready to meet him, and Yen with his men moved on to another place.

That was the last time that they evaded a clash. One day the Japanese came on two trucks with two machine guns and a small cannon but did not find the guerrillas, who then took the initiative and ambushed them. In this first fight Yen lost three killed and four or five wounded; but the Japanese lost more, and the two Chinese truck drivers of the enemy unit went over to Yen.

"That was in May, 1938, and from then on my little group expanded rapidly," Yen continued. "We were soon over 1,000 men strong and collected more and more contributions of arms, food, and money from the villages, strictly according to the amount of land owned by the people. But even then we told all those who did not belong to us that we were only fighting the bandits, whose numbers had in fact increased very much since all government officials had run away.

"Just when I felt our need for better military training, I heard of another landlord, some thirty miles away, a younger man who had organized a similar guerrilla band. He was in contact with a colonel of the Kuomintang army who had been left behind with his regiment when our troops fled. I began to collaborate with that landlord and through him with the colonel."

Yen laughed when he recalled how his new-found ally had been careful not to tell him at that time that he and the Kuomintang colonel were already in close relationship with the Eighth Route Army of the Communists. "I am glad he did not tell me then. It might have been too early for me, considering all the prejudice I, like everybody else, had against the Communists. But he told me soon afterward and I did not mind very much belonging to the Eighth Route Army myself, in a way; because I saw they were good people and fought the enemy well. More and more men joined up, either with groups like mine or directly with units of the Communist forces. That was how the Eighth Route Army grew out of popular resistance."

"What became of that Kuomintang colonel?" I interrupted.

"He is one of the leading officers in the Eighth Route Army today. His name is famous. He is Lu Cheng-tsao, Commander in Chief of the important Anti-Japanese War Base of Shansi-Suiyuan on the Yellow River, adjoining this Border Region. He has long since become a Communist. An excellent man.

"By the way, his chief of staff is a former Kuomintang general whom the National Government sent against Lu, to attack and destroy his powerful army when the Kuomintang began again to fight the Communists."

"And what became of your original guerrillas?"

381

VILLAGE DEFENSE AGAINST THE JAPANESE

"The majority of them were killed in fighting the Japanese. The lowest ranking one of the survivors is now a company commander in the Eighth Route Army. One is a battalion commander who studies here at the Party School at present. And several others are regimental commanders and staff officers at the front. All were simple peasants and are now fine officers."

I thought of a group of eight Kuomintang soldiers who had made a deep impression on me the winter before at the Central China front: Men with seven to eleven years of service in Generalissimo Chiang Kai-shek's crack 57th Division who had been in most of the large engagements of the Civil War against the Communists and of the war against Japan. Yet they still ranked only from private to sergeant.

"Why don't they let such men become officers?" one of the Allied military attachés in our party had wondered. "Even with little extra training they would be much better commanders than most of those innumerable generals we have met these last ten days. These soldiers made more sense in what they said about the recent campaign than most of the generals, although they had no German instructors at orthodox military academies. I really mean it: in the kind of warfare which the Chinese armies should fight against the technically superior Japanese, in a war in which their only hope is the best use of their human material, the commanders should be men like these experienced, clever, and spirited veterans instead of that type of officer we met. . . ."

The old landlord carried on his story: "We still made many military mistakes during the first big Japanese offensive in October, 1938, when we were only loosely connected with the Eighth Route Army. We had no experience and practically no central direction.

"A terrible thing happened to me at the time when I had increased my force to 1,800 men. I left my unit for a while to meet for the first time my commander in chief, Colonel Lu. I turned over my troops to my chief of staff, a third guerrilla landlord whom I had met during the fighting. But during my absence the Japanese attacked our troops in greatly superior strength. The fellow ordered my men to disperse, forgetting to arrange for a place at which they were to reassemble, and when I returned all of them had vanished. With the greatest difficulty I was able to collect barely 800."

His calm eyes flashed for a moment. "I was very much upset. I had the chief of staff shot.

"Our tactics also left much to be desired at that time. We were good on the defensive but missed many opportunities of taking the initiative ourselves. It was for all these reasons that the need was felt by my commander to turn more and more guerrillas into regular soldiers and give them expert training and leadership. I was asked, therefore, to let my remaining 800 men be taken over by a unit of the regular Eighth Route Army which was well organized and happened to be in urgent need of replenishment after it had suffered heavy losses in the same engagement in which my own troops were dispersed. I gave up my troops because I realized it was right, and returned secretly to my home district to recruit fresh fighters. I succeeded in getting many among the farmers and also from the Japanese-controlled Chinese militia. But when I returned with them, headquarters again decided to absorb them into the regular regiments under the Eighth Route Army.

"That created a problem among some of my men, on account of all those prewar years of anti-Communist propaganda in North China. The people simply did not know what sort of men the Communists were. There had never been any Communists in those districts until the Eighth Route Army went behind the enemy lines to fill the vacuum created by the withdrawal of the government troops. Some of my men were afraid to belong to the Communist armies, and so were their families. Some objected to giving up the free life of guerrillas for the strict discipline in the Eighth Route Army which kept all soldiers busy with regular classes and long training courses during periods of lull. When the people in my home district heard that I had again given my new men to the Eighth Route Army, nobody would join me any more. I myself was somewhat annoyed at all this and said I would collect no more men.

"But all of us changed our attitude pretty soon and things have long been entirely different. Wherever the Eighth Route Army goes, it

384

gets a really warm welcome from all the people because they have come to know the Communists. They realize how well they are treated by the Eighth Route Army and how much they owe it. The days of independent guerrilla units of the early stage of the war are over. Now, there are in North China only Eighth Route Army troops with their own regular guerrilla units and militiamen under the local self-governments. And on the other side, there are the Japanese and their Chinese 'puppets.' . . ."

"Are there no Kuomintang troops whatsoever in North China?" I asked old Yen.

"None," he replied. "They have either joined us or gone over to the enemy with their officers."

Yen had something more to say about the shortcomings of the guerrillas during the earlier period, which sounded surprising from a landlord and non-Communist: "The main trouble at that time was that our political work was not very good. The Eighth Route Army did not have enough political propaganda workers behind the front. And good political propaganda is necessary for a full war effort in the enemy's rear."

By 1940 Yen had become "Vice-General" of the Tenth War District of the large Anti-Japanese War Base Chin-cha-chi (Shansi-Chahar-Hopei) in North China. He was at the same time county magistrate for a while. But things then became extremely difficult in that area. The Japanese attacked in very great force, and the Eighth Route Army did not have sufficient arms and ammunition to defend the large district which temporarily shrank to a mere fifty square miles.

And Yen was getting old and was worrying about his family whom he had sent early in the war to the British Concession in Tientsin. But when his superior officer, the younger landlord with whom he had made contact in 1938, told him to retire because these strenuous and dangerous activities were too much for a man of sixty, he did not accept. He wanted to stay on and help in the war.

That was the moment when the old landlord could have separated with honor from the Eighth Route Army if he had not come to like

385

and respect it. He could have lived quietly in the British Concession of Tientsin, in Chungking, or in Hong Kong. Instead, old Yen brought his elderly wife and all his family from Tientsin, across strongly fortified enemy lines, to live with him at his Tenth District headquarters in Chin-cha-chi. He did not fight any more but directed the medical and supply departments of the very large Eighth Route Army unit which had by now grown out of the initial combination of some small guerrilla bands and the few Eighth Route Army companies originally sent into the enemy's rear from the Border Region.

Late in 1942 the great rationalization movement, started in Yenan by another old landlord, Mr. Li Ting-ming, gripped the army in the north and cut down the rear organization to which Yen belonged. He did not take it wrong: "I had plenty of adventures with the Japanese during those years and many narrow escapes, and I was really getting old. It was time to retire from the army."

The old landlord-guerrilla now became active in politics—as a parliamentarian. "Kuomintang members and Communists and many nonparty people from all social classes had meanwhile learned to cooperate in our regions," he said with emphasis, "and I, as a nonparty man, was elected by a county as delegate to the People's Political Council of the Chin-cha-chi Region with its 20,000,000 people. We nonparty men were in fact a large majority in the council of that so-called 'Red' area. There were between thirty and forty Kuomintang members in it. And all the minorities were represented: Mohammedans and Manchus and Lamas from a Buddhist monastery, and an antimilitaristic Japanese and a Korean. Professor William Band, the Englishman who had fled from Peiping with Mr. Lindsay and was working for Chin-cha-chi, was also a member."

Before the first session of the People's Political Council many voters and candidates thought it would not be much use to participate because the Communist party which had called it would most likely run it, too. But that was all wrong, according to Yen. A great deal of real business was accomplished even in that first session. Everybody talked freely. The delegates did not fight or debate senselessly but got at the essentials of the problems they had to solve and really expressed public opinion. Questions were asked of the government without any restraint and there was also criticism of the government. An Executive Government Committee and a Standing Committee of the People's Political Council were elected. Every fifty of the five hundred delegates elected one candidate to each committee. Both consisted of about one-third Communists, one-third Kuomintang members, and one-third nonparty people. Yen himself became a member of the Standing Committee.

"Is that 'Three-thirds' system really practical in actual government work?" I asked.

"Yes, it is. There is, in fact, no party division at all. We all cooperate very well. In the Standing Committee, which meets once a fortnight, our task is to represent the people vis-à-vis the administration, to collect practical suggestions from them, and to criticize the government if we or the people feel that there is anything wrong. In the end the government always has to accept our opinions and act according to them, although there might at first be an argument about policies that are difficult to carry out under the extremely complicated circumstances of our life and work in the war region where the Japanese keep on attacking us."

"How did the ordinary people react to their first democratic opportunity?"

"Very well indeed. Surprisingly well. We did all we could to make them fully aware of that opportunity. The people were very pleased with the results of the first session and felt that the Council was a promising innovation."

Between sessions, the members of the People's Political Council have two main tasks: to supervise the government's activities and to keep in close touch with the people, encouraging them to criticize and make suggestions. Yen himself often went from district to district, investigating affairs and talking to the people. "Many things are, of course, not quite satisfactory yet," he said, "since the system is so new and so unheard-of in China. And the Japanese again launched a very big offensive just when we started, and burned the village that was the headquarters of the Council."

387

"I Was a Wealthy Landlord . . ."

"Do you believe in this system for postwar times?"

"The new system gives answers to all my old questions about political and social improvements in China to which I found none myself before the war. It is the best way China can go in the future. If we could change the whole country to it, everybody in China would have a good life."

We had already talked for hours and the old man never leaned back in his chair. He showed no sign of being tired. In spite of his quiet dignity, which did not leave him for a moment, he became more and more enthusiastic.

"My feeling is that everybody who wants to resist Japan should be democratic," he said. "For if you want to resist the Japanese it is because you don't want oppression. But if you don't want oppression you must want democracy. I was a very rich man. Most of my own class were not much opposed to oppression of any kind. They were mainly interested in preserving their own property. I did not agree with that and that is why I was willing to die for my country. My house was burned. I do not know what became of my land. But I don't care."

He thought for a while and continued: "But you cannot generalize about landlords. Some oppose progress while others don't. The New Democracy in Chin-cha-chi shows all our landlords that in spite of having to pay full taxes regularly and having their land rents reduced by decree, they can retain the ownership of their land under the Communists and live quite well.

"For the time being there can be no question of socialism in China. We all know that. The only question for a long time will be how to give everybody enough food and other necessities. Look at the success of the production movement which is carried out everywhere under the policy of the Communists. This is a practical policy which can and should be carried out everywhere in China. We can produce much more than we ever did, even with our present primitive means, and that alone will make for a better life for all.

"Yes, China has party quarrels now. But I think our people can co-operate after the war, although the anti-Japanese motive which has

388

united us so strongly in the Anti-Japanese War Bases behind the enemy lines will be gone. Under the present system of the New Democracy the landlords are not being oppressed, just as the people are not being oppressed. This is as it should be.

"The new system actually encourages all people to get richer and own more, as you can see from the example of the Labor Hero, Wu Men-yu, who became rich and famous and useful to the community in which he began as a poor peasant. The only restriction on the landlords under the new system concerns their former special privileges. Those were unjust and outdated. They had to go."

"What do you think of Mao Tse-tung?" I asked.

"I think his leadership is correct. I have not spoken to him personally because I am here only to rest. My experience has been that when you yourself cannot think what should be done in a certain situation, Mao has the right idea. What has impressed me especially in his policies is the production movement that was launched everywhere. That is very important. You cannot resist the Japanese effectively, and you cannot do any reconstruction work in China, whether it is political, military, social, cultural, or anything else, without putting economic reconstruction first and carrying it out thoroughly. And the more difficult the general situation is, the more important is increased production. Plenty of food must always come first."

"And what do you think of Chiang Kai-shek?"

"I always hoped the two parties would cooperate. Not only in my region of Chin-cha-chi in the north but all over China. I am very much afraid of the bad effect of this conflict on our future since it has already had such very bad results in our anti-Japanese war. There should be no reason why the two parties cannot cooperate. The Kuomintang in Chungking say they want to realize Sun Yat-sen's 'Three Principles of the People.' I have studied them, and what the Communists are doing is nothing but carrying out those ideas."

"Whose fault is it that the two parties do not cooperate?"

Yen replied somewhat sharply to my question. "This is easy to answer: While the Communists have been fighting the Japanese as I know so well myself, the Kuomintang has most of the time taken a mere

389

watching attitude toward the enemy. Believe me, the Kuomintang has not fought properly. It has not opposed the enemy properly. And with this I am most dissatisfied."

"From what you have experienced in Chin-cha-chi," I asked, "with Communists and Kuomintang people and landlords and other capitalists —do you really believe that there is no fault with the Communist party in this lack of cooperation?"

"No, it is not the fault of the Communists."

"Have there been difficulties with individual Kuomintang members in Chin-cha-chi, too?"

"Yes," and he repeated the stories I had already heard from Michael Lindsay about Kuomintang people collaborating with the Japanese. "I felt very bad about it since it was all proved. Plain village people testified to it. I saw and heard them myself. Matters were aggravated by the fact that the former head of one of the Kuomintang branches, a liberal and very cooperative man who had been dismissed by Chung-king, was mysteriously killed. He was found dead at the bottom of a cliff and the strange thing was that the Kuomintang did not announce his death."

"How did the prewar government army in your home district compare with the Eighth Route Army?" I asked.

"The two cannot be compared. The prewar soldiers were just for themselves, had no connection with the people, treated them badly, and the people were afraid of them. Even the county magistrates feared the army and did not dare to maintain their rights against it.

"But the people themselves were also quite different from what they are now. At the beginning of the war most of them took the attitude that fighting the enemy was the army's business and not theirs as well. They have changed completely.

"It is not an empty phrase but a fact that the people and the army are now really closely united. Both the regular soldiers of the Eighth Route Army and the militia cooperate with the people, as the people cooperate with them. Everybody in those areas came to know how bad the Japanese are, that they must be fought to the end, and that the people need the army to fight for them and with them."

Yen seemed a little offended when I insisted, "Does the Eighth Route Army really treat the people as well as everybody told us in Yenan?"

"You can believe me the Eighth Route Army treats the people very well. The soldiers actually help them in the fields during the busy season and never do anything harmful to them. I never heard of a single case of killing or burning or bad treatment of the people by the Communists, as the Kuomintang rumors say."

"And what is popular opinion about the Communist party?"

"It is that they mean what they say and do not deceive the people. I know from my experience that the Eighth Route Army and the Communists are interested only in fighting the Japanese and in establishing democracy, but not in extending their own power. After the war the only thing the Communist party has to do to be approved by everybody is to maintain the 'Three-thirds' principle of equal representation for itself, the other parties, and the nonparty people."

"Suppose the Communists were to give up their present New Democracy when the war is over and return to radically revolutionary methods?"

Yen did not hesitate for a moment. "If they wanted to introduce Communism, they would have trouble with various groups of the people. This New Democracy is what the people want, not Communism."

"And what would the people's attitude be toward an attempt of the Kuomintang regime to return to North China when the Japanese are driven out?"

Yen's face became very grave. He thought for a long while and replied slowly, as though it caused him pain—carefully choosing every word and stopping for a while between sentences. "I hope very much that the two parties will find a way to cooperate, to solve the problem by political means. . . . The common people cannot stand any more fighting. . . . You don't know what they have gone through in peace and in war. . . . From everything I know I am certain that the great majority of the people in the war areas are convinced that the Eighth Route Army and the Communist party are really fighting for them. . . ."

There was a long pause before he continued.

"And in case of conflict with the Kuomintang, I do not hesitate to say that the Eighth Route Army and the Communist party would have the people's confidence. . . . The people would support them. . . . Most of the landlords and merchants, too, like the ordinary people. . . . It would be a terrible struggle. . . ."

Chapter Thirty-nine

THE ENEMY'S OPINION

I ASKED a number of Japanese captives what reputation the Eighth Route Army has on the Japanese side. They all agreed that the Imperial Japanese Army considers the Communists' dangerous enemies whose fighting qualities are high and who are the main obstacle to the consolidation of Japan's conquests in China.

The first man I interviewed was a sturdy sergeant, one of the converted antimilitarists of the Japanese People's Emancipation League in Yenan, who had been made prisoner several years ago. He spoke with great gusto.

"When we stood against the troops of the famous Kuomintang general Fu Tso-yi in Suiyuan province," he said, "we always won and we thought the Chinese were very weak. But when we were transferred to another front sector we suddenly faced strong and stubborn Chinese troops and were frequently defeated in skirmishes. We discussed among ourselves the 'new enemy' without knowing what had happened to the Chinese. After a while, our officers told us they were Eighth Route Army men.

"They called them bandits but said those bandits were very strong and we had to fight them harder than the other Chinese. Formerly, when we stood against Fu Tso-yi's troops, we used to have only single soldiers on sentry duty. But then, two or three of our men always had to be on guard together and the rest of us were not allowed any more to sleep at the same time in the night. We had to take turns.

"However, it took us a long while to overcome our old-fashioned superstitions and understand the character of our new enemy. I served in the Fourth Company of our regiment and it happened in six encounters with the Communists that each time four of our men were killed. Our commander said our designation was unlucky because, you know, the word 'four' also means 'death' in Japanese, and that seemed plausible to us. We were therefore renamed Hirose Company, after the family name of the commander, to overcome our bad luck. But the company still remained unlucky and Commander Hirose himself was killed immediately after this change of name. A platoon commander whom we all liked took over. He told us, 'If I lead you, we will not be defeated any more.' But he got sick, and our next commander was killed in action very soon after.

"Eventually, the fourth commander explained to us that we were being defeated because we continued to rely to a considerable extent on political warfare, as we normally did against the Chinese, and that in fighting the Communists we had to concentrate all our strength on military action. But that did not help, either. We suffered more and more defeats and I was soon taken prisoner by the Communists."

Another man, a private who is now one of the star teachers in the Japanese Peasants' and Workers' School at Yenan, which converts and trains suitable captives for practical work at the front against the Japanese Army, had surrendered three or four years ago to the Eighth Route Army. He was even more pleased with his story than the first man.

"I will tell you what my commander said to me when he picked me out to do spy work in the Eighth Route Army," he began.

"He called me to his private room, was very friendly, gave me beer and cigarettes, and said he had a very important task for me which would earn me great glory for the country, a decoration for myself, and also while I was absent a good pension for my parents.

"He said we were facing troops of the Eighth Route Army. This was the first time I heard the Communists called by another name than 'bandits.' The Eighth Route Army was very poorly armed but its men were very strong in spite of that, because they had some 'special thought' which makes our fight against them so very difficult. So we must try to destroy them from within.

"Later, when I was sent to a secret three months' training class for the spy work I was to do, we got long lectures about the Chinese armies. We were told that the Kuomintang troops were much better armed than the Communists because they had foreign equipment, but that their spirit had become low and weak while the Communists with their 'special thought' were fighting us very stubbornly so that we had suffered several defeats.

"The Communists were very dangerous to us, the teachers repeated every day, and inside the Eighth Route Army there were bad Japanese who had been affected by that 'thought' and were fighting against our own Imperial Army.

"Later, they talked no more about the Kuomintang troops but said a lot about the Communists. The Communist armies were led by Stalin and they had very close connection with the Chinese peasants, and our defeats at the hands of the Communists were partly due to the fact that they made the ordinary Chinese peasants fight the Japanese Army everywhere.

" 'You may feel strange at first,' the lecturer at the spy school warned us, 'because you will see that the Communists are not only treating their own peasants well but also that they are very nice to Japanese captives. But this is only propaganda for the domination of China and Japan by Stalin. The Eighth Route Army deceives the people with nice slogans like 'Equality' and 'Freedom,' and this is what makes it so dangerous to us.' "

These and similar stories I heard from the converted Japanese anti-militarists may or may not be true, but they became increasingly plausible to me later when I read many articles about the Eighth Route Army from the Japanese press and Japanese-controlled "puppet" newspapers in the occupied cities of China.

I made some typical extracts from those articles and grouped them according to subjects, to show what the Imperial Japanese Army lets the press write about the Communist enemy.*

* Quoted from the following Japanese and "puppet" newspapers and magazines: *Asahi Shimbun*, Tokyo, January 15, 1944; *Domei Home Service*, February 14, 1944; *Mainichi Shimbun*, Special Supplement, no date; *Tang Chen Monthly*, Vol. 7, No. 1;

The Enemy's Opinion

What is the extent of the Japanese war with the Chinese Communists and of the harm they do the invader? These are some of the enemy's replies:

"During the five years from 1939 to 1943, 78 per cent of our 84,000 engagements in North China were fought with the Eighth Route Army."

"The Imperial Japanese Army and the forces of the New [puppet] Government of China fight the Communists incessantly."

"From the figures on the results of Imperial Japanese Army action against the Chungking and Communist armies since December, 1941 [Pearl Harbor], it is clear that the major hindrance to peace in Eastern Asia is no longer the Chungking government but the Chinese Communist party. The stubbornness of the Communist troops has far surpassed that of the Chungking troops."

"The Communist armies mean fatal injury to North China, and operations against them are the major mission of the Imperial Japanese Army in North China. They hold vast numbers of villages, encircle our strong points, and prevent them from obtaining supplies. They disturb incessantly the rear of the Imperial Japanese Army and disrupt communications in order to isolate and blockade the cities, so that supplies and replenishments of the Imperial Japanese Army are hampered by them."

"With Eastern Hopei [east of Peiping] as their center, they have already expanded into Jehol [in the Japanese puppet state of Manchukuo, G. S.] and they are striving constantly to set up a new Border Region in that area."

"In pacified regions, especially in the big cities, the Communist party works underground, enlarging its organization, carrying on intelligence work, and plotting various activities, all in such subtle ways that it is difficult to discover them."

To what factors is the fighting strength of the Communists ascribed by the enemy?

Hsin Chung Kuo, Shanghai, July 10, 1944; *Wen Yo*, Shanghai, April, 1944; *Yung Pao*, Tientsin, January 7 and 18, 1944.

"The Communist armies are clever in relying upon their guerrilla tactics and their political offensives in harassing us. They absolutely hold the initiative in fighting and always maintain the offensive. Every Communist commander knows how to master conditions and misses no chance. Often, by resorting to attacks and carrying on well-planned, organized fighting, they gain decisive successes in a very short time.

"The main principles of the Communists are to defend their war bases, to maneuver their main forces in control of the outer areas of those war bases, to destroy the communication lines and bridges of the Imperial Japanese Army, and to lay many ambushes to delay its advance. They attack certain of our strong points, exhaust our forces, and make it impossible for us to pay attention elsewhere.

"If conditions are extremely unfavorable to the Communists, they will lead the population to withdraw and to hide their foodstuffs, according to their policy, 'Clean Up and Hide Everything before the Enemy Comes,' so that it is impossible for the Imperial Japanese Army to stay long at any place. After that, they will disperse their troops to disturb and raid us and cut off the supplies of our units, making it impossible for us to live securely and compelling us to withdraw.

"Sometimes, when our troops have broken into the Communist war bases and are searching for foodstuffs or for the Communists themselves who have so mysteriously disappeared, others of our units cannot help leaving their strong points and scattering their men in the vicinity. The Communists always use such opportunities to raid us. They will then employ small detachments of guerrillas to hold our units down in other places and concentrate all their strength and fire power on the annihilation of part of our units. When our units, at last, cannot stand the strain any longer and have to stop their futile search of the villages and withdraw to their original positions, the Communists will pursue them that very moment and attack them severely.

"They use their strength very well, avoid all waste, and concentrate on decisive actions. In those ways they exhaust their adversary and make him scatter his forces, so that he becomes incapable of using his whole strength before the fight actually begins.

"They are nimble in action, never miss opportunities, and never fall into traps. They utilize dark nights, heavy mists, rain, or storm to raid the exhausted or unprepared units of the Imperial Japanese Army. Or they lay ambushes at important spots, inflicting heavy casualties. Or they put our rear into confusion by destroying military stations, depots, communications, telephone lines, etc. . . .

"They have been tempered with special skill through their environment. They are precise in shooting and very skillful in throwing hand grenades very far and accurately. They are extremely fast.

"They may suddenly appear anywhere. They know the roads everywhere, the course, depth, and width of rivers, how many households there are in a village, what kind of houses they have, the character of their inhabitants. They know everything, matters great and small and in every corner.

"In their resistance against a superior army they maintain their troops in rigid organization and strict training. The conditions of their troops are extremely bitter and hard. To overcome their supply difficulties, to face critical situations, to deal with extremities, and to consolidate themselves, they need especially strong will power and strict organization. The Communist armies, in these respects, have attained the peak of achievement."

Finally, how does the enemy judge the political aims and methods of the Communists and the effect of their military and political struggle on the situation in China?

"The Communists are instigating national consciousness and seeking decisive battles against the Imperial Japanese Army in North China.

"To break through the material difficulties of their situation which were created by our military and economic offensives and by the breakup and isolation of their bases, the Communists strove to raise the efficiency of their army and to simplify their administrations.

"The Communist party is extremely stubborn, and this is especially true of its leading groups, which are rich in experience, thorough in reviewing operations and studying tactics, and quick in realizing and readjusting their faults and weaknesses.

"They are enthusiastic in leading the lower party functionaries and the people and are themselves always models to them.

"However, they have the following weaknesses: Although the Communist party gives the people its powerful support, it has to increase the burden of the people to continue its prolonged warfare. Thus discontent is aroused incessantly. They consider Kuomintang-Communist cooperation as a temporary expedient while looking forward to leading the entire Chinese nation in the overthrow of the Kuomintang. Before that is done, the first step of the Communists is to intensify the acuteness of the antagonism between the people and the Kuomintang and also to shake the Kuomintang from within. Herein lies the dangerous character of the Communists.

"The Communist bandits are the only hindrance now existing to the revival of China and the defense of Eastern Asia. We must thoroughly combat them both spiritually and in actual fighting."

The comparative frankness of the enemy about certain aspects of his war with the Chinese Communists may sound suspicious. Does it have ulterior motives? How can it be explained?

These seem to be the reasons.

The Japanese militarists owe a good deal of explanation to their people at home and especially to their puppet supporters in China. Why is it becoming more and more difficult, the longer the war lasts, to exploit the economic resources of the greater part of the so-called occupied regions in North China and northern Central China? Why are the cities' supplies from the interior shrinking all the time, not only those for the Chinese inhabitants but also those for the Japanese themselves? Why are the Japanese-held transportation lines becoming even less safe as time goes on? Why is the recruiting of labor and of puppet soldiers in the interior growing into a greater and greater problem? Why are the 360,000 Japanese and their 780,000 puppet auxiliaries in the "occupied" regions losing more and more territory, including important county seats, to the Communists—instead of recapturing those they lost since 1941?

The Japanese cannot deny the truth of these facts because they are too well known in the big Chinese cities under their occupation, through the Chinese version of the grapevine—popularly called "the bamboo telegraph." They cannot say that the war in the Pacific prevents them from maintaining sufficient strength in "occupied China." For the people, who must daily support the Japanese and puppet armies with all they need, know only too well that the huge number of troops has not decreased. They know of the fighting that goes on incessantly outside the big cities along the railroads and highways and in their own towns and villages. They see the Japanese and puppet troops come and go, bringing back the wounded.

These conditions force the Japanese to give considerable credit to the strength of the Communists by way of apologizing for their own military failure in the rear.

Skeptics might think the Japanese are exaggerating the strength and importance of the Communists as a matter of policy, since the Red bogey has been so useful to them for many years as a means of undermining Chinese unity. Yet this would seem illogical under the present circumstances. A policy of making the Communists appear more powerful than they are would have the contrary effect on every group the Japanese are anxious to influence: first, the Kuomintang; second, the puppets; and third, the common Chinese people in the occupied areas.

First, on the Kuomintang: for it was Chungking's slow though still incomplete realization of the actual strength of the Communists which led to a resumption of negotiations between Chungking and Yenan. The Japanese would only force the National Government a step further toward Chinese national unity and would only strengthen the conciliatory elements in the Kuomintang against its militant anti-Communists if they impressed Chungking more thoroughly with the real power of Yenan.

Second, on the puppets: for the puppets have now come to realize the inevitability of Japan's defeat, the real strength of the Communists outside their very gates. Ever greater numbers of puppet troops are going over to the Communists or cooperating with them secretly. A good many of the smaller political puppets have recently tried to play

400

up to the Communists, asking them for certificates of good political behavior which would give them security after the war. The puppets as a whole would become panicky earlier than necessary if the Japanese gave them an exaggerated picture of Communist power.

Finally, on the common people: for the invaders have every reason to avoid propaganda tactics which would only increase the sympathies for the patriotic Communist fighters among the common people in the Japanese-controlled areas and their hope for eventual liberation through the Eighth Route and New Fourth Armies.

All this forced the enemy to keep his publicity on the fighting with the Communists as closely to the truth as possible; to admit that they are powerful adversaries of the Imperial Japanese Army; to explain at least to some extent why this is so; but not to give an exaggerated impression of their strength and their successes.

The frankness of the enemy about the main reason for his fear of the Chinese Communists is self-explanatory. He fears them not so much because *"they are seeking decisive battles with the Imperial Japanese Army"*—which evidently the Communists cannot wage until the Chinese war effort as a whole is revived on the basis of national unity—as because *"the Communists are instigating national consciousness."*

He fears them not only because *"the stubbornness of the Communist armies has far surpassed that of the Chungking troops"*—so that *"the major hindrance to [Japan's] peace in Eastern Asia is no longer the Chungking government but the Chinese Communist party"*—but because the Communists *"intensify the acuteness of the antagonism between the people and the Kuomintang and shake the Kuomintang from within."*

In the Communists' endeavor to make the liberals in the Kuomintang help them shake up the Chungking government, which the Japanese no longer consider the major hindrance to their aims in China, and to strengthen the Chinese war effort by democratization of the Kuomintang regime—*"herein lay the dangerous character of the Communists"*—their danger to the Japanese.

Part Eight

YENAN'S JAPANESE ALLIES

POLITICAL DEBATE IN A VILLAGE

Chapter Forty

JAPANESE IN CHINESE UNIFORM

THE guests were the U. S. Army Observer Section and hundreds of the leaders and plain people of Yenan's New Democracy. . . .

The hosts were seventy Japanese—not long ago soldiers in Hirohito's Imperial Army and now in the blue cotton uniforms of the Communist Eighth Route Army of China. . . .

The place where they entertained us with a theatrical show was the assembly hall of Yenan's People's Political Council, gaily decorated with flags and banners.

Side by side with the flags of the United Nations was one I had never seen before—a red flag with a yellow star in the upper left corner and a white horizontal stripe across its lower half.

On the stage stood a small, grave Japanese—Susumo Okano, one of the founders of the Communist party of Japan, a former student of the London School of Economics, veteran of Japanese jails and underground antimilitaristic work—and the brains behind a movement which may come to play a role in postwar Japan.

"I welcome our Allied friends," he said in fluent English, "in the name of the Japanese People's Emancipation League, the Japanese Peasants' and Workers' School in Yenan—and the underground fighters against militarism and Fascism inside Japan.

"In the fight for the complete and permanent destruction of Japanese militarism and Fascism the armed forces of the Allies are certainly the decisive factor. But there are other forces whose importance must not be underestimated: those of the people in the Japanese-occupied areas and colonies; and those of the anti-Fascist opposition in Japan.

405

"That opposition reaches far beyond the membership of the Communist party and its sympathizers. It includes workers, farmers, intellectuals, and small businessmen of other political views. But it is still weak because it lacks unity and organization. So far, only the Japanese Communist party has determinedly and consistently struggled against the militarists.

"To achieve unity among the opposition is the aim of the Japanese People's Emancipation League which was established in the territories of Communist-controlled China by Japanese war prisoners who have turned antimilitarist and anti-Fascist. We are organizing for that unity, not on a Communist party basis, but on a democratic basis on which all opponents of Fascism and militarism can be brought together and activated. . . .

"While we endeavor to extend our influence into Japan itself, we are working and actually fighting against the Japanese Army in China, in close cooperation with the Communist-led armies.

"We hope your presence here will provide us with an opportunity to establish a first contact with the Allied governments and nations, so that we can help to accomplish the common aim of defeating and uprooting Japanese militarism and of establishing a genuinely peaceful and democratic Japan.

"Our gathering here has therefore special significance. I hope that already tonight—in the plays our students are going to perform—you will breathe something of the atmosphere of that future Japan.

"And I hope the next time we may invite you to a show it will be in the Imperial Theater in Tokyo. . . ."

The hundreds of Chinese in the audience, army, party, and government leaders and the rank and file, applauded enthusiastically.

Colonel David D. Barrett replied with a short speech:

"Possibly American Army officers never found themselves in such an unusual and interesting situation as we do tonight," he said, looking down at his U. S. Army uniform with the characteristic grin that enlivens even his most serious talk.

He spoke about the tasks of the U. S. Army Observer Section and

406

the ways in which his Japanese hosts could be of help to the American Army in carrying them out, and thus in winning the war against Japan.

"I am glad to say," he ended to the lively applause of Chinese, Japanese, and Americans, "that Mr. Okano and the Japanese antiwar organizations have already rendered us valuable assistance in our work here in Yenan. . . ."

The theatricals the Japanese soldiers staged for us were vivid and instructive.

The first play was "Pfc. Shimada." Okano said it was based on two incidents that took place in 1943 and characterized in a realistic manner part of the work the J.P.E.L. has been doing at the front for several years.

First scene. In no man's land between Eighth Route Army territory and a Japanese position. A group of soldiers: in Japanese uniform Pfc. Shimada who had been wounded and captured a few months earlier; and in Eighth Route Army uniform several Chinese soldiers and Japanese members of the J.P.E.L.

Shimada thanks everybody for the good treatment he had been given during his three months in an Eighth Route Army hospital: "We were told in the Japanese Army you killed prisoners. But my return will show them it is not true. I am glad that you understand my wish to return to my army unit, to do my duty as a patriot, in spite of what you have told me about Japanese militarism."

A Chinese peasant leads him away, to the Japanese side.

Second scene. The room of a Japanese company commander in a small occupied town. Some Japanese and a Chinese traitor are discussing the business of distributing booty they have just stolen from the people.

Shimada comes in, reporting for duty to the company commander. He explains what happened to him and shows the bullet wound in his leg. The commander curses him for having disgraced the Imperial Japanese Army by having been captured alive. His name has been struck from the company roll. He has been dead for months. He is to commit suicide: "Off you go. . . . You *have* to be dead by tonight."

407

Japanese in Chinese Uniform

Third scene. A group of Japanese soldiers in their barracks. Shimada tells them his story, gives them leaflets of the Eighth Route Army, and sings them a song of the J.P.E.L.

"They don't kill prisoners as our officers tell us," Shimada says, "and as we were often made to do ourselves.

"This is the order of their army commander: * '(1) Injury and insults to Japanese captives are strictly forbidden. (2) Special care is to be given to wounded. (3) Those who wish to return to their own units must be sent back. (4) Those who want to stay and work with us against Japanese imperialism or who want to stay with us to study must be helped to do so. (5) They must be given facilities to send letters to comrades in the Japanese Army or their families if they desire to write to them.'

"They were good to me, cared for me, and taught me many things. Our own comrades who decided to stay with them when they were taken prisoner are working against Japanese militarism. They think our cause is unjust. Maybe they are right. I am not quite sure yet. But I felt I had to return and do my duty."

Some soldiers disapprove of Shimada's praise of the Eighth Route Army or seem indifferent, but most of them show an interest in his experiences.

Fourth scene. The same soldiers, without Shimada. They grumble about the bad food and treatment they get and the cruelty of their company commander when he comes in with a sergeant, searching for Shimada.

The soldiers deny having seen him and are punished by the elaborate methods of petty, degrading torture customary in the Imperial Japanese Army. Once more alone, the soldiers angrily discuss ways of revenge on the company commander.

Last scene. An open field in front of a Japanese blockhouse. Soldiers on night duty. Shimada is with them, glancing expectantly in the direction of the Communist areas.

A Chinese peasant brings a message from the puppet chief of his

* From General Chu Teh's order to the Eighth Route Army issued early in the war.

408

near-by village, warning the Japanese of an imminent attack on their blockhouse by Communist troops. But he also brings for Shimada and the others some of those "comfort bags" with little gifts, news sheets about world developments, and propaganda leaflets, which the J.P.E.L. systematically smuggles into the Japanese Army.

Voices are heard from a distance: a propaganda unit of the J.P.E.L. with the advancing Eighth Route Army shouts antimilitaristic slogans through megaphones. The company commander comes on the scene and orders the hesitating soldiers to open fire. Shimada shouts, "Don't fight them. . . ."

The commander notices Shimada, points his pistol at him, but is killed by one of his soldiers before he can shoot. . . .

Another short play, based on the personal experience of one of the men of the J.P.E.L. who is himself on the stage, sketches a scene somewhere in a poor district of Tokyo during General Doolittle's first bombing of Japan on that historic day, April 18, 1942.

The play castigates the brutality and cowardice of a typical Tokyo policeman and the hypocrisy of ultra-patriotic wardens during the raid, pictures the confusion and helpless despair of the common people, and shows the only way by which they can rid themselves of their sufferings —by opposition to militarism.

A bomb, marked with an American flag, comes down on the scene— like a symbol of liberation—hitting the spot where the policeman had sought shelter. . . .

"It is all so strange," one of the American officers remarked to me. "These Japs really seem to want their own country bombed. Are they really so different from what we think all Japs are?"

"Do you want Japan bombed?" I asked one of the Japanese.

"Certainly," he beamed, "since we cannot defeat our militarists without your help. They are the enemies of our people."

The Japanese People's Emancipation League had about 400 active members in Communist-controlled China in September, 1944, most of whom were working at the front, while some were learning and teaching in the Japanese Peasants' and Workers' School in Yenan and its branches in the war areas. (Okano was of course unable to disclose anything about the organizational contacts of the League inside Japanese-controlled China and Japan proper.)

Over thirty of the group in Communist-controlled China were killed in action against the Japanese Army during the last few years.

"The great majority of the prisoners taken by the Eighth Route and New Fourth Armies since the war began, about 2,000 out of a total of over 2,400, were sent back to the Japanese Army," Okano said, "because they wanted to return. But, every month now, more captives are made than ever before, and their numbers will grow steadily. A considerable number not included in those figures are at present on their way to our training schools, and more are still at the various war fronts.*

"These days most of them don't want to be sent back any more. They know of the recent Japanese order to kill returning prisoners at once because what they usually tell their comrades about the J.P.E.L. and the Chinese Communists began to undermine morale in the army. All the captives are kept now and sent to school. I believe that almost all of them can be reeducated."

"I thought nothing would be more difficult than to change the ideology of Japanese soldiers," I said.

"It is not so very difficult," Okano said, "although it often takes many months, and a year or even more in some hard cases. I confess I myself was surprised how much easier it is to be successful in reeducation work than I had expected. This is of course partly due to the favorable conditions under which we work in the New Democracy of the Chinese Communists, which is a living illustration and example to the students of all we teach them.

"They live and work here in an atmosphere of liberty they never knew before. As you see, the Eighth Route Army does not treat them as prisoners. They are just military students and have the same freedom

* By early 1945 the total of the Communists' Japanese war prisoners had increased to 3,880; and the number of active members of the J.P.E.L. is supposed to have risen considerably since September, 1944.

as Chinese military students and wear the same uniform. This in itself makes a deep impression on them.

"In school they are together with converted men who have worked already at the front with the Eighth Route Army and are studying here to raise their qualifications. The genuine anti-Fascist enthusiasm of those advanced students is a most effective influence on the new-comers.

"As a rule, the belief of the captives in the divine descent of the Emperor and in the whole system of Japanese ideology collapses very soon when their own comrades, eager to convince them of the logical new truth they found, make them think for the first time in their lives. And the teachers, having been ordinary soldiers who came the same way as they did, are ideally qualified to help the new men along."

"Do you consider all your converts reliable?"

"No, some are not. But the other students and the teachers observe them closely. They want to be certain of their success and can judge the honesty of everyone. They continue working patiently on those who may not be firm yet or who may only pretend to shed their old ideology. You must understand that there is no pressure. The change of thought of the student develops naturally in the course of the theoretical and practical studies in preparation for our work during and after the war.

"To most students this means the first real education they ever had: 34 per cent were factory workers, 32 per cent peasants, 21 per cent petty merchants and clerks, the type of people who know very little when they join the army. The superstitions inculcated in them in their youth cannot long survive the factual knowledge we give them."

The school, in rows of tidy caves in the center of Yenan, had seventy students. I visited them several times and talked with at least a dozen individually. They seemed quite different from men of similar types whom I had known in Japan.

Their answers to my questions gave me the impression that they had not mechanically exchanged their imperial Nipponism for Marxian materialism along the lines of Mao Tse-tung's New Democracy, but that they had learned to think more naturally and logically in terms of their new ideology.

They seemed genuinely happy to have found in it a key to the understanding of many questions they would have been unable to answer in the past. Some of them reminded me of newly literate adults I had met in the USSR who could not quite overcome their astonishment at the results of a few months' reading course which suddenly "made pieces of paper tell them all kinds of stories about new, interesting things"—as a peasant-turned-factory-worker once told me.

A good part of the students had already worked at the front—doing "megaphone propaganda" near the Japanese lines, instructing Chinese troops on Japanese Army tactics, teaching them the use of captured Japanese infantry guns or mortars, helping in intelligence tasks, and working on new prisoners.

They were in Yenan for advanced studies, getting courses in enemy intelligence, learning improved propaganda methods, and intensifying their knowledge of Japanese politics and economics. At the same time they prepared themselves to teach those many prisoners who would fall into the hands of the Chinese when the Communist counteroffensive began—in order to make as many of them as possible into pioneers for that New Democracy which the J.P.E.L. wants to build up in Japan after the defeat of the militarists.

"This is what the Allies should also do with their Japanese war prisoners," Okano said. "Educate them to democratic thought before they return them to Japan after the war.

"Every Japanese war prisoner who goes back without being prepared for the changes that have to take place in Japan will be a force against the Allies and the progressive elements in our country which will have to bring about those changes; while everyone who comes home with new ideas, like our men, will lead dozens or hundreds to work actively for a peaceful, democratic Japan and for its cooperation with the democratic world. . . ."

412

Chapter Forty-one

A PROGRAM FOR DEFEATED JAPAN

THE Chinese Communists in Yenan think highly of Susumo Okano and consider him fully reliable and very capable. They treat him as one of them and seem to consult him regularly on important matters connected with Japan. He has his offices at Eighth Route Army headquarters and lives with his Chinese wife close to General Chu Teh's caves. There seemed to be no public functions of importance at which he was not present among Yenan's leaders.

His speech before a mass meeting of 40,000 on United Nations Day, ending with the exclamation, "Long live the unity of the Chinese and Japanese peoples," drew great applause. For he is well known and popular among the people of Yenan, like the students of the Japanese Peasants' and Workers' School who move freely in the town and of whom one or two were elected members of the People's Political Council of the Border Region.

Okano—a quiet man of about fifty whose real name is Tetsu Nosaka —is not one of those Japanese who try to impress foreigners with smiles, false modesty, and exquisite politeness. Nor does he have any of the disturbing mannerisms of most Japanese, like the sucking in of the breath and the long hissing "s-s-a-a-a" that follows—apparently intended to gain time for the vaguest possible answer to any question. He is direct, outspoken, and almost impersonal in his careful analysis of things Japanese—cool, dry, systematic, and precise.

Okano's outward appearance, in the simple Yenan cotton uniform he wears, seemed to me closer to the description of a sober, slightly pedantic business executive or scientist of some prominence than that of a professional revolutionary with a long record of prison and underground life.

413

A Program for Defeated Japan

His studies in the London School of Economics, his journeys in Europe, and years of residence in Moscow, where he was delegate of the Japanese Communist party to the Communist International, have given him a cosmopolitan outlook which is rare even in the most widely traveled Japanese.

Because of his impersonal manner it takes long to get to know him, but the more I saw of him and heard his opinions, the more inclined I felt to trust his intellectual honesty and the sense of responsibility that seems to dominate his personality.

Outside Japan today Okano is probably the only Japanese of any potential importance to the future development of his country, and he is certainly one of the very few Japanese politicians anywhere who cannot be suspected of ever having assisted Japanese militarism or given in to it. He seems to be the only Japanese antimilitarist abroad still able to maintain some contacts with Japan proper, and whose organization may be able to participate in the reform movement that is to change the political character of Japan after the defeat of her militarists. Finally, Okano and his group seem to have the moral support of the Chinese Communists who are bound to play a role in postwar East Asia.

It may be worth while therefore to print here my record of the final, programmatic interview I had with him at the end of September, 1944.

My first question was about the ideas which guide the propaganda policies of the Japanese People's Emancipation League for the last stages of the war.

"Our propaganda strategy during the war must be to divide the enemy camp in Japan and concentrate all the force of our attack on the militarists who are the decisive group among the Japanese ruling classes. For this reason we must avoid the slogan 'Down with the Emperor,' although we are of course as much as ever opposed to the monarchy. To use that slogan now would only help the various groups among the Japanese ruling classes to compose their increasing conflicts by rallying behind the Emperor and to make the hesitating elements

414

among the people follow suit. Our members who work at the front with Chinese troops agree from their experience that if we demanded the overthrow of the monarchy now, most Japanese soldiers would oppose the J.P.E.L. without giving it a hearing. And this is symptomatic for the attitude of the great majority of the Japanese people at the present time.

"But the Emperor is merely the figurehead of the militarists. Once we have overthrown the militarists, we can overthrow the Emperor easily. On the back of the militarist horse ride not only the Emperor, but also big business and the big landlords. If you want to kill the riders, you have to kill the horse first.

"This does not mean that we abstain even now from all propaganda against the Emperor. We aim at undermining his prestige by making it clear to the soldiers and the people that he is not an unsullied divine power but shares responsibility for what is happening to Japan now.

"Developments in Japan help us in this respect. For the domestic power of the militarists in Tokyo is not so real and absolute as that of the Nazis in Berlin, and this is why they had to get the Emperor down from heaven to help them out with his prestige. Every eighth day of each month, at the 'memorial day' of the outbreak of the Pacific War, all the papers have to reprint the Emperor's declaration of war and the people have to read it aloud—which identifies the Emperor with those responsible for the war.

"It would also be wrong for us now to use the slogan 'Down with Big Business.' For it would divert attention from the main enemy, the militarists. And it would promise the Japanese people a socialist revolution of which there can be no question for a long time to come. But we advocate the control of monopolistic big business by a liberalized government and the confiscation of war profits.

"Nor do we propagandize the independence of Korea and the return of Formosa to China—yet. Naturally, we fully agree with those as with all other points of the Cairo resolution of the Big Three. But such a slogan is unsuited for us at present since the Japanese people still believe those colonies to be under the Emperor's divine sway, and we leave the issue alone for the time being."

A Program for Defeated Japan

I asked Okano about his ideas on the treatment of Japan when hostilities come to an end.

"It would be very dangerous for world peace if the Allies were to deal with a Japanese Badoglio, such as General Ugaki, and with the Emperor or with big business.

"The primary need at the end of hostilities will be for the Allies to make certain that the main elements in a new Japanese government shall be people who opposed the war or at least did not actively support it. The Communist party must be represented in the new government. Otherwise a liberal regime would be weak internally and might easily become reactionary and the instrument of militaristic elements once again.

"During the last thirteen years of Japan's war of aggression since the conquest of Manchuria, the Japanese Communist party was the only active and reliable group in opposing the war. The common people in Japan know that. On the basis of freedom of speech and press, the Communist party would gain considerable influence among them and would thus be able to help the Allies and all progressive elements in Japan in the uprooting of the remnants of militarism.

"At the armistice, the Allies should be absolutely uncompromising in their demand for a democratic government—preferably on a republican basis."

Okano welcomes the prospect of Allied military occupation of Japan and of an Allied military government for a transition period, because both will help the Japanese people to work for the necessary political changes.

But he warns that the Allies should restrict themselves in both respects to a modicum of interference. He fears that Allied occupation of more than some strategic parts of Japan and an undue prolongation of the control of the Allied military government over a liberal postwar Japanese government might make the pacification of the country and its progress toward democracy much more, instead of less, difficult.

"These are the dangers which might arise if the Allies went too far," Okano said. "The spirit of revenge might be strengthened and spread to parts of the Japanese people who otherwise would not be influenced by it. The guerrilla warfare which militant elements will most probably organize against the Allied occupation forces in Japan and against progressive Japanese might be intensified and prolonged. And the necessary political reforms the postwar Japanese government will have to carry through might be discredited in the eyes of many who would wholeheartedly approve of them as long as those reforms did not appear to be due to constant Allied military pressure."

This is what Okano said about the program of the Japanese People's Emancipation League for postwar Japan:

"I want to stress that the J.P.E.L. is not identical with the Communist party of Japan. It is an organization intended to activate and unify the antimilitaristic and anti-Fascist groups and individuals in Japan—whatever political views they may hold on other subjects—in cooperation with the Communist party, the most active element among the opposition forces. It is so far only a propaganda movement and by no means intended to provide a ready-made government for postwar Japan.

"The absolute minimum of what the J.P.E.L. wants to achieve immediately after the downfall of militarism includes the following main points:

"(1) The overthrow of the political power of the militarists, (2) a very considerable limitation of the political power of the monarchy, (3) a new, liberalized election law, giving general suffrage to men and women over eighteen years of age, (4) the guarantee of more power to parliament, (5) government control over big monopoly capitalists.

"As to the Communist party of Japan, it must be given freedom for its work, no matter whether its present name will be used after the war or not.

"In other words, the minimum program of the J.P.E.L. implies no more than the creation of a liberal government immediately after the defeat of the militarists.

"Our maximum program, however, aims at the establishment of a

417

genuine democracy, roughly in the sense of the New Democracy under which the Chinese Communists are uniting all progressive forces.

"Even the Communist party of Japan as such will not go further in its demands than the maximum program of the J.P.E.L. The reason why we, as Communists, shall not aspire to more than a New Democracy for a long time to come lies in the present economic and social structure of Japan. The time is not ripe in Japan for Socialism, so that it would be futile to aim at a socialist revolution.

"Japan, in spite of being one of the big capitalistic countries, has at the same time remained semifeudal in many important respects. It would be impossible to attempt the introduction of Socialism before those strong semifeudal features of Japanese society have been overcome in a genuinely democratic system—that is, before semifeudal forms of production, especially in agriculture but also in large parts of industry, have been changed to those of modern capitalism.

"In Japan—as in China or elsewhere—the inevitable development toward socialism can be achieved by way of peaceful progress, once a genuinely democratic regime is established. It will take very long, but not so long as in China where capitalism is still much less developed than in Japan.

"In the democratization of Japan's political structure, the development of self-government from the bottom up will be of the greatest importance.

"On this, we have much to learn from the New Democracy of the Chinese Communists who, as you have seen here, succeeded in introducing really democratic village, borough, town, district, and region governments. To awaken and activate the people for self-government and social progress will be one of the essential tasks of the J.P.E.L. in the future.

"The various mass organizations, like peasants' and workers' unions, the cooperative movement, women's and cultural associations, must be revived and given full democratic rights. They will have to play equally important roles in Japan as they do in China's New Democracy.

"New political parties will arise, but the old parties *Minseito* and

418

Seiyukai cannot and should not be revived. They have been too long and too closely connected with Japanese militarism and imperialism and are too much discredited in the eyes of the people. It may be possible to reform the *Shakaitaishuto* ['proletarian party'] for cooperation in a democratic popular front. The Communist party will certainly come to play an important, although not a dominant, role.

"At the top, all political power must rest with parliament. But the House of Peers must be abolished, like the Privy Council, although it might be replaced by a Senate.

"Our maximum program requires the abolition of the monarchy. Our minimum demand is its change into a constitutional monarchy, together with the resignation of Hirohito as one of the men personally responsible for the wars of Japanese aggression during the last thirteen years.

"We would certainly offer no opposition if the Allies were to try him as a war criminal. The punishment of war criminals is one of our basic demands and we are keeping lists of all cases that come to our knowledge.

"But I want to emphasize that the most effective means of getting rid of the monarchy for good is to give the Japanese people full freedom of speech and press and the necessary democratic rights to deal with it themselves.

"For, once they have the necessary democratic freedom to come to know its real character, the Japanese people will not retain the monarchy but will abolish it, either immediately or gradually.

"Too drastic Allied action of a direct nature against the monarchy—especially before the necessary democratic rights have been given to the Japanese people to enable them to play an active part in its overthrow—may easily make martyrs of the Imperial House and hold up that natural progress by which it is bound to lose all popular sympathy under a democratic regime.

"Yet it would be even more dangerous for Japan herself and for world peace if the Allies were to support the monarchy against progressive forces in Japan, or if they tried to prevent the Japanese people from getting ready for its overthrow—because that would once more make the imperial tradition and its representative on the throne the rallying point for militarists and imperialistic elements in the country.

"Proper educational policies will be of the greatest importance for the reform of Japan. To carry them through without compromise on any essentials will be among the greatest tasks of the J.P.E.L. We *must* bring about a fundamental change of the psychology of the Japanese people in order to guarantee the development of a truly democratic and peaceful Japan. And to bring about that change, there must be freedom of speech and of the press.

"I believe from my experience with the reeducation of Japanese soldiers that such a change, although far from easy, will not be so difficult as many people think—if it is done with determination. In our Japanese Peasants' and Workers' School here in Yenan a fundamental change of the psychology of most of our students from that of traditionally indoctrinated soldiers of the 'divine Emperor' to progressive antimilitaristic citizens takes place within two or three months.

"It will of course be necessary to expose in school textbooks the crimes of the Imperial House and also the untruth of its divine descent —although belief in that dogma should not be a punishable offense since that would only produce martyrs.

"The fight against the hatred of foreigners must also begin in school textbooks. The Shinto and Buddhist religions need not be touched. Long-range reeducation, freedom of speech and press, and general democratic progress will cause them to die out. Direct action against those religions and their institutions might also cause unnecessary provocation and friction. But propaganda against superstition in general will be needed.

"The Japanese system of script (Chinese characters) must be simplified, with the eventual aim of its Latinization—in order to raise the educational level of the masses. This will be somewhat easier in Japanese than in the Chinese language."

These are Okano's ideas on economic policies in postwar Japan.

"The first long-term consideration must be to raise the level of con-

420

sumption of the people and thus to strengthen political democracy by the creation of economic democracy.

"The production of arms and munitions must be prohibited.

"Further industrialization will be necessary. It should take place especially in high-quality industries—mechanical, electric, chemical—of the type characteristic of Switzerland.

"We must help the numerous small manufacturers who have been badly suppressed and in many cases thrown out of work during the war, so that they are enabled to resume production, compete with larger enterprises, and become the auxiliaries of high-quality industries.

"The development of a larger home market for industrial products, by means of improving the living standard of the masses of the people, is necessary. But a peaceful Japan can help China much in her industrialization, and this will provide additional employment for Japanese industries. In the first period after the war China will probably be the main market and supplier of Japan.

"A special task for Japanese industry after the war will be the production of good, cheap agricultural machinery. For some measure of mechanization of Japanese agriculture has to be achieved. It will help to increase food supplies, not only in the northern parts of the country where considerable agricultural development work is still possible, but everywhere.

"In agriculture, food production must be expanded at the expense of silk. The introduction of cooperative methods of farming of the kind that has been so successful in Communist-controlled China is of extreme importance. These methods will contribute further to an increase of production, so that the Japanese masses will then be able to live on a higher level of nutrition, yet without food imports.

"A thorough reform of the system of land tenure has to be carried out immediately. The government must buy up the land of absentee landlords—compulsorily and at low prices—and distribute it to poor peasants against payment of low annual rents to the government. Our minimum program also requires the confiscation of crown lands and the land holdings of war criminals for distribution to poor farmers. Part of such land is to be used for the establishment of government model

421

farms which are to develop and teach the farmers improved methods of production.

"Resident landlords must be obliged by law to reduce the rents they charge their tenants, and creditors of farmers will have to reduce interest rates. In this as in other respects, we can learn much from the successes of China's New Democracy.

"Banks have to be controlled by the government, so that their policies are made to fit into its general economic and social policies."

"Wasn't there a time when the Communist party of Japan advocated a socialist revolution," I asked Okano, "while your aim today is a democratic revolution?"

"In the Communist International in Moscow in 1930-31, American Communists denied the need for Japan to pass first through a democratic revolution before Socialism could be aimed at. The Russian Communists, at that time, understood the peculiar Japanese position better, but also not easily. And especially a number of comrades in our own Japanese Communist party had wrong ideas about the subject, under the influence of Trotskyism.

"Our late party leader Katayama, however, was correct in what he wrote at that time about the tasks of the Japanese Communist party on the basis of a democratic-revolutionary program.

"Eventually, in 1932, the question about the character of the revolution at which our party should aim was submitted to the Communist International for discussion.

"I was in Moscow then and helped the Western European Bureau of the Comintern write the Fundamental Theses on the Japanese Question which arose from that discussion and eventually became the basic principles for the policies of the Japanese Communist party.

"Those principles declare that the Japanese revolution must be a bourgeois-democratic revolution, aiming at the overthrow of the monarchy, the distribution of land to the peasantry, and the radical improvement of working-class conditions including the eight-hour day.

"Based on these principles, I wrote a pamphlet on tactical questions in 1936, advocating a wider United Front against war and the militarists, and for the establishment of a New Democracy in Japan. My proposals were adopted by the Japanese Communist party, against very few dissenters.

"Our party program had always demanded a bourgeois, not a socialist revolution, although our analysis of the complicated high-capitalistic and semifeudal character of Japanese capitalism was not thorough until 1932."

"What is the strength of the Communist party in Japan now?" I asked Okano.

"I am sorry, I cannot give you any actual figures," he said, "in view of the conditions of underground work under which the party has to exist in Japan. This is all I can say: a few thousand active party members are free, working especially in munitions factories where they had a hand in a number of strikes in recent years.

"At least four thousand people convicted for political crimes were in various Japanese jails a year ago, according to a comrade who recently arrived here from Japan. Even larger numbers are still awaiting trial in police prisons—including some three or four thousand who were arrested immediately after Pearl Harbor. The larger part of all those prisoners are Communists or sympathizers. Some very good Communists have already been in jail for twelve or even fifteen years.

"But underground activities continue in spite of the great difficulties. I have information also that sabotage in war factories has been fairly widespread recently. It was originally spontaneous but has gradually become somewhat more organized."

Okano had no doubt that the consequences of the defeat of Japan's militaristic dictatorship would automatically strengthen the Communist party and make it an important factor in Japanese politics.

Part Nine

PERSPECTIVES OF A WORLD PROBLEM

"Puppet" Traitors

Chapter Forty-two

JAPAN PREPARES FOR A COMEBACK

THE Japanese militarists seem to have worked out a plan for Japan's gradual return to world power and another round of conquest. It may sound fantastic. But it is no more fantastic than the chain of programs for the establishment of world dominion worked out by former generations of Japanese militarists—from Lord Hotta's 1858 program in which he outlined how the great Western powers must be used to teach and help a weak Japan to get strong enough to conquer the world from them, to the 1921 Tanaka Memorial with its detailed itinerary of aggression to Pearl Harbor and beyond.

Japan's military leaders have evidently realized for some time that defeat in the present war is inevitable. But they seem unwilling to accept their coming disaster as the end of a brilliant seventy years' career of conquest. It is only natural for them to lay their plans for the next round before the present one is finished.

Their new plan centers on the subtle use of China for the comeback of Japanese militarism.

Its initial requirement is political—to prevent China from becoming a true democracy devoted to the peaceful social progress of her people and the stabilization of world peace in close cooperation with the United Nations. For such a China would be of no use to the Japanese militarists.

Nor is a weak and disunited China any longer what they need. On the contrary, they must try to help China get strong and unified—on the basis of a reactionary regime which would direct its domestic efforts toward militarization, its international influence toward the disturbance

427

of the new world equilibrium, and its search for an ally toward a harm-lessly weak but potentially very useful Japan.

From what General Chou En-lai told me in Yenan on the basis of captured documents, the Japanese in China may already have taken the first step in carrying out their plan. They seem to have made prep-arations for leaving behind a powerful Fifth Column when they are eventually forced out of China.

This Fifth Column is to be built up within the ranks of their Chinese puppets. It is to work for the first Japanese requirement—the strength-ening of the reactionary elements in China. It is to become heir to as much of the arms, munitions, and supplies of the defeated or surren-dering Japanese armies in China as can be played into their hands. And this Fifth Column is to be used against the Chinese Communists.

To make clear what the Japanese are aiming at, a few words about the political character of their Chinese puppets are necessary.

The composition of the huge camp of collaborationists in the occu-pied areas of China is particularly complex. It will be extremely diffi-cult, when Japanese power in China collapses, to distinguish between the disguised patriots, the harmless meek, and the various kinds of outright allies of the Japanese among those innumerable Chinese poli-ticians, businessmen, landlords, and army officers who have been work-ing for many years with the enemy.

On both extreme wings of the puppet camp a good number of cases are clear enough to cause no problem and no disagreement when the time comes for patriotic China to rehabilitate or punish them.

Genuine patriots in disguise are by no means infrequent, at least in the lower categories of political and military puppets. A good number of them have done devoted and useful work against the Japanese for the Kuomintang and especially the Communist forces; some of them since the very beginning of their puppet careers and others since they saw the inevitability of Japan's defeat.

Similarly, some of the worst traitors among the high-ranking political puppets should have no hope of disguising themselves and some have been marked out for trial by the National Government in Chungking. Various statements to that effect were made to us in reply to our persistent questions at the foreign press conferences in Chungking. But government spokesmen used to be very reluctant about the collaborationists. They refused to give the names of the prominent puppet leaders who were to be brought to trial. And they hinted on every occasion that not all of the former high Kuomintang officials among the puppets who might appear to be traitors could be considered as such.

It seems that the main problem will arise in those numerous cases in which military puppets worked for the Japanese but did not attack Chungking troops and even rendered valuable services to the Kuomintang by acting against the Chinese Communists in the Japanese rear.

The Communist leaders in Yenan and several high-ranking Eighth Route and New Fourth Army officers from various war areas told us they had definite proof that many of the Kuomintang generals who went over to the Japanese with their troops had actually been under orders to do so. In some cases, we were informed, the orders for going over to the enemy could actually be traced back to high military authorities in Chungking. In others, they were issued by war area commanders or other responsible officers of the National Government armies at the front. Such surrenders, according to the Communists, were always preceded by agreements between the Chinese and Japanese sides about the specific use of those troops in their new role as puppets.

The Communists allege that there is a definite Kuomintang policy behind this—the so-called "Policy of National Salvation in a Roundabout Way." According to the Communists, this policy was openly explained and propagandized in various areas; for example, in Shantung province. It is supposed to be determined by the following considerations.

The national salvation of China requires not only the eventual defeat of the Japanese, which will take place anyway sooner or later with the help of the Western powers; but it requires also the defeat of the Chinese Communists who built up powerful positions in their fight against the Japanese in the occupied territories. And with the Communists the National Government itself would have to deal.

The over-all interest of national salvation makes it necessary, in view of the steadily growing strength of the Communists, to use some National Government troops against them—even while the war with Japan lasts. Such action would do no harm to the prestige of the National Government either in Free China or abroad, since little news about it would seep out from the enemy's rear, while the Yenan Border Region itself was firmly blockaded against the outside.

The first category of National Government troops considered suitable for this task were those left behind in the enemy's rear. For their usefulness against the enemy was impaired by their isolation from Free China and their failure to organize a popular war effort in the areas they occupied, as the Communists did. Yet the inability of those troops to obtain popular assistance also made them more or less ineffective in their fight against the Communists.

The Japanese were willing to take them over as puppets, offering to keep their units intact under their old commanders and to supply, reequip, retrain, and advise them—for the sole purpose of continuing the anti-Communist fight on which the Japanese have always been at least as keen as the Kuomintang.

Similar Japanese offers were apparently made to units of the National Government Army which found themselves in a precarious situation at the regular fronts and whose fighting power against the Japanese was reduced by supply difficulties and poor leadership.

This, according to Yenan, is how some 450,000 National Government troops came to serve both the Japanese and the Kuomintang against the Communists; in their original units, with their old commanders and staffs, but strengthened by Japanese aid; in contact and cooperation not only with the Japanese but also with the main body of the National Government armies on the other side of the front lines and with Chungking itself.

It is of course impossible to prove by whose orders and on the basis of what reasoning National Government generals with their troops went over to the Japanese, why they fight the Communists under Japanese direction, or how many of the National Government troops which surrendered in the course of the war became Japanese puppets. But Chungking government spokesmen admitted on several occasions that certain well-known generals were "captured" with their units by the Japanese; that some of those generals who used to broadcast from Japanese-occupied cities seemed to have risen to prominence in the puppet camps, although "probably under duress"; and that "some" former National Government troops were serving the Japanese as puppets.

I know of at least two instances in which military officers in Chungking frankly asserted to Allied officers that there was contact and cooperation with puppets of National Army origin in various areas. It is also definitely established that those and other puppet troops are daily fighting the Communists; while it seems from Chungking's war communiqués that puppets other than some locally recruited plain-clothes men are indeed rarely used against the forces of the National Government.

This is why Yenan suspects very strongly that Chungking's conception of "treason" will scarcely be broad enough to try and punish a good part of the commanders of the puppet armies when the Japanese are defeated. They and their troops may be publicly rehabilitated or even honored, reincorporated into the National Army, and used for further action against the Communists.

For the aim of Chungking's alleged "Policy of National Salvation by a Roundabout Way" is to make sure that Chinese troops loyal to the Kuomintang will be all around the Communist-controlled areas in the enemy's rear at the time when the Japanese are eventually forced out of the country.

Those commanders and their troops will be there when the national enemy is defeated. And it seems that they will be a considerable force. They are supposed to be better nourished, better trained, and now already better equipped than the average units of Chungking's own armies. Moreover, they are strongly indoctrinated with an anti-Communist and antiforeign ideology. Captured Japanese propaganda materials I saw in

Yenan show clearly that the enemy lays special emphasis on the anti-Communist and antiforeign education of his puppets, based on the most reactionary version of Kuomintang ideology. Criticism of Generalissimo Chiang Kai-shek is avoided or restricts itself to his policy of having "made Chungking dependent upon the Western enemies of the peoples of Asia."

These puppets, according to the captured documents mentioned by General Chou En-lai, are the forces to which the Japanese want to bequeath the legacy of arms, munitions, and supplies when disaster overtakes their military power. With these puppets they want to establish their Fifth Column in postwar China.

What would the Japanese have to gain if their plan were to succeed? In what "roundabout way" could those troops be used to promote the "national salvation"—of Japan?

First, a generous supply of Japanese war materials to them might make the outbreak of civil war in China more likely. The position of the reactionaries in the National Government, who are anxious to liquidate the Communists as quickly as possible, would be greatly strengthened by the veteran anti-Communist fighters among the puppet generals. The Japanese legacy of arms, munitions, and supplies would give those puppet generals a favorable bargaining position against any possible "appeasers of Yenan" in the political or military councils of the National Government. They might even create a *fait accompli* by starting a large-scale offensive against the Communists in order to force the regular Kuomintang armies to support them.

Second, a civil war would necessarily be bitter and prolonged because of the great strength of the Communists. A civil war would naturally cancel the liberalization of the Kuomintang regime which Generalissimo Chiang Kai-shek has promised the Chinese nation and the Allies. It would tend to enhance and perpetuate its reactionary features and give it a stronger militaristic note.

Third, the Allies would probably press the National Government to stop the civil war in the interest of world peace, and such action would certainly be resented by the right-wing Kuomintang. Allied pressure, even if it did not go to the extent of preventing the flow of supplies into Kuomintang China, would strengthen the anti-Russian bias and the general antiforeign tendencies in rightist Kuomintang quarters. And this might pave the way toward the second prerequisite of Japan's plan for a comeback: an increasing aversion of a reactionary Chinese regime to the Western powers and an increasing desire to oppose them.

The line along which the Japanese will try to foster antiforeign feelings in the Kuomintang in connection with Allied attempts to prevent civil war and foster democracy in China is clear from an article in Tokyo's *Nippon Times* which was broadcast by *Domei* on February 4, 1945.

"American efforts to force Chungking to collaborate with Yenan," the editorial stated, "will be disastrous to Chungking because of the fundamentally incompatible character of the two regimes. There can be no real fusion of interests of the two, since Chiang Kai-shek's power rests upon the support of the money power of banking interests, large landowners, and the bourgeoisie in general, as well as of bureaucratic careerists—while Yenan's power rests on the proletarian dictatorship of doctrinaire radicals springing from a revolutionary agricultural movement.

"Chiang Kai-shek wails, for he well realizes that for him to compromise with Yenan along the lines of American desires would be to admit the Trojan horse of Yenan within the walls of Chungking.

"If [American pressure] results in the eventual defiance of Chungking by Yenan, it will conveniently mean so much less Chinese nationalistic resistance to the economic penetration and exploitation of China which America envisages for the future. For that, after all, is the ultimate goal of the United States in her machinations in China as well as her war against Japan, the champion of Asia's resistance to American imperialism."

In other words, Japan argues that only the defeat of the Communists by means of civil war can make China strong enough to resist America's "imperialist designs" on the country. This view has long existed in certain reactionary Kuomintang circles in Chungking.

433

Some Japanese in the occupied territories of China seem to have already developed a further line of argument in favor of an understanding between militaristic remnants in postwar Japan and reactionary elements in China. They try to absolve the "champion of Asia's resistance to American imperialism" from his sins toward China, and to explain his temporary defeat, by stressing the existence in Japan of capitalistic and bureaucratic corruption which impaired the purity of her Asiatic idealism. Defeat will purify that idealism.

China has therefore nothing to fear from Japan any more. On the contrary, she has everything to gain from true cooperation with her against the common enemies in the West who made China bleed for them and who will rob her of the fruits of victory over Japan.

In this way, the Japanese would wish to arrive at the next stage of their plan—at a Sino-Japanese "Rapallo Treaty" on the pattern of the 1921 agreement between two ex-enemies of the First World War, that is, the victorious but civil-war-torn Russia which, like China, possessed great man power and undeveloped natural wealth but no technical skill to make use of either; and the defeated Germany which had no such wealth but the industrial and military skill to help Russia overcome her weakness.

The wish of the Japanese militarists for mutual Sino-Japanese rearmament after the war seems foreshadowed in the document of which General Chou En-lai told me.

The Japanese seem to have required only one *quid pro quo* for their offer to leave arms, munitions, and supplies to the "reliable" puppet armies: Certain Japanese property, machinery, and technical experts are to be hidden safely in China. . . .

We must count on the probability of some form of cooperation between China and Japan after the war. For enmity between the two nations, in spite of many years of conflict and war, may prove less lasting than that between ourselves and Japan or ourselves and Germany.

The Japanese as a nation do not seem to hate the Chinese people as they hate us. And they will probably find less reason to ascribe their eventual defeat to China than to us. On the other hand, more people in China than in America and Britain seem unafraid of cooperation with one or another group in postwar Japan and even anxious to develop it. Economically, the two neighboring countries are in many respects complementary to one another and there will be opportunities for mutually beneficial trade on a much larger scale than before the war. Culturally, they have more in common than either of them has with any of the Western powers. The reactionary elements in both countries think very much along the same lines. And this may come to be even more true of the progressives on both sides when the Japanese liberals gain more intellectual and political freedom. Politically, the development of each country in the postwar world will to a considerable extent depend upon that of the other.

A genuinely democratic China can do more than any Western country to foster true democracy in Japan, if only because of the geographical and cultural proximity between the two. A reactionary China, on the other hand, would make it more difficult than any other factor—both for ourselves and for the progressive elements in Japan—to destroy the deep ideological and organizational roots of Japanese militarism quickly and thoroughly.

The same holds true in reverse. A well cleaned-up Japan, put safely on the way toward democratic reform, would rob the reactionary elements in China of the only potential helpmates they can hope to find in Asia, and by weakening the Chinese reactionaries would thus assist China in her own democratic progress.

Yet an incompletely democratized Japan, handicapped by Allied endeavors to prevent the development of a popular revolt against the monarchy, big business, and landlordism, would certainly strengthen the reactionary elements in China, who have an old tradition of contact and sympathy with their opposite numbers in Japan.

The mutual influence on one another of the political systems of China and Japan will be of far-reaching consequence to the development of postwar Asia. This consideration must determine the Allies' future policies toward China as well as Japan.

Chapter Forty-three

YENAN, MOSCOW, AND OURSELVES

THE land mass of Asiatic Russia looms large over the thousands of miles of China's vast geographic boundaries in the north and the east. And China's outlying provinces, between those borders and the Great Wall, all have a history of Russian influence.

Manchuria in the east—large, rich, and populous, under Czarist control until Japan beat out the Russians and became first its claimant and then its conqueror—would once more see Russian troops on its soil if the USSR entered the war against Japan.

Outer Mongolia in the center—a vast semidesert territory sparsely populated by Mongolian nomads and never effectively controlled by their hated Chinese overlords—became an autonomous republic during the Russian Civil War and then an ally and buffer of the USSR against Japan.

Chinese Turkestan in the west—huge and arid, with a small population of Moslems of various alien races—was recently even more estranged from China than normally, yet friendly with Russia and under her influence until a year or two ago.

In the heart of North and Central China there are the large regions under Yenan's Communists which extend in the north close to Russian-controlled Outer Mongolia and in the east to areas where Russian armies may come to fight the Japanese.

This telescoped picture of Sino-Russian political geography—correct as far as it goes, but open to misinterpretation—is frequently used to make the following allegations plausible: Moscow is out to dominate China and is behind Yenan materially as well as morally. Russia interferes in Chinese internal affairs. The Chinese Communists, as their

436

agents, are ready to hand over to their Russian comrades whatever territory Moscow wants to annex in China. And a world front of the democracies both against the Russian and the Chinese Communists is the only way of saving Asia and the world from being turned Red.

What are the connections between the Chinese and the Russian Communists?

On several occasions responsible government officials in Chungking told me that they had never had any evidence or even serious suspicion of material Russian assistance to the Chinese Communists and that, to their knowledge, no connections existed between Yenan and Moscow, possibly excepting radio contacts.

Land communications between the territories under the control of Moscow and Yenan seem indeed impossible. A vast belt of roadless semidesert country—several hundred to about one thousand miles deep —separates Russian-controlled Outer Mongolia from the Inner Mongolian fringes of Yenan's Anti-Japanese War Bases and the Border Region.

That belt is strictly guarded: in the west by troops of the Chinese National Government; and in the east by the Japanese Army. Both forces are said to be equipped with sound detectors against aircraft, so that any Soviet planes flying to the Chinese Communist regions would be noticed; and neither side would be likely to keep its discovery secret.

The USSR, evidently, has been most anxious not to antagonize either the Kuomintang government in Chungking or the Japanese. That in itself makes it likely that people in Yenan were right in denying the existence of any kind of traffic between Russian territories and the Yenan areas.

Sino-Russian diplomatic and military contacts, too, seem to be exclusively those between Chungking and Moscow. The Russians have two *Tass* correspondents and an army surgeon in Yenan who went there years ago with Chungking visas, over the normal air route from the USSR via Kuomintang-controlled China, and those three men seem to be the only Soviet citizens in the Yenan regions.

All I was able to find out about radio contacts is that Soviet broadcasts are received in Yenan and distributed to newspapers and government offices by the *Tass* representatives, very much in the same way as foreign branches of the Office of War Information and the British Ministry of Information distribute their home broadcasts in China and elsewhere.

But what about Moscow's attitude toward Chungking?

During the first years of the Sino-Japanese war, which were the most dangerous for her, China received considerably larger military supplies from Russia than from America and Britain, as cabinet ministers in Chungking used to tell me when they criticized American and British timidity toward Japan which prevented them from aiding China more and from depriving Japan of war-essential American and British export goods.

At General Chiang Kai-shek's request, the Russians sent not only a large group of pilots but also military advisers to the Kuomintang armies—under a general who later, during the battle of Stalingrad, proved to be one of their ablest strategists. And part of them stayed on after Russia was attacked by Germany. But no Russian military advisers were ever alleged to have been with the Chinese Communists.

Sino-Russian relations became cooler as the United Front in China waned, giving rise to increasing mutual suspicions between Moscow and Chungking.

Against this background, minor friction over Sinkiang (Chinese Turkestan) led to considerable irritation on both sides.

A peculiar situation, characteristic of the old political vacuum in China's outlying Frontier regions, had developed in that vast semi-desert province which links the USSR and China by land and air but has never been under the effective control of the National Government.

Its local war-lord ruler, a Manchurian general who had exploited civil strife between various racial groups in Sinkiang to make himself supreme in the province in the early 1930's, was strongly opposed to Chungking—like the local people who had long resented the over-lordship of the alien Chinese. He asked for, and received, Russian help for the economic development of his domain. Trade with the near-by

USSR flourished and the long-dormant province achieved a new measure of prosperity.

Chungking objected to Russian influence in Sinkiang and the presence of Soviet troops which had apparently been brought in because of the prevailing insecurity from tribal unrest. Rumors about Russian territorial designs became more insistent in Chungking as relations with Moscow cooled down.

The denouement came when the Sinkiang war lord, believing that Russia was about to be defeated by Germany, broke with Moscow and made his peace with Chungking.

The Russians, apparently, made no attempt to resist the establishment of Chungking control over the province. All Russian economic advisers, technical experts, medical personnel, and what now proved to have been no more than one or two regiments of Soviet troops, withdrew at Generalissimo Chiang Kai-shek's request. But mutual distrust was too deep for the solution of the much-exaggerated Sinkiang problem to become the basis for an improvement of Sino-Russian relations.

No open friction ever arose between Chungking and Moscow on the Kuomintang-Communist conflict. As a matter of fact, Moscow's diplomacy seems to have been infinitely more reticent than Washington's on this issue, although the USSR, wanting a strong China at her Japanese flank, was as interested as the United States in Chinese national unity.

I did not hear even in confidential talks with Chungking leaders and Chinese and foreign diplomats that the Kuomintang-Communist question had ever been officially raised by the USSR, as it was with increasing insistence by the U. S. State Department.

But it may easily become an acute issue between Moscow and Chungking—more acute even than it did between Washington and Chungking during the crisis over the Generalissimo's demand for the dismissal of General Joseph W. Stilwell, the Commander in Chief of U. S. Army forces in the China-Burma-India theater, the nominal Allied Chief of

Staff to Chiang Kai-shek, and the most ardent advocate of Kuomintang-Communist reconciliation.

If the USSR enters the war against Japan, Moscow may press Chungking for permission to cooperate with the strong military forces of the Chinese Communists in Japan's rear, press harder than Washington did, and be less prepared to resign herself to failure.

And at the postwar settlement of Far Eastern problems—no matter in what form the USSR might have contributed to the defeat of Japan—Moscow may raise its familiar demand for friendly, democratic regimes in neighboring countries and at last bring up the delicate problems centering around the conflict between Chungking and Yenan.

Washington seems to have been aware of those prospects for a long time. The State Department apparently had three reasons for trying in 1943 and 1944 to bring the Chinese Communist forces into the Allied front against Japan and to help toward an understanding between the Kuomintang and Communist parties by democratization of the National Government.

First, in order to revive the Chinese war effort and facilitate American strategy.

Second, in order to forestall the outbreak of an acute Moscow-Chungking crisis in case of Russia's entry into the Pacific War; for that would automatically lead to contact and presumably cooperation between Russian and Chinese Communist troops at the Japanese flanks.

Third, in order to pave the way for a solid peace settlement in East Asia by preventing the strife between the two political and military camps in China from developing into an international problem more dangerous than those which arose over similar situations in Yugoslavia, Greece, and Poland. China might in fact become a second Spain.

This is why former Vice-President Henry Wallace, on his visit last year, as well as the State Department, has been trying hard in Chungking to sponsor better relations between China and the USSR and why President Roosevelt took a great personal interest in the matter.

The Chinese Communists do not deny their wish for friendlier and closer relations between China and the USSR. They are openly critical

440

of the attitude of the National Government toward the USSR. Its ideological aversion to Sovietism, the Communists say, has blinded Chungking's judgment of the aims and the international position of the USSR. It has given Chinese foreign policy a strong anti-Russian bias and has been responsible for the steady deterioration of Sino-Russian relations, which can only be detrimental to China and to the peace of the world.

The leaders in Yenan are far too realistic and much too keen on close Sino-American and Sino-British cooperation to demand for China a policy of exclusive or even predominant reliance upon the USSR.

"China cannot restrict herself to friendly relations with only one power or group of powers," Mao Tse-tung said to me. "It would be just as wrong for China to rely only on the USSR and snub the USA and Britain as it has been for Chungking, in recent years, to rely only on the USA while showing antipathy, suspicion, and actual unfriendliness toward the USSR.

"To count on the aggravation of the differences between the capitalistic countries and the USSR and to try to benefit from it, as the National Government in Chungking does, is very dangerous. It is equally against China's own interests and the interests of world peace.

"I do not believe for one moment that conflict between the capitalistic world and the USSR is inevitable. On the contrary, we Chinese Communists—who are making a success of the New Democracy which brings all social strata in our areas into close cooperation—are convinced that the capitalistic world and the USSR can and will learn to cooperate closely in peace as in war, in spite of occasional difficulties. We must not give in to an attitude which implies a defeatist denial of the possibility of stable world peace and thereby in itself hampers progress toward real peace.

"China can and must be one of the bridges between the two camps, instead of hoping to win foreign support as one of the zones of friction.

"China's progress depends upon real world peace, and the international role of our country can be enhanced only by sincere cooperation with all countries and by helping them overcome their differences."

441

The Communists are by no means the only Chinese who are strongly critical of the right-wing Kuomintang's attitude toward the USSR. Practically the same ideas have for years been expressed by many liberals with greater knowledge of world affairs than the right-wing Kuomintang leaders have.

Outstanding among them is Dr. Sun Fo, the son of the late Kuomintang leader Dr. Sun Yat-sen and himself a high-ranking member of the Kuomintang and the government.

He is by no means a "sympathizer" of the Chinese Communists but has always maintained that the Russian attitude toward Chungking was not determined by the existence of a strong Communist camp in China and that Chungking was only doing itself harm by not taking a friendlier attitude toward the USSR, which had often proved its readiness to improve relations with China and to help Chiang Kai-shek's government.

Nationalism is so strong and genuine in the Communist-led armies and in the party itself, and it is so much the foundation of the entire political system under which Yenan gained the cooperation of the people in its war areas, that it would have been ridiculous to ask the Communists whether they were willing to help the USSR to annex Chinese soil.

But I asked Mao Tse-tung's opinion about the problem of Outer Mongolia, nominally still under the suzerainty of China although it has been cut off from her for over twenty years and is administered in alliance with the USSR by a revolutionary government of its own. Did he want Outer Mongolia returned to China?

"Our National Government must first recognize Outer Mongolia as an autonomous national state," he said, "in accordance with the promise Dr. Sun Yat-sen gave all national minorities—the people of Outer Mongolia as well as the Tibetans. The Mongolians are not Chinese; they are a nation of their own.

"When they took that right for themselves and set up their own democratic republic, the Outer Mongolians issued a declaration to the effect that they would rejoin China as soon as they were recognized as

442

one of the national entities which, according to Dr. Sun Yat-sen, are to enjoy equal autonomous rights under the Chinese Republic.

"I hope and have no doubt that they will rejoin China the moment the National Government lives up to the promise of the founder of the Republic and the Kuomintang."

Nor are the moderate elements in the Kuomintang anxious to force Outer Mongolia back into its old relationship to China. They do not seem to ascribe immediate importance to the problem of suzerainty over an area which has never been under China's effective control and has in fact a theoretical right to autonomy under the principles Dr. Sun Yat-sen laid down for the fundamental policies of the Kuomintang.

Internal reforms in China and an improvement of Sino-Russian relations would help to solve the problem without difficulty, they believe, especially when Japan is defeated; for the strategic importance of Outer Mongolia in her long smoldering conflict with Japan was the real reason why the USSR gained such a strong influence on that territory.

"Let us be realistic: Would China have gained if she had been in control of Outer Mongolia in 1937?" one of the Chungking liberals once remarked to me. "The Japanese would have occupied it without difficulty. They would have threatened the very heart of Siberia. This might have changed the course of world events in favor of the aggressors."

But is Yenan's attitude toward world events independent from that of Moscow? Did not the Chinese Communists follow the political line of the Communist International in 1939 when they denounced the European War as an "imperialist war"? And did they not, like other Communist parties, change it the moment Russia was attacked by Germany?

I challenged Bo Ku, editor of Yenan's *Liberation Daily*, member of the Politburo of the Communist party and probably of equal importance in Yenan's world-affairs council with its main "diplomat," General Chou En-lai.

"We don't like to talk about that chapter of recent history any more,"

443

he said. "For that involves reference to Britain's policy toward China at that time, which we can forget since we have become allies. But if you are interested in it, I shall have to give you our views.

"From the beginning of the war with Japan in 1937, we had the slogan 'Alliance with all democratic countries, especially with Britain and the United States.' We were strongly against Germany and Italy—much more so than Chungking was—since both were already the close friends of our enemy Japan. We wanted support for China only from the democratic countries. But developments disappointed us.

"To recall only a few symptomatic details: The deliberate Japanese air attack on the car of the British Ambassador to China, Sir Hugh Montgomery Knatchbull-Hugessen, did not cause London to take a strong stand against Tokyo. After the fall of Hankow, the British embassy did not go to Chungking, the wartime capital of China, but to Shanghai, which was partly occupied by the Japanese.

"Worst of all, the British Prime Minister, Mr. Neville Chamberlain, made that shocking, programmatic declaration in the House of Commons in November, 1938, which virtually gave up China to Japan. He said he was optimistic about the future of British trade in China in spite of the Japanese conquest of our country, giving the reason that Japan would need the cooperation of British capital to develop it."

I looked up in an old copy of the *China Weekly Review* a report on Mr. Chamberlain's speech in the House of Commons on November 1, 1938. It reads: "He declared he was optimistic on the future of British trade in China. He said there could be no development in China without a great deal of capital, 'and for that [capital] Japan would have to go to other countries, including Britain.' He added that whoever reconstructed China could not do so without some help from Great Britain."

"Eventually," Bo Ku continued, "Britain unnecessarily closed the Burma Road under Japanese pressure. Britain gave up Chinese silver to the Japanese. The London *Times* carried on the most outspoken appeasement policy toward Japan. There was the definite danger of an Eastern Munich. And the attitude of the French Government toward

444

China, both in the French Concession in Shanghai and in French Indo-China, was even worse.

"I am not reproaching Britain and France now. I only want you to understand that nothing but those events and our general estimate of British and French policies influenced our attitude toward the European war. We never said for one moment that Germany was right. All we said was that the policies of the British and French Governments were still fundamentally determined by imperialistic considerations."

"But was not Britain too weak in the Far East to take a strong line toward Japan?" I asked.

"I admit that we did not know then that Britain was so weak. Her weakness surprised us later. But the main point is that all the weaknesses of Britain arose from her wrong imperialistic policies in general. And Chamberlain's attitude toward China was determined more by that general character of his policies than by Britain's military weakness.

"Now about the timing of our statement. Comrade Mao Tse-tung was the first of any Communist party leaders to denounce the war as imperialistic. He gave an interview on September 1, 1939. If he had done it at the order of the Communist International, why was that order not first given to Pollit of the British Communist party, who supported the war at first, or to the French or American parties, which had much more to do with the issue?"

"But how did the German attack on Russia in 1941 change the character of the Anglo-German war?"

"Mr. Churchill immediately renounced Britain's antagonism to the USSR. That meant a definite reversal of Chamberlain's imperialistic policy—also toward China.

"As a matter of fact, we already began changing our attitude in May, 1941. Yes, certainly without orders from the Communist International. The *Liberation Daily* stated then that there was no danger of an Eastern Munich any more.

"Churchill's new policy was a progressive policy in favor of mankind. Therefore we were able to support it. It changed the whole character of the war, influencing not only Europe but the entire world."

I wondered whether Yenan's original denunciation of the European

445

war as imperialistic was not a wrong step from the present point of view of the Chinese Communists: wrong because it seemed to have been treated as a matter of ideological publicity rather than of practical politics.

Bo Ku only smiled.

The Communist International has since been dissolved.

But it will probably still happen in the future that Chinese Communist party reaction to important international developments will be the same as that of Communist parties in other countries.

To some people this might then prove that another organization in Moscow has taken the place of the Communist International in order to keep Communist attitudes uniform all over the world. That may or may not be so; but from my experiences in Yenan and Moscow it seems just as likely to me that the common political philosophy of the Chinese and Russian Communist parties is sufficient explanation for similar reactions to general world events.

I would not be surprised, however, to learn someday that the Chinese Communist party is taking a different view from other Communist parties—possibly even from that of the USSR—on issues on which China's national interests might differ from those of other countries.

That would confirm my impression of the way in which the Chinese Communists arrive at their judgment of foreign affairs, that is, by a method of analyzing world developments which is Marxist, but from a viewpoint which is determined by China's national requirements.

I refuse to believe that any of the Chinese Communists I came to know considers his party and the area under its control in any way subordinate to Moscow, or that it would come to his mind to be guided by interests other than those of his own country.

The Chinese Communists are nationalists. Probably more so today than they were, say, five years ago. The steady intensification of their nationalism seems due not to the waning and eventual death of the Communist International, which probably influenced them much less than was often believed, but mainly to the introduction by Yenan of the New Democracy in 1941.

That new political system, it seems, democratized the minds of the Communists to a considerable extent. It made them think less in the old "class" terms of the Communist party and more in terms of the Chinese nation as a whole.

Among the questions for which American and British friends in Chungking had wanted me to find answers in Yenan was this: How would the Chinese Communists and their views on foreign policy fit into the postwar world if they were either to gain decisive influence on the National Government or if Communist-controlled China were to become a separate entity?

I found that Yenan's ideas on foreign policy do not differ from the principles which the foreign policy of the National Government professes. Even friendship between China and the USSR is one of the avowed aims of Chungking's foreign-policy program.

These are the main points of general criticism of Chungking's foreign policy that I heard in Yenan. They characterize Yenan's outlook on foreign affairs.

First, the fundamental assertion that Chungking's foreign policy lacks the necessary foundation of democratic government and therefore of correct domestic policies—for "foreign policy begins at home."

Second, the resultant personal interference of Generalissimo Chiang Kai-shek—and through him of certain reactionary elements in the party—with the diplomacy of men of more liberal leanings and greater knowledge of world affairs who are responsible for the Ministry of Foreign Affairs.

Third, the discrepancies between Chungking's professed principles of foreign policy and their application in actual diplomatic practice which are caused by those factors.

The Communists seem to have a stronger belief than the decisive persons and groups in the Kuomintang in the logic of international developments which should make world democracy triumph over balance-of-power politics when this war is won. Defeatism on the winning

447

of the peace is to them as blameworthy as defeatism on the winning of the war, as Mao Tse-tung implied in what he told me.

They have less fear than the Kuomintang leaders that China may remain at a dangerous international disadvantage because of her military weakness. For they are more strongly of the opinion that China's position in the world depends primarily upon her success or failure in the achievement of national unity and democracy—rather than on her military strength, her international prestige, and the credit she can at one time or another command in foreign countries.

Chungking's failures in domestic policies—in the war effort as well as in political, economic, and social reforms—are held responsible for its failures in foreign policy during the war, especially for China's nominal status in the councils of the Allies, which is so deeply resented by the Kuomintang leaders.

In consequence, the Communists are of the opinion that China must emulate the Big Three in the opportunities they have given their common people for developing into modern citizens—on the basis of genuine national unity and democracy—in order to become the Big Fourth in fact as well as in name.

The Communists believe that China's relationship with the USSR is not the only one which suffered from discrepancies between the theory and practice of Chungking's foreign policy and from personal interference of the Generalissimo and reactionaries behind him with the logical execution of policies on which he had decided.

China's relations with the United States and Britain also suffered in these ways. Chungking misinterpreted the principle of international cooperation in a one-sided manner, especially where the United States was concerned. The Kuomintang took it for granted, the Communists say, that China had nothing more to offer the Allies than her determination to continue in the war to the end—not even the urgently needed internal reforms the Allies expected the Generalissimo to carry out years ago, reforms which would have benefited China at least as much as the Allies.

It was equally taken for granted that the Allies' "Hitler First Strategy" put Washington under an obligation to compensate Chungking—not only by whatever direct military help was possible but also by submitting to a general Chinese attitude which was often as clamorous as it was uncooperative and which was apparently designed to take advantage of Washington's endeavor to please and calm Chungking.

This "undemocratic" Chinese attitude toward the United States, and to some extent also toward Britain, makes Yenan fear that China has been losing much of her good-will fund in both countries—if not yet with the general public, which is still unaware of a great deal that happened, at least with the American and British officials involved in many unpleasant controversies.

Mao Tse-tung summarized his views as follows:

"The international position of China at present is basically quite good. But we must learn to rely mainly on our own efforts. If we rely only upon a favorable international situation, we will never be able to solve any of the problems of China.

"The aims of the programmatic manifestoes proclaimed by the Allies, like the Atlantic Charter and the resolutions of the Moscow, Cairo, and Teheran conferences, are precisely the aims we are working for.

"The new international relationships which are necessary after the present anti-Fascist war require a new League of Nations built on a basis of democracy.

"However, to make it successful and to achieve world peace, we must have democracy inside each country, as well as democratic relationships between all countries.

"We expect foreign countries to take a democratic attitude toward China. But we ourselves must also take a democratic attitude toward them, an attitude of mutual help—in our own interest."

Part Ten

ONE CHINA—OR TWO?

MARRIAGE REGISTRATION IN VILLAGE

Chapter Forty-four

CAN CHINA UNITE?

THE fresh negotiations for an understanding between the Kuomintang and Communist parties were dragging on in Chungking during the time I spent in Yenan—month after month, as former talks had dragged on year after year. The two parties were as far apart as ever.

Over and over again, the Communist representative repeated Yenan's fundamental thesis: The effective democratization of General Chiang Kai-shek's one-party regime is the irrevocable prerequisite for bringing the Communist-controlled armies and local administrations under a truly national government.

Over and over again, the Chungking authorities repeated their basic demand on Yenan—unqualified submission of the Communists' armies and administrations to the lawful National Government. The legalization of the outlawed Communist party would follow, together with gradual political reforms to be determined by the government.

The intervals between discussion meetings grew longer and longer and their subjects remained as unrealistic as ever. The Kuomintang negotiator would offer recognition and army pay for a small number of Communist-led divisions, provided a temporary agreement on other points could be reached. The Communist representative would raise the number of divisions which were to be recognized and paid. But he would reiterate what Yenan had stated many times before—that the unrecognized majority of the Communist-controlled troops would of course continue to fight the Japanese. The Kuomintang negotiator would repeat the equally old retort: All unrecognized troops and all Communist-led militiamen must be disbanded, no matter what Yenan's opinion is about the influence of such a measure on the war situation in the Communist-controlled areas. Deadlock.

Or, after weeks of waiting, the Kuomintang would offer some more or less decorative post in the National Government in Chungking to an appointee of the Communist party, provided agreement were possible on other subjects. The Communist would point out that such a "concession" was meaningless and that Yenan was not out for jobs in Chungking but for the democratic reform of the Kuomintang dictatorship. Again deadlock.

But the leaders in Yenan were not surprised. Like that, negotiations had been going on for years, with intervals of weeks and months and sometimes half-years between meetings. The time had apparently not yet come, they said, for Chiang Kai-shek to want an understanding. He still felt that Yenan had to submit to his will—as even powerful Washington did when he was firm enough on some refusal of an American request. They would have to be patient.

These were the proposals the Communists made to Generalissimo Chiang Kai-shek in the fall of 1944 when negotiations were to be revived once more.

First, a national emergency conference should be called of representatives elected by the following groups: (a) the Kuomintang, the Communist party, and the democratic parties; (b) the Kuomintang-led armies, the Communist-led armies, and various provincial armies nominally under Generalissimo Chiang Kai-shek but in fact of a semiautonomous character; (c) local governments both in the Kuomintang- and Communist-controlled areas; (d) people's organizations in Kuomintang- and Communist-controlled territories. Seats at that conference should be apportioned according to the number of members represented by the various groups.

Second, this conference should formulate an administrative program on the basis of the Three Principles of the People of Dr. Sun Yat-sen, the late leader of the Kuomintang and the original United Front— with the aim of overcoming China's military, political, and economic crisis.

Third, a coalition government should be formed of all those parties and groups, embracing their leading persons, but excluding defeatist and Fascist individuals.

Fourth, the coalition government should form a United Supreme Command of all the armed Chinese forces of resistance.

Fifth, the coalition government should prepare for the earliest possible convocation of a People's Congress based on genuinely universal elections.

I asked Mao Tse-tung for a formal interview on Kuomintang-Communist relations.

"The possibility of an improvement of relations between the two parties still exists," he said. "It does exist in spite of all difficulties. And we are confident of being right in continuing our clear-cut, concrete, and definite policies that strive for closer cooperation with the Kuomintang, because of three reasons.

"First, Kuomintang-Communist cooperation is the categorical demand of the vast majority of the Chinese people, a demand they make on both parties.

"Second, the progressive elements in the Kuomintang itself are also working for such cooperation, as you know.

"Third, our endeavor for closer cooperation with the Kuomintang is in line with the policies of the principal Allied powers, the United States, Britain, and the USSR; with the fundamental policies of the Atlantic Charter and of the Moscow, Cairo, and Teheran resolutions; and with what the Allies expect and demand of China for the sake of establishing democratic, peaceful relationships in the international sphere.

"China is backward. China is many years behind the progressive countries of the West, particularly in economic development. But when the Japanese are driven out and if democratic reforms are carried through in our political and economic life, China as a country with great man power and considerable natural resources will be able to provide a better living for its masses. This will be highly beneficial to all nations and to their peaceful political and economic cooperation.

"We have not given up all hope yet that the Kuomintang may still carry out democracy. However, in order to attain a real understanding with the Communist and democratic parties the Kuomintang should agree with them on a program containing the fundamentals of democracy on the basis of Dr. Sun Yat-sen's principles, and should carry it out seriously.

"Once that were settled and the present one-party dictatorship of the Kuomintang gave place to democracy, there would be no more need for the Kuomintang blockade of our Border Region. Our democratically elected local governments would be automatically recognized as such. And everybody would be happy to see the Border Region and our Anti-Japanese War Bases in the enemy's rear continue to organize and improve in the interest of the nation."

I asked about the Communists' attitude toward Chungking's demand that the size of their armies be reduced.

"Chungking is now willing to 'grant' us ten divisions, which means 100,000 men; while the other 370,000 men of our armies and all our militia, over 2,000,000 men, are to be disbanded. They are willing, once more, to recognize our Border Region but none of our Anti-Japanese War Bases. Even that of Shansi-Chahar-Hopei, which we originally established in agreement with the National Government, is to be recognized only nominally. It would just mean handing over to the enemy all the territories our troops are denying him, and with them 90,000,000 people. . . ."

I told Mao Tse-tung of the fear in certain circles in Chungking that it was the ambition of the Communists to occupy Manchuria at the end of the war against Japan.

He smiled. "If we are strong enough when the time comes, we shall of course take up the task of driving the Japanese out of Manchuria as well as out of other parts of China. We hope that Allied troops and ours will do it together.

"Ever since 1937 our slogan has been to fight until we reach the Yalu River at the eastern border of Manchuria. The people in Manchuria

456

have been isolated from the rest of China for many years; they have been oppressed during all those years and deceived and poisoned by the Japanese with wrong ideas; but they are against the Japanese because of their cruelty.

"Our guerrillas have already penetrated into Jehol, the southernmost province of Japan's puppet state, Manchukuo. And the people there, through our correct propaganda and explanations, have responded enthusiastically to our call for the fight against Japan. Long before this, we organized in Manchuria a broad movement of anti-Japanese pioneers which still has considerable influence."

"To what extent do you intend to demobilize the Communist armies when the war is over?"

"When the Japanese are driven out, we are willing to demobilize our armies in proportion to the demobilization of the Kuomintang Army."

"And what are your demands on the Kuomintang for postwar times?"

"For the time after the war our irrevocable demand is that all strata of government in the country be popularly elected. We have some 19,000 lower administrative units, that is, rural subdistricts, towns, and cities in the whole of China. Let the people elect 19,000 local governments.

"As for the governments above, for the counties and provinces and for the nation as a whole, let them be elected either by direct suffrage or by the elected representatives of the people in the lower government units, according to Dr. Sun Yat-sen's demands.

"With free elections it will be very easy to solve all problems. There will be no trouble if we follow the real meaning of Dr. Sun Yat-sen's program, for the Kuomintang Manifesto of 1924 about his *new* Three Principles of the People says clearly that the government is to belong to the people and must not be monopolized by the few."

Mao Tse-tung paused for a moment. His face took on a sad, almost melancholic expression. He spoke with unusual emphasis.

457

"Yet the possibility of a large-scale civil war in China, started from the Kuomintang side, unfortunately still exists. There are two powerful cliques within the Kuomintang which are working for it all the time. The opportune moment they may choose to start a civil war against us will be in the future rather than in the present time. But this danger must be taken into consideration.

"The demands we make on the Kuomintang of which I have told you are not just the demands of the Communist party of China. They are the demands the late Dr. Sun Yat-sen himself made on the Kuomintang a long time ago.

"We hope sincerely for a fresh understanding with the Kuomintang. But this is possible only if the Kuomintang reforms its policies in the direction toward democracy. It would be an unworkable proposition for us to ignore the existence of the Kuomintang. But it is an equally unworkable proposition for the Kuomintang to ignore the existence of the Communist party and of the small democratic parties."

Shortly before I left Yenan I asked Mao Tse-tung what the Communists would do if, after the war, National Government troops tried to seize the areas liberated by the Communist-led forces and administered under the New Democracy—in case no understanding were by then reached by the two parties.

"I shall answer you with what I told General Chiang Kai-shek's liaison officer here in Yenan last year, at the time when the Kuomintang armies of General Hu Chung-nan prepared to attack this Border Region.

"Referring to the fact that Chungking always accuses us of speaking in 'un-Chinese, Marxist terms,' I said I could equally well express what I wanted to tell him in terms of quotations from the Chinese classics, as the Kuomintang like to do.

"First, I reminded him of Lao-tse's 'I would never want to be the first in the world,' which conveys the meaning that we shall never shoot first.

Second, I quoted a famous saying from ancient Chinese history, 'When you attack us, we shall retreat thirty miles. . . .'"

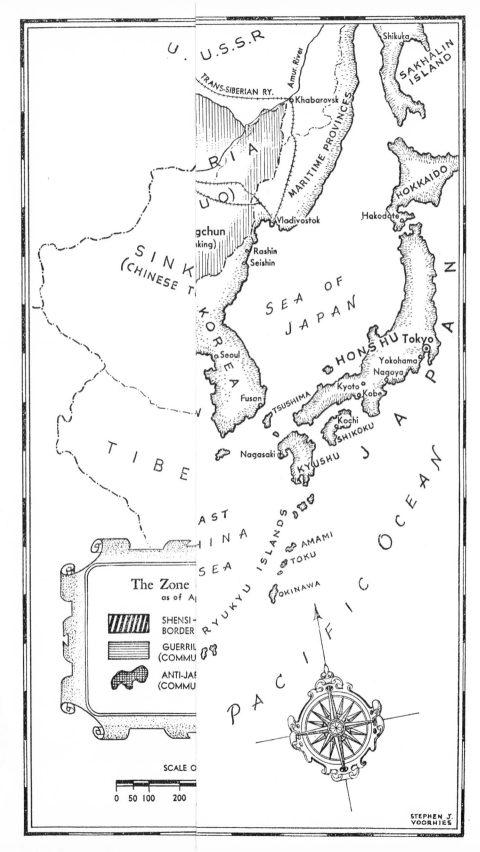

U. U.S.S.R

SAKHALIN ISLAND
Shikuka

TRANS-SIBERIAN RY.
Amur River
Khabarovsk

BIA
MARITIME PROVINCES

UO)
HOKKAIDO

gchun
nking)
Vladivostok
Hakodate

SINK
(CHINESE T
Rashin
Seishin

KOREA
SEA OF JAPAN

HONSHU
Tokyo
Yokohama
Nagoya
Kyoto
Kobe

Seoul

TIBE
Fusan
TSUSHIMA

Kochi
SHIKOKU

Nagasaki
KYUSHU
JAPAN

AST
HINA
SEA
AMAMI
TOKU

RYUKYU ISLANDS
OKINAWA

PACIFIC OCEAN

The Zone
as of A

SHENSI-
BORDER

GUERRIL
(COMMU

ANTI-JAP
(COMMU

SCALE O

0 50 100   200

STEPHEN J.
VOORHIES

"And then?"

Mao Tse-tung said quietly: "Of course, after having shown our willingness to avoid conflict and having retreated thirty miles—we shall fight back."

Chapter Forty-five

REACTION IN CHUNGKING

I LEFT Yenan on a crisp October morning—together with some high-ranking American officers from General Stilwell's headquarters who came on a week-end visit to the Eighth Route Army, and with Brooks Atkinson of *The New York Times*, who had arrived a fortnight before.

On the airfield were Mao Tse-tung, Chu Teh, and many other Yenan leaders, to say good-by to the first American general they had ever met, and to watch a simple military ceremony.

Against the background of an Eighth Route Army guard of honor stood Dave Barrett, the colonel in command of the U. S. Army Observer Section and by now the friend of all Yenan. The American general read a citation on the colonel's distinguished services in his liaison work with Chinese troops and pinned a decoration on his broad chest.

We flew over endless chains of yellow loess hills, sprinkled with green fields on the side of the Border Region, barren and empty on the Kuomintang side; over the blockade belt with its forbidding rows of blockhouses where large Kuomintang armies beleaguer the Communist "bandits"; over Sian, General Hu Chung-nan's anti-Communist headquarters; and at last, almost skimming some trees on the low Yangtsze hills, into the fog of Chungking.

Three hours from one Chinese world to another. . . .

I found only one change in Chungking, which was as listless and as skeptical of the likelihood of genuine government reform as ever, suffering from still higher prices and waiting for the war to end.

The change was this: some of the truth about Yenan had seeped into the consciousness of high officials who, five months ago, had evidently been quite unaware of the real character, the achievements, and the strength of the Chinese Communists—victims of the propaganda of their own government.

"Yes, we know it is true that much of what the Communists do is good and that they are making progress" was the tenor of what I was told by almost everyone in high Kuomintang quarters to whom I spoke about my impressions of Yenan.

The liberals among them seemed willing to accept most of my favorable estimates of Communist policies, even on aspects of which they had not heard. They were in a way proud of what ordinary Chinese people were able to accomplish under conditions even more difficult than those in the Kuomintang areas.

Yet there was an undertone of discomfort in their admission of the superiority of Yenan's methods over those of Chungking. The lives of the liberals, after all, are linked with the Kuomintang, however critical they may be of its present leadership. They fear that the Kuomintang may prove too far gone on the downward path to reform itself and too ossified to cooperate on anything like equal, democratic terms with the new power in China which has grown up in the "bandit" regions, and with the small democratic parties in the Kuomintang areas.

The Kuomintang liberals know well from their own experience of holding "responsible" positions, without being given either real authority or a voice in the inner party councils, what the Kuomintang leaders' conception of cooperation is. They know that a political party as strong as that of the Communists cannot be expected to submit to Chiang Kai-shek, as some liberals do as individuals. They were skeptical about an understanding between the Kuomintang and the Communists.

The moderates among the high government officials—men who are willing to loosen the Kuomintang's political monopoly somewhat instead of wanting to maintain it rigidly under the disguise of sham reforms, like the reactionaries—conceded that the Communists were efficient and hard-working and could teach the Kuomintang a great deal.

461

But they denied the genuineness of Yenan's democratic intentions and showed neither much hope nor real desire for Kuomintang-Communist cooperation. They were as opposed as they had been before to any attempt at armed suppression of the Communists. Yet they seemed more adamant than ever in their old enmity toward Yenan because they had in the meantime realized its growing strength and the increasing weakness of the Kuomintang which, most probably, would make the Kuomintang lose out under conditions of democratic freedom of speech, press, association, and election.

The reactionaries who had briefed me generously on the sins and lies of the Communists before I left for Yenan, were not keen on seeing me when I returned. The few I met looked a bit sheepish when I spoke of various experiences, including that with the "murdered Kuomintang intellectuals" whom we had found very much alive in Yenan and evidently on good terms with their Communist "executioners."

Even those sworn enemies of the Communists volunteered statements that "in some respects," as for example in their production drives, the Communists seemed to be "quite good." But Yenan's democracy, they said, was fake; the people in its areas were badly suppressed; and Yenan wanted and would always want to dominate the whole of China.

As to Kuomintang-Communist cooperation, they maintained that this was a wrong term. The issue was that the Communists had to obey the government. The reactionaries did not deny any longer that Yenan had built up a position of considerable strength; for they, too, seemed to have learned a good deal more than they might have known before about the real situation in the Yenan areas.

Their "authority" on Yenan—General Hu Chung-nan, the Strong Man of Sian—had apparently lost his reputation for truthful reporting on the Communist situation and had come under a cloud.

On the whole, the opening of the door to Yenan had served to correct the utterly distorted picture which official Chungking used to have of the Communist-controlled regions. Some of the Kuomintang newspapermen who were with us in Yenan at the beginning seemed to have written comparatively objective accounts of part of what they saw and had apparently divulged more in their private talks. The impressions of the American Army officers in Yenan had become known in Chungking and attracted considerable attention in official circles.

And our messages from Yenan—filed via Chungking where the censorship suppressed the best part of what we reported to our newspapers—seemed to have provided some additional information to high government quarters and possibly caused some more objective investigation into the real situation in the Communist areas.

In the meantime, China's small democratic parties had become more outspoken in their criticism of the Kuomintang government and their support of the demands of the Communist party on Chungking. Their political importance increased with the crisis of the Kuomintang regime and the growing popular recognition of the achievements of the Communists and of the need for national unity. For the logical role of these small democratic parties is to act as mediators between the Kuomintang and Communist camps.

These parties—federated in the Democratic League—lead a semi-illegal Cinderella existence in the Kuomintang areas, in spite of the fact that they made their peace with the Kuomintang when the war broke out, recognized the leadership of Chiang Kai-shek, and were given a few seats in Chungking's so-called People's Political Council.

The Democratic League consists mainly of these elements: the National-Socialist Party, whose name has no connection whatever with Hitler Fascism; the China Youth Party; the Third Party, which is led by early Communist and Kuomintang dissenters who wanted to build a bridge between the two main political camps; the National Salvation Group; several vocational organizations and a considerable number of individual nonparty intellectuals with reformist ideas. Its total membership is probably under 100,000—for it is not permitted to lead a normal party life—but it is strong among the faculties of Chinese universities and in intellectual, professional, and clerical circles in the big cities.

For years in Chungking I had kept contact with those respectable and moderate intellectuals who had to lead lives of isolation and semi-legality, as if they were dangerous revolutionaries.

This is what two of their responsible leaders told me, asking me to tone down their criticism of the Kuomintang in what I wrote and not to mention their names. . . .

"Ever since the war broke out, the small parties as well as the Communists recognized the leadership of the Generalissimo. But we regret to say that the cooperation of the Kuomintang with any of the other parties has been far from adequate. The Kuomintang did not respond with equal sincerity to our readiness for cooperation.

"Progress toward the realization of democratic policies has been too slow. And there has not been sufficient freedom of thought, speech, press, and assembly, nor sufficient observance of human rights.

"Most of the personnel in the government are not satisfactory to the public. But the Kuomintang does not satisfy the people by discharging all those who are not respected. On the other hand, most of the good and fairly liberal officials—even those of very high rank—are not in a position of real influence.

"This fact and especially the inadequacy of interparty cooperation is responsible for the weakness and the gradual waning of the war effort and for the growing crisis and disillusionment in which the people live. If the Kuomintang had accepted the sincere support of all the other political parties, things would have been quite different and China would have been strengthened by the war."

I asked the two men about the cooperation between the Democratic League and the Communist party.

"Cooperation between us in the opposition has made progress ever since the war broke out. Those years have brought all of us closer together. And the people expect and hope for even closer cooperation between us when the time for real action comes."

"We quite agree with the Communist party on China's need for democracy. Since the Communists modified their economic policies on the basis of definite recognition of private property, we agree with them

464

also on that subject. Their economic policies coincide with China's needs on the basis of existing conditions.

"Our impression of the present activities of the Communists in the regions they control is that they are doing their best with all sincerity, that they are working hard, that their organization is very solid, and that there is no dissension among them.

"In other words, we are in agreement with the policies the Communists have been carrying out during the war. There are some minor unsatisfactory points, but they can be ignored. It is part of the cooperation between the Communist party and ourselves that these points are being discussed frankly.

"We are also of the conviction that the Communists will not revert to their more radical prewar policies when the war is over. As a matter of fact, although we have no assurance on that point, we believe that after the war the Communist party may become even more democratic than it already is—provided the Communists are not again attacked by the Kuomintang armies.

"If the Kuomintang changes its present policy toward the Communist party and takes a more friendly attitude toward it, there will be the possibility of full cooperation between the two great parties and ourselves for the realization of genuine democracy all over China."

"Are you not afraid that the Communists may want to become supreme in China once their party is legalized everywhere?"

"No. The Communists have no ambition of being the sole leaders of the nation. Of this we are convinced and we know them very well. They are realists and know that the Chinese people will never really support and help a one-party dictatorship. We are certain the Communists want to cooperate with the Kuomintang if only the Kuomintang is serious about practicing democracy."

"But what about the fact that the Communists have their own armies and governments?" I asked.

"On principle we do not agree with the Communist party, or any party, having its own armies and governments. But it is not their fault that they have to have them. If they did not, they could not exist at all under the circumstances prevailing in China. Do not forget that the

465

Kuomintang has not given a legal position to any political party but itself and that its 'National Army' is in fact a party army, too."

"Look at ourselves," one of the party leaders added with a sad smile, "where we are as opposition parties, without armies and governments of our own. You know the conditions under which we must try to work. You know what Chungking's People's Political Council, and our few seats in it, amount to.

"On the other hand, our members in the Communist-controlled territories—there are not many because we were always weak outside the big cities—enjoy full democratic rights and cooperation under the 'Three-thirds system' of representation practiced by the Communists."

I had met several members of the Democratic League in Yenan who served in responsible government positions and gave equally favorable opinions about the attitude of the Communists toward the small democratic parties.

The wider realization among Chinese and foreigners that the "bandits" in Yenan were in fact honest patriotic fighters and good administrators and had gained the cooperation of the people in their own regions had increased domestic and American pressure on Chiang Kai-shek for a real settlement with Yenan.

In various cities in the Kuomintang areas the rumbling of public opinion, the criticism of the National Government, and the demand for democracy became more audible. Some members of the well-selected and tame People's Political Council of Chungking made more than normal use of their "advisory power" to emphasize the need for an understanding with the Communists on the basis of a democratization of the regime.

The Generalissimo and those close to him, I was told, were alarmed. They, too, had probably underestimated the power of the Communists —both material and moral—and the popular demand for democracy.

Chapter Forty-six

STILWELL HAD TO GO

WASHINGTON—apparently reflecting the opinions of the American Army officers in Yenan—insisted more strongly on bringing the Communist-led forces into the Allied fold and on a political understanding between Yenan and Chungking. These points were part of the American plan for reviving the Chinese war effort—and beyond that for helping China to enter the new era of peace in a state of genuine national unity.

For two months negotiations had been going on between Chiang Kai-shek and President Roosevelt's personal representative, Major General Patrick J. Hurley, on the subject of giving substance to General Joseph W. Stilwell's position as Allied Chief of Staff to the Chinese armies by letting him command all Chinese forces under the Generalissimo.

At first Chiang Kai-shek was inclined to agree. But gradually his attitude stiffened, became negative, and eventually adamant. He decided to assert his authority—for all at home and abroad to see that he would not let himself be coerced by anybody into army or government reforms or into an agreement with the Communists. He sent a personal ultimatum to President Roosevelt, demanding the recall of General Stilwell—shortly before the presidential elections.

"Uncle Joe" had to go—the most competent and devoted officer the Generalissimo had ever had at his disposal to help him raise the combat efficiency of his troops and make the best use of them against the enemy.

"The Chinese Government hedges and hesitates over anything involving the use of its armies. Foreigners can only conclude that the Chinese Government wants to save its armies to secure its political power after the war. . . . No diplomatic genius could have overcome the Generalissimo's basic unwillingness to risk his armies in battle with the Japanese."

This is what Brooks Atkinson, the calm and balanced correspondent of *The New York Times,* reported. He was the only one of the Chungking correspondents who got the real story of the Stilwell affair out; for he left China together with Uncle Joe. His article caused a sensation in Chungking when it was cabled back. At last, somebody had been able to tell the basic truth about what was wrong with Chungking.

The hope of many Chinese that Stilwell might be able to help Chiang Kai-shek reform the army, coordinate the Kuomintang and Communist forces, and thus bring about national unity as well as a revival of the war effort, was dashed. But wasn't there hope that the American public, informed at last of the true situation in China, would strengthen the hand of the Administration in helping China toward national unity, both for the last stages of the war and for true peace after victory?

"Joe Stilwell has now concluded a busy, constantly frustrated attempt to help China stay in the war and to improve the combat efficiency of the Chinese forces," Brooks Atkinson wrote.* "Uncle Joe speaks Chinese. He knows more about China than most foreigners. He is more intimately acquainted with the needs and capacities of the Chinese Army than the Generalissimo and General Ho Ying-chin, Minister of War and Chief of Staff, because he has repeatedly been in the field with the troops. He is commonly regarded as the ablest field commander in China since 'China' Gordon.

"The decision to relieve Stilwell . . . may mean that the United States has decided from now on to discount China's part in a counter-offensive.

"Inside China it represents the political triumph of a moribund anti-democratic regime that is more concerned with maintaining its political supremacy than in driving the Japanese out of China.

"America is now committed at least passively to supporting a regime that has become increasingly unpopular and distrusted in China, that

* *The New York Times,* Oct. 31, 1944.

maintains three secret police services and concentration camps for political prisoners, that stifles free speech, and resists democratic forces.

"The fundamental difference between the Generalissimo and General Stilwell has been that Stilwell has been eager to fight the Japanese in China without delay, and the Generalissimo has hoped that he would not have to. In no other way is it possible to understand the long series of obstructions and delays that have made it impossible for Stilwell to fulfill his original mission of equipping and training the 'unlimited man-power' resources of the Chinese Army.

"The Generalissimo has one positive virtue for which America is now indebted: he has never made peace with the Japanese although there have been times when his ministers thought the future looked hopeless.

"But the technique of preserving his ticklish balance of political power in China keeps him a passive man. Although he is the acknowledged leader of China, he has no record of personal military achievement and his basic ideas of political leadership are those of a war lord. He conceives of armies as political forces.

"The Chinese Communists, whom the Generalissimo started trying to liquidate in 1927, have good armies that are now fighting guerrilla warfare against the Japanese in northeast China. The Generalissimo regards these armies as the chief threat to his supremacy. For several years he has immobilized 300,000 to 500,000 (no one knows just how many) Central Government troops to blockade the Communists and keep them from expanding.

"Distrusting the Communists, the Generalissimo has made no sincere attempt to arrange at least a truce with them for the duration of the war. The Generalissimo's regime, based on the support and subservience of General Ho Ying-chin, Dr. H. H. Kung, Minister of Finance, and Dr. Chen Li-fu, Minister of Education, has remained fundamentally unchanged over a long period of time and has become bureaucratic, inefficient, and corrupt.

"Most of the armies are poorly fed and shockingly maltreated. In some parts of the country the peasants regard the armies as bandits and

469

thieves. In Honan last spring the peasants turned against the Chinese armies during the Japanese offensive in revenge for the ruthlessness with which the armies collected grain during the famine years.

"The reason why nothing is done to alleviate the miseries is that the Generalissimo is determined to maintain his group of aging reactionaries in power until the war is over when, it is commonly believed, he will resume his war against the Chinese Communists without distraction.

"Bewildered and alarmed by the rapidity with which China is now falling apart, he feels secure only with associates who obey him implicitly. His rages become more and more ungovernable and attack the symptoms rather than the causes of China's troubles.

"Inside China everything Stilwell has tried to do has been obstructed and delayed. . . .

"Now he has been forced out of China by the political system that has been consistently blocking him; and America is acquiescing in a system that is undemocratic in spirit as well as fact and is also unrepresentative of the Chinese people, who are good allies.

"Relieving General Stilwell and appointing a successor has the effect of making us acquiesce in an unenlightened, cold-hearted, autocratic political regime."

I left China soon after the Stilwell affair had broken. The censorship made truthful reporting impossible.

The dismissal of Stilwell meant a great blow to hopes for the creation of Chinese national unity under the stimulus of last-minute revival of the Chinese war effort. It meant more than the dismissal of a person. It seemed to indicate the abandonment of a policy for the salvation of China which had at long last begun to take shape—its abandonment by Chiang Kai-shek and by President Roosevelt.

Stilwell, the able soldier and rare expert on China, the sincere friend of the Chinese people and loyal supporter of Generalissimo Chiang Kai-shek, was ideally suited to help him. Stilwell the man perhaps was not. He was as blunt as he was honest, as hard-driving as he was efficient. He did not appreciate Chinese decorum and may have ignored it

470

purposely. It had been too long in the way of Chinese progress and had cost too many lives. His heart was with the soldiers and the common people whom he wanted to help win their war and their peace, and his manner, although modest and thoroughly correct, is not that of a courtier.

I think nothing characterizes the fundamental difference of character between Chiang Kai-shek and Stilwell better than a little sequel to his dismissal.

The Ledo-Burma highway had at last been finished some time after Stilwell, the initiator and executor of the plan for a new supply route from India into China, had gone in disgrace, followed by harsh words. With the blood and sweat of Chinese and American fighters and coolies it had been pushed through swampy, disease-infested, Japanese-held jungle positions, under incredible difficulties of fighting and road-building work and with great, heroic human sacrifice. It had been the men, much more than the generals, who accomplished this feat. The Generalissimo solemnly gave it the name Stilwell Road.

Uncle Joe was asked at a press conference in Washington what he thought of Chiang Kai-shek's gesture.

"I'm against it," he said gruffly. "I think they ought to find some means of indicating the contribution made by the people who built it."

The clash of personalities was the reason given for Chiang Kai-shek's demand to have Stilwell recalled and for President Roosevelt's acceptance. But it was clear from the moment his successor Lieutenant General Albert C. Wedemeyer was appointed by Washington and welcomed in Chungking that the new man was to play a different role—to help in a repair job for limited ends rather than in fundamental reform, and not to press for national unity.

Having won his point, the Generalissimo announced a "government reform." The three main targets of Chinese and Allied attack in his cabinet were "removed." General Ho Ying-chin ceased to be Minister of War but retained the vital position of Chief of Staff he had held concurrently for ten years; and he was given great additional power once more after a little while, as Commander in Chief of all Chinese land forces.

Chen Li-fu, one of the two brothers who lead the powerful Fascist "CC group" in the Kuomintang, ceased to be Minister of Education— only to be given the more important Kuomintang Ministry of Organization (outside the cabinet), which carries with it complete control over the party membership.

Dr. H. H. Kung, the Minister of Finance and Vice-Premier, left for the United States to undergo a major operation—but the great influence he wields through his powerful group in the financial, economic, and political fields remained.

Dr. T. V. Soong, the able liberal, was made Premier in addition to his post of Foreign Minister under Kuomintang party leader, Generalissimo and President Chiang Kai-shek—to impress domestic and foreign opinion with his prestige.

"T. V.," who had so often been pushed aside by the whims and jealous suspicions of his two brothers-in-law, Chiang Kai-shek and Dr. Kung, and who had so often overcome his pride when he was prevailed upon to come back because he was urgently needed to help them out, was ready once more.

But would the Generalissimo, who had so long proved unable to delegate power, give T. V. Soong the authority that should go with this post at a time when drastic internal reforms were of such vital importance and when the maintenance of Soong's prestige as a liberal and an efficient administrator would depend upon his opportunities of living up to his avowed political ideals? There was no real change in Chungking's government and its policies. Things remained fundamentally as they had been in spite of much-advertised reform schemes.

The Generalissimo next turned to the Communist problem.

Major General Patrick J. Hurley, now the United States Ambassador in Chungking, acted as godfather to intensified negotiations between the two parties, flew to Yenan, and carried proposals from one camp to the other.

Again the alarmed voice of Tokyo was heard over the air.

A *Domei* broadcast quoted the complaint of the Tokyo newspaper *Mainichi Shimbun* that "the activities of the Yenan regime have become more vigorous in coordination with America's Pacific offensive" and that "Communist attacks on the Imperial Japanese Army have recently been especially marked in Central China" where, for example, "the New Fourth Army is swarming into the Anhwei sector."

It continued with an editorial from the *Nippon Times*, expressing sympathy with Chiang Kai-shek's "wailing" at American pressure for an understanding with Yenan and warning Chungking that, "if it results in the eventual defiance of Chungking by Yenan, it will mean so much less nationalistic resistance to the economic penetration and exploitation of China which America envisages for the future; for that, after all, is the ultimate goal of the United States, both in her machinations in China and her war against Japan, the champion of Asia's resistance to American imperialism.

"The United States pretends that a Chungking-Yenan *rapprochement* is necessary for the prevention of civil war in China," the *Nippon Times* added, "but a compromise sponsored by the United States would only make civil war inevitable."

The fresh talks led to nothing. They stranded, as always, on fundamentals. Chiang Kai-shek refused to recognize the actual situation that exists in China. He stuck to the view that he is the government and that the Communist party has no right to anything like political equality with the Kuomintang. And he refused to consider a genuine democratization of the regime. The Communist fighting forces were not brought into the Allied fold. The blockade of the Border Region was not lifted.

Dave Barrett was recalled from Yenan.

General Wedemeyer stated at a press conference in Chungking that "he was not empowered to give military aid to the guerrilla fighters of the Chinese Communists," and that "all United States officers in China are required to sign a statement that they will not give assistance to individuals or organizations other than those affiliated with the Chungking government.

473

"I hope with all my heart," General Wedemeyer said, "that the Chinese can get together."

"But it was the consensus of most observers," a United Press dispatch from Chungking added, "that those hopes had once more been dashed." (Months later, in the summer of 1945, when General Wedemeyer made a 2,100-mile inspection tour of Chinese and American installations in northwest China—according to the *Associated Press*—he visited the anti-Communist headquarters, Sian and Tungkwan at the Yellow River bend, "across which he stood within rifle range of Japanese soldiers"; but "at no point did the American commander touch Communist-controlled territory.")

The political results of the present American policy which "appears to be to ignore the Communists and to work in closest cooperation with the Kuomintang . . . have such grave implications for the future in the event of civil war in China that they are giving nightmares to most Americans familiar with the Orient," the *New York Herald Tribune* wrote in its editorial of June 29, 1945. "It seems preposterous to continue drifting in the direction of involvement in a Chinese civil war."

And Walter Lippmann wrote the day before in his column:

"An understanding with China and about China has the first and highest priority. There was open civil war in China for many years before the Japanese invasion. There has been latent civil war during the Japanese invasion. There will be no peace in Eastern Asia if civil war breaks out after the defeat of Japan.

"The Chinese civil war is not a purely Chinese affair: it is a threat to the peace of the world. The United States, out of loyalty to an ally, as a matter of good faith, and for military reasons in this war, is giving full support to the Chungking government. It is committed to taking a leading part in assisting the reconstruction of China and its industrialization.

"But the United States can have no interest in building up the military power of Chungking in order that it may then wage civil war after the Japanese war is concluded. That could hardly fail to bring

Chungking into conflict with the Soviet Union, and to entangle the United States in that conflict."

The Generalissimo eventually announced that at the end of 1945 "constitutional government" would be established by calling a National Assembly for the adoption of the draft constitution which the Kuomintang had worked out in the early 1930's.

Everybody in China realized that this "concession" did not mean what it seemed to imply; that it meant, on the contrary, a bid for the perpetuation of unchanged Kuomintang rule over China and an attempt to mislead foreign opinion.

For the delegates to that "National Assembly" were chosen in 1936, before the war with Japan broke out. Their "election" took place through the party-cum-government organizations of the Kuomintang, without consultation of the people. The Civil War was still going on at the time and the Kuomintang was then, as it is once more today, under the rigid control of its most reactionary clique, the Fascist "CC group."

All questions concerning the membership and powers of the National Assembly, according to Chungking's *Chinese News Service* (New York, May 7, 1945), will be "left to the Central Executive Committee of the Kuomintang"—that is, to the monopoly party which the National Assembly, ostensibly, is to dethrone in favor of a democratic regime.

And what about the draft constitution which this sham National Assembly is to adopt? This instrument, for many years under attack from all liberal elements in China, is nothing but a legalistic disguise for the continuation of the Kuomintang dictatorship. Under its provisions, the President of China holds greater powers than the head of state of any democratic country in history; and he is elected for six years, not by the people, but by the National Assembly which convenes for—one month once every three years. Its bill of rights, like that of the Japanese constitution, qualifies and destroys every civic freedom by the ominous clause, "except in accordance with law." And it contains a blanket provision for virtually dictatorial emergency rule by decree, fashioned after the fatal Article 48 of the Weimar Republic which helped Hitler into power in Germany.

This move of the Generalissimo must be fresh proof to all those in China who oppose the one-party dictatorship of the Kuomintang that Chiang Kai-shek is unwilling to give in to the nation's demand for democracy. It has deepened the rift between the Kuomintang and Communist parties—more than any action Chiang Kai-shek has taken against the Communists since the war with Japan began.

But no protest became audible from Chungking. The Kuomintang censorship—as ruthless as ever—saw to that.

In San Francisco, however, one of the members of China's delegation to the United Nations Conference on International Organization spoke up. Li Hwang, the highly reputed chairman of the China Youth Party, which belongs to the Democratic League, told a correspondent of the *Overseas News Agency:* "It is the same old story. Nine years ago, the Kuomintang government appointed twelve hundred men to membership in the National Assembly. They were supposed to represent the people of China. Actually, they represented the Kuomintang.

"It is unfair. It is undemocratic and illegal. There are no elections. It is simply a one-party dictatorship."

And he stressed that he wanted it known that the people of China were not represented at the San Francisco Conference, either—in spite of the diplomatic gesture of Chiang Kai-shek to include a Communist and several representatives of the democratic parties in the large Kuomintang delegation to the United Nations Conference on International Organization—since there are no free elections and the people have no opportunity to select the representatives they want. The non-Kuomintang delegates, he said, had been kept in virtual seclusion, newsmen had been elaborately shooed away from them, and their opinions had been ignored.

The Communists—according to Yenan's Morse broadcasts which are directed to the United States in English and daily recorded by the Federal Communications Commission—regard this action of Chiang

Kai-shek as a move "to split the Chinese people and to prepare for civil war."

They announced that they are preparing their countermove: They will hold a popular congress of their own in Yenan, at the time the Kuomintang's National Assembly is to take place in Chungking.

That congress will give reality to the over-all United Front organization of all the territories under the New Democracy which has been in the process of development for some time—the Chinese People's Liberation Union.

It will represent not only the 90,000,000 people under the democratically elected administrations of the Anti-Japanese War Bases and Yenan's own Border Region, but also a good part of the people in the Japanese-occupied areas, and it will be open to the people in the areas under the National Government.

An ominous *United Press* dispatch which indicates what may result from the deepening rift between the Kuomintang and Communist camps came through the otherwise so strict Chungking censorship on June 6, 1945:

"Reports reaching Chungking from several sources today indicated that Chinese Communists from the north were infiltrating toward such cities as Shanghai and Changsha in Central China, apparently in the hope of occupying them if the Japanese should withdraw.

"Some quarters expressed fear of clashes between government and Communist troops should the government regulars, following the Japanese, come into areas in which the Communists have established themselves.

"Two Communist divisions were said to be established in the area northwest of Changsha after marching from Shensi through penetrated Japanese lines."

The Communist troops which fought their way through many Japanese lines, marching more than 1,000 miles from Yenan through North China to the Hunan capital Changsha in Central China, in order to challenge the enemy at one of his most vulnerable front sectors, were

477

part of those I had seen in the Border Region—on the great army model farm of Nanniwan.

They were led by their old commander, Brigadier General Wang Chen.

He had confided to me on the day of my departure from Yenan that he was at last ordered to go back to the front and, once more, fight the Japanese . . .

I was in the United States by then, watching the aftermath of the Stilwell crisis from a distance, assessing my experiences in Yenan and Chungking in terms of a world elated by the march of victory over aggression yet increasingly apprehensive of the problems of the coming peace—problems among which that of China's disunity is taking shape as one of the greatest and most delicate.

Chapter Forty-seven

OUR TASK IN CHINA

WE MUST face facts.

There are *two* Chinas today—not only the one we recognize.

And there will be two Chinas in the future unless the regime of the Kuomintang, following the trend of the time and the desires of the vast majority of the awakening people all over the country, liberalizes itself sufficiently to merge with the China of the New Democracy into a nationwide system of true self-government.

By the side of the internationally recognized and nurtured China of the Kuomintang, the wild-growth China of the Communist-initiated New Democracy has come to stay—no matter whether it gains from the defeated enemy much or little of the territories he held between the Communists' Anti-Japanese War Bases; no matter whether its share in the Japanese heritage of arms and munitions is greater or smaller than that of the Kuomintang; no matter whether or not it remains blockaded and isolated from the outside world.

Its fundamental strength lies not so much in territory, arms, and outside supplies as in the fact that the New Democracy answers the needs of the Chinese people and solves their basic problems. This progressive reform system has gained for the Communists and their leading United Front collaborators a degree of active mass support such as no regime in China has ever been able to obtain. More than that: the people have come to regard that system as their own.

They will, if need be, fight in its defense.

Chiang Kai-shek's armies, even if they were equipped with foreign arms, would be no more likely to succeed decisively against that combi-

479

nation of Communists-led troops and politically conscious people than hundreds of thousands of well-equipped Japanese troops with plentiful puppet support did during eight years of incessant war and terror.

The Kuomintang regime, on the other side, is certainly weak and in a deep internal crisis, but it will not collapse within a short time or voluntarily give place to the popular forces that oppose it.

On the contrary, the Kuomintang is preparing itself for a stubborn struggle against those forces.

There are already signs that it responds more vigorously to the danger of its own political eclipse in postwar China than it did to the grim fact of preventable national decline during the war. It has begun to improve the efficiency of its administration and especially of its armies —not by democratic means, of which it is incapable as at present constituted, but by stricter application of its old autocratic methods.

It will, no doubt, continue to make the greatest possible use of its high-pressure publicity machine—supported by censorship of its own press as well as news reports that leave its capital, and by the continued news blackout against the Communist-controlled areas—in order to impress the world in its own favor.

For the Kuomintang regime—inclined to rely upon foreign aid since its very inception with the help of foreign capital—is now hoping for much American support to overcome its economic and financial crisis, and to strengthen itself in its struggle against the China of the New Democracy.

During the last phases of the war, considerable quantities of American arms and military and other supplies were given to China, of which little could be used any more against Japan. Some of those arms have already been fired against the Communists before Japan surrendered.*

Chungking hopes that President Truman will not invoke the clause

* In July, 1945, the Communists alleged to have captured American Lend-Lease arms of recent make from Kuomintang troops fighting them not far from Yenan. And Lt.-General Albert C. Wedemeyer, according to United Press, stated in Chungking on August 3, "it was 'probably true' that some Chinese government troops fighting Chinese Communist troops were using American weapons . . . implying that they had been obtained through irregular channels."

of the Lend-Lease agreement which entitles him to recall such materials after the war; that, on the contrary, certain Lend-Lease contracts may still be fulfilled; and that the United States can be prevailed upon to help the National Government carry out its ambitious postwar plans for the expansion of its air force and the general modernization of its armies and armament industries—no matter if there is a danger of civil war or not.

These two Chinas will continue to compete with one another in the outside world.

Each will try to strengthen itself by enlisting international moral support—Kuomintang-controlled China among the conservative and reactionary elements in each country, and Communist-controlled China among the progressive forces all over the world.

We must try, actively, to prevent a situation in which there would only be these grim alternatives: the perpetuation of China's split in two, and its reunification by force, as the final result of open civil war.

We must help these two Chinas become one—one China that fits into a progressive, democratic world.

Legalistic considerations—such as nonintervention in the affairs of a sovereign state, and the continuation of trade with a recognized government, even though it finds itself in a civil war—must not be allowed to stand in our way of preventing fresh disaster for China and ourselves.

To help China become *one* is the collective task of American, British, and Russian statesmanship.

It is the first constructive task the Big Three have to face together in this challenging new age of atomic energy in which there is only the choice between world-wide disaster and world-wide peace and human progress.

INDEX

Active Elements, 97

Administration in Communist areas: principles of development, 129-130; officials produce most of their needs, 133-134; methods applicable to big cities, 135; deficiencies, 136-137; recruitment of officials, 137-138; salaries, 138-139; comparison with Kuomintang areas, 200

Agriculture: Mao Tse-tung about agrarian reform, 110-113; new methods and progress, 162-166; land reclamation, 166

American attitude toward Chinese internal conflict, in 1927, 9-10; in 1944-1945, 26, 467, 470, 473-475

Antiforeignism of Kuomintang official, 79, 82

Anti-Japanese Association, People's, in Communist areas, 335-336

Anti-Japanese War Bases of Communists, 97, 328-332, 368-378

Antisemitism of Kuomintang official, 79, 82

Armies, Chinese "puppet": strength, 327; to become Japanese Fifth Column after the war, 428, 431-433; many consist of Kuomintang deserters, 429-431

Armies, Communist-controlled (*see also* Eighth Route and New Fourth Armies): battle records, 3, 333-334; tasks given by National Government in 1937, 18; battle records suppressed by Chungking, 19; pay stoppage by National Government, 1941, 21, 140; Kuomintang accusations, 35, 38; deserters, 46, 67; production work, 66-70, 198; military performance records, 73; political education, 74, 152; headquarters in Yenan, 85; cooperation with people, 161; military setbacks in 1940-1941, 322-324; losses in fights with Kuomintang troops, 334; total strength, 338; Japanese estimate of fighting power, 395-401

Armies, Japanese, in China: strategy against Kuomintang, 1939-1943, 319-320; strategy against Communists, 322-323; distribution, 327-328; fortifications against Communists, 341-342

Armies, Kuomintang-controlled: in Civil War, 11; attacks on Communist regions, 1944, 126; in summer, 1945, 477, 480; bad attitude toward people in own regions, 126, 469; owe first loyalty to party, 149; reasons for failure against Japanese in Honan, 307; total strength, 327-328; losses in fights with Communists, 334; many became Japanese puppets, 429-431

Arms, captured by Communists from Japanese, 72, 334, 344

Atkinson, Brooks, 26, 27, 460, 467-470

483

Index

Index

Index